W9-DFO-545

A COMPLETE GUIDE

FIRST EDITION

DOMINICAN REPUBLIC

Great Destinations

Christopher P. Baker

The Countryman Press
Woodstock, Vermont

This book is dedicated to my friend Daymaris Bencomo. May you fulfill your dreams.

Copyright © 2009 by Christopher P. Baker

First Edition

All rights reserved. No part of this book may be reproduced in any way by any electronic or mechanical means, including information storage and retrieval systems, without permission in writing from the publisher, except by a reviewer, who may quote brief passages.

ISBN 978-1-58157-103-5

Cover photo © Chistopher P. Baker
Interior photos by the author unless otherwise specified
Book design by Bodenweber Design
Page composition by Chelsea Cloeter
Maps by Mapping Specialists Ltd., Madison, WI, © The Countryman Press

Published by The Countryman Press, P.O. Box 748, Woodstock, VT 05091

Distributed by W. W. Norton & Company, Inc., 500 Fifth Ave., New York, NY 10110

Printed in the United States of America

10 9 8 7 6 5 4 3 2 1

DOMINICAN REPUBLIC

Palm trees and turquoise ocean, Playa Bavaro

GREAT DESTINATIONS TRAVEL GUIDEBOOK SERIES

Recommended by *National Geographic Traveler* and *Travel + Leisure* magazines

A crisp and critical approach, for travelers who want to live like locals.
—*USA Today*

Great Destinations™ guidebooks are known for their comprehensive, critical coverage of regions of extraordinary cultural interest and natural beauty. Each title in this series is continuously updated with each printing to ensure accurate and timely information. All the books contain more than one hundred photographs and maps.

Current titles available:

The Adirondack Book
The Alaska Panhandle
Atlanta
Austin, San Antonio
  & the Texas Hill Country
Baltimore, Annapolis & the Chesapeake Bay
The Berkshire Book
Big Sur, Monterey Bay
  & Gold Coast Wine Country
Cape Canaveral, Cocoa Beach
  & Florida's Space Coast
The Charleston, Savannah
  & Coastal Islands Book
The Coast of Maine Book
Colorado's Classic Mountain Towns
Costa Rica
Dominican Republic
The Erie Canal
The Finger Lakes Book
The Four Corners Region
Galveston, South Padre Island
  & the Texas Gulf Coast
Glacier National Park & the Canadian Rockies
Guatemala
The Hamptons Book
Hawaii's Big Island
Honolulu & Oahu
The Jersey Shore: Atlantic City to Cape May
Kauai
Lake Tahoe & Reno
Las Vegas
Los Cabos & Baja California Sur
Maui
Memphis and the Delta Blues Trail
Mexico City, Puebla & Cuernavaca

Michigan's Upper Peninsula
Montreal & Quebec City
The Nantucket Book
The Napa & Sonoma Book
North Carolina's Outer Banks
  & the Crystal Coast
Nova Scotia & Prince Edward Island
Oaxaca
Oregon Wine Country
Palm Beach, Fort Lauderdale, Miami
  & the Florida Keys
Palm Springs & Desert Resorts
Philadelphia, Brandywine Valley
  & Bucks County
Phoenix, Scottsdale, Sedona
  & Central Arizona
Playa del Carmen, Tulum & the Riviera Maya
Salt Lake City, Park City, Provo
  & Utah's High Country Resorts
San Diego & Tijuana
San Juan, Vieques & Culebra
San Miguel de Allende & Guanajuato
The Santa Fe & Taos Book
Santa Barbara and California's Central Coast
The Sarasota, Sanibel Island & Naples Book
The Seattle & Vancouver Book
The Shenandoah Valley Book
Touring East Coast Wine Country
Tucson
Virginia Beach, Richmond & Tidewater Virginia
Washington, D.C., and Northern Virginia
Yellowstone & Grand Teton National Parks
  & Jackson Hole
Yosemite & the Southern Sierra Nevada

The authors in this series are professional travel writers who have lived for many years in the regions they describe. Honest and painstakingly critical, full of information only a local can provide, Great Destinations guidebooks give you all the practical knowledge you need to enjoy the best of each region.

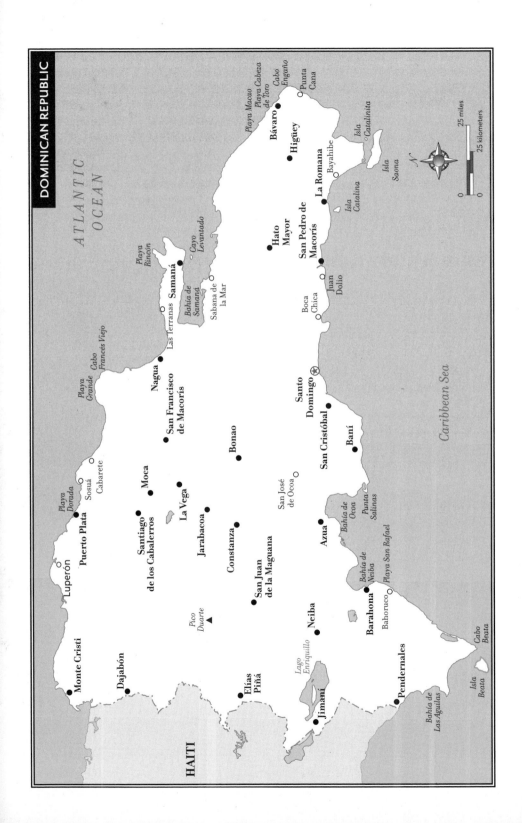

Contents

Maps

General Index   361

ACKNOWLEDGMENTS

I could not have prepared this book without the help of a coterie of other people.

Particular thanks go to Arturo Fuentes, of Fuentes & Co.; Kathy Hernández, of Kathy Hernández Associates; and Sonja Loges, Laura Tanin, Patricia Tazalla, Vanessa Walter, and Holly Werblow, of BVK Public Relations; and the executives and staff of the Dominican Republic Tourist Board.

I also wish to thank the following for miscellaneous assistance: Alberto Abreu and Germán Gómez Pellerano, of Puntacana Resort & Club; Ayesha Abreu, or VH Hotels & Resorts; Linday Ayares, of M. Silver Associates; Enzo Bonarelli, of Vesuvio; Madeline Camps and Jenny Corporán, of Ocean World; Marí Checo and Gina Eli, of Renaissance Jaragua Hotel & Casino; Yamirca Faña, of Agualina Kite Resort; Lissette Gil, of Asociación Hotels La Romana-Bayahibe; Norina Gómez Herrera, of HotelBeds; Tim Hall, of CafeCaribe; Sultan Karim, of Spirit Airlines; Claire Kunzman, of Y Partnership; Vân Lê, of Caliente Resort; Sandra López, Kim Hutchinson, and Joselyn Nuñez, of Casa de Campo; Saraida de Marchena Kalucha, of CapCana; Marco, Rocky's Rock & Blues Bar; Steve Morris, of Casino Dominicus; Elizabeth Ortega, of YPB&R Public Relations; Paula Pascale, of Villa Serena; Jean Le Priellec and Mayka Rodríguez, of Sofitel Nicolás de Ovando; Elizabeth Rosario, of Casa Bonita Tropical Lodge; Soledad Terc García, of Museo Infantil Trampolín; Pedro Vegas, of Europcar; plus the owners and/or public relations/managerial staff of the Gran Bahía Principe Cayo Levantado; Gran Bahía Principe Cayacoa; Hotel Alto Cerro; Hotel Las Salinas; Hotel Villa Taina; Paraíso Caño Hondo; Rancho Cascada; Sivory Punta Cana; and Viva Wyndham Samaná.

INTRODUCTION

There's a good reason almost 4 million foreigners visited the Dominican Republic in 2007, outstripping arrivals to any other Caribbean destination by a wide margin (Cuba was number two, with 2.1 million). There's Santo Domingo, with its ancient cathedrals and convents and castles evocative of the once mighty power of Spain. Then there are the bottle green mountains and emerald valleys full of dramatic formations... and the talcum-white, talcum-fine beaches dissolving into bathtub-warm waters of impossible, jaw-dropping turquoise hues. The Crayola colors have to be seen to be believed!

Scenically the soulful DR, as the nation is colloquially known, is mind-blowing in its sensational beauty (several roads have been designated as panoramic routes). You'd expect such of the island that boasts the highest mountains in the Antilles. While roughly triangular in shape, the republic's vital stats—242 miles (390 km) wide by 165 miles (265 km) north-south—are the geographic equivalent of a 36–24–36 figure. No other Caribbean isle (except Cuba) has so much to offer. Nor such contrasts in terrain and scenery. Hispaniola—the Caribbean isle that the Dominican Republic shares with Haiti, to the west—is sculpted to show off the full beauty of the tropics. You can journey, as it were, from the Arizona desert to a Swiss alpine forest simply by starting at Lago Enriquillo—at 115 feet (35 m) below sea level, the Caribbean's lowest point—and walking uphill. Neighboring and depauperate Haiti, with its unstable government and deforested mountains, contrasts sharply with the Dominican Republic's stable democracy, fecund slopes, and fertile *vegas* (fields) where the world's finest tobacco and coffee is grown.

Where you find forests, you find wildlife. At 18,680 square miles (48,380 sq km), slightly smaller than West Virginia, the republic is a veritable Noah's Ark. Birders' spirits soar at the nation's encyclopedic profusion of endemic species, easily seen in protected wetlands and rugged mountain reserves, while flamingoes strut around in jade shallows. Endangered Ricord's and rhinoceros iguanas plod around the cactus-studded southwest, where crocodiles congregate thick as sardines in the super-saline waters of Lago Enriquillo. Rare mammals such as the solenodon (a nocturnal insectivore resembling a giant longhaired shrew) and hutia (an overgrown guinea-pig-like rodent) inhabit unmolested terrain. And the marine environment is no less enthralling. Manatees thrive in coastal lagoons such as Caño Estero Hondo. Marine turtles crawl ashore to lay their eggs in diamond-dust sands. Humpback whales frolic in Samaná bay during winter months, when they arrive to mate and give birth. And the coral and pelagic sea life help define the Dominican Republic's nearshore waters as Nirvana for scuba divers no less enamored of the numerous Spanish galleons and latter-day vessels a few fathoms down.

Above the surface, water sports are as good as it gets. Hobie Cats? Aqua-Bikes? Most beach resorts have them, while the north shore resort of Cabarete is considered the finest spot in the entire Caribbean for kiteboarding and surf action. Golfing here is unsurpassed, too. More than 20 championship courses by the likes of Pete Dye, Nick Faldo, Tom Fazio, Jack Nicklaus, and Arnold Palmer boast rippling fairways overhanging teal blue seas. Hiking trails lace the isle, reaching their pinnacle atop the summit of Pico Duarte (10,164 feet, 3,098 m). The spectacular waterfalls that tumble from the mountains even provide for whitewater rafting.

While the vast majority of visitors come for the spectacular beaches, the Dominican Republic also abounds in historical charm. Nowhere else in the Caribbean boasts such a plethora of pre-Columbian sites, with dozens of caverns full of pre-Columbian Taíno art. Albeit scant, the ruins of La Isabela and La Vega Vieja (the first two permanent Spanish settlements in the New World) are mementoes of the arrival of Christopher Columbus in 1492. The Zona Colonial of Santo Domingo, the capital, echoes with the chants of friars and the footsteps of conquistadores. Still cobbled in places, the old city boasts the Western hemisphere's first cathedral and fortress among its early colonial treasures. By contrast, Santiago de los Caballeros (the republic's second largest city) and the charming north coast town of Puerto Plata are replete with quaint gingerbread structures erected during the 19th-century boom days of tobacco.

If it's hip modernity you're seeking, fear not. Santo Domingo is a thoroughly modern metropolis, full of casinos, fine-dining restaurants, art galleries, nightclubs...and endless traffic! Glittering high-rise condominiums, banks, and hotels scratch the sky while below, colonial plazas teem with trendy youth sipping cocktails and dancing to merengue alfresco.

The beach resorts are no less hip to the times. The Dominican Republic's hotels are world class...and getting better, drawing a stellar crop of hip celebrities from the international A-list. World-renowned for the quality of its all-inclusive resorts, the country is now making a splash with fashionable new boutique hotels. Foreign and Dominican chefs have opened chic beachfront restaurants. Tour operators offer all manner of exciting excursions. And a wave of super-deluxe new resorts in the making guarantees that the Dominican Republic will continue to set the standard to beat. Best yet, the keen competition on the island keeps prices well within reach. Combined with a superb level of service, the result is true value for money.

Then there are the people. Visitors return raving about the vivacious Dominican people, gracious to a fault. And the art and music scene is astounding, reflecting a lively Latin spirit hot enough to cook the pork.

Nonetheless, there's no escaping the harsh realities of life throughout the republic, where overt wealth abuts grinding poverty. To drive is to take your life into your hands (Dominicans surely rank as among the world's most reckless and dangerous drivers). The infrastructure—the electricity, the water supply—are, shall we say, somewhat dysfunctional. And prostitution, drug trafficking, and even police corruption are rife. Fortunately, most tourists return home without having encountered the downside of the DR. The lingering memories are of blazing white beaches...turquoise waters...swaying palm trees...heady rum cocktails...and satisfying accommodations offering service with a smile.

Is it any wonder that tourism to the Caribbean's most-visited isle is increasing in leaps and bounds?

THE WAY THIS BOOK WORKS

This book is divided into 10 chapters. Entries within each regional chapter are broken down geographically according to the names of towns or distinct geographic entities, such as valleys or beach zones. The same order of headings—Lodgings, Dining, Attractions... etc.—is used for each regional chapter.

Some entries include specific information—telephone numbers, websites, addresses, business hours, and the like—organized for easy reference in blocks at the top of each entry.

For the same reasons, we have routinely avoided listing specific prices, indicating instead a range. Lodging price codes are based on a per-room rate, double occupancy during winter months (high season). Off-season rates are often cheaper. Restaurant price ratings indicate the cost of an individual meal, including appetizer, entrée, and dessert but not cocktails, wine, tax, or tip.

All information was checked as close to the publication date as possible. Even so, since details can change without warning, it is always wise to call ahead. Finally, I'd like to hear from you if you have suggestions for ways to improve this book. Also, please let us know about your experiences, both good and bad, with hotels, restaurants, and other businesses listed. If they don't live up to their recommendations, let me know.

Price Codes

Code	Lodging	Dining
Inexpensive ($)	Up to $100	Up to $10
Moderate ($$)	$100–150	$10–20
Expensive ($$$)	$150–250	$20–35
Very expensive ($$$$)	Over $250	$35 or more

Some prices are in Dominican Republic pesos: RD.

The following abbreviations are used for credit card information:

AE: American Express
CB: Carte Blanche
D: Discover Card
DC: Diner's Club
MC: MasterCard
V: Visa

1

HISTORY

"All of us . . . have benefited greatly from the Dominican Republic.
We must find a way to give back to the people."

—C. Carlito Fuente, Arturo Fuente & Co.

NATURAL HISTORY

Blessed with virtually every attribute for which the region is known, this Spanish-speaking nation combines a fascinating colonial history and architectural legacy with magnificent mountain scenery and stupendous beaches melding into reef-protected, bathtub-warm, electric-blue shallows. Its landscapes are kaleidoscopic. Shaped like an arrowhead—the Dominican Republic tapers eastward—and fringed by the Atlantic (to the north) and Caribbean (to the south), the nation shares the island of Hispaniola with neighboring Haiti, which takes up the westernmost third of the isle. Hispaniola, which lies entirely within the tropics between 17 and 19 degrees north of the equator, is cusped betwixt Cuba (to the west) and Puerto Rico (to the east) and boasts both the Caribbean's highest point, Pico Duarte at 10,164 feet (3,098 m) and its lowest, Lago Enriquillo at 115 feet (35 m) below sea level.

Enclosing the Caribbean like a shepherd's crook, the paternoster of islands that comprise the Lesser Antilles is of volcanic origin. Hispaniola is part of the Greater Antilles, the larger and westernmost isles of tectonic origin—landmasses thrust from the sea by the cataclysmic collision of tectonic plates that make up the Earth's surface, like a moveable jigsaw puzzle. The island rides atop the Caribbean plate at its jostling juncture with the North American plate. Deep below the Earth's crust, viscous molten rock flows in slow-moving convection currents that well up from deep within the Earth's core, carrying the plates on their backs. The Greater Antilles first began to emerge some 50 million years ago, in the Eocene. They are still rising, as evidenced by the violent earthquakes that still frequently rattle Hispaniola.

No surprise, then, that the 18,816-square-mile (48,734 sq km) island is exceedingly mountainous. A four-fold concertina of parallel ranges rises in east-west waves that begin with the narrow Cordillera Septentrional, running parallel to, and a short distance inland of, the northern seaboard. Though scenic, this chain is a mere shadow of the Cordillera Central, a dauntingly rugged mountain massif rising from the heart of the isle and boasting three peaks—Pico Duarte, Pico La Pelona, and Pico La Rucilla—exceeding 10,000 feet. To the southwest, the republic's Sierra de Neiba and Sierra de Bahoruco are blanketed in primary forest—a far cry from the deforested westerly extensions across the Haitian border (in fact, forest cover has *increased* in the republic, from 27 percent in 1997 to 33 percent in

Pine forests in the Cordillera Central

2008). The mountain ranges are separated by broad lowland vales whose loamy soils are fed by waters teeming out of the highlands. Tractors till the cinnamon soils into furrows, notably in the Valle del Yaque, which opens east to the broad Valle del Río Camú (colloquially known as El Cibao), a breadbasket where some of the world's finest tobacco is grown. The nation's real breadbasket, however, is El Valle de Culata, a temperate high-mountain vale deep in the Cordillera Central and centered on the alpine town of Constanza.

The relatively narrow southeastern third of the island comprises a plain, framed inland of the north shore by the rugged Cordillera Oriental, full of dramatic limestone formations. The flatlands of the southeast (and much of the narrow coastal plain elsewhere in the nation) are farmed in sugar—a gently undulating sea of chartreuse. This region is renowned for the blazing magnesium-white beaches that limn these shores, tapering to the sharp naze of Cabo Engaño, the island's easternmost point. The nation's foremost beaches are here, centered on Punta Cana.

There are only two seasons: wet (May to November) and dry (December to April), though the nation is a quiltwork of regional variations. Despite the republic's location within the tropics, the extremes of elevation and relief spawn a profusion of microclimates. The climate differs markedly between Atlantic and Caribbean—the former receives the moisture-laden trade winds and, thereby, considerably more rainfall. The arid flatlands of the southwest and the sodden coastal plains of the northeast could belong to different worlds, never mind the same nation, notwithstanding their similar elevation. The Cordillera Central and twin *sierras* of the southwest form rain shadows over much of that region. Moist trade winds bearing down from the east spill their water on the windward slopes, while the lowlands at the base of the leeward slopes are left to thirst. Thus, much of the extreme southwest is scrub covered, with cacti poking up from the parched earth. And though temperatures in any one place scarcely vary year-round, the smothering heat of the lowlands contrasts markedly with the crisp cool of the highlands.

Almost one-quarter of the country's land area is safeguarded within 70 registered Protected Areas that include 16 national parks, 9 natural monuments, and 6 scientific reserves under the direction of the Dirección Nacional de Parques.

Flora

Relatively small it may be, but the Dominican Republic is clad in multiple shades of green, from coastal mangrove forests and swampy wetlands to cloud forests and alpine meadows soaked in ethereal mists atop the higher peaks. The diverse canvas is even dun-colored: pockets of dry deciduous forest merge into cactus-pinned semi-desert in the parched plains of the southwest. Unlike neighboring Haiti, where impoverished and landless peasants have stripped the land bare, more than one third of the Dominican Republic is still covered in forest typical of original Antillean vegetation, much thanks to a ban on commercial logging enacted in the 1960s. The picture isn't all roses, of course; much of the land has been denuded by landless peasants, who continue to gnaw at the forests at lower slopes.

The republic steeps in humidity and, except the upper mountain slopes, near-constant high temperatures, with the sun lasering down from directly overhead throughout the year. The greenhouse effect is aided by drenching rainfall that fuels extraordinarily luxuriant growth. In fact, the republic boasts the most impressive species diversity in the Antilles. More than 5,500 separate species of flora have been identified locally. The country is especially rich in endemic flora. In a tropical climate, trees, shrubs, and flowers are always in

View of Caribbean from near Punta Balandra, Samana Peninsula

Mangroves at Laguna Oviedo, Parque Nacional Jaragua

bloom: Ruby-pink begonias. Saucily shaped anthuriums in pinks, reds, and whites... Torch-like gingers... Pendulous heliconias, the latter boasting more than 30 species.

Most abundant are the ferns (690 species), found from sea level to the highest eleva-tions. Notable, too, are orchid species: About 300 have been catalogued so far, many of them now endangered. Thriving on moisture, these exquisite plants are also found at every elevation, from sea level to the misty upper slopes of Pico Duarte (orchids especially abound on the cloud-wrapped slopes of the Sierra de Bahoruco). At any time of year, dozens of species are in bloom, many of them barely bigger than a pinhead, such as the endemic *Lepanthes trilobata*. Most orchid species are epiphytes (Greek for air plants), arbo-real nesters that root on tree trunks or branches and use sponge-like roots to tap moisture directly from the air. Walking the sodden forests, you'll also chance upon bromeliads fes-tooning tree trunks and boughs. These epiphytes have thick spiky leaves that are tightly whorled to form cisterns that capture both water and falling leaf litter (and the occasional unfortunate bug) whose decay feeds the plant. Parasitic dwarf mistletoe, which draws nutrients directly from its host tree, is also quite common in the mountains.

Ironically, given the abundance of exorbitant plants, the national flower is the diminu-tive February to April bloom of the *caoba* (West Indian mahogany), which soars skyward to form an umbrella above the canopy of lowland and mid-elevation moist subtropical forests. Silvery-gray *Palma real* (royal palm), another quintessential tree of the Greater Antilles, studs the lowlands like petrified Corinthian columns. With its slightly bulbous trunk, this graceful palm is beloved for its utilitarianism, including thatch for roofing, and is even a symbol on the national coat of arms, as well as its coins (and less honorably as the symbol of Dictator Rafael Leonidas Trujillo's Partido Dominicano). At least a dozen other species of palm are used for construction and crafts, including the sabal or *Palma cana* (like the royal,

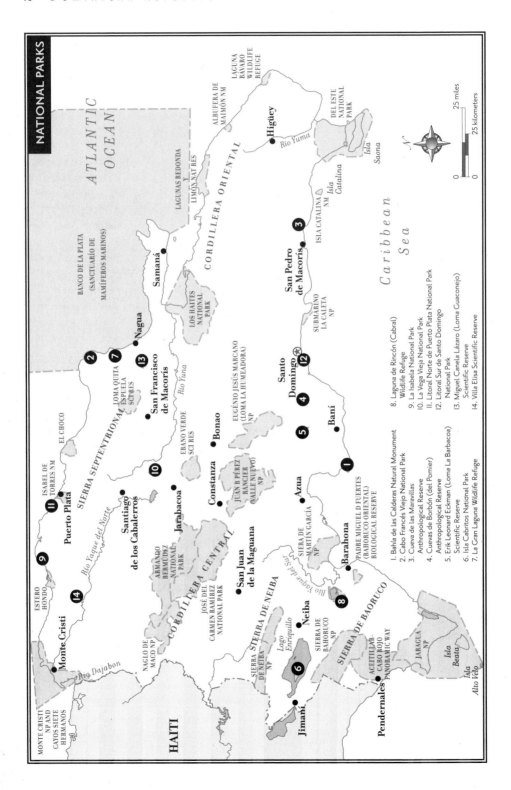

NATIONAL PARKS

ATLANTIC OCEAN

Caribbean Sea

HAITI

1. Bahía de las Calderas Natural Monument
2. Cabo Francés Viejo National Park
3. Cueva de las Maravillas Anthropological Reserve
4. Cuevas de Borbón (del Pomier) Anthropological Reserve
5. Erik Leonard Eckman (Loma La Barbacoa) Scientific Reserve
6. Isla Cabritos National Park
7. La Gran Laguna Wildlife Refuge
8. Laguna de Rincón (Cabral) Wildlife Refuge
9. La Isabela National Park
10. La Vega Vieja National Park
11. Litoral Norte de Puerto Plata National Park
12. Litoral Sur de Santo Domingo National Park
13. Miguel Canela Lázaro (Loma Guaconejo) Scientific Reserve
14. Villa Elisa Scientific Reserve

a towering giant), and the more slender silver thatch or *guano*. Most notable along the shore is the gracefully curving coconut palm. Despite its ubiquity, it is actually an Old World species introduced to the Dominican Republic by the Spanish in the 16th century. Some palms are even adapted for cooler heights, such as the 13-foot (4 m) tall, mountain-dwelling sierra palm, whose branches unfurl from a cello-like fiddlehead.

Vegetation zones vary with elevation. At lower levels are broad-leafed subtropical humid forests with species such as statuesque ceiba, West Indian cedar, walnut, wild olive *(Palo amargo)*, baobabs with trunks like pregnant bellies, and *yagruma*, whose silvery leaves seem frosted. Above about 4,000 feet (1,219 m), feathery-leafed parrot tree *(Palo de cotorra)* and *Palo de cruz* pine precede the mist-soaked cloud forest—officially known as tropical mon-tane rain forest, with an abundance of epiphytes. Higher still, wild avocado is found, although Creolean pine predominates, while wildflowers emblazon soggy alpine meadows. At the highest elevations of the Cordillera Central, wind-scoured savannas intersperse with forests of stunted trees skulking low against howling rains.

The forests, dry and moist alike, flame with Cezanne color: Almost fluorescent yellow *corteza amarilla* ... Purple jacaranda ... Snow-white frangipani ... Bougainvillea in a rain-bow assortment of colors ... And flame-red *Spathodea,* or African flame-of-the-forest, emblazoning the Dominican landscape before dropping their petals like colored confetti. Many are the species, too, that produce succulent fruits—a bounty for hotel dining rooms. Familiar to most visitors are bananas, papayas (locally called *lechosas*), and mangoes, but you'll also find—and should try—guavas *(guyaba)*, *limoncillos* (resembling a lime, but far more delicious), plum-like passion fruit *(chinola)*, oval-shaped *sapote,* and tamarind, which is cusped within a long peanut-shell pod and, like *guanabano,* mostly finds its way into drinks.

Dry Forests

The three geographic extremes of this triangular nation have in common a paucity of rain. Thus the land encompassed within Parque Nacional Jaragua (to the southwest), Parque Nacional del Este (to the southeast), and Parque Nacional Monte Cristi (in the northwest) are semi-arid and abound in cactus. Great care is required when hiking these regions due to the cactus spines, which range from tiny hairlike glochids that penetrate into the skin like invisible splinters, to stiff, needle-like spikes that can easily pierce a boot or tire.

Seasonally dry deciduous forest covers much of the land, which in Parque Nacional Jaragua and Parque Nacional del Este comprises limestone dangerously eroded into knife-sharp ridges known as iron shore or "dog's tooth." Despite thin soils and little rain, these parsimonious regions teem with the glories of nature. Many species lie dormant through-out the dry season before exploding in riotous color with the onset of rain; an hour-long deluge can resurrect flora from sun-scorched torpor.

Palma guanito or *macaco*, a fan palm (named for the shape of its long fronds) endemic to the dry forests of Hispaniola, grows on the sunny, south-facing side of deep crevices and canyons, forming shady oases wherever sufficient water exists. *Roble,* or yokewood, also thrives in the seasonally dry environment, as does the steel-strong lignum vitae *(guayacán)*, with its mottled peeling bark and winged seed capsules. *Guayacán* is the dens-est of any known wood in the world, so hard and durable that it was once used for bearings as well as British police truncheons. And the indigenous Taíno used its resin to treat med-ical conditions, including arthritis. The logwood *(campache)* they used against dysentery and as a black dye. Favoring the dry forests, too, the contorted gumbo-limbo, with its stout,

Cactus at Bahia de la Aguilas, Parque Nacional Jaragua

massive branches and a spreading, rounded crown; it's also known as "burned tourist" due to its shiny, smooth, reddish exfoliating bark, like the peeling skin of sunburned tourists. The smooth, papery thin bark peels off in sheets to reveal a greenish layer beneath. The oily bark gives off a gummy, turpentine-scented resin that has long been used locally for glues and varnish, handy in the manufacture of canoes. The Taíno also used the gumbo-limbo's aromatic sap for medicinal teas. Intriguingly, the soft, spongy wood, if chopped and planted, easily takes root in the ground, for which reason it is used for fence posts.

These dry forest trees are draped with wispy tendrils of Spanish moss, like Fidel Castro's beard, that draw water from the air during rare rainfalls. Dodder vines also twine up tree trunks and usurp nutrients until they kill their host trees. And orchids are also present, often growing on the tops of cactus pads.

The Dominican Republic has 14 species of cactus. Hispaniolan cacti display a high degree of endemism. For example, the clambering moonlight cactus (so named because their giant funnel-shaped, sweetly scented flowers open at night) is an arborealist, endemic to Hispaniola, coiling around its host like serpents around Eden's tree.

The hardiest and most adaptable plants in the cacti family are the six species of opuntias, which includes the prickly pears (*chayotes*), fast growing even in the poorest of desert soil. They grow in a succession of fleshy oval pads, protected by long spines and short barbed glochids. The plant is anchored by a deep-reaching taproot. Other wide-spreading roots near the surface soak up light rains. In winter, these roots take up the role of the pads by storing water. They come in a variety of forms, all of which burst into glorious bloom (from yellow to deep carmine, depending on species) and give off a seedy and nutritious pomegranate-like purplish fruit. Alas, the local opuntia population is threatened by the cactus moth, an invasive non-native species that has spread through the Caribbean since being introduced to the Lesser Antilles in 1957. The adult female lays her eggs in the cactus pads, whose succulent flesh provides food for the hatched larvae. The larvae consume the entire cactus from within, leaving a desiccated shell.

Mangroves and Wetlands

Dense thickets and forests of mangroves line much of the coast. Five species of these tropical halophytes (salt-tolerant plants) grow in the Dominican Republic, thriving at the margin of land and sea on silts brought down from the mountains. Thus they are frequent around river estuaries. These shrubby pioneer land-builders trap sediment flowing out to sea from the slow-moving rivers and form a bulwark against wave action and tidal erosion (by filtering out sediment, they are also important contributors to the health of coral reefs). They rise from the dark water on a tangle of interlocking stilt roots that give them the appearance of walking on water. The dense, waterlogged mud bears little oxygen. Hence the mangroves have evolved aerial roots, drawing oxygen directly from the air through pores in the bark (black mangroves, however, breathe through pneumatophores, specialized roots that stick up from the mud like snorkel tubes). The roots of red mangroves, the most common species in Hispaniola, have evolved to filter out salt before taking up water; any salt entering via the shoot is carried to the leaves, which are then shed. White mangroves even excrete salt directly through special glands for that purpose, hence its name.

Mangals—mangrove communities—are a vital habitat for all manner of animal and marine life. Rich in organic content, the mud is the base in a unique ecosystem in which

Rosa de Bayahíbe

algae and other small organisms thrive, providing sustenance for oysters, shrimp, sponges, and other creatures higher up the food chain. Small stingrays flap slowly through the shallow waters, while baby sharks and tiny fishes flit about in their tens of thousands, shielded from larger predators by the protective tangle of roots. Tiny arboreal mangrove crabs mulch the leaves and are preyed upon by larger, mostly terrestrial, species. Mangals are also important breeding grounds for ibis, frigate birds, pelicans, and other waterbirds, which nest here en masse. Herons and egrets pick among the braided channels and tidal creeks. Arboreal snakes slither along the branches. Turtles bask on the mud banks. Crocodiles lurk in the silty waters, while West Indian manatees are constantly on the forage for food. (Crab-eating raccoons were once common, too, until exterminated for their meat following Columbus's arrival in 1492—the great explorer called them *perro mastin,* or clownlike dog.)

Aggressive colonizers, mangroves have evolved a remarkable propagation technique. The shrub blooms briefly in spring, and from the resulting fruit grows a seedling sprout. The large, heavy, elongated seeds shaped like a hydrometer, or plumb bob, germinate while still on the tree. Growing to a length of 6–12 inches (15–30 cm), they drop like darts. Landing in mud, they begin to develop immediately. If they hit water, they float on the currents until they touch a muddy floor. The seeds can survive months at sea without desiccation and are thus capable of traveling hundreds of miles to begin a new colony. With each successive

Big Bully!

The bully of tropical trees is the giant strangler fig, or ficus, called *higo* in the Dominican Republic. This exquisite yet murderous tree (there are actually almost one thousand species throughout the tropics) is like something from *The Lord of the Rings.* Birthed on the branches of other trees when birds deposit their guano containing the seeds, the sprouting fig sends roots creeping along the branches while long tendril roots drop to the ground and begin to take nutrients from the soil. Over decades, the roots thicken and merge, twining in an eerie latticework around the host tree. Eventually the latter is choked to death (the process can take a century) and rots away, leaving a complete yet hollow mature fig. Often several fig plants will grow on the same host tree, eventually fusing together to form a compound organism with genetically distinct branches. Pocked with abundant nooks and crannies, the hollow trunk provides a perfect home for bats and other invertebrates, plus birds and lizards, all of them gifted with an abundant food source in the plentiful fig fruits (galls) that grow in clusters directly from the tree branches.

The tree owes its life to a remarkable symbiotic (mutually dependent) relationship with the tiny gall or fig wasp. Pregnant females are drawn to the tree's fruity galls, each of which has a tiny hole through which the wasp enters. She tears off her wings as she squeezes in to lay her eggs in the stigma of the tiny flowers (both male and female) that grow within the gall; the flowers can't pollinate each other, as they mature at different times. Duty performed, the female wasp dies. The hole seals itself. And the eggs are left to hatch. First to emerge are the males, which crawl from their eggs pre-programmed and ready to mate. They chew open the eggs of the females and inseminate them in their natal sleep. Hatching at the exact moment that the male flowers mature, the already pregnant (and winged) females get covered with pollen as they chew a hole in the gall and fly off to find their own tree. (The males also depart the gall and proceed to die.) Locating their own galls on other trees in the right stage of development, each female burrows in to begin the process anew. The pollen she carries is brushed onto the female fig flowers, completing the pollination. In her sole day of life, the female wasp thus ensures a new generation of wasps and of ficus.

Manatees

Looking like swollen wineskins, or tuskless walruses, manatees are gentle herbivorous mammals that have adapted completely to a life in warm water. These highly intelligent animals lack hind limbs entirely. Instead, they propel themselves gracefully with a single spatulate tail that surely gave rise to the myth of the mermaid.

Manatís (the word is a native Taíno word for breast) inhabit shallow tropical coastal waters and are particularly fond of river estuaries, but they move freely between fresh and saline waters. The West Indian manatee is now an endangered species following centuries of being hunted for meat, disturbance of its habitats, entanglement with fishing gear and, increasingly, collisions with speeding boats. However, they are easy to spot in the sheltered waters of Refugio de Manatís Estero Hondo and in the coastal lagoons of Parque Nacional del Este, Parque Nacional Monte Cristi, Parque Nacional Jaragua, and the Bahía de Samaná.

Adult manatees average about 1,000 pounds (454 kg) and 9 feet (2.7 m) in length, although much larger individuals have been sighted. Females are slightly larger than males and reach sexual maturity at about four years old. Males gather to compete to mate with ovulating females, who give birth to a single calf (and occasional twins) only once every two to five years. While males contribute no parental care, mother and calf remain together for up to two years throughout weaning. Manatees can live to be 60 years old.

They have tough gray skin, tiny beady eyes, and fleshy and pendulous upper lips like a shortened trunk, similar to the elephant, to which they are closely related. This they use to gather vegetation. Opportunistic, non-territorial feeders, they are capable of chomping up to 75 pounds or more of sea grasses, water hyacinths, and other aquatic vegetation daily. Uniquely among mammals, they have only six pairs of dentures—all molars and premolars—that are constantly replaced throughout life.

generation, the colony expands out to sea, eventually forming a great forest. The oldest mangroves, often soaring 60 feet (18 m) high, exist high and dry and eventually die on land the mangroves themselves have created.

The Dominican Republic has significant (and easily explored) mangals at Parque Nacional del Este, Parque Nacional Jaragua, Refugio de Manatís Estero Hondo, and Parque Nacional Los Haitises.

Many other coastal wetland systems support profuse bird life. The swampy freshwater bayous of Lagunas Redonda y Limón teem with waterfowl: Black-crowned night herons... Common gallinule... Pied-billed grebe... Roseate spoonbills. Jade-colored Laguna de Oviedo (in Parque Nacional Jaragua) is a precious habitat for flamingoes, roseate spoonbills, and more than 130 other bird species. And Lago Enriquillo, the nation's prime wetland ecosystem, combines freshwater marshes and hyper-saline waters where flamingoes and spoonbills wade warily under the hungry stare of the densest population of crocodiles in the Americas.

Fauna

The Dominican Republic is an A-list destination for international birders. Reptiles abound and are easily seen. And life beneath the waves gives snorkelers and divers raptures of the deep. By contrast, mammalian life is relatively sparse, at least in terms of numbers of species. The republic has 27 mammal species, of which 16 are bats and 8 are marine mammals (see

Hispaniolan parrot at Jellyfish Restaurant, Playa Bavaro

Beneath the Waves, below). At least 7 other mammal species are now extinct.

The bats range from the Jamaican fruit-eating bat to the giant greater bulldog bat, or fishing bat: Named for its feeding habits, it uses echolocation to detect water ripples made by fish, which it snatches on the wing with its sharp claws as an eagle snatches salmon. Other bats emerge at night to feast on insects, which they echolocate in the darkness by emitting an ultrasonic squeak whose echo is picked up by their oversize ears.

Hispaniola's only two surviving endemic ground-dwelling mammals are the solenodon and the hutia. The former is a shy, nocturnal, cat-sized giant of the shrew family. Emerging by night from its burrow or hideaway in hollowed-out logs or caves, it uses its Pinocchio nose and sharp claws to grub around in the undergrowth for insects, worms, and tiny reptiles. Remarkable in mammals, it has a venomous bite. It also gives off a pungent odor from glands in the armpits and groin. Alas, it is now an endangered species due to predation by mongeese, and feral cats and dogs—all introduced since Columbus's arrival to devastating effect on the local fauna. Today, it is restricted to remote wilderness regions enshrined as national parks. The Hispaniolan hutia is also endangered and considered locally extinct except in Parque Nacional Jaragua and Parque Nacional del Este, and perhaps a few other national parks. Also the size of a small house cat, this grayish-brown, forest-dwelling, short-limbed rodent also makes its home in burrows and hollowed-out logs or caves. Sharp-nosed like a rat (other hutia species, such as the raccoon-sized hutia of neighboring

Cuba, are blunt-nosed, like capybaras), it is omnivorous and survives on fruits, leaves, bark, and tiny reptiles and grubs, which it digests in a triptych stomach.

Birds

Ornithologists' hearts take flight in the Dominican Republic. The coos, calls, and cater-wauling of avian fauna draw serious birders from far and wide to one of the Western Hemisphere's premier birding locales. Its kaleidoscopic habitats provide a home to 306 bird species, including 32 endemics—more than at any other Caribbean island. In fact, an entire endemic family (the palm chats, the republic's national bird) is found only here, where they inhabit low- to mid-elevations with an abundance of palm savannas. These gregarious and voluble songsters form vast communal nests amid the palm fronds; dozens of pairs live in their individual compartments within their treetop condominiums.

The forests are alive with the squawks and screeches of the endemic Hispaniolan para-keet (*perico*) barreling overhead in jet-fighter formation. This ubiquitous bird is even found within city limits, unlike the Day-Glo green Hispaniola parrot (*cotica*), now much reduced in habitat and only occasionally seen. Other uniquely Dominican birds include the Hispaniolan oriole, the Antillean siskin, and Hispaniolan woodpecker, a lovable bird with a yellow-and-black-striped back, a blood-red hairdo, olive gray rump, and a black tail tipped as if dipped in red paint. A social creature at heart, the Hispaniolan woodpecker

Kleptomaniacs of the Sky

What's that sinister looking black bird with 6-foot (2 m) wide Stuka wings, a long hooked beak, and a devilish forked tail hanging motionless over the ocean on warm updrafts? Truly one of a kind, the frigate bird is the pirate of the sky (it's colloquially called the Man-o'-War bird). This kleptoparasite uses its lofty perch from which to harry gulls and terns until they release their catch, which the frigate bird then scoops up on the wing as it falls. These pelagic piscivores are not above snatching other seabird chicks from their nests. However, they catch most of their food by skimming the ocean surface and snatching fish.

Boasting the largest wingspan-to-body-weight ratio of any bird, frigate birds are supreme aerial performers and expend little energy while gliding the thermals. Thus they can stay aloft for days on end, landing solely to roost or breed. They nest in colonies, usually building rough individual nests atop mangroves in areas with a strong wind for lift on take-off.

Despite its sinister appearance, this eagle-size bird is quite beautiful, thanks to the iridescent purplish green sheen of the male's otherwise jet-black plumage. The male displays a bloodred gular sac that he inflates into a heart-shaped balloon during mating season, when males sit atop their mangrove roosts ululating and preening as the larger females wing around overhead, inspecting the goods. The female wears a bib of white on her abdomen and breast, plus a ring of blue around her eyes, all the better to impress her would-be mate. Each pair is seasonally monogamous. The female lays one or two eggs each breeding season. Weaning takes a full year—the longest of any bird—as the chicks spend day after day exposed to the sun.

Unlike pelicans and other diving birds, frigate birds lack the small preen gland that produces water-resistant oil for the feathers; thus, they need to stay dry. Nor can they swim or walk, nor take off from a flat surface. If they submerge or hit the water, their feathers get waterlogged and they are doomed.

nests in colonies unlike other, individualist woodpecker species. The Hispaniolan crossbill feeds almost exclusively on the seeds of the endemic Hispaniolan pine, found above 3,000 feet (914 m). The Hispaniolan trogon is another highland forest dweller, with green blue back and tail, a gray breast and red belly, and black-and-white banded wings.

The island's very own hummingbird—a family restricted to the Americas—is the Hispaniolan emerald, whose preference is for upland regions. Scintillating green of cloak, the male has an iridescent black chest patch and a slightly forked tail; the female is paler. Other hummers found on Hispaniola are the Antillean mango, purple-throated Carib, ruby-throated hummingbird, and the diminutive vervain hummingbird, the world's second smallest bird. These tiny, high-speed creatures are named for the buzz of the blurringly fast beat of their wings: at 10–70 beats per second, so fast that they can hover and even fly backwards. Their metabolic rate (a hummers' heart rate can exceed 1,000 beats a minute) is so prodigious that they must consume vast quantities of high-power nectar and tiny insects. In fact, they typically eat the equivalent of their own body weight in a day (they also choose only flowers whose nectar has a sugar content above about 20 percent)! They're a delight to watch, hovering in flight, sipping nectar drawn through a hollow extensile tongue that darts in and out of their long narrow bills.

Most threatened of the nation's endemics is the critically endangered Ridgway's hawk, a raptor now restricted entirely to the rugged terrain of Parque Nacional Los Haitises. Now down to around 115 pairs, it is erroneously thought by local farmers to prey on domestic fowl, for which reason it is illegally hunted. The **Peregrine Fund** (208-362-3716; www.peregrine fund.org) has a conservation program aimed at saving this magnificent bird known for its loud, musical call. Eighteen other endemic bird species are considered threatened or endangered, including the bay-breasted cuckoo, which like several other endemics is virtually restricted today to the Sierra de Bahoruco mountain range. Here, the island's largest area of intact native pine and broadleaf forest provides a sheltered habitat relatively untouched by the destruction of woodland that has affected many other regions.

Thirty-seven species of New World warblers sing a calliope on the avian scales. Turkey vultures are common throughout the country. So are cattle egrets, easily seen in pastures. In fact, the republic is home to 12 species of herons and egrets. There are as 24 species of ducks; 9 species of coots and rails; 9 species of raptors, including osprey and American kestrel; 12 species of terns, including sooty terns and brown noddys; 6 species of cuckoo; and 5 of owls, plus the closely related northern potoo. The list goes on and on.

About half of the Dominican Republic's bird species are migrants, the majority of which are waterfowl, shorebirds, and warblers. Most are snowbirds, fleeing the North American winter. Baikal teal, king eiders, and white-cheeked pintail flood the shallow lakes and wetlands in multitudinous thousands. Northern jacana trot across the lily pads on their widely spread and oversized feet. Glossy ibis, white ibis, roseate spoonbills, and flamingoes pick for tidbits in freshwater and briny lagoons, while coastal mangroves are ideal nesting sites for pelicans, Neotropic cormorants, and anhingas, colloquially known as snake-birds for their long slender necks cocked in a S-shape, like a cobra. And down by the shore, sandpipers, whimbrels, willets and American oystercatchers scurry in search of small crustaceans and similar tasty morsels.

Seabirds, too, are well represented. Red-billed tropic birds grace the sky with their snow-white plumage and trailing tails. Frigate birds hang in the air like kites on invisible strings. Masked, red-footed, and brown boobies—quintessential maritime birds—nest on various offshore isles. Others on the must-see wish list of birding enthusiasts include

Wilson's storm-petrel, Pomarine jaeger, and Audubon's shearwater, a small, stocky seabird named for John James Audubon (1785–1851), the gifted wildlife artist and author of the seminal *Birds of America* who was born on Hispaniola.

See Birding, in the Tours section of the Information chapter, for information on birding, including companies offering birding tours in the Dominican Republic.

Born with a Watertight Skin

Other than birds, it's the reptiles that you're likely to see. The Dominican Republic boasts 26 snake species, 63 frog species, and 114 lizard species, all of them shared with Haiti.

Let's start with the snakes. Commonly seen, the large Hispaniolan boa is colored with somber tones of chestnut and dusky brown; it feeds primarily on rodents, birds, and bats. Like many boas, its skin displays a remarkable pearly blue green iridescence when seen in sunlight (the sheen results from the molecular structure of the skin cells and is unrelated to the skin's pigmentation). It prefers moist forests and open savannas and, like all boas, surprises its prey with a biting lunge that precedes constricting the poor beast to death. The Hispaniolan boa can grow to 8 feet (2.4 m) in length, significantly longer than the smaller arboreal boas: the Dominican clouded boa, Hispaniolan vine boa, Haitian tree boa, and Hispaniolan desert boa, which prefer the more arid regions. These species typically average no more than about 1–2 feet (30–60 cm) in length. Most are capable of changing color from dark to light to suit their background, like chameleons. Unlike most snake species, which lay eggs, female boas produce live offspring.

Unique to the Greater Antilles, dwarf boas, such as the shy, strikingly colored Hispaniolan trope, aren't actually boas. These tiny snakes have the strange habit of bleeding from their mouths when they feel threatened.

Unlike boas, which lie in ambush, the racers, which range in size from 2 to 7 feet (.6–2 m) in length, are alert and high-strung hunters that pursue their prey with great bursts of speed. Thus, they have excellent eyesight. Arboreal species can often be seen hiding in bromeliads in wait of frogs or other prey to come to drink or lay eggs in the cisterns. These

Crocodile   The Dominican Republic Ministry of Tourism

Defying Gravity

Scratch your head as you might, you can puzzle all day and night about how the Dickens geckos cling to ceilings and scurry along upside down without falling off. Sticky feet? Nah! Suction cups? Forget it! Surface tension? Getting warmer!

Touch a gecko's foot and you'll find it dry and smooth. No gummy adhesive or clasping hooks or Spiderman-like suction cups. The gecko's astounding adhesive ability is actually due to pure physics. The feat is accomplished by specialized toe pads covered with millions of spatula-tipped filaments, each a mere hundred nanometers thick—a diameter less than the wavelength of visible light. The spatulae themselves tip millions of microscopic hairs that blanket curling ridges on each toe pad on the gecko's five-toed feet. The nanofilaments are so small that they tap into the van der Waals force, the transient negative and positive electrical charges that draw adjacent molecules together. The attractive force that holds a gecko to a surface is thus an electrical bond between the spatulae and the molecules of whatever surface the gecko nimbly scampers across.

The grip, however, is highly directional and self-releasing. The toes bond to a surface when placed downward and are released when the gecko changes its toes' angle, breaking the geometric relationship of spatulae and surface molecule.

include the three species of pencil-thin, bottle and lime green Hispaniolan tree snakes—the sharp-nosed vine snake, sharp-nosed green tree snake, and blunt-headed green tree snake—that mimic thin branches and vines. Most numerous of all snakes on the island is the Hispaniola lesser racer, which can also be found on Cuba, Jamaica, and the Bahamas. Two of the Hispaniolan racers are called hognose racers, for their upturned snouts. All the racers are mildly to moderately venomous and carry just enough venom to kill small birds or mammals.

Other snakes include a pink-hued blind snake, *rabo de gato,* looking like a giant worm.

Most snakes are predominantly nocturnal and spend the days cozying underground or beneath leaf litter. They are shy, retiring animals and avoid confrontation with man whenever possible. However, they will bite if cornered or restrained. The fangs of a full-grown boa can inflict considerable damage. And although the venom of racers is not deadly to humans, that of some species is sufficiently potent to send hypersensitive folks to the hospital.

Alas, snake populations throughout the island have been decimated by habitat loss and predation by the ferret-like mongoose.

Lizards are everywhere, darting from rock to rock or staring you down from a shady crevice. The semi-arboreal green and brown anoles are easily recognizable by the way males bob their heads and extend and retract their throat dewlaps, as if opening and closing a Spanish mantilla fan. Anoles can change their skin color, much like chameleons, which are also found on Hispaniola. You'll fall in love with geckos—undeniably cute, bright green, and almost rubberlike, like the charming Cockney-speaking gecko of the Geico ads. You'll probably hear them before you see them, as they love to vocalize with cheeping sounds. Don't be surprised to find them scurrying across your hotel room ceiling! Geckos feed on tiny insects, such as mosquitoes, for which reason house geckos (which live in thatched roofs or crevices in ceilings) are happily tolerated by Dominican families. The world's smallest lizard—no bigger than the width of a quarter—is a dwarf gecko endemic to

Isla Beata, off the southernmost tip of Hispaniola, where it was only discovered in 1998.

Iguanas—fearsome-looking, dragon-like lizards—are plentiful and commonly seen in lower elevation forests. Despite their size—up to 5 feet (1.5 m) long—and *One Million Years B.C.* appearance, they're harmless herbivores and frugivores. The Dominican Republic has four species, including the green iguana, common to many Caribbean islands and countries of Central America. Iguanas have a row of protective spines running down their back and along their whiplike tails, which they use to deliver painful lashes if attacked. Males have large dewlaps that hang below their chins, to help regulate their body temperature and for use in courtship displays. Most remarkable is the parietal eye, a rudimentary third eye, or photosensory organ, atop the head to detect motion from above. The endemic banded rock iguana, rhinoceros iguana, and Ricord's iguana are rock iguanas specific to the Dominican Republic's dry forests (the endangered Ricord is found solely in the southwestern region). They are both a dark gray brown, merging into turquoise toward the tail. The rhinoceros iguana (which has a royal blue mouth!) is named for the small horn on the male's nose; they also have a helmetlike pad atop their head in place of the parietal eye.

The Dominican Republic also boasts the Caribbean's largest population of American crocodiles, which can attain a whopping length of 16 feet (4.9 m) on a diet of fish. Once numerous throughout coastal waters, today they are relegated to Lago Enriquillo. See the

What a Croc!

The olive green American crocodile (*cocodrilo* to Dominicans), one of four species of New World crocodiles with a lineage dating back 200 million years, is a true giant of the reptile kingdom. Males are capable of attaining 20 feet (6 m) of saurian splendor. Their favored habitat is freshwater or brackish coastal lagoons, estuaries, and mangrove swamps, although in the Dominican Republic they are now restricted almost entirely to Lago Enriquillo, a landlocked hypersaline lake that was once linked to the open sea. They spend most of their mornings basking on mud banks, soaking up the sun and regulating their body temperature by opening or closing their gaping mouths. Come nightfall, they slink off into the water for the hunt. The American crocodile exists on a diet of fish (crocodiles are vital to aquatic ecology, for they wean out weak and diseased fish) and the occasional careless waterfowl and small mammals. Crocs cannot chew. They simply chomp down with their hydraulic-pressure-like jaws, then tear and swallow, often consuming half their body weight at one sitting. Powerful stomach acids dissolve bones 'n' all.

Crocodiles may look lumbering but they are capable of amazing bursts of speed. They're also supremely adapted to water. Their eyes and nostrils protrude from atop their heads to permit easy vision and breathing while they otherwise lurk entirely concealed underwater. A swish of their thick muscular tails provides tremendous propulsion.

They make their homes in burrows accessed by underwater tunnels, much like a beaver's. They reach sexual maturity at about eight years of age. Winter is mating season. The mature males battle it out for harems, then protect their breeding turf from rival suitors with bare-toothed gusto. The ardent male gets very excited over estrous females and roars like a lion while pounding the water with his lashing tail. Mating can last up to an hour, with the couple intertwined like Romeo and Juliet. Females lay their eggs during dry season in a sandy nest covered with moist, heat-creating compost. They guard their nests with gusto. Once the wee ones hatch, Mum uncovers the eggs and takes the squeaking babies into her mouth and swims off with the youngsters peeking out between a palisade of teeth. Dad assists until all the hatchlings are in their special nursery, which the dutiful parents guard.

Other reptilians include two species of freshwater turtles. They're easily seen basking on logs or mud banks in lagoons and wetland ponds. Four of the world's eight species of marine turtles—green, hawksbill, leatherback, and loggerhead—lumber out of the surf to lay the seeds of tomorrow's turtles in the republic's sugar-fine sands. Most females typically time their arrival to coincide with full moons, when there is less distance to travel beyond the high water mark. Finding an elevated spot in the sand, she digs out a 3-foot deep (1 m) hole with her rear flippers, drops in her 100 or so golf-ball-sized and -shaped eggs, then laboriously fills in the hole, tamps it down, scatters sand about to disguise it and, exhausted after this hours-long labor, crawls back down the beach and swims off through the surf. All four species are endangered, threatening a demise for creatures that have been swimming the oceans for 100 million years. Unlike its smaller cousins, which have an external skeleton in the form of their calcareous carapace, the leatherback (which can measure 8 feet (2.4 m) long and weigh up to 1,000 pounds) has an internal skeleton and an exterior of leathery, cartilaginous skin. Tapered for hydrodynamic efficiency and insulated by a layer of thick oily fat, it has evolved to survive staggeringly deep cold-water dives and migrations of thousands of miles.

Amphibians also have watertight skins. They range from the thimble-size olive-brown Dominican tree frog, which chirps through the night (especially after a heavy downpour), to the giant cane toad, which can grow to an astounding 8 inches (20 cm) long. The latter, with its brown skin covered with warty toxin glands, was introduced to the Caribbean islands during the colonial era to control insect pests in the sugarcane fields. Instead, it developed a taste for virtually anything that moves and it can get down its gullet. It outcompetes native amphibians and has been an ecological disaster. It laughs off snakes with its toxic secretions (even cats sicken and can die), which it can squirt over 3 feet (.9 m) when threatened.

Arachnids, Insects, and Relatives

The Dominican tropics are abuzz with bees, wasps, and flies. There are at least 6,000 known species, including 126 known species of ant . . . and counting. Dragonflies flit back and forth across the surface of pools. Some 200 species of butterflies—swallowtails, heliconius, Julia longwings, white peacocks, stinky leaf wings—brighten the landscapes of Hispaniola, dancing like floating leaves on the wind. There are mantids. Cockroaches. Venomous centipedes. Big stink bugs. Katydids 3 inches long. Stick insects as long as your forearm. And beetles galore in a kaleidoscope of shimmering greens, neon blues, startling reds, and impossible silvers and golds.

Probing around with your hands amid rocks is never a good idea, as scorpions (*alacrán* to Dominicans) spend the daylight hours hiding in shady crevices. They stir around dusk, when they emerge to hunt crickets, cockroaches, and other insects, which they subdue with a venomous sting. With their fearsome looking claws and sharp-curving stinging tail, scorpions should be treated with due trepidation. Hispaniola has an amazing 32 distinct species of scorpions! Some are virtually harmless to humans; others have venom as deadly as any viper.

The Dominican Republic even boasts its own endemic species of tarantula (*cacata*). The black Greater Hispaniola tarantula—a true giant of the spider kingdom—is as big as your hand and furry as a teddy bear (its cousins, the Barychelid tarantula and the Dominican trap-door tarantula, are considerably smaller). These nocturnal critters are nonaggressive and will bite only if provoked, except during mating season, when the males are particularly ill tempered. The chief enemy of the tarantula and other spiders is the enormous tarantula hawk wasp, unmistakably adorned with an iridescent blue body and brilliant orange wings. Though they feed on nectar, the females paralyze large spiders with their powerful sting. Dragging the paralyzed spider into her burrow, she then lays an egg upon it and seals the entrance to the hole. When the larvae hatch, they eat the inert yet still-alive host.

Beneath the Waves

The seas around Hispaniola are a pelagic playpen, prodigiously populated by fish and marine mammals. Coral reefs rim much of the isle. Sheets of purple staghorn sway to the rhythms of the ocean current. Leaflike orange gorgonians spread their fingers upwards toward the light. And lacy crops of black coral resemble delicately woven Spanish mantillas. Kaleidoscopic extravaganzas of fish as strikingly bejeweled as damsels in an exotic harem play tag in the coral-laced waters. Palometo. Sargassum triggerfish. Stoplight parrotfish. Redlip blenny and scores of other rainbow-hued species whose names you may forget but whose beauty you will remember forever. Spiny lobsters the size of house cats crawl over the seabed while small rays flap by and moray eels peer out from their hideaways. Sharks, of course, are ever-present, though most are harmless nurse sharks. Farther out, the aquamarine oceans teem with game fish, luring anglers keen to snag dorado, tuna, wahoo, swordfish, and marlin.

The stars of the show, however, are undoubtedly the humpback whales that migrate from colder northern waters and gather each winter to frolic in the bathtub-warm waters of Samaná Bay and, off the northeast coast, in the shallow crystal-clear waters of the Silver Bank. Here, they gather for courtship and to mate and give birth.

Majestic Humpback whales in Dominican Republic The Dominican Republic Ministry of Tourism

SOCIAL HISTORY

First Inhabitants

Although Hispaniola's recorded history began on December 12, 1492, when the Genoese explorer Cristóbal Colón (Christopher Columbus, 1451–1506) stepped ashore to claim the isle for Spain, the land had already been occupied for at least two thousand years. The first known occupants were the Archaics, a primitive pre-ceramist, nomadic culture of hunters and gatherers who seem to have settled Hispaniola around 1000 B.C. and are thought to have originated in Central America. They were displaced by the Ciboney, the first of several Arawak (Amerindian) tribes that originated in the Orinoco basin of South America and populated the Caribbean during the next two millennia. The Ciboney were ceramists. Physical evidence of their presence is paltry and little is certain about their culture. The docile Ciboney were assimilated by the more advanced Ignerí around 100 A.D. These people, also from South America, introduced *bateyes,* ballparks and ceremonial plazas most prominently seen today as archaeological remains in Puerto Rico. The Ignerí, in turn, were displaced and enslaved, perhaps as early as 500 A.D., by the Taíno who, like their predecessors, had pursued a gradual migration north through the Caribbean using giant *canoas* (dugout canoes) hewn by fire and adze from massive mahogany and ceiba trees.

The peaceable Taíno (the word means good or noble) called their new home Quisqueya. They lived in clan villages centered on *bateyes* under the leadership of caciques—chieftains whose large, square, thatched huts, or *caneyes,* were surrounded by circular *bohíos* occupied communally by *naborias* (common people) and *nitainos* (nobles). Although caciques were invariably male, Taíno society was matriarchal. The polygamous, non-hereditary chieftains were selected democratically by women. Each cacique's importance within the tribe was determined by the size of his clan. Agglomerations of clans were arranged into five tribes owing allegiance and tribute to high caciques. Both males and females went about naked or wore a tiny breechcloth over the genitals; tattooed their bodies with black dye from the *jagua* fruit; and considered a receding forehead such a mark of beauty that they flattened babies' foreheads by pressing the head between boards to restrict development.

The Taíno dried the leaves of a domestic plant called *cohiba* to burn and inhale into the nostrils, through long tubes called *tabacos,* to induce hallucination. Religion was integral to their lives. An entire pantheon was believed to control nature's forces, including *cemís* (spirit gods of the ancestors), minor gods such as *Huracán* (god of violent storms), and two supreme gods—*Yúcahu* (of agriculture and the sea) and his mother *Atabey* (goddess of fertility and water). Taíno adorned their artifacts, *bateyes,* rock faces, and caverns with depictions (also called *cemís*) of gods and spirits, often represented by animals and/or abstract and humanlike faces. They believed in rebirth and thus buried their dead in a fetal position for the afterlife.

The Taíno had neither a written language nor knowledge of metals. Nor did they use the wheel or employ beasts of burden. Nonetheless, they evolved a rudimentary astrological calendar. They were also skilled weavers and conjured *henequen* (hemp) and wild cotton into ropes, mats, and *hamacas* (hammocks). They were also gifted potters and farmers and evolved a sophisticated cultivation technique of raised mounds, called *conucos,* to grow squash, beans, and yuca (their staple crop), a starchy edible root that they used to make cassava flour for bread. They also grew *maíz* (corn) using slash-and-burn methods.

On the eve of Christopher Columbus's arrival, the Taíno (who are thought to have numbered between 100,000 and 500,000 on Hispaniola) were being threatened by Caribs, a warlike Arawak race that had swept north through the Lesser Antilles like a plague. The Caribs would lend their name to the entire region.

Columbus Arrives

On August 3, 1492, Columbus sailed from Spain on the first of his four voyages in search of a westward route to the Orient, under the patronage of King Ferdinand and Queen Isabela. His three-ship flotilla, manned by 90 crewmembers, was comprised of the caravels *Santa Maria, Niña,* and *Pinta*. After 33 days, the cry of *"Tierra!"* rang out as land shadowed the moonlit horizon. After making his first landfall in the Bahamas, Columbus continued on to Cuba (the Taíno name, which Columbus mistook for Kublai Khan) before turning east. On December 12, 1492, he anchored off the north coast of Hispaniola, believing that he had reached Japan. He voyaged along the north coast for two weeks until, on Christmas Day, the *Santa Maria* struck a reef and sank. A colony of Spaniards was left behind to found Puerto de la Navidad, the first settlement in the New World, while Columbus returned to Spain. Since Columbus was convinced that he had reached the Indies, as the Orient was then known, he collectively named the islands the West Indies.

Columbus returned to Hispaniola in 1493 to discover all the stranded colonists were dead. A new settlement, La Isabela, was consecrated on November 22, 1493 in honor of the Spanish queen, and Columbus's brother Bartolomé (1461–1515) was named governor of

Remains of Columbus's house, Isabel

Casa Ponce de León

Hispaniola. La Isabela's marshy locale was malarial. Thus, in 1498 Bartolomé relocated the settlement to the south coast, where Nueva Isabela was built on the east bank of the Río Ozama. That year, on his third voyage, Christopher Columbus returned to discover civil unrest among the Spanish colonists. When word reached Spain, a royal representative was sent to investigate. He arrested the brothers, who were sent back to Spain (Christopher Columbus soon won a pardon). In 1502, Nicolás de Ovando (1460–1518) arrived to reestablish order and govern the Indies. He was accompanied by 30 ships bearing 2,500 Spanish settlers. When that year a hurricane leveled Nueva Isabela, Ovando moved the settlement to the south coast, where a new settlement was laid out on the east (and later the west) bank of the Ozama river as Santo Domingo de Gúzman. (Columbus never found the precious metals, stones, and spices that his backers had sought. He eventually died a dispirited man in Valladolid, Spain, on May 20, 1506.)

Meanwhile, the peaceable Taíno were suffering greatly. The medieval conquistadores were not on a holy mission. They came in quest of gold and fortune. The "Indians" were seen as pathetic heathen to be used as chattel under the *encomienda* system (a modified form of slavery, which the Pope had banned in the New World), in which conquistadores received land grants and usufruct rights to Taíno labor, ostensibly with the purpose of converting the heathen to Christianity. However, the aborigines were not inclined to harsh labor. Cacique Guarionex led ill-fated rebellions in 1495 and in 1497. They were brutally suppressed. Those Taíno not slaughtered by musket and sword succumbed to smallpox, measles, and tuberculosis—Old World diseases to which they had no immunity—while others withered spiritually and committed mass suicides. A Dominican friar, Bartolomé de las Casas (1474–1566), defended their cause: *"The Indians came to meete us, and to receive us with victuals, and delicate cheere—the Devill put himselfe into the Spaniards, to put them all to the edge of the sword in my presence, without any cause whatsoever, more than three thousand soules, which were set before us, men, women and children. I saw there so great cruelties, that never any man living either have or shall see the like."* Beseeching authorities on their behalf, the Apostle of the Indians was instrumental in the abolition of the *encomienda* system in 1542. Nonetheless, within a hundred years of Columbus's arrival, the Taíno had been virtually exterminated.

Named Governor of the Indies, Columbus's firstborn son Diego Colón (1479–1523) replaced Nicolás de Ovando in 1508. He laid the foundation stone of the first cathedral in the Americas and lived with his wife Doña María de Toledo, King Ferdinand's niece, in the grand, 22-room Palacio Alcazar. Santo Domingo attained its regular grid pattern and became the center of Spanish authority in the Americas. Although the city was soon eclipsed in wealth and real power by Havana, Lima, and Veracruz, Santo Domingo remained the seat of the *Real Audiencia,* or Supreme Court, in the Americas until the function was transferred to Cuba in 1799.

Hispaniola had precious little gold to give up. The primitive mines that the Spanish established were soon exhausted. Santo Domingo became a staging post for expeditions to conquer and colonize the lands of Central and South America. In 1519, Hernán Cortés (1485–1547) subdued Montezuma, opening the astonishing wealth of the Aztecs to plunder. Within 15 years, conquistador Francisco Pizarro (1476–1541) had similarly vanquished the opulent Incas. Treasure ships groaning from the weight of their bullion converged on Havana (assembly point for twice-yearly treasure fleets—*flotas*—en route to Spain), which had a strategically advantageous position that sent Santo Domingo into decline.

Although administrative authority over the Indies remained with Hispaniola, the island evolved primarily as an agricultural base to supply Spain with hardwoods, cattle hides, sugar, and tobacco (a smoking craze quickly took hold in Europe in emulation of the Taíno habit). The lowland forests were felled to raise cattle and sugarcane, which Christopher Columbus introduced to the isle. Canefields multiplied to feed Europe's collective sweet tooth. With the Taíno workforce decimated, the Spanish turned to West Africa to supply labor for the sugarcane fields. The first *asientos*—contracts—to import and trade African slaves were granted as early as 1505. A lucrative new trade developed. By the mid-16th century, the island's population of 50,000 was comprised two thirds of slaves. Once ashore, the Africans were sold to plantation owners or to work as domestics. No attention was paid to family relationships: Parents and offspring were torn asunder. Life as a domestic held few rights, but was immensely preferable to the brutal work and brutality of the canefields, where slaves toiled as beasts of burden under the searing of both sun and lash. Understandably, rebellion was always around the corner. Hispaniola's first slave revolt erupted in 1522 on a plantation owned by Diego Colón. Its brutal suppression set an unforgiving pattern.

Despite the immense wealth being generated, the Spanish crown disdained the colonies, which they treated as a cash cow to milk. Spain applied a rigid monopoly forbidding manufacture in the Americas, which were forced under threat of punishment to import virtually all their necessities from Spain at inflated prices. Even exports to Spain were taxed. Not surprisingly, smuggling took hold quickly, not least in slaves: The trade was so profitable it defied regulation. Many a famous pirate got his start smuggling slaves, including famous cousins John Hawkins (1532–95) and Francis Drake (1540–1596), who supplied Hispaniola and smuggled out sugar and silver under the noses of corrupt officials.

Piracy and Revolution

During the 16th and 17th centuries, piracy became the scourge of Spain's Caribbean possessions. Although the majority of pirates were freelancers like Walt Disney's fictional Captain Jack Sparrow, many were corsairs (corsarios) officially licensed by Spain's rivals—England, France, and Holland—to harass and plunder Spanish shipping and possessions. No vessel, city, or plantation was safe from these bloodthirsty predators. For example, the image of Sir Francis Drake as genteel hero is pure myth; he was a ruthless cutthroat. In 1586, Drake attacked Santo Domingo with a fleet of 18 ships. Although the city had been enclosed by a fortified wall, Drake quickly captured the city. It was duly plundered, and most of the churches (along with one-third of the city) were destroyed.

In 1588, King Philip of Spain determined to end England's growing sea power and reinstate Catholicism. A great armada of 160 ships was assembled for an invasion, but the larger and heavier Spanish galleons proved no match for England's smaller, nimbler and more advanced "racers" under the command of Drake, Hawkins, and Sir Walter Raleigh. The Armada was destroyed. Spain's seafaring abilities were shattered. Her colonies were impotent as piracy and smuggling gained new zeal. The Spanish-born authorities (peninsulares) thus decided to raze the smuggling centers of Bayajá, La Yaguana, Monte Cristi, and Puerto Plata. In 1605, these towns were burned to the ground, resulting in the collapse of the island's economy. Hispaniola was weakened prey. Thus, in 1655, England's archly anti-Papist Lord Protector Oliver Cromwell (1599–1658) launched an ill-fated campaign to seize Spain's Caribbean islands. Alas, the badly equipped and disorganized fleet led by Admiral William Penn was easily repulsed in its assault on Hispaniola in April 1655. (The English forces managed to capture the weakly defended Spanish colony of Jamaica the following month).

Meanwhile, a new breed of pirate—the buccaneers—swept the Caribbean like a plague. This band of seafaring cutthroats had begun as a motley band of international (mostly Dutch, French, and English) ne'er-do-wells who had gravitated to Tortuga, a small French-held isle off the northwest coast of Hispaniola, where they worked the land, hunted wild boars on Hispaniola, and traded boucan (smoked meat, from which the buccaneers took their name) to passing ships. Suppressed by the Spanish, they turned to piracy and eventually set up base in Port Royal, Jamaica, where they were given official sanction and attained infamy for their cruelty and daring under the leadership of Welsh pirate, Henry Morgan (1635–88). Many other buccaneers shunned piracy in favor of farming. They settled western Hispaniola in increasing numbers and established French-speaking settlements that Spanish cincuéntenas (squads of 50 troops) sent from Santo Domingo were unable to squash. Finally, by the Treaty of Ryswick of 1697, Spain ceded to France the western third of Hispaniola, which was divided into Santo Domingo and Saint-Domingue. The treaty also banned privateering.

The French government took an entirely different approach to its colony than Spain did to increasingly depauperate Santo Domingo. The latter stagnated, while the French invested vast sums in efficient and up-to-date plantations. By 1775, Saint-Domingue's sugar exports exceeded those of all the other Caribbean islands' combined, while its wealth was exceeded by none. *Les grandes blancs* (the wealthy white class) lived luxuriantly and decadently, supported in their wealth by half a million impoverished and brutalized slaves. News of the French Revolution in 1789 caused consternation as arrivals from France stated that the National Assembly had declared all men free and equal. The powerful white planters, however, still in charge of the local assemblies, were in no mood to grant slaves their freedom. In October 1790, a brief rebellion broke out in southern Saint-Domingue as mulattos attempted to assert voting rights of free people of color. Then, on August 22, 1791, the much-feared slave uprising boiled over. Northern Saint-Domingue exploded, plunging the nation into civil war between supporters of the Ancien Régime and those of the Paris Communes (made up principally of *petites blancs*—white petty merchants, scribes, artisans, and the like who saw an opportunity to claim spoils heretofore reserved to the planters). An attempt by revolutionary troops sent from France failed to restore order. The situation was worsened as French commissioner Léger-Félicité Sonthonax (1763–1813) suppressed both white planters and slaves while enforcing the rights of social equality recently granted to free people of color.

In 1792, the Revolutionary Wars broke out in Europe, pitting France against England and Spain. Saint-Domingue's insurrectionist leaders, led by former slave Toussaint L'Ouverture (circa 1743–1803), joined forces with the Spanish troops of Santo Domingo. L'Ouverture, a brilliant strategist, led a successful conquest of northern Saint-Domingue against the French. Meanwhile, British troops seized Port-au-Prince. With Sonthonax on the verge of surrender came word that on February 4, 1794, the Jacobin National Convention in Paris had declared the emancipation of slaves. Sonthonax declared Saint-Domingue's slaves free. L'Ouverture then switched sides. In quick succession, he defeated the Spanish and British and essentially took power of the island. In 1795, the Treaty of Bale, Spain surrendered Santo Domingo to France.

An astute politician, L'Ouverture consolidated his popularity and power and ran his own fiefdom, outmaneuvering a succession of governors sent from France to administer the entire island. In January 1801, he easily overran Santo Domingo, whose population of 80,000 people was a mere tenth that of Saint-Domingue. He seized control of the former Spanish possessions (where slavery was still in effect), declared slave emancipation, and dictated a constitution that made him governor-general for life over all Hispaniola. France was now under the rule of Napoléon Bonaparte (1769–1821), as First Consul. Bonaparte deemed L'Ouverture a threat to the isle's restoration as a profitable colony. A fleet of 22,000 troops was therefore dispatched to depose L'Ouverture, who was captured and imprisoned in France. However, France was unable to secure peace on the isle. A brutal guerrilla war led by black General Jean-Jacques Dessalines (1758–1806) ensued. On November 18, 1803, at the Battle of Vertières the French were finally pushed out of western Hispaniola. On January 1, 1804, Dessalines declared independence for the former colony of Saint-Domingue, naming the world's first black republic Haiti.

Invasion and Independence

Meanwhile, France continued to rule over Santo Domingo. The Spanish populace, however, resented French rule and sought help to restore Spanish sovereignty. In 1808, the British blockaded the port of Santo Domingo and occupied Samaná. The following year, France ceded Santo Domingo back to the Spanish, who reverted to brutal and inept rule, including the reinstatement of slavery. The ensuing period (1809–21) of colonial government earned the derisory epithet, *españa boba* (foolish Spain). The Spanish-born *peninsulares* were increasingly resented by island-born *criollos* who, not least, chafed at undue taxation. Thus, the epoch coincided with the rise of a national independence movement. On December 1, 1821, anti-colonial gentry led by José Núñez de Cáceres declared independence and petitioned to join Gran Colombia, Simón Bolívar's (1783–1830) newly formed federation of liberated Spanish colonies. The period that would later be known as the *La independencia efímera* (Ephemeral Independence) was short-lived. While Santo Domingo awaited a reply, a Haitian army led by President Jean-Pierre Boyer (1776–1850) invaded. Santo Domingo would be absorbed into and ruled by Haiti for 22 years. The period witnessed a reign of terror against whites and mulattos that left the region economically shattered (large estates were broken up and distributed to former slaves) and instilled in Dominicans a hatred for their Haitian neighbors.

The *independistas'* efforts were now focused on freeing Santo Domingo from Haitian rule. Key among these was La Trinitaria, a secret organization founded in 1838 and led by a young nationalist, Juan Pablo Duarte (1813–73). Finding an unlikely ally in embittered troops under Haitian General Charles Hérard, they supported an insurrection of March 1843 that toppled Boyer and named Hérard as president. However, Hérard betrayed La Trinitaria. Duarte was exiled to Venezuela. Other *independistas* were shot. When independence wasn't forthcoming, the *independistas* seized Santo Domingo's Fortaleza Ozama, and on February 28, 1844, declared independence from Haiti. Although Hérard returned with an army of 25,000 soldiers, he was repulsed and retreated back to Haiti, leaving the white, red, and green flag of the República Dominicana to flutter over Santo Domingo.

Duarte returned as a hero and was favored as a candidate for the presidency of the newborn republic. Before a vote could be held, Pedro Santana (1801–64), a powerful pro-Span-

Statue of of Juan Pablo Duarte, Universidad Autónoma de Santo Domingo

Juan Pablo Duarte and La Trinitaria

The Dominican Republic's foremost national hero, Juan Pablo Duarte y Díez, was born on January 26, 1813, in a small house on Calle El Tejera, in Santo Domingo. His father, Juan José Duarte, was a shopkeeper born in Spain. His mother, Manuela Diez Jiménez, was from El Ceibo. Duarte studied philosophy at the University of Santo Domingo and, later, studied languages in New York following which he traveled to London, Paris, and Barcelona. He returned to Santo Domingo in 1831 already fired with romanticism, liberalism, and ideals for the nationalist cause.

On July 16, 1838, Duarte was a principal founder of La Trinitaria, a secret patriotic society dedicated to overthrowing Haitian rule and establishing independence. Its motto was *"Dios, patria y libertad"* (God, Mother Country and Freedom). He also founded La Filantrópica, a radical theater group that spread the liberation message. In 1843 La Trinitaria launched its revolution to repel Jean-Pierre Boyer and the Haitians. When it failed, Duarte was briefly jailed, then exiled to Caracas, Venezuela, where he penned the Constitution. On February 27, 1844, another uprising expelled Boyer, and Duarte was summoned. He was nominated by the Liberal party as a candidate for the presidency of the newborn republic. His opponent, General Pedro Santana, of the Reactionary party, preempted the election with a coup and banished Duarte. In 1845, the entire Duarte family was exiled by Santana.

Duarte returned briefly to the island in 1864 to partake in the War of Restoration against Spain. He returned to Venezuela as the Dominican Consul. Duarte died in Caracas on July 15, 1876, at the age of 63. His remains were transferred to the republic in 1884 and he was buried with full honors beneath a mausoleum in Parque Independencia. Duarte—author, philosopher, poet, soldier, and independence hero—has come to be acknowledged as the Father of the Country (*padre de la patria*). His birthday is commemorated as a national holiday.

ish cattle rancher from the eastern lowlands, marched a private army on Santo Domingo and quashed the *independistas*. Duarte was exiled again, never to return to his homeland. The next two decades witnessed a state of near constant civil war as rural patriarchs with large peasant armies fought among themselves for control of the nation. They were assisted in their efforts by a succession of Haitian invasions that permitted the *caudillos* (strongmen) to rescue the republic and assume power. These constant wars devastated the cities and countryside, which were constantly put to the torch. The country was left destitute. Meanwhile, Santana and his arch rival Buanaventura Báez (1812–84) helped bankrupt the nation with their military spending and grandiose frauds as they succeeded each other in alternate periods of power

In 1861, Santana appealed to Spain to re-annex the Dominican Republic. They agreed. Thus, on March 18, 1861, the 17-year-old republic again became a Spanish colony with Santana serving briefly as governor before being dismissed from office. Spain attempted to run its new ex-colony in the same repressive way as before, and popular protests were brutally crushed. In February 1863 an armed uprising was launched. On August 16 insurrectionists led by Gregorio Luperón (1839–97) raised their flag at Capotillo in an act known as *el grito de capotillo* (cry of Capotillo) declaring the second republic. The War of Restoration (Santana led the Spanish forces) dragged on for two more years until Spain eventually gave up and departed in July 1865.

Hope for stability and recovery, however, were once again dashed. Self-serving *caudillos* reasserted authority in a sordid five-decade-long epoch of coup, counter-coup, and civil strife. The revolving door of warlord-presidents included Buenaventura Báez (1812–84), who after several terms in power eventually sold out the country to foreign commercial interests. In 1869, he offered to sell the republic to the United States for US$150,000. President Ulysses S. Grant (1822–85) agreed and an annexation treaty was drawn up. However, the U.S. Senate rejected the deal. Báez then leased the Bay of Samaná, one of the Caribbean's finest natural harbors, to the New York-based Samana Bay Company for $150,000 a year. The company intended to lease the bay to the U.S. government as a naval base but immediately fell behind in its payments and the contract was soon rescinded. Popular dissatisfaction with the deal forced Báez from office.

Luperón became president in 1879, ushering in a rare period of economic stability and relatively clean government based in Puerto Plata. The calm was short-lived. After Luperón stepped down in 1882, one of his former lieutenants, black General Ulises Hereaux (1845–99), manipulated a series of incompetent and corrupt presidents until eventually seizing (and maintaining) power by intimidation and assassination. He established a model of extreme corruption that blurred the distinction between the States' and his personal finances—a forerunner of worse to come in the following century. Nonetheless, his tenure saw the electrification of Santo Domingo, construction of the nation's first railway, and other grand modernization schemes. Hereaux also gave land grants to a wave of émigrés fleeing Cuba's Ten Years War; they set up the Dominican Republic's first mechanized sugar mills and a tobacco industry today considered to exceed in quality even that of their homeland. Heureaux, however, succeeded in bringing the entire country to the brink of bankruptcy before being assassinated in Moca in July 1899.

Washington's S.O.B.

The 20th century promised more of the same. A succession of short-lived governments led by provincial caudillos oversaw a bankrupt nation threatened with military intervention by European powers seeking redress. The United States had followed fractious events on the island with growing concern (the U.S. had already been granted control of Dominican Customs), which heightened after completion of the Panama Canal raised the region's strategic importance. Neighboring Haiti had already descended into even worse anarchy, resulting in President Woodrow Wilson (1856–1924) dispatching U.S. Marines in 1915. The Dominican Republic, meanwhile, was crippled by internecine conflicts and mayhem. When an army revolt in April 1916 overthrew the elected president, Wilson ordered Marines ashore there also. A formal military occupation was declared. It lasted eight years, during which schools, hospitals, and highways were built, and a functional system of local government established. The occupation meant a boom time for U.S. investors, who bought up much of the land at bottom dollar from desperate peasant farmers. The ranks of embittered urban masses swelled. Most Dominicans despised the occupation as an insult to national sovereignty by foreigners who looked down on them. A guerrilla resistance army—los gavilleros—enjoyed popular support. The guerrillas were countered by a brutal repression enacted by the U.S.-established (and heavily militarized) Guardia Nacional police force, a forerunner of the National Army, or Ejército Nacional.

U.S. forces departed in 1924 following the election of relatively scrupulous and progressive Horacio Vázquez Lajara (1860–1936). Lajara promoted public works schemes and fostered the democratic system. But the darker currents of the republic's malaise proved insurmountable. In February 1930 Lajara was overthrown. His successor, Rafael Estrella Urena (1889–1945) had worked out a deal with Ejército Nacional chief, General Rafael

Bottlecaps

Rafael Leónidas Trujillo Molina was born in San Cristobal, west of Santo Domingo, on October 24, 1891. His father, José Trujillo Valdez, was a small retailer from the Canary Islands. His mother, Altagracia Julia Molina Chevalier, was half Haitian. Trujillo was an unremarkable scholar. He began work at 16 years old as a telegraph operator and, later, as a security guard and an enforcer against sugarcane workers (rumors that he was a forger, embezzler, and cattle rustler circulated but were never proven). In 1918, he joined the Dominican army as a cadet and was trained by the U.S. Marine Corps. He rose rapidly through the ranks and by 1927 was a brigadier general and commander-in-chief of the army. He was also a psychopath with an uncanny psychological grasp of manipulation and terror.

Trujillo was also supremely vain. Projecting a messianic figure, he billed himself as The Great Benefactor of the Nation and Father of the New Dominion. He donned flamboyant uniforms and adorned himself with so many medals that he earned the moniker *chapitas* (bottlecaps). In 1936, the psychophantic congress voted to rename the capital Ciudad Trujillo while Pico Duarte was renamed Pico Trujillo. Bridges and important buildings took his name. And busts and monuments of his likeness sprouted throughout the nation. Churches were required to post the slogan, *Dios en cielo, Trujillo en tierra* (God in Heaven, Trujillo on Earth). Even car license plates featured the slogan *Viva Trujillo!*

Trujillo *was* a well-known philanderer and adulterer, a fact he did nothing to disguise. In 1913, he married Aminta Ledesma, a peasant girl whom he had got pregnant. They divorced in 1924 and a year later Trujillo married Bienvenida Ricardo, a wealthy (and non-too-pretty) socialite from Montecristi. This marriage also failed and in 1937 Trujillo divorced his pregnant wife to marry his new girlfriend, María Martínez, whose son, Ramfis, Trujillo took as his own.

Trujillo was also immensely insecure with being a mulatto in a class-conscious society. Hence, he used powder to lighten his skin. Although he himself was quarter Haitian, he adopted the Dominicans' ingrained racism against the mostly black (and supposedly inferior) Haitians, resulting in the horrific 1937 pogrom. Despite his clear fascist leanings (and overt admiration for Adolf Hitler and Benito Mussolini), Trujillo welcomed Jewish refugees from Nazi Europe and leftist Spaniards escaping Franco's execution squads as part of a policy of *blanquismo*, intended to "whiten" the republic's mixed-race population.

Following his assassination, Trujillo was buried at Cimetière du Père Lachaise Cemetery in Paris at the request of his relatives, who were forced into exile in Paris.

Leónidas Trujillo (1891–1961), who had promised to support Estrella in elections scheduled following the revolt. However, Trujillo betrayed Estrella and put himself on the ballot. His squads (known as La 42) set out to assassinate and terrorize his opponents. Soon he alone remained on the ballot. Trujillo was elected unopposed. It was the beginning of three decades of brutal depravity. (Trujillo actually held the office of president 1930–38 and 1942–52; during the interregnums, he held absolute power but left ceremonial affairs to puppet presidents, including his brother Héctor Bienvenido Trujillo Molina, president 1952–60, and protégé Joaquín Balaguer Ricardo, 1960–61.) However, Trujillo endeared himself when three weeks after the election, a massive hurricane leveled much of the city: Trujillo used U.S. aid money to rebuild the city.

Taking a cue from Hereaux, Trujillo shaped the government and entire national economy to serve his own pocket. Manufacturing businesses and vast landholdings were confiscated or otherwise manipulated into his hands. Huge public work schemes were mere inventions to feed his corporate fiefdoms. The terrorized workforce even went along with a

10 percent tax on public employees' salaries that directly fattened his pockets. Any opposition to his dictatorship was quashed without mercy. Trujillo created a true police state. Anyone deemed an opponent was eliminated. Thousands were murdered, or simply "disappeared." Military checkpoints were established every few miles, while every citizen had to carry an identification card and account for his or her movements. And the media came under strict State control. In October, 1937, Trujillo ordered the massacre of Haitians living in the Dominican Republic. At least 20,000 Haitians were murdered—many hacked to death by machete—in ensuing weeks in what came to be known as El Corte (The Cutting, for the machete chops) and the Parsley Massacre (to determine if a person were Haitian, Trujillo's thugs held up a sprig of parsley, or *perejil,* which Haitians couldn't pronounce; they couldn't trill the "r").

Even this depravity was insufficient to turn the U.S. against him. An ardent anti-communist who welcomed U.S. business, the republic's gangster-tyrant dictator was one of Washington's darlings. "He may be a S.O.B., but he's our S.O.B.," United States Secretary of State, Cordell Hull, famously quipped. For sure, Trujillo helped lubricate Washington's cynical support with a healthy dose of financial largesse and a clever public relations campaign. Nonetheless, he eventually overreached himself. Washington's tacit acceptance turned sour following Trujillo's explicit support for an assassination attempt on respected Venezuelan president Rómulo Betancourt (1908–81). Then, in March 1856, anti-Trujillo Dominican exile Jesús Galíndez was kidnapped in New York by Trujillo's thugs. He was flown to the Dominican Republic, where he was tortured and brutally murdered.

International disgust with Trujillo's regime attained an apogee in June 1959 when Cuban-trained anti-Trujillo rebels—the 14J, for *catorce de junio* (14th of June)—landed in the Cordillera Central. The popular uprising they hoped to inspire never materialized, however. The brigade was captured and tortured to death. Still, domestic opposition to Trujillo was beginning to crystallize. The underground resistance movement was led by an unlikely trio: three upper-class sisters, Antonia María, Patricia, and Minerva Mirabel, who formed the Fourteenth of June Movement. On November 25, 1960, Trujillo's thugs ambushed the sisters, who were handcuffed and clubbed to death in a canefield. Public outrage boiled over and Trujillo met his just end on May 30, 1961, when CIA-supplied assassins machine-gunned the dictator after a dramatic car chase down Santo Domingo's Malecón.

The Last Half Century

The dictator's adopted son, Ramfis Trujillo (1929–69) returned from his Parisian playground and seized power following his father's assassination. His brief six-month tenure saw a wave of recriminations against his father's political enemies. Ramfis—a dilettante playboy with a taste for mink coats, luxury cars, and Hollywood starlets (his lovers included Kim Novak)—was soon forced out by popular reaction and he fled back to Paris with the Trujillo family. The republic descended into chaos. Joaquín Balaguer (1906–2002) served mere months as president before begin toppled by another coup. Ensuing elections, in December 1962, were won convincingly by Juan Bosch (1909–2001), a left-leaning reformer and founder of the Partido Revolucionario Dominicano (PRD). His efforts to tame the military and an attempt at land redistribution antagonized the army and conservative church elites. A right-wing coup forced him out in September 1963. A rightist triumvirate then ruled for two years until pro-Bosch Constitutionalist officers staged their own coup, which sparked a right-wing counter-coup and mayhem. On April 28, 1965, U.S. Marines landed to stomp out the brief civil war and forestall what President Lyndon Johnson (1908–73) termed "a second Cuba," referring to Bosch's perceived socialism.

The June 1966 elections, overseen by the U.S., were won by Balaguer, who went on to serve three terms. This period of stability witnessed massive infrastructure projects (mostly a means for Balaguer to reward his political supporters with lucrative public works contracts) and an economic boom—the Dominican Miracle—that concentrated wealth while the poor, whose agitation for fair wages and greater inclusiveness were coined communist, were dealt with harshly by Balaguer's barbarous secret police, La Banda. Alas, he had been well trained by Trujillo. A wily *caudillo*-style politician, Balaguer portrayed himself as a benevolent father figure while using intimidation and fraud to cling to power for most of the next 35 years. He banned opposition parties except the PRD (Balaguer's chief rival, Juan Bosch, was forced into exile, where he founded the Partido de la Liberación Dominicana, PLD). In May 1978, Balaguer lost his bid for a fourth term. Unwilling to accept defeat, he had the ballots destroyed and declared victory. President Jimmy Carter (1924–), however, supported the true winner, Antonio Guzmán Fernández (1911–82) of the PRD, and Balaguer was forced to step down.

The 1980s witnessed renewed economic malaise. Rising unemployment and hardship fostered a wave of migration from the Dominican Republic to New York. The situation was exacerbated when the U.S. cut its sugar quotas and the International Monetary Fund (IMF) imposed stiff conditions on the new PRD government of Salvador Jorge Blanco (1926–), the vice president who succeeded Guzmán following his suicide on July 4, 1982. The hardships led to massive riots and scores of deaths. By 1986, Balaguer was back in power. He launched a tirade of denunciation against Blanco, who was charged with corruption and sentenced in absentia to 23 years in prison (Blanco was undergoing medical treatment in the United States at the time); the Supreme Court later overruled the sentence. Balaguer, who had merged his party with the Social Christian Revolutionary Party to form the Social Christian Reformist Party, turned to populist measures. He reversed the IMF austerity plan, printed unsecured money, and cast the republic back on the path to ruin. Inflation ran wild. In 1989, the country reneged on its debt and was subsequently cut off from international credit.

Robocop!

The Dominican National Police and 32,000-member military—both once hated and brutal entities—have been cleaned up to a large degree and are no longer automatically feared. However, incidents of excessive force and attempts to solicit bribes continue to be reported. Often this involves tourists who are stopped while driving by someone who appears to be a police officer (frequently they approach by motorcycle from behind) and who demand an on-the-spot fine. On-the-spot fines are not allowed. If you're stopped for a violation, demand a traffic ticket. If the person looks too young, or his uniform seems ill fitting and lacking a name badge, there's a good chance the uniform is stolen. If the motorcycle is not an official police motorcycle, there's a good chance you're about to be robbed by a *tíguere* (tiger)—a hustler who makes a living by deceit and cunning. Ask for police identification: Never hand over your driving license or other documents until you're sure the person is actually a policeman. Leave yourself an escape route when you stop. Incidents involving police should be reported to the Internal Affairs Department of the National Police; 809-688-1777 or 809-688-0777.

Soy Dominicano

Cubans, Puerto Ricans, and Dominicans are all Spanish-speaking Caribbean peoples, but just like Gravenstein, Cox, and golden delicious apples have their distinct tones and flavors, these Afro-Latin peoples each have their own unique culture and characteristics.

A POTPOURRI

The 9.5 million Dominicans are a potpourri—an exotic blend of various shades from white through mulatto to black. Only the faintest elements of pre-Columbian Taíno blood course through the veins of Dominicans, who trace their heritage principally to the earliest days of Spanish occupation. Pure whites are extremely rare—almost everyone carries DNA passed down by miscegenation of Spanish (and French) colonialist and African slave during three centuries, while English and Dutch pirates added their singular traits to the bouillabaisse.

In the 19th century, settlers from the Canary Islands arrived in large numbers. On their heels came traders (colloquially known today as *turcos*) from the Levantine, as well as English-speaking Caribbean islanders (their descendants are called *cocolos*) of African heritage imported for backbreaking work in the canefields. During the 20th century, Dictator Rafael Trujillo sponsored the migration of Japanese farmers, and of Jewish refugees fleeing Nazi Germany. They established communities in Constanza and Sosúa, respectively. And Americans and Europeans have settled in recent decades in increasing numbers. Meanwhile, Haitians (mostly pure black) have continued to pour over the border in search of work (usually illicit and ill paying).

In colonial era Santo Domingo, the institution of slavery was relatively weak and the percentage of slaves in the larger population relatively low in comparison to neighboring Haiti. The Dominicans' individual and communal sense of *dominicanidad* (Dominicanness) is largely shaped by a long and antagonistic relationship with Haiti. (Dominicans have no soft spot for Haitians, who face discrimination without the protection of legal rights. Most live in poverty in urban shantytowns, makeshift rural shacks, and in *bateys*—substandard housing associated with the canefields.) The dislike of Haitians, derogatively termed *negros*, or blacks, has produced in Dominicans a warped concept of color that attributes subtle distinctions of status according to gradations of shade varying from *oscuro* (dark) and *quemado* (burnt), to *canela* (cinnamon) and *lavado* (washed), and *trigueno* (olive-skinned). Dominicans negate their black heritage and implausibly cling to the myth of Taíno blood. Although the Spanish conquistadores wiped out the Taínos, 90 percent of the population is officially lumped together as *indio*; in fact, 90 percent of the population is actually mulatto (mixed blood of white and black). The social elite is comprised almost entirely of *blancos* (whites) or *la gente primera* (first people, or upper crust) descended from the colonial landowning gentry with a traditional power base in Santiago de los Caballeros and El Cibao. Whiteness is considered an ideal. Trujillo (a mulatto) exemplified this insecurity by lightening his skin with creams.

WAY OF LIFE

Two-thirds of Dominicans live in towns and cities, including 2 million in Santo Domingo and 1 million in Santiago de los Caballeros, the second city. Despite a robust middle and upper class and the republic's estimated $8,200 annual per capita income (2007), almost one-third of the population lives below the poverty line, including *marginados* comprising an urban underclass living in slum shacks. In the countryside, most people are landless and often live in humbling poverty, a fact not lost on visitors. One-fifth of the populace is unemployed; jobs for the unskilled (15 percent of the population is illiterate) often pay barely above slave labor wages; and the government provides only the most meager social safety net. Thousands of young women have turned to prostitution, while many families rely on remittances sent from the 2 million or so Dominicans living abroad.

Social life revolves around the family. Families gather on weekends, often heading to the beach or to riverside *balnearios* to swig rum, smoke cigars, play dominoes, and dance to twangy *bachata* country music and fast-paced merengue. While the urban middle class has adopted overtly U.S. values, many social traditions remain strong. *Compadrazgo* (god-parentage) is still a powerful force in the countryside. And Roman Catholicism is a unifying element of the culture. Nonetheless, many Dominicans are superstitious and believe to greater or lesser degree in *vodú dominicana*, brought from Africa by slaves and synchronistically merging Catholic elements with spirit worship. *Fucú*—omens portending bad luck—are generally feared.

Despite Catholicism, common-law marriages and unwed motherhood are the norm in rural areas and among *marginados*. Women have equality before the law and make the most of newfound freedoms. But while many females have risen to positions of power and influence in business and politics, wages and salaries are well below those for males in comparative positions, and laws meant to protect women against sexual harassment and violence are only loosely enforced. Machismo—an overt exertion of masculinity—is ingrained in the culture. Women are expected to be submissive and chaste, while males bolster their sense of masculinity by philandering, devil-may-care driving, and a passion for cockfighting—the national *criollo* pastime. Seducing women is the special art form of *sankys* (from sanky-pankys), male hustlers who feign love to woo female tourists for pecuniary gain.

Merengue dancers The Dominican Republic Ministry of Tourism

Balaguer clung to power through two more electoral terms, notwithstanding that he was now nearly blind. He wasted millions of dollars completing El Faro—a massive 10-storey monument, the Columbus Lighthouse—completed in 1992 for the visit of Pope John Paul II to celebrate the 500th anniversary of Columbus's landing in the Americas. In 1994, at 90 years old, Balaguer won another term after a vicious campaign marked by blatant electoral fraud. His term was cut short under pressure from Washington. In the 1996 election, he inexplicably cast his support to Bosch protégé, 42-year-old lawyer Leonel Fernández Reyna (1953–), of the Partido de la Liberación Dominicana, before emerging from semi-retirement to run for an eighth term as president in the 2000 elections at the age of 93 (he failed and died on July 14, in 2002).

Fernández's term was unusually clean by Dominican standards. He sold off several state-owned industries, reformed the judiciary, and wrote a new constitution banning presidential consecutive terms. Remarkably, he was able to tame the military. Fernández oversaw a resurgent economy, not least in thanks to the diversification of agriculture and industry (principally of textiles and processed foodstuffs) and the beginnings of a tourism boom centered on Puerto Plata and Punta Cana. Fernández's achievements were undone by his successor, the PRD's Rafael Hipólito Mejía (1941–), whose 2000–2004 term was marked by inflation, a devastating financial scandal, and spiraling debt, much of it incurred when the Dominican Republic hosted the Pan-American Games in 2003. Fernández was returned to power in 2004 by a landslide following a constitutional amendment allowing presidents to serve more than one term.

The past few years have been marked by a massive increase in tourist arrivals (the Dominican Republic is now by far the most important destination in the Caribbean by volume) and by construction of the Santo Domingo Metro subway system. The country's economic growth registered an astounding 11.7 percent in 2006, and although it fell to a still-impressive 7 percent in 2007, it was bolstered by a sharp increase in the price of nickel, a major export. Inflation had also been reduced to 6 percent in 2007, not least due to strict targets established by the IMF. Service industries (principally tourism) have overtaken the agriculture sector as the country's largest employer and income earner, while free trade zones have drawn dozens of major international corporations.

Nonetheless, all is not well. The nation was battered in September 2004 by Hurricane Jeanne and again in October 2007 by Tropical Storm Noel, both of which killed dozens across Hispaniola and did considerable damage. Impoverished Haitians have continued to flood the Dominican Republic in search of opportunity. Companies operating within the free trade zones are exempt from paying the nation's minimum wage and most workers earn mere subsistence wages. Unemployment above 15 percent continues to plague the nation, and 42 percent of the population lives below the poverty line. Meanwhile, crime and drugs trafficking have reached frightening proportions (on a positive note, Fernández's campaign to eradicate police corruption has met with considerable success). In the May 2008 election, Fernández was reelected to another four-year term.

Democracy at Last!

After a century-and-a-half of corrupt dictatorships, this tormented nation has settled into a period of calm as a pluralist democracy. The 1966 Constitution closely resembles that of the United States. The republic is headed by an elected president, limited to two 4-year terms. The legislature, or National Congress, comprises the 178-member Chamber of Deputies (*Cámara de Diputados*) representing the 31 provinces plus Santo Domingo, elected by proportional representation; and the 32-member Senate. Alternating biannual elections choose representatives for the twin chambers. Every citizen 18 years or older is obliged to vote. A governor appointed by the president oversees each province, while elected municipal councils, each overseen by a mayor, run local affairs.

The conservative and nationalistic Social Christian Reformist Party (PRSC), founded by Joaquín Balaguer, is the weakest of the three major parties. The two main rivals are the leftist Dominican Revolutionary Party (PRD), founded by Juan Bosch in 1961, and the centrist Dominican Liberation Party (PLD), also founded by Bosch (in 1973) and led by current president, Leonel Fernández Reyna. Although paternalism and corruption remain ingrained in the national political psyche, Fernández's relatively transparent and clean administration has characterized a strengthening of accountable and responsible government.

Fishing boat, Playa Saladilla

2

Planning Your Trip

The Checklist

The island of Hispaniola is the second largest of the Greater Antilles. The Dominican Republic, which takes up the eastern two-thirds of the island, is much larger than many visitors conceive. Having the basics at hand provides peace of mind and goes a long way to helping you enjoy the Dominican Republic without worry. Providing information running the gamut from weather reports to visitors bureaus, this chapter covers planning and everyday practical matters, as well as emergencies.

CLIMATE

There's a reason that midwinter is the Caribbean's peak season for tourism. It's fabulous to be soaking up the rays on a glorious beach or playing a round of golf beneath gorgeous blue skies while the most of North America and northern Europe is digging out from under the snow. In fact, the Dominican Republic lies south of the Tropic of Cancer and has a deliciously warm tropical climate year-round. The northeast trade winds blow steadily from the Atlantic all year long, helping take the edge off the pirate sun.

The winter months (ironically called *verano*, or summer, in the republic) average a balmy 75–80 degrees F (23–26 degrees C) in Santo Domingo. This is also a dry season (November through April), when you can expect relatively little rain. An exception is the

In an Emergency
Ambulance (private): 809-535-1080 (Movimed) or 809-541-3000 ext. 2825 (ClinicAssist)
Ambulance (public): 911
Fire: 911
Police: 911, in Santo Domingo; 1-200-3500, in the provinces; www.adn.gov.do/PoliciaTuristica.asp;
    Bloque D, 30 de Marzo, at Avenida México, Santo Domingo
Canadian Embassy: 809-685-1136; Calle Eugenio de Marchena 39, Santo Domingo
U.S. Embassy: 809-221-2171; www.usemb.gov.do; Calle César Nicolás Penson and Calle Leopoldo
    Navarro, Santo Domingo
U.K. Embassy: 809-471-7111; www.britishembassy.gov.uk/dominicanrepublic; Avenida 27 de Febrero
    233, Santo Domingo

northern coast, which receives the bulk of rains November to January. Summer months (called *invierno*, or winter, in the republic) average 86–90 degrees F (30–32 degrees C) May through October; this is also the rainy season when humidity increases until a half-hour walk can leave you dripping wet. While prolonged thunderstorms and severe tropical storms are common, rains typically fall in mid- to late-afternoon following clear mornings.

Regional variations abound. Plan accordingly. The mountain regions enjoy mild temperatures: Jarabacoa (with a mean temperature of 64 degrees F (18 degrees C) and Constanza, in the Central Cordillera, are blessed with a springlike climate year-round. Higher still, the climate is distinctly alpine: You'll want warm clothing for hiking Pico Duarte! Meanwhile, the lowlands of the southwest lie in rain shadows of the high mountains (the Cordillera Central, Sierra Neiba, and Sierra Bahoruco). Here, the climate is semi-arid, cactus stud the plains, and residents broil under a sun that beats down hard as a nail.

The Dominican Republic lies within the hurricane belt: June through October is hurricane season. In 1998, Hurricane Georges left 300 Dominicans dead; Hurricane Dean struck in 2007, when Hurricane Noel also came ashore, leaving 87 people dead. However, hurricanes actually strike the island only infrequently and most summer vacationers enjoy their time without mishap.

When to Go

Apart from factoring the weather, consider prices and availability when choosing when to go. Since winter months are high season, many hotels sell out and rental cars can be in short supply. Airfares, hotel rates, and even car rental rates are also generally higher in prime travel season. You can save money by traveling off-season. Christmas and New Year's are considered peak weeks, and prices are spiked. Dominicans take to the beaches en masse for Lenten week, when much of the country shuts down; this is especially true for cities such as Santiago de los Caballeros that host *carnavales*.

Weather Reports

A good resource is the World Meteorological Organization website (www.worldweather.org /132/m132.htm), which shows real-time weather, short-term projections, and climatological patterns for eight locations in the Dominican Republic.

The Weather Channel (www.weather.com) has a similar service.

TRANSPORTATION: GETTING THERE

No surprise: A nation this size is served by various international airports and preplanning is required to ensure you choose the best airport for your principal destination in the republic.

Well-paved highways link the main towns and beach resorts, but once you begin to stray, road conditions often deteriorate rapidly. Don't trust your map! Many roads shown as B-roads are actually little more than dirt tracks. Be warned: Santo Domingo's chaotic traffic and appalling rush-hour congestion can make even Los Angeles look like Utopia.

There are numerous ways to get to and around the Dominican Republic.

Teeth of the Dog Golf Course at Casa de Campo The Dominican Republic Ministry of Tourism

By Air

The Dominican Republic has several international airports and where you land will depend on which part of the country you wish to visit. The main airport is Santo Domingo's somewhat chaotic **Aeropuerto Internacional Las Américas** (SDQ), 10 miles (16 km) and a 30-minute taxi ride east of the city and close to the beach resort of Boca Chica. Some flights arrive and depart **Aeropuerto Internacional La Isabela** (JBQ), on the northwest outskirts

Sample Air Travel Times to Santo Domingo			
From Miami	2 hours	From Chicago	4.5 hours
From New York	3.5 hours	From Los Angeles	7 hours

of Santo Domingo. The airport, officially called Aeropuerto Internacional Joaquín Balaguer, replaced the dangerously crowded Aeropuerto Internacional de Herrera, on the west side of the city, which closed in 2006.

Most vacationers bound for the Dominican Republic, however, arrive and depart the private **Punta Cana International Airport** (PUJ), the nation's busiest airport, serving the beach resorts of the southeastern corner of the republic. Most major North American airlines offer direct service, and during peak winter months as many as 250 flights arrive from throughout North America, Europe, and Latin America.

The privately operated **Aeropuerto Internacional La Romana** (LRM) serves Casa de Campo and the beach resorts of Juan Dolio and Bayahibe. If you plan on staying at the north coast resorts, consider flights that arrive and depart Puerto Plata's **Aeropuerto Internacional Gregorio Luperón** (POP). In 2006, **Aeropuerto Internacional "El Catey" Presidente Juan Bosch** (AZS) opened to serve the beach resorts of Samaná. Relatively few flights arrive and depart the small **Aeropuerto Internacional María Montez** (BRX), at Barahona, in the southwest of the republic.

Air Canada (888-247-2262, www.aircanada.com), American Airlines (800-433-7300; www.aa.com), Continental Airlines (800-231-0856; www.continental.com), Delta Airlines (800-221-1212; www.delta.com), JetBlue Airlines (800-538-2583; www.jetblue.com), Spirit Airlines (800-772-7117; www.spiritair.com), and US Airways (800-428-4322; www.usairways.com) all offer regular service from North America, as do numerous charter airlines. American Airlines has the most frequent service, with more than a dozen daily flights to Santo Domingo, Punta Cana, and Puerto Plata. Air Europe, Iberia, and Air France are among the European airlines with direct service. Air Dominicana (809-732-6517, www.airdominicana.com.do) was created in 2007 and initiated service between Europe and the republic in 2008.

Aeropuerto Internacional Gregorio Luperón: 809-586-0107 or 586-0278; La Unión, 10 miles east of Puerto Plata; www.aerodom.com

Aeropuerto Internacional La Isabela: 809-826-4019

Aeropuerto Internacional La Romana: 809-550-5088 or 813-9119; Carretera La Romana-Higüey, La Romana.

Aeropuerto Internacional Las Américas: 809-947-2225 or 809-947-2222; Carretera A3, Punta Caucedo; www.aerodom.com

Aeropuerto Internacional María Montez: 809-524-4144; Av. C. Damirón, Barahona; www.aerodom.com

Aeropuerto Internacional Presidente Juan Bosch: 809-338-5888 ext. 100; Carretera 5, El Catey, 20 miles west of Samaná; www.aerodom.com

Punta Cana International Airport: 809-668-4749; Punta Cana; www.puntacana.com

By Sea

To be borne on the seas to the isle discovered by Christopher Columbus can only add to the drama of your arrival. Yet despite its popularity as the Caribbean's most visited destination, the Dominican Republic is a second tier player when it comes to cruising. Surprisingly few cruise ships make stops. Casa de Campo/La Romana is the main destination, while a few ships call in at Santo Domingo, Puerto Plata, and/or Samaná. Your cruise will feature day-long excursions (or occasionally an overnight in port) before sailing off to the next destination.

More than a dozen major cruise lines include Dominican Republic on their itineraries, including Carnival Cruise Lines, Celebrity Cruises, Costa Cruises, Crystal Cruises, Holland America Line, Norwegian Cruise Line, P&O Cruises, and Royal Caribbean. For information, contact the **Cruise Lines International Association**; 212-921-0066; www.cruising.org.

Ferries del Caribe (809-688-4400 in Santo Domingo, 787-725-2643 or 787-832-4800 in Puerto Rico; www.ferriesdelcaribe.com) operates car-and-passenger ferries between Santo Domingo and Mayagüez, in Puerto Rico. The M/S *Caribbean Express* sails from Santo Domingo on Sunday, Tuesday, and Thursday, and from Mayagüez on Monday, Wednesday, and Friday. The ticket office and berth in Santo Domingo is on Avenida del Puerto, opposite Fortaleza Ozama. The overnight passage takes about 12 hours. It operates much like a regular cruise ship, with a nightclub, casino, shows, and kids' programs. One-way fares begin at about $190 in an airplane-style seat, or from $217 in a cabin (depending on the number of people in the cabin).

Cruise ship near Santo Domingo   The Dominican Republic Ministry of Tourism

By Package Tour

Many companies sell air/hotel packages that are all-inclusive and focus exclusively on the beach resorts. The key advantage is their low cost. However, relatively few companies offer motor coach sightseeing tours as you might find in, say, Europe. The exception is special interests tours, such as for birders and scuba divers. The Dominican Republic Ministry of Tourism publishes a list of recommended tour companies that offer such tours from North America and Europe.

TRANSPORTATION: GETTING AROUND

By Air

The Dominican Republic is large enough to make domestic flights between destinations a viable option. There is no domestic scheduled airline. However, you can charter small planes (or join other passengers) with private companies such as **AeroDomca** (809-826-4141, www.aerodomca.com) and **Air Century** (809-846-4222, www.aircentury.com). **Carib Air** (809-542-6688, http://caribair.com.do) has also offered service in the republic; however, its license was suspended in January, 2009. **Destination Service Take-Off Travel Agency** (809-552-1333; http://takeoffweb.com) has scheduled service between key tourist resorts using 10-passenger Cessna Grand Caravans.

No public buses or shuttles serve any of the international airports. Many of the major hotels make life easy by providing free airport shuttles for arriving and departing visitors. Tour package operators usually include such transfers in their one-price-for-everything rates. Check ahead. Trustworthy freelance guide Rafael Silva (809-330-1262, www.dominicanairporttransfers.com) offers airport transfers throughout the Dominican Republic with a minimum 24 hours notice. And an English-based company, **Resorthoppa** (0871-855-0350, www.resorthoppa.com), arranges transfers throughout republic.

Licensed tourist taxis (they are painted yellow and feature a Taxi Turístico logo) charge around US$20 into Santo Domingo from Santo Domingo international airport, depending on your bargaining skills, as there is no government-regulated fare. (Taxis from Aeropuerto Internacional La Isabela will cost US$10–15.) The following are typical minimum fares to other destinations: Bayahibe US$75; Boca Chica, US$20; Cabarete US$100; Casa de Campo US$70; Higüey US$95; Jarabacoa US$95; Juan Dolio US$30; Puerto Plata US$80; Punta Cana and Playa Bávaro US$120; Río San Juan US$140; Santiago de los Caballeros US$95; Samaná peninsula US$140–150; Sosuá US$130. To avoid being ripped off, be sure to ask and agree to a price *before* you get in a cab.

Exiting the airport, expect to be hustled by any number of individuals offering to carry your bags or even open the door to your taxi. If you accept, you'll be expected to tip.

Car rentals are available at all the international airports, as are taxis.

Renting a Car

Although aircraft and ships will bring you to the island, a car is a virtual necessity once you arrive if you seek flexibility and wish to explore far beyond the beach resorts or Santo Domingo. Public transportation is somewhat limited, especially to outlying attractions, and distances are considerably greater than many visitors may imagine. Unfortunately, driving in the Dominican Republic is not for the faint of heart, and extreme caution is required.

Although the major roads are well paved (with the occasional pothole), conditions rapidly deteriorate on many minor roads, where a 4WD vehicle (*carro con doble*) is essential. Dominicans are extremely reckless and aggressive drivers, and pay little heed to traffic rules. Running through red traffic lights is common! And a dog-eat-dog mentality often snarls traffic in cities, where drivers block junctions in their jostling for an advantage. Avoid driving at night, as the many hazards include poor (or no) lighting, unmarked verges, other vehicles lacking headlights or taillights, lots of stray animals and pedestrians, and the possibility of a nighttime highway robbery.

Most major international car rental companies have offices at the Santo Domingo and Puerto Plata airports, as well as in downtown Santo Domingo. Several also have offices in Punta Cana and at other regional airports and cities. Local information and reservations numbers are listed below. Advance reservations are recommended for the winter high season. You'll need to be 21 years of age (25 for some companies) and hold a Canadian, U.S., or European driver's license, plus a credit card. Expect to pay at least US$70–150 daily for an automatic, with unlimited mileage, compulsory Loss Damage Waiver (*enuncia a daños o perdida*), and liability insurance. Don't park under coconut palms, as your rental insurance does not cover damage caused by falling coconuts.

Local firms' vehicles aren't always as modern or well maintained as the major companies (you don't want to break down in the boondocks), but rates are often cheaper. Try **McAuto Rental Cars** (809-549-8911. www.mccarrental.com).

Alamo Rent-a-Car: 809-562-1444 or 800-462-5266; www.alamo.com.
Avis: 809-535-7191 or 800-331-1212; www.avis.com.
Budget Rent-a-Car: 809-566-6666 or 800-472-3325; www.budget.com.
Dollar Rent-a-Car: 809-221-7368 or 800-800-6000; www.dollar.com.
Hertz: 809-221-5333 or 800-654-3001; www.hertz.com.
National Rent-a-Car: 809-562-1444 or 800-227-7368; www.nationalcar.com.

Rental cars cannot be taken into Haiti. Police paramilitary roadblocks are located on many highways near the Haitian border; have your passport handy.

In rural areas, top up your tank as often as possible, as gasoline station are often few and far between. Many stations also close after sundown; and many don't accept credit card payment.

The main highways are patrolled by traffic police, and radar guns are in use to enforce the 50 mph (80 kph) limit; alas, locals pay little heed to the limits. Although police corruption is not what it once was, tourists are occasionally stopped by unscrupulous traffic cops (or bogus individuals dressed in stolen police jackets) intent on extracting a "fine" on the spot. Paying an on-the-spot fine is not permitted: If stopped, request a traffic ticket and official identification (police are required to wear a name tag on their uniform). Such incidents should be reported to the police (Internal Affairs Department, 809-688-1777 or 809-688-0777) and your nation's consulate.

By Bus

For independent travelers, the easiest (and safest) means of long-distance travel between cities and resorts is by bus. Three private companies compete: **Caribe Tours** (809-221-4422; www.caribetours.com.do) offers service nationwide; buses depart Avenida 27 Febrero and Leopoldo Navarro, in Santo Domingo. **Metro Expreso** (809-227-0101 Santo Domingo; 809-582-9111 Santiago de los Caballeros; 809-586-6062 Puerto Plata;

www.metroserviciosturisticos.com) connects Santo Domingo to Santiago de los Caballeros and Puerto Plata; buses depart Santo Domingo from Avenida Winston Churchill and Avenida Hatuey, near Avenida 27 de Febrero. **Terra Bus** (809-472-1080) has service between Santo Domingo and Puerto Plata (about US$8) plus Haiti (US$25 each way); buses depart Avenida 27 de Febrero at Maximo Gomez at Plaza Criolla. And **Expreso Bávaro** (809-682-9670) buses serve La Romana and Bávaro/Punta Cana (see the Punta Cana and Southeast chapter); buses depart Avenida Juan Sánchez Ruiz at Avenida Máximo Gómez, in Santo Domingo.

These above companies' modern, air-conditioned buses have comfortable, reclining seats, although they are usually overly air conditioned (take a jacket) and noisy with canned music played far too loud for comfort. For many destinations, you can choose either fast (*directo*) or slower (*regular*) service. Most destinations in the country cost less than US$10 to reach. Book your ticket in advance.

Short-haul service between towns and *within* Santo Domingo and other large cities is by minivans (*guaguas*, pronounced wuag-wahs). Dozens of freelance operators compete. The routes are posted on the windshield or door. They stop anywhere along their route, dropping off and picking up passengers. Departure time is usually whenever the van is filled to overflowing, and not before. Most vehicles are poorly maintained (often a euphemism for falling apart) and since time is money, they are driven at reckless speed while the *cobrador* (fare collector and driver's assistant) often hangs outside the door. Pickup trucks serve the same purpose in the more remote mountain regions. Needless to say, *guaguas* are best avoided, despite their extreme low cost (most short hops in towns cost RD$20; rarely will you pay more than RD$400 for town-to-town travel). Pay upon boarding, and have the correct change. Keep a very close eye on your luggage, as theft is rife. And beware of pick-pockets.

By Taxi

Licensed tourist taxis operate in most beach resorts and in Santo Domingo, and can be found around central plazas in most towns and outside most hotels. The safest bet is always to opt for a radio taxi, or a modern, air-conditioned tourist taxi hailed from outside your hotel. Radio taxis usually arrive within 10 minutes of being called (there are few free-roaming taxis in cities). They charge from RD$95. Fares for most destinations are generally posted at taxi stands or in hotels; short-journey rates are usually non-negotiable with tourist taxis, but you can certainly negotiate a rate for long-term use and with taxis hailed away from tourist venues. Ask your concierge for the going rate and agree in advance with your taxi driver (some drivers try to overcharge tourists), and make sure whether you're talking U.S. dollars or local pesos. It helps to have the correct change. If you're dining, your restaurant will call a radio taxi for you.

Most drivers carry very little change, so have the correct change and plenty of bills (either U.S. or Dominican dollars) at hand. You can pay in U.S. dollars, or even Euros, but don't expect change. Confirm whether the rate is in U.S. dollars or *pesos* before setting off.

Legal taxis display a brown certificate in the windshield. Women should use only radio taxis or tourist taxis connected with a hotel. *Never* take an unmarked (and therefore unlicensed) taxi. Many tourists have been robbed. In all events, ask your driver for his taxi number and jot it down. No number? No go! And even if there's a problem with a licensed taxi, you'll be able to present the police or other authorities with the driver's ID. Most Dominican taxi drivers have a good reputation, although many may try to overcharge you.

Motoconchos in Higuey

However, few drivers speak English, so a smattering of Spanish plus handwritten directions to your destination will help.

In Santo Domingo, try **Aero Taxi** (809-686-1212), **Apolo Taxi** (809-537-0000), **Taxi Express** (809-537-7777), or **Tecni-Taxi** (809-567-2010), which also operates in Puerto Plata (809-320-7621).

Carros Públicos

For a real Dominican experience (and if you're frugal), consider *carros públicos* (also called *conchos*)—shared taxis that operate along fixed routes, like buses. They pick up and drop off passengers along the route; passing *públicos* honk at pedestrians to solicit business, but you can wave one down. Few vehicles are roadworthy; many are dangerous pieces of junk. They're usually always packed to the gills with passengers, and always driven recklessly.

They usually have either a green or a yellow top, and a white seal on the front door stating their route. Still, tell the driver your destination when you're picked up to ensure the *público* is going there. RD$10.00 is the standard fare. Ensure that the car has a picture and ID number of the driver displayed in the car. Never take a *público* at night.

By Motoconcho

Motoconchos—small, privately owned motorcycles that act as short-distance taxis—are the

Dominican Republic Access
Approximate mileage and times by car between towns and cities

SANTO DOMINGO TO:	TIME	MILES/KM
Baní	60 min	40/65
Barahona	3 hrs	124/200
Boca Chica	30 min	19/31
Constanza	2.5 hrs	87/140
Higüey	2 hrs	90/145
Jarabacoa	2 hrs	96/155
La Romana	1.5 hrs	68/110
La Vega	1.25 hrs	78/125
Las Terrenas	3.5 hrs	140/225
Monte Cristi	4 hrs	168/270
Pedernales	6 hrs	221/355
Puerto Plata	3.25 hrs	134/215
Punta Cana	3 hrs	127/205
Sabana de la Mar	2 hrs	96/155
Samaná	3.5 hrs	152/245
San Pedro de Macorís	1 hr	43/70
Santiago de los Caballeros	2 hrs	96/155
Sosuá	3.5 hrs	149/240

staple of rapid transit outside Santo Domingo. They're everywhere. They look like fun. They're dirt cheap. They're also extremely dangerous. In most towns and resorts, they're so numerous they become a road hazard in themselves, not least because they're ridden with brazen disregard for safety as they weave in and out of traffic at breakneck speed. Rides typical cost $20–30 pesos and up, depending on distance, per passenger (fares are double after dusk).

Leave this form of transport to the locals, who often pack the entire family aboard the pillion (small kids even go atop the handlebars), and often their chickens and pigs, too!

By Excursions
Once you arrive in the Dominican Republic, it's easy to explore the country by stitching together a series of excursions. There's no shortage of tour operators to choose from, many of which are local to specific resort areas.

The largest company, and also one of the most respected, is **Prieto Tours** (809-685-0102 in Santo Domingo, 809-221-1335 in Punta Cana; www.prieto-tours.com), with offices in Santo Domingo, Puerto Plata, and Punta Cana. Also recommended is **Turinter** (809-686-4020; www.turinter.com). **Outback Safari** (809-455-1573; www.outbacksafari.com.do), with outlets in Cabarete and Playa Bávaro (Punta Cana) offers exciting adventure tours focusing on culture and ecology. And **Tours Trips Treks & Travel** (809-867-8884; www.4t domrep.com; Calle Principal, Cabarete) specializes in customized educational and cultural tours. Heck, you can even take helicopter excursions with **Helidosa** (809-826-4100; www .helidosa.com), with bases in Santo Domingo, Punta Cana, Puerto Plata, La Romana, and

Las Terrenas.

See regional chapters for other tour and excursion operators.

ENTRY AND EXIT FORMALITIES

All visitors, including those from the United States, Canada, and Europe, require a valid passport to enter the Dominican Republic. No visas are required. Upon arrival, visitors are issued a Tourist Card (US$10) good for a 90-day stay. They can be extended for an additional 90 days (US$5) and longer stays by applying to the Departamento de Inmigración (809-508-2555), Avenida 30 de Mayo and Avenida Héroes de Luperón, Santo Domingo.

A US$20 tax is payable upon departure.

RECREATION

The Dominican Republic is replete with exciting recreational activities. The fabulous never-winter weather spells Nirvana for outdoorsy folks. The scenery is breathtaking, and far more diverse than you might imagine, ranging from below sea level to more than 10,000 feet (3,048 me) atop Pico Duarte. The birding is out of this world. Water sports are off the hook. Hiking is as good as anywhere else in the Caribbean. The golf is the best in the Caribbean. Offshore, big game fish seem to line up to get a bite of your hook. And the diving? You wouldn't believe it unless you see the underwater wrecks and stupendous corals with your own eyes. You get the picture. There's even paragliding, offered throughout the republic by **Caribbean Free Flying** (www.caribbeanfreeflying.com).

Most upscale hotels have swimming pools and tennis (**Casa de Campo**—809-523-8800; www.casadecampo.com.do—has a large tennis academy).

Iguana Mama (809-571-0908; www.iguanamama.com; Calle Principal 74, Cabarete) specializes in adventure tours, including canyoning, hiking, and mountain biking.

ATV and Jeep Tours

Exploring by ATV or Jeep is a popular excursion offered at most beach resorts. Numerous companies offer trips, although the biggest outfitter is **Bávaro Runners** (www.bavaro runners.com), which offers Jeep (it's actually an open-bed truck) safaris from Bayahibe (809-686-1260), Bávaro/Punta Cana (809-455-1135), Puerto Plata (809-320-1061), and Samaná (809-538-2499). **Outback Safari** (809-455-1573 in Bávaro/Punta Cana; 809-244-4886 in Puerto Plata) competes.

Bicycling

Although the republic's paved highways are no place for cyclists (they're *far* too dangerous), the rugged off-road terrain is tailor-made for mountain bicycles. Most major beach resorts have at least one tour operator specializing in organized mountain bike trips. Notable among them are **Iguana Mama** (see above), in Cabarete; and **Rancho Cascada** (809-890-2332; www.ranchocascada.com), on the southern slopes of the Cordillera Central.

If you're in great shape, consider tackling the gruelling eight-day **Gira Dominicana Transalp**, (www.giradominicana.com/Event-dt.htm) mountain-bike challenge.

Serious road racers are served by the **Federación Dominicana de Ciclismo** (809-565-5209; http://fedoci.org).

Birding

No other Caribbean isle can compete when it comes to birding. The republic's kaleido-scopic habitats are home to 306 bird species—the most of any isle in the region. The country is replete with great birding spots. Flamingoes strut about in Lago Enriquillo, Lago Oviedo, and the lagoons of Isla Saona. Frigate birds are a dime a dozen in Parque Nacional Los Haitises. The Hispaniolan parrot is a sure-bet sighting while hiking Pico Duarte. Serious birders, however, know to focus their time (and binoculars) on the southwest, especially Parque Nacional Sierra de Bahoruco, where almost all Hispaniola's endemics can be seen. This region boasts every kind of terrain, from coastal marshes and inland salt lakes to lowland and montane rain forests.

February through April is the best time, when the weather is good and migrant species are still present.

Ornithologist Kate Wallace's **Tody Tours** (809-686-0882; www.todytours.com; Calle José Gabriel García 105, Zona Colonial, Santo Domingo) specializes in birding.

Birding expert **Miguel Angel Landestoy** (809-705-2430; E-mail: mango_land@yahoo .com) hires out as a guide for personalized tours.

Foreign tour agencies such as **Eagle Eye** (250-342-8640 or 1-800-373-5678; www.eagle -eye.com; 4711 Galena Street, Windermere, BC, V0B 2L0, Canada) and **Victor Emanuel** (512-328-5221 or 1-800-328-8368; http://ventbird.com; 2525 Wallingwood Drive, Suite

Palm trees and ocean at Playa Bavaro

Where to Lay Your Towel

Gorgeous white beaches (*playas*) dissolving into bathtub-warm shallows of Maxfield Parrish turquoise blues are the main reason most visitors choose to visit the Dominican Republic. The Punta Cana area, centered on Playa Bávaro, is the fifth most popular warm-weather destination in the world, according to a recent study by the American Society of Travel Agents. No wonder! At the island's southeastern tip, this region—a 40-mile stretch of sands commonly called the Costa del Coco (Coconut Coast) for the coconut plantations—boasts the nation's most spectacular beaches, as well as the lion's share of its all-inclusive hotels. And the north coast—the so-called Amber Coast (named for the semi-precious gem found in the mountains)—and Samaná peninsula have so many beaches it's hard to know where to begin.

Here's a guide to help you decide where to sun and swim.

SANTO DOMINGO AND SOUTH CENTRAL

Boca Chica. About 18.6 miles (30 km) east of Santo Domingo, this is the most popular beach with locals. It has a seedy side; sex tourism is well developed. Positives include good snorkeling and excellent scuba diving, and a lively nightlife.

Najayo and **Palenque**, about 8.7 miles (14 km) and 12.4 miles (20 km) west of Santo Domingo, respectively, are also almost exclusively used by *capitalenos*. The sands are attractive. There is a modicum of midpriced hotels and seafood restaurants, but few water sports.

THE SOUTHWEST

Bahía de Águilas. Remote white-sand beach in a gorgeous bay on the west shores of Parque Nacional Jaragua. No accommodation; camping is permitted. Sturdy 4WD required for access, or rented boat from Las Cuevas.

Playa Los Corbanitos. On the Bahía de las Calderas, this lovely white-sand beach fringed by mangroves and palms is slated for future development, with a marina and deluxe resort hotel.

Playa San Rafael. This shingly beach—one of a half dozen similar beaches south of Barahona—is popular with locals for its walled pools fed by natural springs. There are few facilities, but it's a great place to interact with local families.

THE SOUTHEAST

Bávaro/Punta Cana. The most-developed resort area in the republic and the heart of the Punta Cana region. **Playa Bávaro** melds seamlessly into **Playa El Cortecito** and **Playa Arena Gorda**, which together have dozens of all-inclusive resorts, heaps of water sports and golf courses, and plenty of fine restaurants. Separated by a headland to the south, **Playa Cabeza del Toro** is similarly blessed. Beyond, **Punta Cana** is reserved for the eponymous resort hotel. Farther south, astonishing white sands and turquoise waters are a major draw at the exclusive **Cap Cana** development, a 10-year project that will eventually add four golf courses, at least five super-exclusive hotels, and the Caribbean's largest marina.

Bayahibe/Dominicus. The once sleepy fishing village is now jam-packed with new hotels and ancillary services. Unregulated development is a major drawback. But several deluxe all-inclusive resorts command the major part of the two beautiful beaches. Superb scuba diving. At the gateway to Parque Nacional del Este.

Isla Catalina. Beautiful beach-fringed island popular for day-tripping excursions from La Romana/Casa de Campo. No accommodation.

Juan Dolio. East of Boca Chica. The sands are beautiful, and several   [continued next page] all-inclusive resorts appeal. Development stalled here a decade ago. While major new development is slated, including a marina, Juan Dolio lacks the pizzazz of the Punta Cana region.

Playa Lavacama. One of the loveliest of the as-yet-undeveloped northerly beaches along the Costa del Coco. Neighboring beaches include **Playa del Muerte**, **Playa Nisibón**, and **Playa Esmeralda**. They're connected by a rugged sand track and are backed by coconut plantations. Facilities are minimal. Perfect for a day trip from the Punta Cana area.

Macao/Uvero Alto. North of the Bávaro region, this newly evolving resort area of the Costa del Coco will get a major boost when the Phase I of the Roco Ki project opens in 2010, with a deluxe Westin hotel and Nick Price-designed golf course. Uvero Alto has tangerine sands and rougher waters than the Bávaro region. A plus here is the Sivory Punta Cana boutique hotel. This region is a one-hour drive from Punta Cana.

THE NORTH COAST

Cabarete. Long known as the Caribbean's foremost center for wind-sport action, it has traditionally drawn a young, active traveler. Scores of surfers' hotels, cool beach bars, and kiteboard and surf outfitters line the triptych of beaches. Upscale development has begun to stir.

Luperón. West of Puerto Plata. Beaches here have an as-yet-unfulfilled potential (the long-touted Atlantida deluxe resort and marina project is stalled). Superb scuba diving offshore.

Monte Cristi. In the extreme northwest. Remote, yet gorgeous talcum-white beaches are sheltered by a barrier reef. Turquoise shallows offer spectacular diving. Budget accommodations only, currently, and few services, but a new highway to be launched in 2009 should put this area on the map. Expect this region to boom within a decade.

Playa Dorada/Puerto Plata. The historic town of Puerto Plata is lined by gorgeous **Playa Long Beach**, used by locals, as are nearby **Playa Costámbar** and **Playa Cofresí**. Foreigners congregate east at **Playa Dorada**, with a world-class golf course, plus a dozen all-inclusive resorts and boutique hotels for all budgets. Puerto Plata also has a large marina, plus Ocean World Adventure Park theme park. There's plenty to do away from the beach, too. The sands and waters here don't live up to those of the Costa del Coco.

1003, Austin, TX 78746) also come here.

The following organizations may prove helpful to birding enthusiasts:

Hispaniola eBird: http://ebird.org/content/hispaniola. Documents bird sightings through checklist data. The website has an intuitive web interface permitting thousands of participants to submit their observations or view results.

Society for the Conservation and Study of Caribbean Birds: www.scscb.org. Publishes the *Journal of Caribbean Ornithology* and organizes the annual Caribbean Endemic Bird Festival.

Sociedad Ornitológica de la Hispaniola: www.geocities.com/sociedad_ornitologica _hispaniola; E-mail: falco67_99@yahoo.com. The Hispaniola Ornithological Society.

Fundación Moscoso Puello: 809-566-4898; E-mail moscoso.puello@codetel.net.do; Avenida J. F. Kennedy, Km. 7.5, Los Jardines del Norte, Santo Domingo. Works to protect the critically endangered Ridgway's falcon.

Caving and Canyoning

Caverns riddle Hispaniola, luring spelunkers and others keen to explore underground.

Punta Rucia. A lonesome yet beautiful beach used principally by day-trippers on excursions from Puerto Plata. Nearby **Playa Enseñada** is one of the liveliest beaches, drawing locals exclusively. A nearby wildlife refuge shelters manatees. Major development is on the books.

Río Grande. This area, in the far northeast of the country, boasts a string of diverse beaches. White. Coral colored. Golden. Even brown. Few are developed for tourism. The big enchilada is golden **Playa Grande**, 9.3 miles (15 km) east of Río San Juan, known for its golf course. It's favored by locals. But seas here are rough, as they are southward along a string of undeveloped beaches such as wave-pounded **Playa Preciosa**. An exception is **Playa Diamante**, near Cabrera, with sugar-white sands and turquoise shallows within a reef-protected flask-shaped cove.

Sosuá. Despite its attractive cliff top village, Sosuá struggles to overcome its long-standing reputation as a capital of Caribbean sex tourism. It has accommodations for every budget. Deluxe options are outside town, with their own beaches. **Playa Sosuá**, the cliff-framed main beach, is a colorful node for local life; smaller, more exposed **Playita Alicia** mostly serves tourists at the adjoining hotels.

SAMANÁ

Cayo Levantado. A pearl of an isle off the southern shore of the peninsula. Surrounded by turquoise waters. The public beach is talcum white and talcum fine. The Gran Bahía Principe Cayo Levantado hotel takes up half the island and has its own beaches.

Las Galeras. Part fishing village, part resort village with heaps of charm and a gorgeous setting. Small charming accommodations, plus a second-rate all-inclusive resort at **Playa Frontón**. Nearby **Playa Rincón** offers a scenic, as yet untapped alternative. Splendid scuba diving.

Las Terrenas. The most appealing of all beach resorts in the Dominican Republic for its combination of down-to-earth lifestyle, scenic beauty, gorgeous beaches, and combination of boutique hotels and all-inclusive resorts. In town, **Playa Las Ballenas** ranks as my favorite beach of all. To the east, **Playa Punta Popy** draws kitesurfers. Separated from town by a headland are **Playa Bonita** and **Playa Cosón**, lovely beaches with a choice of boutique and large-scale all-inclusive hotels.

Many caves are adorned with Taíno pictographs. Above ground, the canyons that cut through the Cordillera Septentrional and Cordillera Central provide an adrenaline rush for canyoneers—folks who like to hike and rappel down cascades.

A good resource is Domingo Abréu Collado, of **Espeleogrupo** (809-682-1577; E-mail: domingoespele@hotmail.com). He's considered the republic's preeminent caving guide.

To view and learn about Taíno art, sign up with **Tours Trips Treks & Travel** (809-867-8884; www.4tdomrep.com), which specializes in cave tours.

Iguana Mama offers guided canyoning trips.

Golf

On all points of the Dominican compass, celebrity golf-pro designers have been laying out sublime fairways studded by palms. Nick Faldo, Tom Fazio, Pete Dye, Jack Nicklaus, Gary Player, Nick Price, and Robert Trent Jones Jr., have all lent their hallowed names and design skills. It's all part of a green revolution that has elevated the Dominican Republic into the undisputed golf capital of the region, with more courses (25 and counting) than any Caribbean competitor. And at the time of writing, at least another dozen were in various stages of development. Here are your options:

SANTO DOMINGO

Las Lagunas Country Club (809-372-7441; www.laslagunas.com.do) Originally designed by Pete Dye, then modified by Jack Corrie, this hilly 18-hole course has scenic lake views.

Santo Domingo Country Club (809-530-6606; www.santodomingocc.com) On the eastern outskirts of Santo Domingo, this Robert Trent Jones-designed course opened in 1920 with sloping hills and scenic views.

Isabel Villas Country Club (809-385-0066) Good for beginners, this 9-hole course on the northern Santo Domingo is laid out alongside the Isabela River. Floodlit for evening play.

THE SOUTHEAST

Catalonia Caribe Golf Club (809-412-0000; www.cataloniabavaro.com) This 18-hole course at the Catalonia Bávaro Resort, at Playa Bávaro, features lakes. The resort's Cabeza de Toro Golf Club is a 9-hole layout.

Cocotal Golf and Country Club (809-687-4653; www.cocotalgolf.com) Designed by six-time Spanish champion José Pepe Gancedo, who makes the most of this old coconut plantation. At Playa Bávaro.

Corales Golf Course. (809-959-4653; www.puntacana.com) Currently being laid out by Tom Fazio as the second course at the Puntacana Resort and Club, with holes perched atop cliffs.

Dye Fore. (809-523-8800; www.casadecampo.com.do) Debuted in 2004 at Casa de Campo, this 7,770-yard, Pete Dye-designed course features rippling fairways overlooking the dizzying 300-foot-deep Río Chavón gorge.

Faldo Legacy Course (www.rocoki.com) Set to open in early 2009 at the Westin Roco Ki Beach and Golf Resort with some of the most dramatic golf holes in the Caribbean. The par-five 18th hole requires finite precision over two ocean inlets to make it to the tiny green perched atop a rocky, wind-blown peninsula battered by waves. This mega-resort currently in development will eventually boast *four* Nick Faldo-designed courses.

Golf de Bávaro. (809-686-5797 ext. 1859; www.barcelo.com) Located at the Barcelo Bávaro Beach Resort. A good beginner's course designed to accommodate tourists.

Guavaberry Golf and Country Club (809-333-4653; www.guavaberrygolf.com) Gary Player-designed championship course opened in 2002 near Juan Dolio. Known for its coral rock formations rising up from the fairways.

La Cana Golf Club. (809-959-4653; www.puntacana.com) A P. B. Dye course at Punta Cana Resort and Club. Spectacular ocean vistas, with 14 ocean view and 4 ocean front holes. A voluptuous favorite of President Bill Clinton.

La Hacienda Golf Course. (809-959-4653; www.puntacana.com) Puntacana Resort and Club. Scheduled for completion in late 2009, this P. B. Dye-designed layout will be inland.

Las Iguanas Golf Course (www.capcana.com) A Jack Nicklaus course expected to open by early 2010.

Links. (809-523-8800; www.casadecampo.com.do) Another Dye course at Casa de Campo. Opened in 1975, it has been compared to traditional British and Scottish courses. Lagoons on five holes add an extra challenge.

Los Marlins Golf Course. (809-526-3315; www.groupmetro.com) At Juan Dolio, this 6,396-yard (5,848 m) Charles Ankrom layout opened in 1995 at the Metro Country Club and is known for its many sand bunkers.

Punta Blanca. (809-221-9898; www.punta-blanca.com) Nick Price-designed course winding through the grounds of the snazzy Majestic Colonial Beach Resort. Opened in 2007.

Punta Espada. (809-227-2262; www.capcana.com/site/puntaespada.htm) Jack Nicklaus-designed course that opened for play in September 2006 at Cap Cana, with ocean views from every hole. Eight holes flank the ocean. Two additional Nicklaus courses are in the works at Cap Cana.

Teeth of the Dog. (809-523-8800; www.casadecampo.com.do) Pete Dye-designed course at Casa de Campo resort. Named for the sharp limestone that locals call *diente del perro* (teeth of the dog), this spectacular course is the only Caribbean course ranked in the world's top 50. Dye sharpened the Dog's fabled coral-fanged bite in 2005 with new tees, greens, and bunkers.

White Sands Golf Course. (809-562-6266; www.whitesands.com.do) This Pepe-Gancedo-designed course was completed in 2008 at the White Sands Golf and Beach Resort, in Playa Bávaro.

THE NORTH COAST

Playa Dorada Golf Course. (809-320-3472; www.playadoradagolf.com) A Robert Trent Jones-designed golf course at the Playa Dorada Resort Complex, in Puerto Plata. The 6,730-yard layout opened in 1976.

Playa Grande Golf Course. (809-582-0860 ext. 21; www.playagrande.com) Considered to be the best of Robert Trent Jones' layouts, this beautiful course is commonly referred to as the Pebble Beach of the Caribbean. Ten holes are cliff-top.

Horseback riders and sea grapes, Playa Macao

Las Aromas Golf Club. (809-836-3064.) A par-70, Pete Dye-designed course also known as the Santiago Golf Club. Mountain views.

Jarabacoa Golf Club. (809-782-9883 or 251-2507) Also known as Quintas de Primavera. The only course in the mountain region. Nine holes surrounded by pine trees, with fabulous mountain views.

Hiking

Hikers are in their element in the Dominican Republic, where four major mountain chains and a fistful of lowland national parks are laced with trails. There's something for everyone: from level hikes through Parque Nacional del Este, for example, to more challenging sojourns in, say, the Reserva Científica Quita Espuela. Many visitors arrive in the DR simply to tackle Pico Duarte, the Caribbean's highest peak. The three-day round-trip hikes depart La Ciénaga, where guides can be hired.

Permits for hikes in forest reserves can be obtained from the **Dirección Nacional de Parques** (809-472-4204; www.medioambiente.gov.do; Avenida Reyes Católicos, at Avenida Máximo Gómez, Santo Domingo).

Horseback Riding

Horseback rides along the beach guarantee a fun-filled few hours. Rides are offered at most beach resorts. Trips into the rugged Cordillera Septentrional are popular out of Cabarete, Sosuá, and Puerto Plata; and the ride to El Salto de Limón waterfall from Santí Rancho, in the Samaná peninsula, is thrilling. The republic's short yet strong Creole breed is perfectly adapted for the island's rugged conditions.

More serious equestrians will find superb facilities at **Casa de Campo Equestrian Center** (809-523-3333; www.casadecampo.com.do), which has horses for English or Western-style riding, jumping, and polo, plus ponies for kids. On the north coast, **Sea Horse Ranch Equestrian Center** (809-571-3880; www.sea-horse-ranch.com) has similar facilities, *sans* polo.

Scuba Diving

Scuba aficionados get figurative raptures of the deep when talk turns to dives in Dominican waters, which abound with wrecks and stupendous coral formations. There are dozens of experienced dive outfits, and many large resort hotels have on-site scuba facilities.

Key sites include Parque Nacional Submarino La Caleta with four wrecks; the wreck of the *St. George* just off Playa Bayahibe; and the waters off Isla Catalina, where key draws are a spectacular wall dive and the chance to see humpback whales in winter months. On the north coast, prime sites include the *Zingara* wreck off Sosuá, where Airport Wall is also a world-class dive; and the sheltered waters off Monte Cristi, known for both wrecks and spectacular coral.

ScubaCaribe (809-555-1435; www.scubacaribe.com) is the major outfitter, with more than 20 outlets throughout the country. The **Fundación Espeleobuceo Hispaniola** (809-472-2248; www.espeleobuceo.com) represents dive operators that specialize in underwater caving.

There are decompression chambers at **Hospiten** (809-686-1414.) in Punta Cana, and **Clínica San Rafael** (809-689-8775) in Santo Domingo.

Windsurfer in Cabarete The Dominican Republic Ministry of Tourism

Sportfishing and Sailing

Anglers are hooked big-time on sportfishing in the Dominican Republic. The offshore waters teem with feisty game fish—tuna, wahoo, marlin, sailfish, etc.—that give a rod-bending fight you'll remember! The nutrient-rich Mona Passage separating Hispaniola from Puerto Rico is especially fertile ground.

Charter sportfishing vessels operate from all the major marinas, more of which are coming on line every year (see regional chapters for details). Charters typically cost about $375 a half day, $575 a full day for up to four people. Stick with accredited charter operators rather than local fishermen, whose boats often lack shade and may not meet adequate safety standards.

No license is required to fish freshwater lakes, which offer good fishing for bass, carp, and tilapia. Bring your own tackle.

You can charter sailboats and motor yachts at marinas throughout the country. Party and sunset cruises are offered at key tourist beach resorts. Two of the best are **Bávaro Splash** (809-688-1615; E-mail: bavarosplash@hotmail.com), a self-drive speedboat tour at Playa Bávaro; and, on the north coast, a high-speed catamaran excursion to Punta Rucia offered by **El Paraíso Tours** (809-612-8499 in Punta Rucia, 809-320-7606 in Puerta Plata; www.cayoparaiso.com).

Water Sports

Bring your boards! Along northern shores, brisk trade winds whip up the excitement for surfers, windsurfers, and kiteboarders, who flock to Cabarete—the all-round water sport capital of the Caribbean, with perfect conditions for novice and expert alike. You'll find dozens of surf camps and hotels for kiteboarders here, and in Las Terrenas, on the Samaná peninsula. Surfers should refer to the **Asociación Dominicana de Surfing** (809-682-5466 or 682-7714; www.fedosurf.org).

Elsewhere, dozens of resort hotels provide free use of Hobie Cats, Aqua-Bikes, kayaks, and other non-motorized equipment, while commercial outfitters rent Jet Skis and/or offer paragliding off the beach.

Whitewater Rafting

The Dominican Republic is the only Caribbean nation that offers whitewater rafting—the ultimate combination of beauty and thrill. Trips on the Río Yaque del Norte begin in Jarabaco, where several outfitters offer tours; see the Cordillera Central chapter.

WHAT TO EAT

When in Rome...

Despite the ubiquity of gourmet international outlets tempting deep-pocketed Dominicans, your average island-born diner prefers to stick with *comida criollo*—local fare. That means simple dishes that hark back to the land. Call it peasant fare, or fare of *el campo*. Think fried food, sparingly spiced. The staple dishes, found on menus throughout the island, are roast pork *(cerdo asado)* and fried or roast chicken *(pollo frito* or *pollo asado)*, invariably accompanied by white rice *(arroz)*, black beans *(frijoles negra)*, fried plantains

Seafood paella

A Dominican Republic meal The Dominican Republic Ministry of Tourism

(*plátanos*), and sometimes a starch vegetable such as cassava (*yuca*), yam (*malanga*), or sweet potato (*boniato*). Dominicans seem never to tire of these basic yet tasty dishes.

Forget Wheaties or granola for breakfast. Locals typically start their day with *mangú*, boiled plantain mashed with milk, cheese, and pieces of bacon; or *mofongo*, fried plantain mashed with sautéed garlic and *chicharrones* (deep-fried pork rinds). These dishes often reappear later in the day as appetizers, or often as main dishes when stuffed with seafood. Crispy *chicharrones*, including chicken *chicharrón* (*pica-pollo*), are also eaten as a stand-alone snack, in various soups and stews, or battered and seasoned and served with *tostones*. A popular variant, *chimichurris*, are sandwiches filled with slices of seasoned roast pork typically served at roadside stands. Count the ways, too, that sweet plantain—a vegetable relative of the banana—is used. As a side dish it most frequently appears fried in strips or soft-fried chips (*fritos maduros*), sometimes eaten like French fries sprinkled with salt. Unripe plantains are diced and fried and served as crunchy rounds called *tostones*. A similar snack treat, *batatas* are baked sweet potatoes eaten out of the skin while still hot. Locals also stave off hunger pangs with *yaniqueques* (hot round corn breads resembling Johnny cakes), *quipes* (small wheat rissoles stuffed with meat), and *pastelitos* (tiny turnover pastries filled with cheese, chicken, or minced beef).

The national dish is *bandera dominicana* (Dominican flag), a variant on Cuba's *ropa vieja*—marinated and spiced shredded beef accompanied with white rice, red beans, fried plantain, and salad. Beef is also a key ingredient of *sancocho*, a heavily spiced stew that also features chicken and pork along with various vegetables. Otherwise, beef isn't a big deal with Dominicans, who far prefer pork and chicken. The many goats (*chivos*) that nibble roadside margins are a bony substitute, especially on holidays when goat meat marinated with rum and spices is traditionally roasted (*chivo asado*). No edible parts are wasted. Pork

Price Codes		LODGING	DINING		Credit Card Abbreviations
$	Inexpensive	Up to $50	Up to $15		AE—American Express
$$	Moderate	$50–100	$15–30		DC—Diner's Club
$$$	Expensive	$100–200	$30–50		CB—Carte Blanche
$$$$	Very Expensive	Over $200	$50 or more		MC—MasterCard
					D—Discover Card
					V—Visa

tripe (stomach lining), for example, is a local fave, especially as the base for *mondongo*, a stew typically made with onions, bell peppers, celery, tomatoes, and garlic. Dominicans swear that it can cure a hangover. Another flavorful stew that can be considered a national dish is *asopao*, a kind of spicy shrimp and seafood gumbo.

The republic is an island nation, fulsome with the bounty of King Neptune's larder. The Dominicans first love is *lambi*, or conch. This rubbery giant sea snail ain't much to look at (seeing it pried from its lustrous shell will put you off food for a week), but it's delicious when marinated in a vinaigrette and served as *escabeche*, or with garlic in a hot tomato stew. Lobster (*langosta*) and shrimp (*camarones*) are also great dishes, buttered with lots of garlic. When it comes to fish, you usually can't go wrong with the local fave: sea bass (*mero*), also best enjoyed with butter and garlic (*ajo*). Snapper (*chillo*), swordfish (*emperador*), and dolphin fish (*dorado*) are other popular species.

Local sugar sweetens a dozen or so delicious puddings, including rice with milk (*arroz con leche*), corn pudding (*majareta*), baked coconut and cornmeal cake (*arepa*), soft Dominican cake with a baked-in pineapple filling (*bizcocho dominicano*), and *dulce de leche*, a thick cream-like dessert made of whole milk and sugar, usually with coconut or candied fruits.

Buen provecho!

WHAT TO BUY

Leave some room in your suitcase for souvenirs. The Dominican Republic is a veritable potlatch of art and crafts. Then there are the fabulous rum and cigars. No matter where you are, you'll find plenty of fun and fulfilling things to buy.

In Santo Domingo, the focus is on fashions, electronics, and the like. But don't expect bargains. Designer stores and malls are concentrated in the modern shopping district of Naco. In the Zona Colonial, Calle del Sol and the pedestrian-only Calle El Conde are lined with stores selling everything from cheap Haitian art to CDs and cigars. When buying music CDs and DVDs of *bachata* and merengue, avoid the ubiquitous roadside stalls, as the recordings here are usually bootleg and often poor quality.

Towns near the Haitian border have bustling Haitian markets, but these mostly sell household items and cheap clothing.

Arts and Crafts

The distinction is in art. Stores selling Haitian art abound. It's ubiquitous! Most of it is mass-produced kitsch. Colorful, sure. But far from classy! The focus is faux primitive.

However, the Dominican art world itself is quite vibrant and avant-garde. Santo Domingo and many of the deluxe beach resorts feature galleries selling fantastic works by leading artists.

Most tourist hotels also have gift stores selling crafts—usually the highest quality available. Prices here are fixed, however. It's far more fun to bargain for crafts at stalls and artisans' markets, where you're often buying direct from the artisans themselves. Every town has an artisans' market. And all the tourist beaches are lined with crafts outlets selling everything from straw hats, woven baskets, and wooden carvings (animals and nude female figurines are the most popular items) made of lignum vitae and *guayacán*, to the big-ticket local items: simple jewelry made of amber, larimar, and various colored corals. The tourist boom, however, has spawned a great deal of kitsch. Avoid the tacky and politically incorrect products made of marine turtles, sharks, frogs, black coral, etc. Buying these items only contributes to the decimation of already endangered creatures.

Much of the amber jewelry sold at beachside stalls is fake—i.e., made of a polyester resin. Real amber sinks in salt water, changes color under ultraviolet light, and attracts lint and other small items when electrostatically charged (as by rubbing it against your clothes). If you're seeking quality jewelry, head to either a **Museum of Ambar**, a commercial outfit that has store-museums in Santo Domingo, Bávaro, and Puerto Plata; or, for top-quality items, **Harrison's Fine Caribbean Jewelers**, also with outlets throughout the country.

Thatched art gallery on beach at Uvero Alto

Larimar The Dominican Republic Ministry of Tourism

Rum and Smoke

Other good buys are delicious Dominican rum, and some of the finest cigars in the world. Stick with the quality rum brands, such as Bermúdez and Brugal. The older the rum, the higher the quality—*añejos* aged for seven years are best. *Remember that you will not be allowed to pass through airport security with a bottle of rum if you have to transit aircraft in the U.S.A. or Europe!* So pack your liquors in the checked baggage.

When it comes to cigars, you're best to avoid buying from artisans' stalls, as it rarely pays to go cheap. They're usually the lesser brands or fakes, and/or they've been sitting out in the heat. Stick with quality brands that have been properly stored in a humidor. Best yet, visit a cigar factory where you can enjoy learning about the production process. Serious aficionados should head to **Fábrica de Cigarros La Aurora**, in Santiago de los Caballeros, or the outlying town of Tamboril (ground zero for cigar production). The ultimate experience would be a personal tour of **Chateau de la Fuente** (809-575-4739; by appointment only), the private estate of the world famous Arturo Fuentes cigar company.

Another good buy is delicious Dominican coffee from the highlands.

MAJOR HAPPENINGS THROUGHOUT THE YEAR

Whatever time of year you visit the republic, there's sure to be some festival or other fun event going on. The big bash nationwide is *carnaval*, usually (depending on city) held over the four days preceding Ash Wednesday during the last week of February.

Ongoing events include the **Santo Domingo de Fiesta** (May through December), featuring the Ballet Folklórico Nacional, with free performances every Friday and Saturday night in Plaza España.

Daily newspapers plus *Diario Libre* (available free in shops and other outlets) list local festivals and events. The following are among the major happenings to know:

January

Pilgrimage of Virgen de Altagracia: Higüey, January 21. The nation's principal religious pilgrimage. Many supplicants crawl on their knees.

February

Carnaval: La Vega. Considered the most exciting *carnaval* in the country.
Carnaval: Monte Cristi. A variant on other *carnavals*, this one includes a battle between two sides of town, using fireworks and water bombs.
Carnaval: Santiago de los Caballeros. The country's principal *carnaval*.

Mamajuana . . . It's made of *what?*

If there's one product that is uniquely Dominican, it must be *mamajuana*—an infamous rum cocktail immensely popular among the nation's lower classes for its supposed medicinal and aphrodisiacal qualities. This near-mythical sex potion is accredited with being able to cure everything from backache to infertility. Markets and *botánicas* are full of bottles sold to improve health or sexual functions. And it's a staple of working-class bars, where it's downed in shots. I cannot attest to the aforementioned qualities.

It's actually quite tasty and reminds me of a potent *sangría*. It derives from an herbal tea prepared by the Taíno peoples. Following colonization, rum and wine got added to the mix. There's no specific recipe. Everyone has their own. But the key ingredients involve various leaves, roots, and sticks steeped in rum and red wine. Herbs, and even honey (and sometimes fruits), find their way into the mix, as occasionally do marine turtle penises, said to impart the necessary qualities to turn *mamajuana* into a liquid Viagra.

Get your mamajuana here! Playa Bayahibe

Wooden carvings for sale on Playa Dorada

Carnaval: Santo Domingo. The capital's colorful parade is held along Avenida George
   Washington and culminates with the Día de la Independencia (February 27) celebration.
Master of the Ocean: Cabarete. Triathlon featuring kiteboarding, surfing, and windsurfing.

March

Cabarete Art Festival: Cabarete. Local and national artists display their works in Plaza
   Lunatic.
Fiesta Patriótica de la Batalla de Azua del 19 de Marzo: Azua, March 19. Formal celebration
   of the Dominican Republic's victory over Haiti in 1844.
International Sand Castle Competition: Cabarete (www.castillosdearena.com).
Music Festival. Santo Domingo. Biannual 10-day program of classical music concerts.

June

Expo Mango: Baní. This festival honors the mango, an important local crop.

July

Merengue Festival: Santo Domingo. This vivacious festival on Avenida George Washington
   demonstrates the national passion for merengue.

August

Festival of the Bulls: Higüey. Traditional rodeo and *topes*—displays of equestrian skills.
   Cowboys hit town en masse, along with their cattle.
Restoration Day: Nationwide, August 16. Celebrates the country's second independence.

October

Merengue Festival: Puerto Plata. The town comes alive for this weeklong party focused on Dominicans' favorite music.

November

Dominican Jazz Festival: Puerto Plata and Sosúa (809-571-3880 or 571-0882; www.drjazzfestival.com). International and local celebrities play.
International Film Festival: Puerto Plata (809-646/723-0135; www.dominicaninternationalfilmfestival.com). Even Hollywood celebrities fly in. Includes films screened on the sands.
Procession of Nuestra Señora de Regla: Baní, November 21. The town's patron saint is paraded.

December

Día de Santa Bárbara: Santa Bárbara de Samaná; December 4. Colorful parade and music.

PRACTICAL DETAILS

Banks, Money, Etc.

The Dominican *peso* (RD$) is divided into 100 *centavos*. Coins of 1 and 5 pesos, and bills of 10, 20, 50, 100, 500, 1000, and 2000 pesos circulate. The U.S. dollar (which was worth about 34 pesos at press time) is accepted almost everywhere and is the preferred currency in tourist zones.

Most hotels will change U.S. or Canadian dollars or Pounds Sterling or Euros for pesos. Banks and foreign exchange booths (*casas de cambio*) will exchange other currencies. There are BanReservas exchange booths in the major airports. Larger bank branches usually have

---

Patron Saint Festivals

Every year, towns throughout the nation hold festivals (*fiestas patronales*) in honor of each town's patron saint. Although religious in origin, most have adopted elements that are more secular (even pagan), with beauty pageants, rodeos, folkloric music and dance, and plenty of live entertainment and street vendors. Each fiesta varies according to regional proclivities. That of Baní, for example, features *sarandunga*, an Afro-Latin dance form unique to the town.

Key fiestas patronales include:

March: San José de Ocoá; San José de las Matas
May: Luperón; Monte Cristi; San Francisco de Macorís
June: Baní; San Juan de la Maguana; San Pedro de Macorís; Sosúa
July: Puerto Plata; Samaná; Santiago de los Caballeros
August: Higüey; La Vega; San Cristóbal
September: Constanza
October: Dajabón; Elías Piña
November: Boca Chica
December: Las Matas de Farfán

National Holidays

January 1: New Year's Day

January 6: The Epiphany

January 21: Our Lady of Altagracia

January 26: Juan Pablo Duarte's birthday

February 27: Independence from Haitian occupation

May 1: Labor Day

May 26: Corpus Christi

August 16: Dominican Restoration Day

September 24: Our Lady of Mercedes

November 6: Constitution Day

December 25: Christmas Day

Easter Friday, which varies annually, is also a national holiday. Most banks and government offices close during national holidays.

foreign exchange counters. Elsewhere anticipate possible long lines and waits for service. Major credit cards (*tarjetas de crédito*) are accepted everywhere, and you can use them at banks and larger hotels to get cash advances. (BanReservas only gives cash advances against MasterCard.) Most branches also have 24-hour ATMs. However, don't rely on them having cash, as many will run out, especially on weekends. And if possible, use them only during banking hours in case there's a problem, such as your card not being ejected. Banks are usually open Monday through Friday 8:30 to 4 PM; some are also open Saturday 8:30 to noon.

Most shops refuse to accept travelers' checks due to the high incidence of fraud, for which reason banks often put a long hold on such checks; a surcharge may apply.

Never change money on the streets—many people are robbed or scammed!

Child Care

Even the most loving parents like to get away from the kids, especially when night calls for sampling a chilled martini. Most resort hotels provide child care facilities, although don't expect the same from small boutique hotels, many of which don't permit children.

Communications

Postal Service

The **Instituto Postal Dominicano** (809-534-5838; www.inposdom.gob.do) operates post offices throughout the country. They're typically open Monday through Friday 8 to 5:30 PM. However, most hotels sell postage-prepaid letters and postcards, which you can also mail at your hotel reception desk. Service is unreliable and slow. Allow at least 10 days for mail to North America (US$0.30) and about 14 days to Europe (US$0.80).

Theft is common, so if you're going to mail anything of value, use a private courier service such as DHL (809-534-7888; www.dhl.com.do) or FedEx (809-565-3636; www.fedex.com/do), which have offices throughout the republic.

To receive mail, you will need to rent a postal box (apartado postal, abbreviated *Apdo.*), as there is no home delivery in the Dominican Republic.

Telephone Service

The republic's telephone system is efficient. Three telecommunications companies compete: **Claro Codetel** (809-220-1111; www.codetel.net.do), **Orange** (809-859-6555; www.orange.com.do); and **Tricom** (809-476-6000; www.tricom.net). They have call centers nationwide.

There's no shortage of public phones. They use prepaid phone cards, sold at hotels, stores, gas stations, and call centers, and from touts selling them roadside. You insert the card into the phone; the cost of your call is deducted. Local calls cost RD$1 per minute; national calls cost about RD$5 per minute. Phone cards can also be used from most hotel phones—a handy money saver, as tourist hotels typically charge exorbitant fees for direct calls from in-room phones. The cheapest way to call home is from a call center (typical rates to North America are RD$5 per minute, and about RD$15 per minute to Europe).

The Dominican Republic code is 809 (or 829 for cellular phones). To dial the republic from North America, dial 1, then 809 and the local number. There are no regional area codes within the country, although local telephones numbers are preceded by "1" when dialing beyond Santo Domingo. For operator-assisted calls to countries outside the Dominican Republic, dial 0. Call 411 for directory inquiries.

To make free international calls using the Internet, register with Skype (www.skype.com).

You can activate your cellular phone at Claro or Tricom outlets (European GSM phones can be activated at Orange outlets), then purchase a phone plan or prepaid phone card.

Internet Service

Tourist hotels usually have some form of Internet service. Most upscale hotels have Internet modems and/or WiFi reception in guest bedrooms, although many charge for WiFi. Many older all-inclusive resort hotels have Internet booths; charges are usually high and the wait for use can be long. All towns have Internet cafés at reasonable rates; many telephone call centers double as Internet cafés.

Electricity

The Dominican Republic operates on 110 volts and outlets use U.S. two-prong or three-prong plugs (European visitors will need to bring adapters). Some outlets are 220 volt, usually marked as such. Power outages (*apagones*) are common. Fortunately, most resort hotels have their own back-up generators. Bring a surge protector or transformer to protect against power surges.

Handicapped Services

The Dominican Republic is far behind developed nations in terms of handicap accessibility. Few sidewalks have wheelchair ramps, for example. And few buildings have special toilets. Nor are buses adapted for wheelchairs. However, things are changing. The **Consejo Nacional de Discapacidad** (National Council for Disability, 809-687-5480; Arzobispo Portes 554, Santo Domingo) has established wheelchair ramps on major avenues in Santo Domingo, and many new public buildings are handicapped-equipped. So are most major tourist hotels and upscale restaurants built in recent years.

The **Society for Accessible Travel and Hospitality** (212/447-7284; www.sath.org; 347 5th Avenue, Suite 610, New York, NY 10016) is a handy resource for disabled travelers.

In the republic, two organizations to know are the **Asociación Dominicana de Rehabilitación** (809-688-6444; www.adr.org.do; Calle San Francisco de Macorís and Avenida Leopoldo Navarro, Santo Domingo) and the **Fundación Dominicana de Ciegos** (Dominican Foundation for Blind People; 809-245-3444; Avenida Expreso V Centenario and Calle Tunti Cáceres, Edificio 11, Santo Domingo).

Health and Safety

Medical Services

The republic has only a rudimentary public health system; although most towns have *centros de salud* (health centers); standards are well below those of North America and Europe. However, there are plenty of private clinics *(clínicas)* of high standard. In Santo Domingo, the best public facility is **Hospital Padre Bellini** (809-221-8272; Avenida Sánchez between Arzobispo Nouel and Padre Bellini); the best private hospital is **Clínica Abre** (809-688-4411; Avenida Independencia and Burgos). Tourist areas are served by **Clinic Assist** (809-541-3000 ext. 2825, www.hospiten.es), which has ambulance service and full-service clinics in Santo Domingo and Bávaro.

Most large hotels have a nurse on-site and/or maintain a list of recommended doctors and health facilities.

Most towns have well-stocked pharmacies, and many drugs sold as prescription-only in North America and Europe are available over the shelf (however, the name of a specific drug may be different).

Travel Insurance

Travel insurance that covers health service and medical evacuation is a wise investment. Keep receipts for insurance claims. The following companies are recommended: **American Express** (800-234-0375 www.americanexpress.com); **TravelGuard International** (800-826-4919; www.travelguard.com); and **Travelers** (800-243-3174; www.travelers.com).

Assistcard (305-381-9959; www.assist-card.com) offers comprehensive insurance packages and has a regional assistance center in Santo Domingo (809-683-3433 ext. 24).

Health Issues

Your biggest enemy is the climate. The tropical sun is intense. Many foreign (and especially first-time) visitors underestimate the power of the sun and get badly burned. Use lots of sunscreen with a minimum UV rating of 15. And build up your exposure to the sun gradually. Otherwise you risk getting potentially fatal sunstroke as well as sunburn.

You'll be constantly sweating and may not even notice, as your sweat may evaporate instantly. Avoid alcohol by day, and replenish your body fluids by drinking *lots* of water.

In a tropical climate, bacteria breed profusely. Wash cuts and scrapes with bottled water and rubbing alcohol, and use antiseptic creams.

Stomach ailments are common. To avoid them, avoid food from cheap food stalls, as well as uncooked seafoods, unwashed salads, unpeeled fruits, and any meats that have been exposed to flies or left in the heat too long (as at many resort buffet counters).

Don't drink or brush your teeth with tap water—use bottled water. Ensure any ice you drink is made from bottled water. And don't drink water from streams—a sure way to become infected with the giardia parasite.

Mosquitoes are prevalent in humid lowland areas, especially near coastal mangroves. Malaria is present along the Caribbean coast, and outbreaks of dengue fever (an excruciating and debilitating disease) often occur. Both are spread by mosquitoes. Ask your doctor for a prophylactic against malaria (there is no medication or cure for dengue). To reduce the chance of being bitten, use insect repellent liberally and wear light-colored clothing, ideally long-sleeved shirts and pants.

The other biting pest is the no-see-um (Dominicans call them *jejenes, malla,* or *mee mes*), a minuscule flea with a nasty bite that itches like hell and leaves you looking as if you

Tigueres and Sanky-pankys

Tigueres (literally, tigers), or hustlers, are the bane of tourists. Employing all manner of scams, come-ons, and clever pitches, their goal is simple—to part you from your money. These masters of psychology know how to prey on innocent tourists' gullibility. Some sell drugs. Many *tigueres* even pose as police (see Renting a Car, this chapter). Others—called sanky-pankys—seduce foreign females (usually older and loveless) with false declarations of love, or simply serve as gigolos for women looking for love beneath the palms. The ultimate goal is marriage, simply for a foreign visa, as portrayed in Spanish director Jose E. Pintor's 2007 movie, *Sanky Panky*. Many sanky-pankys actually prostitute themselves to males as well as women. Robbery by sanky-pankys and female sex workers is common. Never accept a drink offered by either—they're often drugged.

have chicken pox. They're active on beaches at dawn and dusk. Insect repellent doesn't stop them, but Avon Skin-So-Soft does.

Safety Issues

Let's start with traffic—the biggest safety issue you'll face. Dominicans are lousy drivers! Aggressive...Devil-may-care...Lawless...And just plain dangerous. If you rent a car (or even cross a road as a pedestrian), use utmost caution.

And as for coconuts...there's a reason coconut trees at beach resorts are harvested for their nuts before they fall, and it isn't simply for fresh juice for your piña colada. A falling coconut can seriously ruin your day!

Sexual diseases, especially, HIV/AIDS, are prevalent among the republic's sex workers.

Scorpions and tarantulas are common. The latter are relatively harmless, and usually bite only under severe provocation. Never put your hand under rocks or in crevices, never walk around barefoot at night, and do shake out your shoes and clothes in the morning before putting them on. The Dominican Republic has no venomous snakes, but keep a safe distance from the crocodiles in Lake Enriquillo. And when wading in sandy ocean shallows, shuffle your feet through the sand to scare away any stingrays—if you step on one, their slashing tail can inflict an awesome and excruciating wound.

Don't swim if you've been drinking alcohol. And beware of riptides, which are prevalent on beaches receiving high surf. They cause many people to drown every year. These narrow and ferociously fast currents drain incoming water back to sea. If you get caught in one, swim *parallel* to the shore to escape the current, otherwise you're sure to tire yourself out and panic in a vain effort to swim back to shore. Check local conditions before swimming.

In towns, be guarded at all times against snatch-and-grab theft and/or muggings. Avoid lonely places and impoverished areas, especially at night. Guard your belongings closely in crowded areas, such as buses and markets. Don't drive alone at night. And never leave any possessions in a parked vehicle, or unattended on a beach. To reduce the risk of theft, never carry your camera loose on your shoulder; don't wear fancy jewelry; wear clothing over a money belt; and keep the bulk of your valuables in a hotel safe.

Time Zones

The Dominican Republic operates on Atlantic Standard Time (AST) and is one hour ahead of New York and Miami and four hours behind Greenwich Mean Time (GMT). Daylight Savings is observed April through October.

Getting Married

Many visitors to the republic tie the knot. Some even decide to do it impromptu once they arrive! It's easily arranged. If you plan on staying at a large resort hotel, it's easiest to have the hotel make all your arrangements (usually several weeks notice is required). Many hotels offer complete wedding packages. If you go it alone, you'll need to apply to the local *Oficial del Estado Civil* (City Clerk). Either way, you'll need to provide copies of your passports and birth certificates, plus notarized single-status affidavits, plus any divorce or death certificates, which must be translated into Spanish and certified by a Dominican Republic Consulate.

Tourist Information

The **Ministerio de Turismo** (Ministry of Tourism; 809-221-4660; www.godominicanrepublic.com; Avenida México, corner of 30 de Mayo, Santo Domingo) publishes the *Dominican Republic Vacation Planner*, plus a series of pocket-sized guides on each region and special interest travel such as golf. It has the following offices abroad:

Canada: 514-499-1918 or 1-800-563-1611; 2080 Rue Crescent, Montreal, Quebec H3G 2B8.

United Kingdom: 020-7242-7778; 18–20 Hand Court, High Holbon, London WC1.

U.S.A.: 212-588-1012 or 1-888-374-6361; 136 E. 57th Street, Suite 803, New York, NY 10022.

The ministry's regional tourist information bureaus include:

Boca Chica: 809-529-3644; Calle Domínguez Charzo 8.
Cabarete: 809-571-0962; Plaza Tricom, Calle Principal.
Constanza: 809-539-2900; Calle Matilda Viña 18, corner of Miguel Andrés Abreu.
Jarabacoa: 809-574-7287; Plaza Ramírez, Calle Mario Galán, between Duarte and Calle del Carmen.
La Romana: 809-550-2342; Gobernación, Calle Teniente Amado García.
Las Terrenas: 809-240-6363; La Ceiba 6 at Calle Principal.
Monte Cristi: 809-579-2254; Gobernación, Calle Mella 37.
Puerto Plata: 809-586-5059; Calle José del Arizo 45.
Punta Cana: 809-552-1237, Playa Bávaro
Samaná: 809-538-2332; Avenida La Marina.
Santiago de los Caballeros: 809-582-5885; Gobernación, Parque Duarte at Calle del Sol.
Santo Domingo: 809-686-3858; Palacio Bonde, Calle Isabel la Católica 103.
Sosúa: 809-571-3433; Calle Duarte 1.

BIBLIOGRAPHY

Coffee-table

Borkson, Joseph L. *Reflections on the Spanish Isle: Glories of the Dominican Republic.* Philadelphia: Cyrano Press, 2007. The author/photographer focuses on the island's history and architecture.

Fernández, Eladio, et al. *Hispaniola, A Photographic Journey Through Island Biodiversity.* Cambridge, MA: Harvard U Press, 2007. 396 pages, photos.

Friedel, Michael. *Dominican Republic: The Very Best of Michael Friedel.* Steingau, Germany: Michael Friedel Publishing, 2006. 96 pages, photos.

Cookery

González, Clara, R., and Ilana Benady. *Traditional Dominican Cookery.* Hialeah, FL: Lunch Club Press, 2007. 128 pages, photos.

Culture, History, Economics, and Politics

Brennan, Denise. *What's Love Got to Do with It? Transnational Desires and Sex Tourism in the Dominican Republic.* Durham, NC: Duke University Press, 2004. 272 pages. An academic's study of the complex world of Sosúa's sex business.

Brown, Isabel Zakrzewski. *Culture and Customs of the Dominican Republic.* Westport, CT: Greenwood Press, 1999. 224 pages.

Crandall, Russell. *Gunboat Democracy: U.S. Interventions in the Dominican Republic, Grenada, and Panama.* Lanham, MD: Rowman & Littlefield Publishers, 2006. 256 pages, photos.

Diederich, Bernard. *Trujillo: The Death of the Dictator.* Princeton, NJ: Markus Wiener Publishing, 2000. 264 pages. A study of Trujillo's brutal regime and his assassination.

Howard, David John. *Dominican Republic In Focus: A Guide to the People, Politics and Culture.* Northampton, MA: Interlink Books, 1999. 94 pages

Kaplan, Marion A. *Dominican Haven: The Jewish Refugee Settlement in Sosúa, 1940–1945.* New York: Museum of Jewish Heritage, 2008. 255 pages, photos.

Moya Pons, Frank. *The Dominican Republic: A National History.* Princeton, NJ: Markus Wiener Publishing, 1998. 543 pages.

Roorda, Eric Paul. *The Dictator Next Door: The Good Neighbor Policy and the Trujillo Regime in the Dominican Republic, 1930–1945.* Durham, NC: Duke University Press, 1998. 312 pages.

Sagas, Ernesto. *The Dominican People: A Documentary History.* Princeton, NJ: Markus Wiener Publishing, 2003. 278 pages.

Sellers, Julie. *Merengue and Dominican Identity: Music as National Unifier.* Jefferson, NC: McFarland & Company, 2004. 239 pages.

Torres-Saillant, Silvio, and Ramona Hernandez. *The Dominican Americans.* Westport, CT: Greenwood Press, 1998. 208 pages.

Wucker, Michele. *Why the Cocks Fight: Dominicans, Haitians, and the Struggle for Hispaniola.* New York: Hill and Wang, 2000. 304 pages

Literature

Álvarez, Julia. *How the Garcia Girls Lost Their Accents.* Chapel Hill, NC: Algonquin Books, 1991. 308 pages. Fifteen short tales of a Dominican family trying to establish a new identity in the U.S.A.

Álvarez, Julia. *In the Time of the Butterflies.* New York: Plume, 1995. 353 pages. This profound novel fictionalizes the true-life account of the Mirabal sister's fateful and futile fights against the Batista regime.

Vargas Llosa, Mario. *The Feast of the Goat.* New York, Picador, 2002. 416 pages. A novel with three parallel stories set during the final days of General Rafael Trujillo's wicked regime.

Natural History

Jiménez, Francisco, Juan Llamacho and James Ackerman. *Orchids of Dominican Republic and Haiti.* Santo Domingo: Curva Vertical, 2007. Photos, illustrations.

Latta, Steve, et al. *The Birds of the Dominican Republic and Haiti.* Princeton, NJ: Princeton University Press, 2006. 360 pages, photos, illustrations.

Raffaele, Herbert et al. *The Birds of the West Indies.* Princeton, NJ: Princeton University Press, 1998. 208 pages, photos, illustrations.

Ferguson, James. *The Dominican Republic: An Introduction and Guide.* Oxford, UK: Macmillan Caribbean. 154 pages, maps, photos.

Lane, Peter. *Dominican Days.* Bury St. Edmunds, UK: Arima Publishing, 2006. 312 pages. A personalized account of Dominican history and society.

Nave of the Catedral Primada de América, Santo Domingo

Santo Domingo

The Americas' First City

Founded in 1502 as the first colonial city in the Americas, Santo Domingo wears its history on its sleeve. Its Zona Colonial (declared a UNESCO World Heritage Site in 1990) is a lived-in museum, with enough attractions to enthrall for days. Beyond sprawls the modern metropolis of 2.2 million people. Contemporary sophistication and old-world charm merge in a sultry amalgam.

The precursor city of Nueva Isabela was originally founded in 1498 by Bartolomé Colón (Bartholomy Columbus) on the east bank of the Río Ozama, on Hispaniola's southern coast. In 1502 a hurricane swept through, destroying the settlement of wooden houses. The new governor, Nicolás de Ovando, chose to rebuild above the more propitious west bank of the river, where a new city—Santo Domingo de Guzmán—was laid out in a neat grid protected by a *muralla* (curtain wall) with 20 *baluartes* (sentry towers) and six entrance gates.

Conquistadores of future renown (Hernán Córtes and Diego Velásquez among them) set out from Santo Domingo to conquer the Americas for Spain. The city's early importance drew pirates. In 1586, a fleet of 20 ships led by Sir Francis Drake ransacked the city. When they left a month later, much of Santo Domingo lay in ruins. Despite continuing to serve as the administrative capital of the New World (in 1799, jurisdiction was finally transferred to Cuba), Santo Domingo never gained Havana's stature, nor even that of Lima, Cartagena, or Mexico City—majestic cities whose elaborate edifices were funded by the traffic in vast quantities of gold and silver.

While Havana prospered through the colonial epoch, Santo Domingo struggled, and never more so than in the 19th century, when the city fell first to French, British, then Haitian forces (see the History chapter). The Haitian occupation (1822–43) was followed by turmoil. The city was a prize plum in the constant warring between Dominican *caudillos*. Neglected, much of the early colonial city fell into ruin, and much of its old walls crumbled to dust. Further damage was done when Hurricane San Xenon pummeled Santo Domingo in 1930. The hurricane came only three weeks after Trujillo seized power. Although it might have been an omen of tempestuous decades to come, Trujillo (who in 1936 renamed the city for himself) seized the opportunity by launching massive reconstruction. Magnificent buildings went up, including the Palacio Nacional. Thereafter, the city expanded exponentially in every direction.

Today, Santo Domingo—the second largest city in the Caribbean after Havana—is home to one-fifth of the Dominican Republic's total population.

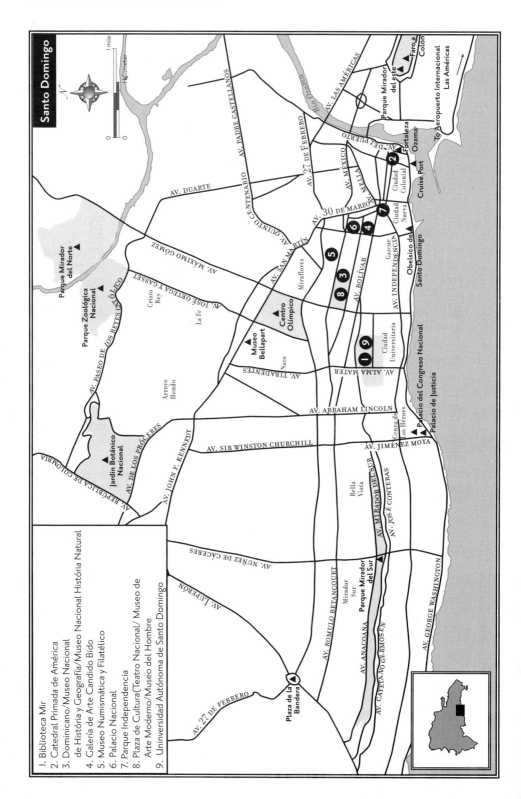

Santo Domingo

1 mile

0

kilometer

0

1. Biblioteca Mir
2. Catedral Primada de América
3. Dominicano/Museo Nacional
de História y Geografía/Museo Nacional História Natural
4. Galería de Arte Candido Bido
5. Museo Numismática y Filatélico
6. Palacio Nacional
7. Parque Independencia
8. Plaza de Cultura(Teatro Nacional/ Museo de
Arte Moderno/Museo del Hombre
9. Universidad Autónoma de Santo Domingo

Getting Your Bearings

Santo Domingo slopes gently north from the Caribbean shore and comprises distinct neighborhoods. It pays to have a sense of what's where to make the most of your time in the city.

Most of the sights of interest are in the **Zona Colonial**, the historic and cultural heart of the city dating back to 1503 and defined by the extent of the old city walls. The principal landmarks of interest are here, concentrated within the southeast quadrant. You could fill two days exploring around Parque Colón, Plaza España, Plaza Juan Duarte, and along Calle Las Damas and Calle Hostos.

Immediately west of Zona Colonial is late-19th-century **Ciudad Nueva** and, farther west, the 1930s-era **Gazcue**, together a predominantly middle-class residential district laid out in a grid. The twin regions lie inland of the Caribbean shore. Running along the oceanfront is Avenida George Washington (the Malecón), a broad and undistinguished boulevard lined with high-rise upscale hotels, casinos, and several fine restaurants. Sites of touristic interest are relatively few: the Palacio Nacional (on the north side of Ciudad Nueva) and Plaza de la Cultura (on the north side of Gazcue), with the city's major museums. The few beaches are disgustingly littered and are to be avoided (fortunately, in 2008, the government announced plans to build a 500-dock marina—Sans Souci Port—to occupy the shorefront between Calle Vicini Burgos and 19 de Marzo). The section between Calle Pasteur and Avenida Máximo Gómez is closed to vehicles on Sunday evenings, when youth cruise with their ghetto blasters cranked up. Strolling the Malecón is best avoided after dusk.

To the northwest of Gazcue lies **Naco**, the sprawling heart of the modern city. Here are the major banks, shopping malls, and nightclubs. Traffic can be a nightmare.

Together, the above regions comprise the city's core. The polygon is roughly bordered by the Río Ozama (east), Avenida George Washington (south), Avenida Abraham Lincoln (west), and the Autopista Kennedy (north).

Beyond these distinct neighborhoods, the sprawling metropolis extends to west, north, and east in a hotpotch of districts. Many are difficult-to-navigate warrens, including economically depressed areas, such as Villa Mella, Los Alcarrizos, and Herrera that are best avoided. The poorest *barrios* (districts) are virtual shantytowns, found on the city outskirts.

Aeropuerto Internacional Las Américas: To find your way to Santo Domingo from the nation's largest airport, take the Autopista San Isidro (A3), a fast-paced toll highway (RD$30) that lies immediately north of the airport. The highway becomes Avenida las Américas and crosses the Río Ozama by the Puente Juan Pablo Duarte bridge; exit immediately on the west side to loop around onto Avenida del Puerto to reach the Zona Colonial and the modern hotels along the shoreline Malecón (Avenida George Washington). East from the airport, the A3 becomes a two-lane highway that hugs the coast and passes through Boca Chica en route to San Pedro de Macorís. The 10-mile trip to downtown Santo Domingo will take 30 minutes minimum, depending on traffic conditions.

TOURING IN THE ZONA COLONIAL AND BEYOND

Santo Domingo's transportation is, er, shall we say a tad chaotic. A little planning goes a long way. Please note that prices for transportation fares quoted in this book were based on fuel costs at the time of research and may be subject to volatility, including surcharges. The two major bus drivers' unions staged various work stoppages in 2008 to protest rising fuel prices, adding to the chaos. And a major refurbishing of the colonial zone's historic attractions has also been announced for 2009 and onwards.

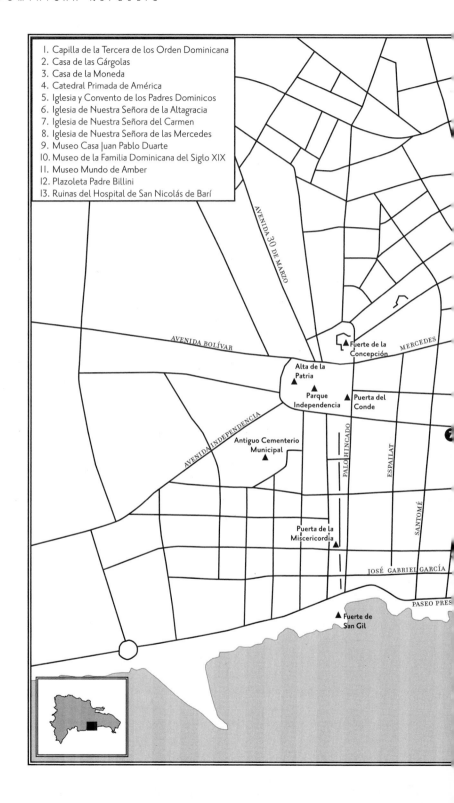

1. Capilla de la Tercera de los Orden Dominicana
2. Casa de las Gárgolas
3. Casa de la Moneda
4. Catedral Primada de América
5. Iglesia y Convento de los Padres Dominicos
6. Iglesia de Nuestra Señora de la Altagracia
7. Iglesia de Nuestra Señora del Carmen
8. Iglesia de Nuestra Señora de las Mercedes
9. Museo Casa Juan Pablo Duarte
10. Museo de la Familia Dominicana del Siglo XIX
11. Museo Mundo de Amber
12. Plazoleta Padre Billini
13. Ruinas del Hospital de San Nicolás de Barí

AVENIDA 30 DE MARZO

AVENIDA BOLÍVAR

Fuerte de la
Concepción

MERCEDES

Alta de la
Patria

Parque
Independencia

Puerta del
Conde

AVENIDA INDEPENDENCIA

Antiguo Cementerio
Municipal

PALO HINCADO

ESPAILLAT

SANTOMÉ

Puerta de la
Miscericordia

JOSÉ GABRIEL GARCÍA

PASEO PRES

Fuerte de
San Gil

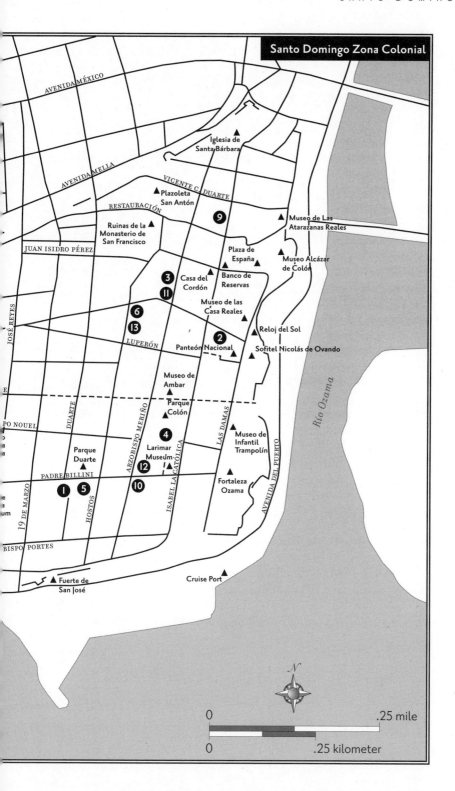

Santo Domingo Zona Colonial

AVENIDA MÉXICO

AVENIDA MELLA

VICENTE C. DUARTE

Iglesia de
Santa Bárbara

Plazoleta
San Antón

RESTAURACIÓN

9

Museo de Las
Atarazanas Reales

Ruinas de la
Monasterio de
San Francisco

JUAN ISIDRO PÉREZ

Plaza de
España

Museo Alcázar
de Colón

3

Casa del
Cordón

Banco de
Reservas

11

JOSÉ REYES

6

Museo de las
Casa Reales

13

LUPERÓN

Reloj del Sol

2

Panteón Nacional

Sofitel Nicolás de Ovando

Museo de
Ambar

E

Parque
Colón

PO NOUEL

DUARTE

ARZOBISPO MERIÑO

LAS DAMAS

4

Museo de
Infantil
Trampolín

Parque
Duarte

Larimar
Museum

AVENIDA DEL PUERTO

Río Ozama

PADRE BILLINI

12

ISABEL LA CATÓLICA

1   **5**

10

Fortaleza
Ozama

19 DE MARZO

HOSTOS

um

BISPO PORTES

Fuerte de
San José

Cruise Port

N

0   .25 mile

0   .25 kilometer

Nehemias Zarzuela plays acoustic guitar at the Hotel Sofitel Nicolas de Ovando, Santo Domingo

By Bus or Público

Santo Domingo has a fairly efficient or dysfunctional public bus system, depending on your perspective. OMSA (Metropolitan Office of Buses Services) operates large Metropolitan buses along the major avenues (RD$5.00 for gray buses, or RD$10.00 for yellow air-conditioned buses). Most bus stops (*paradas*) are signed, and it is easy to transfer between buses at major intersections. The downside is that public buses are usually crowded and hot and run on no fixed schedule. They operate 6 AM to 9:30 PM.

Even more crowded minibuses (*públicos* or *guaguas*) connect city neighborhoods along set routes. Parque Independencia, on the western edge of Zona Colonial, is the main hub for *públicos,* but most passing *públicos* will honk their horns at you to see if you want a ride. These buses are always jam-packed, with passengers like proverbial pilchards—definitely not for claustrophobics! While most are modern, others are nearly derelict. Regardless, they're sure to be driven by a madman. Most charge RD$5 and require exact change. To hail one, hold your arm out and point downwards.

There is no central bus terminal for travel beyond Santo Domingo. See Transport: Getting Around, in the Planning Your Trip chapter, for details.

By Carriage

You can hire a horse-drawn carriage for a slow-paced, romantic exploration of the Zona

Colonial and along the Malecón. Typical fares are about $20 per hour (and no fuel surcharge), but can be negotiated. Don't expect your guide to speak English, however. You can usually pick one up outside the Hotel Sofitel Nicolás de Ovando, or on the Malecón (Avenida George Washington).

By Foot

Pack your walking shoes for exploring Zona Colonial. The grid of easily navigated and narrow (and thereby shaded) streets is tailor-made for perambulation. However, stick within the walled zone. Beyond, distances make walking a pain in the butt; traffic makes crossing streets a hazard; and walking in some zones is an open invitation to snatch-and-grab thieves and even muggers.

By Subway

Finally, after much anticipation, the city has a spanking new Metro underground system. The first line (serving Avenidas Máximo Gómez and Hermanas Mirabal) was inaugurated on February 27, 2008, to connect Villa Mella (north of the city) with La Feria (south of the city); commercial passenger service was initiated in January 2009. Trains currently operate every five minutes 6:30 AM–10 PM between Villa Mella station (in the northwest) and Centro de los Heroes, with 16 stations. You buy a coded ticket-card that can be recharged with any amount of money (RD$20 per ride).

Five other lines were currently in various stages of construction at press time.

LODGING

Santo Domingo's hotel scene is wide-ranging. There is something for everyone, from inexpensive hostels to intimate boutique hotels, and ritzy resort hotels with every amenity from tennis and disco to casinos and spas. Most of the latter line the Malecón or are found in the western part of town, in the business district, far from the Zona Colonial. Fortunately, most of the intimate boutique style hotels *are* within the Zona Colonial. Choose accordingly.

Bed and Breakfast Inns / Boutique Hotels

EL BEATRIO GUEST HOUSE
809-687-8657
www.elbeaterio.com
Calle Duarte 8, Ciudad Colonial
Credit Cards: None

This restful charmer is in a colonial structure—a 16th-century convent—made of limestone and stucco. The vestibule retains its original floral-patterned tile floor and is fitted with overstuffed armchairs and sofas, making a delightful space to relax. The air-conditioned guest rooms are perfectly delightful, with their beamed ceilings and simple wrought-iron furniture, including four-poster beds. Each has a ceiling fan, cable TV, and in-room safe, and opens to a balcony or terrace overlooking the palm-filled patio. WiFi is available. Breakfast is served in a quaint dining area. $.

COCO BOUTIQUE HOTEL
809-685-8467 or 829-968-4767
www.cocoboutiquehotel.com
E-mail: reservations@cocoboutiquehotel.com
Calle Arzobispo Portes 7
Credit Cards: MC, V

What a gem! Travelers who appreciate a touch of class in their decor will love this little place, tucked into the very southeast corner of the Zona Colonial. Small and intimate, it has just four air-conditioned rooms, each decorated in its own style and color scheme. They're sophisticated enough, I would think, for the pages of *Architectural Digest*. The Black Vanilla room is, you guessed, all blacks and whites with a twist of 1950s kitsch. Eastern Spice blends gold brocades with Middle Eastern lanterns and similar touches. Morning Dew is a blaze of whites. Silver Musk plays on its silver fabrics and decor. All feature fluffy down pillows and Egyptian cotton towels, plus designer toiletries, and glossy hardwood floors. Some have king beds. And there's high-speed WiFi. Breakfast is served on a small rooftop terrace offering views of the Caribbean Sea and the mouth of the Río Ozama. Cocktails are served in the intimate Coco Lounge Bar. The rate includes breakfast. $$.

FOREIGNERS CLUB HOTEL
809-689-3017
www.casanewyorker.com
Calle Canela 102
Credit Cards: MC, V

It could be love at first sight, especially at night, when the Art Deco facade topped by a 1940s-era neon sign lends a wholly unique aspect to this gay-focused boutique hotel. Formerly the gay-oriented Casa New Yorker, it reopened in April 2008 under new owners: Americans Dorothy Simms, Doran Mooney, and Daniel Ziebarth. Alas, the rooms don't live up to the potential offered by the Art Deco exterior and lobby, with its black-and-white-checkered floor. The 10 rooms (on two levels) are all named for New York boroughs and are simply appointed with clinical whites and modest furnishings. No frills here, although mosquito net drapes over the beds add a romantic touch to some rooms. All have air-conditioning, ceiling fans, cable TVs, and in-room safes.

It has a no-frills rooftop sundeck, and WiFi access. The best thing about this hotel is the location one block south of Parque Independencia, on the western fringe of Zona Colonial—handy for both exploring the Zona Colonial and for the restaurants and nightlife of Ciudad Nueva and Gazcue. Guests are welcome at no extra charge. $.

HODELPA CARIBE COLONIAL
809-688-7799
fax: 809-685-8128
www.hodelpa.com
E-mail: infocolonial@hodelpa.com
Calle Isabel La Católica 159
Credit Cards: AE, MC, V

This is one example of a hotel that doesn't quite live up to the images portrayed on its website. Still, it has plenty of pluses for none-too-fussy vacationers seeking modest-priced digs in the heart of the Zona Colonial. Just 164 feet (50 m) from Parque Colón, this 1950s Art Deco building is situated on a slightly shabby block that teems with noisy nightlife (some of it, shall we say, questionable). The colorful and tiny lobby has a small Internet booth (free), and there's a small bar and restaurant to one side. A major plus is the consistently friendly and gracious staff. However, the parking area is tiny and once parked, retrieving your car can take a while. Guest rooms vary markedly. Some are mere cubbyholes made more cramped by the flowing drapes overhanging the beds. All 54 rooms and suites are air-conditioned and have telephones, tiny cable TVs (with a half-dozen channels), minibars, in-room safes, plus irons and ironing boards. Decor ranges from clinical whites with colorful accents in some rooms, to overdone golds and blues in others. The roof has a sundeck. $$.

HOSTAL NICOLÁS NADER
809-687-6674
fax: 809-535-5142

www.naderenterprises.com/hostal
E-mail: hostalnicolas-
nader@naderenterprises.com
Calle Luperón, corner of Duarte
Credit Cards: AE, MC, V

Yet another delightful conversion of a former, two-storey 16th-century convent, and
erstwhile home of poet Pedro Henríquez
Ureña. The exquisite mood is enhanced by
the weathered limestone columns, oak
beams, and cool courtyard full of palms and
other tropical foliage. A thoughtful remodel
has converted the building into a gracious
and cozy hotel. Hardwood floors gleam
underfoot in the guest rooms, where the
eclectic decor spans early colonial antiques
and Spanish mahogany antique reproductions to Art Deco pieces. Rooms vary in size
and decor. The courtyard doubles as an art
gallery. And the Bar Don Roberto, which
draws a loyal local crowd, stays open until
the last customer departs, and live musicians often perform...so expect some
noise! The rates are a total steal. $$.

HOTEL ATARAZANA
809-688-3693
www.hotel-atarazana.com
Calle Vicente Celestino Duarte 19
Credit Cards: MC, V

Call it the most intimate hotel in the city.
And possibly the find of the century! At
least if you're on a budget. Even deep-
pocket travelers with a taste for contempo-
rary chic may find satisfaction in the
sensational good taste of the German own-
ers. The setting is a rose-tinted 18th-cen-
tury townhouse towards the northern end of
Zona Colonial, just one block north of Plaza
de España. Ah, but step inside and what a
shock! Bit by bit—it's been a long process—
Susanne and Bernardo (Bernie) have graced
this boutique gem with a colorful 21st-cen-
tury minimalist aesthetic that would make
hotel design guru Ian Schrager green with
envy. Fabulous travertine touches are every-

where, including new floors, plus a backlit
wall in the breakfast patio, where guests get
kitchen use. Bold blood reds and banana
yellows against frosted glass and stainless
steel. Get the impression? All beautifully
executed. The six small bedrooms are
accessed by a curving, contemporary hard-
wood staircase. Nice! All have ceiling fans
and cable TV. Rooms to the front catch the
noise from the nearby bars and traffic. The
rooftop deck is a cool place for a chilled
Presidente. Guests get free breakfast and
use of Internet, and Susanne and Bernie
(and their staff) go overboard to make your
stay in the DR as satisfying as possible. If
ever the term cute applied to a hotel, this is
it. $–$$.

HOTEL DOÑA ELVIRA
809-221-7415
fax: 809-221-7369
www.dona-elvira.com
E-mail: reservations@dona-elvira.com
Calle Padre Billini 207, Zona Colonial
Credit Cards: AE, DC, MC, V

Seeking an intimate bed and breakfast?
Look no further. With just 15 rooms tucked
into a courtyard, this renovated 16th-cen-
tury mansion exudes old-world charm. The
unassuming entrance and façade belie the
intimacy and aged charm within. The
exquisite lobby-lounge retains its original
colonial tile work and redbrick details, and
teems with antiques. It opens directly onto
the small courtyard, with a tree-shaded
swimming pool. Ocher-toned rooms to
each side are on two levels. Modestly yet
charmingly furnished, all have air-conditioning, ceiling fans, cable TV, and WiFi
connection. Some have king beds; others
have mezzanine bedrooms (which can get
hot). The place is owned and run by a
bohemian couple: Marc, a former Belgian
diplomat, and his Spanish-Filipina wife,
Elvira. They grant guests privileges to use a
kitchen. $$.

SOFITEL FRANCES

809-685-9331
Fax: 809-685-1289
www.sofitel.com.
E-mail: h2137@accor.com
Calle de las Mercedes, corner of Arzobispo
Merino
Credit Cards: AE, MC, V.

An historic property operated by the French
Accor hotel group, this atmospheric hotel in
the heart of the Zona Colonial doesn't reach
the standards of its sibling, the Sofitel
Nicolás de Ovando. It's a charmer nonetheless. The aged, direct-off-the-street
entrance opens to a lovely albeit small lobby
steeped in 17th-century ambience, with
Oriental throw rugs, and wrought-iron
chandeliers hanging from the beamed ceiling. Spanish colonial antiques meld with
contemporary mahogany furnishings, and
potted plants abound. The lovely Le Patio
restaurant serves French cuisine and opens
to a palm-shaded courtyard, surrounded by
a columned arcade with comfy wicker
lounge chairs. It's especially conducive to
romance when candlelit at night and a
pianist performs. The 19 rooms vary in style
and appeal. Decor is of calming reds,
whites, and pinks, and furnishings mix
antique reproductions with simple Edwar-
dian-style hardwood pieces. Some rooms
are small, with equally cramped bathrooms,
and the overall mood of accommodations is
ho-hum. If possible, view several before
choosing a room, all of which have Internet
connectivity, and the lobby has Wi-Fi. Staff
is friendly and willing. An ample breakfast
buffet is included. Several elements detract
from the enjoyment: tiny TVs; loud street
noise (if you're a light sleeper, aim for a
room to the rear); and a $30 fee is charged
for *any* visitor—business colleague or otherwise—to visit your room. Fortunately,
guests get privileges at the nearby Sofitel
Nicolás de Ovando. $$$.

SOFITEL NICOLÁS DE OVANDO

809-685-9955
fax: 809-686-6590
www.sofitel.com.
E-mail: h2975@accor.com.
Calle Las Damas
Price: Very Expensive.
Credit Cards: AE, D, MC, V.

Time seems to stand still in this natty con-
version of the former home of the island's
first governor, Nicolás de Ovando. Built
between 1502 and 1509 of coral stone and
brick, this architectural A-list property
today offers the city's most fancy digs. And
the location, on Calle Las Damas just one
block from Parque Colón, is unmatched.
The 104 rooms of weathered coral stone and
red brick offer a sublime level of luxe.
Refitted in stylish contemporary fashion,
they come with flat-screen TVs, gorgeous
travertine-clad bathrooms, and top-quality
mattresses with plump down duvets as soft
as a sigh. La Résidence restaurant offers
truly gourmet dining beneath weathered
arches lit by ancient wrought-iron chande-
liers, or in air-conditioned rooms done up
in a chic, sophisticated vogue. Afterwards,
savor a divine postprandial smoke in the
Cibao cigar lounge, or the elegant yet casual
poolside (yes, there's a swimming pool) bar
featuring live jazz or bossa nova. Rooms in
the old building are preferable to those in a
newer block. The Sofitel offers 24-hour
room service and is superbly managed by
the French Accor hotel group. $$$$.

Budget Hotels

EL REFUGIO DEL PIRATA GUEST HOUSE

809-687-1572 or cell 809-394-0419
Calle Arzobispo Merino 358
Credit Cards: None

Another colonial-era hotel in the Zona
Colonial, this one serves the serious budget
crowd for whom low price trumps all other
considerations. The air-conditioned rooms

with wood-lined walls are clean, but many elements of this hotel are jury-rigged. The showers here use overhead heating elements, and hot water is never guaranteed. All rooms have cable TV and a small refrigerator. The hotel has a small terrace. $.

HOTEL RESIDENCE

809-412-7298
www.hotelresidencia.com
E-mail: info@hotelresidencia.com
Calle Danae 62, Gazcue
Credit Cards: MC, V

This modest family-run hotel is handily close to key restaurants and nightclubs. Not all rooms have air-conditioning (a wise investment), but those with ceiling fans only are slightly cheaper. All have cable TV, some rooms have a small refrigerator and safe, and there's a common kitchen on the third floor. Decor is none too inspiring, but rooms are kept clean. $.

LA HACIENDA

809-333-5605
www.grupoarena.com/lahaciendasantodom
ingo/frameintrog.htm
E-mail: lahaciendasdq@verizon.net.do
Calle Santiago Rodríguez 68
Credit Cards: None

Catering to gays, this small boutique hotel in Zona Colonial has four studios and eight suites, all with stylish furnishings, plus cable TV, Internet, and in-room safes. A rooftop terrace has views. $–$$.

PLAZA TOLEDO BETTYES GUEST HOUSE

809-688-7649
www.hostels.net
E-mail: bettymarshall@hotmail.com
Calle Isabel la Catolica 163, corner Luperón
Credit Cards: None

A small youth hostel for the backpacking set in a former colonial mansion. Betty Marshall, the friendly owner, is conscientious and keeps a tight rein on her spic-and-span home, with four rooms with bunk beds, and eclectic furnishings that include fantastic artwork. One block from Plaza de España. $.

Generic Hotels

BOUTIQUE HOTEL PALACIO

809-682-4730
fax: 809-687-5535
www.hotel-palacio.com
E Mail: hotelpalacio@verizon.net.do
Calle Duarte 106, corner Salome Ureña
Credit Cards: MC, V

A competitor to the Sofitel Frances, this colonial hotel is just two blocks from Parque Colón and once was the home of dictatorial 19th-century President Buenaventura Báez. It was recently restored as a hotel, with 40 rooms that combine Caribbean tropical luxury and Spanish Castilian decor. The resulting mood is a bit dowdy for my tastes, especially when compared to the sophistication of the Sofitel Nicolás de Ovando. Still, they're spacious and come with terra-cotta tile floors, king or queen beds, cable TVs, two telephones, minibars, in-room safes, high-speed Internet connections, and modern bathrooms, many with his and her sinks. Suites have personal computers and faxes, and antique furnishings play on the Columbus theme. The atrium courtyard is a lovely space to relax with a cocktail or beer. The rooftop deck has a plunge pool. Despite its name, it's hard to classify this as a boutique hotel. $$.

COURTYARD MARRIOTT

809-685-1010
fax: 809-685-2003
www.marriott.com.do
Avenida Máximo Gómez 50a
Credit Cards: AE, D, MC, V

Good for business travelers, this cookie-cutter hotel is on the western side of town, close to upscale restaurants, nightclubs, and the financial and business district. The 145 guest rooms on four levels are elegant and comfy enough, although they win no prizes. $$$.

HOTEL DUQUE DE WELLINGTON

809-682-4525
fax: 809-688-2844
www.hotelduque.com
E-mail: hotelduque@codetel.net.do
Avenida Independencia 304
Credit Cards: AE, DC, MC, V

If you want to be close to the Zona Tropical *and* the nightlife of the modern zone, *and* you're seeking a bargain, then this well-run, 29-room hotel fits the bill. For these prices, you're not getting luxury. Far from it. But it's in a relatively tranquil part of Gazcue and (very important) is secure. The individually styled, air-conditioned bedrooms are graciously if modestly furnished, with colorful decor, although most bathrooms are small. All have tiny TVs. On hot days, you can cool off in a plunge pool in a leafy courtyard. The pleasant restaurant is a bonus, and there's a travel agency in the lobby. $$.

HOTEL CONDE DE PEÑALBA

809-688-7121
fax: 809-688-7375
www.condepenalba.com
Calle El Conde, Corner of Arzobispo Meriño
Credit Cards: AE, DC, MC, V

Looking as if it belongs in Madrid or Barcelona, the Count of Peñalba Hotel stands proudly over the northwest corner of Parque Colón. The four-storey structure, with its Mediterranean architecture enhanced by wrought-iron balustrades and potted plants, has a curving corner containing the entrance, in almost Gaudiesque fashion. The ground-floor open-air restaurant spills onto the square and is a lively spot, drawing expats, tourists, and locals alike. The 20 rooms win no prizes but are comfortable and perfectly adequate. They're furnished in dowdy, grandmotherly fash-

ion, and have cable TV with few channels, but you can't argue with the views from the south-facing rooms over the plaza. $$.

HOTEL DELTA

809-535-9722
http://hoteldelta.com.do/en/default.asp
E-mail: reservaciones@hoteldelta.com.do
Avenida Sarasota 53, Bella Vista
Credit Cards: AE, MC, V

On the west side of Santo Domingo, two blocks north of Parque Mirador del Sur, this modern seven-storey hotel is close to major shopping malls, banks, and restaurants. However, the location offers no advantage if you're going to spend most of your time exploring the colonial city. No surprise, it aims squarely at business travelers. The 141 air-conditioned guest rooms come as standards, junior suites, suites, or penthouse suites (the latter with terraces and private Jacuzzis). All feature stylish contemporary decor with modern accouterments, such as cable TVs, in-room safes, etc.; and some have kitchenettes. It has a café, terrace bar, a pool, and Jacuzzi, and the lobby offers Internet access for a small fee. $-$$.

HOTEL DISCOVERY

809-687-4048
www.discoverygranhotel.com
Calle Arzobispo Meriño 402
Credit Cards: MC, V

For the traveler not too fussy about ambience or decor, and who seeks nothing more than a comfy, value-priced bed for the night. This modern hotel, in rather soulless architectural style, lies at the northern end of Zona Colonial. Guest rooms are spacious enough and have antique reproduction furnishings (choose from rust, olive green, or blue color schemes), ceramic floors, air-conditioning, cable TV, telephone, in-room safe, and refrigerator. The rooftop terrace with plunge pool doubles as a bar, and simple meals are served in the downstairs restaurant. $-$$.

HOTEL EUROPA

809-285-0005
fax: 809-685-1633
www.antiguohoteleuropa.com
Calle Arzobispo Meriño 109, corner of
Emiliano Tejera
Credit Cards: MC, V.

A neo-classical building houses this
recently remodeled hotel in the heart of
Zona Colonial, and the interior has a clinical contemporary take on a colonial theme.
Choose between Standards, Superiors, and
Junior Suite. Simple antique reproductions
are uninspired yet comfy enough, and all 52
rooms feature centralized air-conditioning,
cable TV, telephone, and in-room safe.
Most open to wrought-iron balconies.
Standards are small, however. Rooms to the
back are more spacious, albeit lacking windows. The top-floor Terraza Restaurant
serves Caribbean and *criolla* fare, and has a
terrace that offers a romantic setting at
night over the ruins of the San Francisco
monastery. The free continental breakfasts
here are desultory. It has parking spaces
and guests are allowed. $$.

HOTEL MONUMENTAL

809-682-4747
www.hotelmonumental.com.do
E-mail: hotelmonumental@gmail.com
Calle El Conde 355
Credit Cards:

This relatively modest and Spartan option
has one thing going for it. Location, loca-
tion, location. A newcomer, it opened in
February 2008 on Calle el Conde. The 25
air-conditioned rooms have cable TVs,
telephones, free WiFi, and tasteful, albeit
simple and oddly mismatched, furnishings
that include wrought-iron beds, and place
Day-Glo minimalist chairs against cheap
antique reproductions. $$.

HOTEL RESTAURANT LA CASONA DORADA

809-221-3535
fax: 809-221-3622
www.casonadorada.com
E-mail:
lacasonadorada@casonadorada.com
Avenida Independencia 255
Credit Cards: MC, V

A no-frills option for travelers seeking
nothing more than a secure bed and a modicum of comfort, this hotel in Gazcue has 21
rooms (some are spacious; others not so).
Air-conditioning, cable TVs, telephones,
in-room safes, and small bathrooms with
hot-water showers are standard. Some
rooms have balconies; and some have king
beds. Decor is yesteryear dowdy. The bar
and restaurant is a tad hokey. And the website has to be seen to be believed for its
ridiculous English translation...but that's
another story. It has secure parking, plus a
courtyard pool. $–$$.

HOTEL SANTO DOMINGO

809-221-1511
fax: 809-534-5584
www.hotelsantodomingo.com.do
Avenida Independencia and Avenida
Abraham Lincoln
Credit Cards: AE, DC, MC, V

Unlike the neighboring modern-style high-
rise hotels, this centrally located option is a
rambling oddity that clings to an outdated
classical Spanish design in its public arenas. You either love it or you hate it. The 214
accommodations, however, boast a more
eye-pleasing, albeit simple contemporary
decor. It has a lovely Moroccan-themed bar,
and the Las Palmas Nightclub is here.
$$–$$$.

HOTEL VILLA COLONIAL

809-221-1049
www.villacolonial.net
E-mail: villacolonialsd@yahoo.fr

Calle Sánchez 157 between Padre Billini and Nouel
Credit Cards: MC, V

The latest in a series of colonial conversions in Zona Colonial, the Villa Colonial is a tasteful addition. Its spacious and lofty lobby exudes elegance, although the modern remake has so diluted the original colonial ambience that this hotel is no match for the Sofitel Nicolás de Ovando. A wrought-iron staircase leads to the 215 air-conditioned albeit smallish rooms, all tastefully furnished with antique reproductions and yesteryear styling. Standard features include cable TV, direct dial phone, cable Internet, WiFi, minibar, in-room safe, writing desk, and hair dryer. The hotel is loaded with facilities, including a gift shop, lounge and piano bar, an outdoor pool, and even a tennis court. Room service 24/7 is a plus. $$$.

MERCURE COMERCIAL
809-688-5500
fax: 809-688-5522
www.mercure.com
E-mail: h2974@accor.com
Calle El Conde, corner Hostos
Credit Cards: AE, MC, V

This modern hotel is in the thick of things, right on the El Conde pedestrian walkway just two blocks from Parque Colón. The gracious, simply-appointed lobby sets the tone with its contemporary motif. The 96 rooms are equally stylish, with peach and papaya color schemes, comfy beds (some are kings), and a blend of antique reproductions and hip, almost minimalist furnishings. It has its own air-conditioned restaurant (and there are dozens more close at hand) with retro-themed stainless steel tables and seats overlooking El Conde, good for catching the buzz. Pets are permitted. It has WiFi, plus small conference facilities for business travelers, whom it clearly targets. $$.

Resort Hotels and Spas

HILTON SANTO DOMINGO
809-685-0000
fax: 809-685-0202
www.hiltoncaribbean.com/santodomingo
Avenida George Washington 500
Credit Cards: AE, D, MC, V

Rising 21 storeys above the seafront Malecón boulevard, this hotel appears garish from outside, not least due to the massive neon signs associated with the casino (Santo Domingo's largest). But inside, the interior was recently upgraded in a snazzy contemporary vogue. It has 228 rooms with recessed ceilings lit by hidden halogens, adding to the sense of spaciousness. The lovely decor features deep-blue carpeting, yellow drapes and soft goods, plus king or queen beds with quality mattresses and goose down pillows and duvets. Comfy! South-facing rooms have ocean vistas through a wall of glass. Five entire floors are given over to executive rooms for business travelers. A rooftop lap pool and sundeck is served by a bar, and there's a gym. For eats, La Torre serves light fare, while the chic Sol y Sombra offers Caribbean and Continental fare. $$–$$$.

MELIÁ SANTO DOMINGO
809-221-6666
fax: 809-687-8150
www.solmelia.com
Avenida George Washington 365
Credit Cards: AE, DC, MC, V

Another deluxe high-rise hotel on the Malecón, you can't miss it due to the glittering casino. Inside, the snazzy lobby sets a modish tone. The rooms don't quite come up to par with those at the Renaissance Jaragua or even the Hilton, but they're perfectly comfy and adequate, and have most of the mod cons you could wish for, including Pay-Per-View movies, and Internet modems. A gym, two restaurants, and out-

door pool are among the amenities.
$$$–$$$$.

RENAISSANCE JARAGUA HOTEL AND CASINO

809-221-2222
fax: 809-686-0528
www.renaissancehotels.com
Avenida George Washington 367
Credit Cards: AE, D, MC, V

Towering over the Malecón, this is by far the
nicest resort hotel in town. Its 300 gra-
ciously appointed rooms offer sumptuous
contemporary styling, and supremely com-
fortable beds with deluxe linens. Nice!
Amenities include tennis courts, a large
casino, a gym and spa, and a spacious sun-
deck and large pool in landscaped grounds.
If you seek elegant accommodation with all
the services, this is a wise choice. $$$$.

DINING

The capital city is a veritable potlatch of fine
dining, with something for every taste.
Many of the nation's best restaurants are
here, spanning the globe with their inter-
national flavors. In addition to the full-on
restaurants, including those in the upscale
hotels, consider eating at simple *colmados*
(see the sidebar below).

AKA SUSHI EN ROJO

809-732-9502
www.red.com.do
Avenida Winston Churchill 110
Cuisine: Japanese

Santo Domingo has no shortage of sushi
options, and this intimate option tucked
inside Plaza Nueva Orleáns in the Urbinaz-
ión Fernández district on the west side of
the city, ranks among the best, despite its
small size. The 21st-century decor is suavely
minimalist, with everything accented in
sexy oranges highlighted by stainless steel
chairs and white tables. Contemporary art

pieces festoon the walls, and rows of circu-
lar ceiling lamps form their own art. The
Peruvian-Japanese chef earns high marks
for delivering consistently melt-in-your-
mouth fresh sashimi and sushi. The set
sashimi platter features 24 slices of 6 kinds
of raw seafood, including scallop and
conch, although individual portions are
meager. Among the rolls, try the tuna
tartare and Aka roll. The best bargain is the
Aka 1, with tuna, salmon, and shrimp nigu-
iri, Philadelphia roll, vermicelli roll, and
caterpillar roll. The prices are more than
fair. Free parking. Open: Daily 11 AM–11 PM.
$$–$$$

EL CATADOR

809-540-1644
http://elcatador.com.do
Calle José Brea Peña 43
Price: Expensive
Cuisine: Tapas

OK, I know, it's not a restaurant per se. But
since this fabulous wine-tasting room (*sala
de catas*) serves savory canapes and tapas
from a hors d'oeuvres menu, it deserves a
high recommendation here. This clubby
spot exudes sophistication, tempting the
local business crowd for pre- or postpran-
dial pleasures. It's operated by the El Cata-
dor wine import company, which stocks
more than 500 labels from around the
world. They're sold by the bottle only, but
you can sample tasters from an Enomatic
dispenser serving from 16 different labels.
The cozy lounge has leather lounge chairs
and sofas. Open: Mon. through Sat. 11
AM–midnight. $$$

EL CONUCO

809-686-0129
www.elconuco.com.do
Calle Casimiro de Moya 152, Gazcue
Cuisine: Traditional Dominican

If it's traditional Dominican fare you seek,
you can't do better than this unpretentious

restaurant behind the Jaragua hotel, whose name translates as "the countryside." The contrived and colorful decor is true to the theme, with native crafts, plus woven blankets and hammocks slung beneath the thatch roof. You're served by waiters in country costume, and a folkloric troupe enlivens the place with merengue and *bachata* and country dancing. More than a few Hollywood stars have been known to dine here, although it is often taken over by bussed-in tour groups. (But don't worry, the large number of locals attests to the quality of the bargain-priced fare). The extensive prix fixe buffet has all the traditional favorites, including the national dish, *la bandera* (beef simmered with rice, kidney beans, and fried plantains) plus big bowls of savory *sancocho* stew. You can heap as much food as you wish on your traditional ceramic plate decorated with floral motifs. It also has an a la carte menu of poultry, meat, and seafood dishes. A bargain, and fun to boot. Open: Daily 11 AM–3 PM and 6 PM–midnight. $–$$.

EL MESÓN DE LA CAVA

809-533-2818
www.elmesondelacava.com
Avenida Mirador del Sur 1, Bella Vista
Cuisine: International

And for something completely different... take to this one-of-a-kind restaurant literally in various subterranean caverns in Parque Mirador del Sur. It's a little eerie, dining surrounded by stalagmites and stalactites floodlit to enhance the romantic mood, while jazz and Latin tunes echo around the various caves linked by tunnels. It's worth a visit just for the ambience. But the cuisine is remarkably creative and well prepared. The globe-spanning menu leans strongly towards surf and turf dishes, but features a wide choice of salads, soups, and international dishes, drawing locals since 1967. For starters, I recommend the gazpa-

cho, tuna carpaccio, *sopa de pescado* (red snapper chowder), conch salad with avocado and herb vinaigrette, or the sautéed shrimp in garlic and white wine sauce. For main course? There's lobster served half a dozen ways; charcoal-grilled beef tenderloin; grilled teriyaki salmon; even lamb and chicken marsala. One of my favorites is the steamed shrimp in a coconut and coriander cream sauce. Leave those stiletto heels behind, as you need to negotiate a rickety iron spiral staircase down into the cave. It's essential to make a reservation. And bring something warm to wear: No air-conditioning required here, as the cave is naturally *muy refrescante*—very refreshing. Open: Daily noon–4 PM and 5:30 PM–1 AM. $$–$$$.

FOGARATÉ

809-686-0044
Avenida George Washington 517
Cuisine: International

Norberto Di Vietro has put together a winning combination at his *criolla* restaurant, where the menu features local staples such as *mofongo* and *sancocho*. It also has a *criolla* buffet, and the à la carte menu features roast pork and chicken dishes, as well as beef plates and seafoods. The colorful decor adds to the fun atmosphere, drawing locals. Open: Daily 11:30 AM–10 PM. $$$–$$$$

HARD ROCK CAFÉ

809-686-7771
www.hardrock.com
Calle El Conde 103, Parque Colón
Cuisine: American

When you're in the mood for a social buzz, perhaps some hip music and American fare, check out the Hard Rock Café, the local franchise of the ultra-successful international chain. Set right on Parque Colón, it has a tremendous locale. Don't be misled by the colonial exterior—the interior has been gutted and refitted in a dramatic retro-industrial style, with a broad spiral staircase auguring up to the second floor, open loft style to the main dining area below. Flat-screen TVs. Leather banquette booths. Mahogany paneling. Brushed steel fixtures. And lots of neon. Framed art (including gold discs) playing on the rock 'n' roll theme. Get the picture? The usual Hard Rock menu applies. Hickory-smoked chicken wings, spinach and artichoke dip, and nachos typify the starters menu, while main courses include grilled sirloin steak, blackened chicken pasta, and grilled Alaskan sockeye salmon, as well as sandwiches, salads, and a dozen or so types of burger. Let's not forget the killer shakes, Häagen-Dazs ice cream, and hot fudge sundae… reason enough to visit! Weekends get lively. Open: Sun. through Thurs. 11:30 AM–12:30 AM, Fri. and Sat. 11:30 AM–1 AM. $$–$$$.

LA BRICIOLA
809-688-5055
www.labriciola.co.do
Calle Arzobispo Merino 152-A, at Padre Billini
Cuisine: Italian

Among the more formal and classy fine-dining outlets in Santo Domingo, La Briciola exhilarates with its en vogue decor and lush courtyard where the romantic mood is enhanced by flickering candles and a piano bar. An offshoot of the original La Briciola, in Milan, this is no second-rate option. Minimalist decor and Italian tile work combine with the aged interior (the restaurant occupies a 16th-century mansion on Plazoleta Padre Billini). The menu includes fresh homemade pastas, including gnocchi, ravioli, and other tried-and-true favorites, all prepared with attention to the subtleties, rather than overpowering sauces. Try the spiced and flavorful osso buco. And carnivores are feted with steaks, while fresh seafood dishes rarely disappoint. The extensive wine list is restricted to Italian labels, alas. A business clientele also appreciates the experience. Jackets are required of gentlemen. And reservations are advisable. Open: Mon. through Sat. 11:30 AM–10:30 PM. $$$$–$$$$

LA RÉSIDENCE
809-685-9955
www.sofitel.com
Callas Las Damas
Cuisine: International

One of my favorite venues, this restaurant in the Sofitel Nicolas de Ovando hotel exudes centuries-old colonial charm. It's the perfect venue for romance, especially when nestled in high-back winged rattan chairs on the shaded and columned arcade terrace, beneath weathered arches lit by ancient wrought-iron chandeliers. The candlelight sparkles on quality silverware, and fresh orchids at every table are a nice added touch. Fans whir overhead, helping keep things cool. On super-hot days opt for one of the suave air-conditioned rooms festooned with lively contemporary color schemes and modern art. The well-trained staff can be a little stiff, but are super efficient. Head Chef Gerard Mosiniak prepares a bargain-priced nightly three-course special. The Mediterranean-themed nouvelle fusion menu features such hits as roast lobster with wok-fried vegetables; boned saddle of rabbit stuffed with bacon and mushrooms; and spit-roasted lamb rubbed with spices and served with bacon, garlic, and vinegar sauce. By night, musicians play guitar. After dinner, relax with a cognac and cigar in the lobby lounge. Open: Daily 7 AM–10 PM. $$$–$$$$

LINA RESTAURANT
809-563-5000, ext. 7250
Avenida Máximo Gómez
Cuisine: International

Situated within the Barceló Gran Hotel Lina, now named for the Spanish-born chef, Lina Aguado, who established this modern, fine-dining restaurant years ago. Prior to opening her own restaurant, Lina was personal chef to Dictator Rafael Trujillo, but don't let that put you off. Although Doña Lina no longer oversees the kitchen (now under the compass of four master chefs), the local cognoscenti know this still to be one of the best eateries in town, and the presence of expatriate *españoles* says it all. Lina's recipes are still in play, with Spanish dishes paramount. The *paella valenciana* is divine, as are the casserole-style mixed seafood medley doused with Pernod, and the sea bass flambéed in brandy. Service is top-notch. Open: Daily 11:30 AM–4 PM and 6:30 PM–midnight. $$–$$$$

MESÓN DE BARÍ
809-687-4091
Calle Hostos 302
Cuisine: Dominican

A bohemian shrine and national institution serving tasty *criolla* fare, this is a must at some stage during your visit. Overflowing with ambience, it has a unique charm not least in thanks to its heart-of-Zona-Colonial setting and to wall-to-wall, floor-to-ceiling artwork. It draws an eclectic and passionately loyal clientele ranging from the political and business elite (Dominican fashion designer Oscar de la Renta is a frequent patron) to well-known musicians and artists. Amazingly (and thankfully), tourists are few. The place usually hums. Tasteful decor plays a calliope of color: ochre and turquoise walls; orange and aquamarine tablecloths, and the art. Downstairs has a bar and gets lively on weekends when ensembles perform live jazz, bossa nova, and even Cuban *son*. Upstairs is for diners who are more serious and who appreciate elegant yet unpretentious surrounds. The decades-old menu stays true to local fare that a Dominican grannie might have made.

Empanadas lambi (conch- and yuca-filled pastries) make a good appetizer. The house specialty, *cangrejo guisado* (savory crab stew) is popular, but there are better dishes, not least because the stew usually comes with lots of crab shell floating around. Instead, try the *chivo ripiao*, shredded goat meat in spicy tomato and pepper sauce. Other consistently good dishes include chicken breast with onion, garlic, and peppers. My favorite spot is to dine at the bar. Open: Daily noon–midnight. $$$.

MITRE RESTAURANT AND WINE BAR
809-472-1787
Avenida Abraham Lincoln 1001, at Gustavo Mejía Ricart
Cuisine: Fusion

This chic eatery, acclaimed for its contemporary fusion cuisine, appeals as much for its hip decor, marked by bare cement and travertine walls, and a mosaic wall that forms a water cascade. Owner Giancarlos Bonarelli oversees a tight ship in the kitchen, which delivers such artistically presented delicacies as crab-stuffed jumbo shrimp; *churrasco* satay strips with gorgonzola fondue and porcini mushrooms; and a mixed Asian seafood dish with octopus, shrimp, and squid in a soy-sesame sauce. It even serves baby back ribs for traditionalists. The upstairs bar-lounge features sumptuous leather sofas—a perfect venue for a postprandial cigar and cognac. You can dine outside under umbrellas on a deck. Open: Daily noon–midnight. $$$–$$$$.

MIX
809-472-0100
Calle Gustavo Mejía Ricart 69, between Lincoln and Lope de Vega
Cuisine: International

As sharply contemporary in style as any restaurant in the city, Mix (in the Naco district) is super sexy, if a restaurant can be called that. Beyond the wall-of-glass entrance, the minimalist decor includes white leather half-moon banquettes hard up against a deep-purple wall, with overarching stainless steel lamps. Choose from three distinct rooms, plus a candlelit terrace. Start out at the 1950s-style retro black marble-top bar. No surprise, this restaurant draws young and trendy professionals (or those with deep-pocketed parents). Owner Fernando Queipo loads the menu with appetizers from around the world: You'll find everything from Spanish-style tapas to sushi. It's an eclectic offering (think satay tempura, Mexican quesadillas, meat-stuffed rice balls) supported by salads, sandwiches, burgers, and a smattering of larger entrées. The small portions throughout reflect Queipo's concept of "food to share," tapa-style. Dress to be admired. Open: Daily noon–midnight. $$$–$$$$.

PAT'É PALO
809-687-8089
www.patepalo.com
Calle La Atarazana 25
Cuisine: International

There's a reason the chic young-adult crowd descends on floodlit Plaza España on weekend nights. The balmy open-air mood is conducive to romance. Live bands perform for free in the square. And there's a wide choice of restaurants to dine at before hitting the wildly popular Atarzana disco-bar nearby. The building supposedly dates from 1505 and originally housed the New World's first tavern. Today, antiques and historic prints adorn the aged redbrick walls. On clear nights, most folks opt to dine on the plaza terrace, attended by staff in pirate costume (the restaurant is named after a famous peg legged French pirate, Francois Le Cler). The wide-ranging menu features such starters as sea bass ceviche with avocado cream; tuna carpaccio; and eggplant

with mozzarella and tomato. Carnivores can choose from rib-eye steaks, Black Angus skirt marinated with curry and honey, baby back ribs, etc., while some of the unusually creative seafood dishes include coconut-curry sautéed shrimp, and Chilean sea bass over Spanish sausage risotto in a creamy beer sauce. It opens at 1:30 PM Fri. through Sun., but 4:30 PM on weekdays. Open: Daily 4:30 PM–midnight. $$–$$$$.

PEPPERONI CAFÉ
809-508-1330
Plaza Universitaria Mall, Avenida Winston Churchill, corner Sarasota
Cuisine: Italian

Don't be fooled by the name. It might seem as if this is an Italian restaurant, but this is as international a venue as you'll find. The place is hip and fun, attracting energy-seeking young professionals drawn to the combo of rustic decor and exotic paintings. True, the globe-spanning menu has plenty of Italian dishes, as well as international staples such as Chilean sea bass and perfectly seared Black Angus steak, but the fusion dishes are what catch the eye. I recommend the Peking duck spring rolls, followed by the house special coconut curry Mai Thai crab. Other winners include the Thai noodle dishes, and penne with fresh mushrooms, rock shrimp, prosciutto, and Parmesan. It even has burgers, and sushi. Don't expect gourmet fare. But most dishes are more than passable, and the prices are fair. Open: Daily noon–midnight. $$–$$$.

RED GRILL
809-732-9502
www.red.com.do
Max Henríquez Ureña 50, corner Lope de Vega
Cuisine: International

You guessed it. The restaurant, in the Naco district, is named for its decor and furnishings, which combine café-style tables edged with stainless steel, plus sexy bloodred leather chairs and velveteen banquette booths. This icon to minimalism offers a casual chic, not least its en-vogue glazed cement floor. Give it no awards, however, for the view of the car park through the wall of glass. You can sup at the raised mahogany bar with high stools. The simple menu focuses on gourmet salads, sandwiches, pastas, and grilled dishes. Typical treats include fried calamari, chicken quesadilla, grilled sweetbreads, pork tenderloin, and 14-ounce sirloin. The real treat awaits upstairs, in the low-lit club-lounge, where red leather chaise-lounges and shag carpet-covered walls would be a perfect backdrop for an Austin Powers movie. Big name DJs spin ear-splitting tunes. Open: Daily 11:30 AM–midnight. $$–$$$$.

RESTAURANTE BOGA BOGA
809-472-0950
Avenida Bolívar 203
Cuisine: Spanish

Off Plaza Florida, in the western district of La Esperilla, this cozy Spanish-owned restaurant plays on a nautical theme, with miscellaneous sunken-ship decor. Serrano hams hang from the ceiling. Although Boga Boga specializes in paellas and seafoods, it also serves a broad range of tapas, such as *chorizo* (sausage) and *queso manchego* (La Mancha cheese). The house special is the *paella marinera y valenciana,* chock-full of seafoods and meats. The inviting bar permits cigar smoking. Open: Daily 11 AM–midnight. $–$$.

RESTAURANTE DEL LAGO
809-482-1924
Avenida Anacoa 24, Parque Mirador del Sur
Cuisine: Criolla

This unpretentious restaurant is perfect when you're out west and need a quick but quality fix. Its two levels overlook a small lake with waterfowl on the north side of Parque Mirador del Sur. The menu is pretty simple, with *criolla* staples plus salads, burgers, sandwiches, and a smattering of steak and seafood dishes. But the real reason to visit is for the bargain-priced Sunday buffet served on the upstairs terrace. If the bugs are out and about, opt for the air-conditioned interior. The friendly staff here performs with alacrity. Open: Daily noon–11 PM. $–$$$.

SAMURAI
809-565-1621
http://samurairestaurante.com
Calle Seminario 51, behind Unicentro Plaza
Cuisine: Japanese

Although more expensive than the smaller Aka Sushi, this restaurant has been hailed as the city's finest for Japanese fare. It has the city's most complete *menu japonesa.* You'll dine at low-slung tables (with stylishly contemporary seats), while gazing out upon a Japanese garden from within a series of contemporary themed Japanese rooms divided by sliding rice-paper walls. For a complete night of it, start with *edamame,* move on to miso soup or a *kaiso* algae salad, then savor a selection of niguiri offerings, such as unagi, hamachi, and yellowtail. The menu also includes tempura and hibachi entrées. Don't overdo it, though, as the ice cream flambéed at your table is not to be missed. Expats and locals in the know flock for the Sunday brunch. Open: Daily 11 AM–3 PM and 6 PM–midnight. $$$–$$$$.

SCHEREZADE
809-227-2323
www.scherezade.com.do
Avenida Roberto Pastoriza 226, Naco
Cuisine: Steaks

Whisking you to the Levant with its exotic decor of arches, mosaic tiled floors and walls, cloisonné, and Oriental rugs, Scherezade serves the best Mediterranean fare in town. All the expected dishes are on offer, including staples such as hummus, tabbouleh, and lamb with couscous. But the menu also ranges from garlic octopus and Madagascar shrimp, to lobster prepared any of 11 ways. There's even salmon, and 16-ounce Chateaubriand. The executive luncheon buffet is a bargain. Leave room for sweet flan or baklava. Live musicians and occasional belly dancers perform. Open: Daily noon–midnight. $$$–$$$$.

VESUVIO DEL MALECÓN

809-221-1954

www.vesuvio.com.do

Avenida George Washington 521

Cuisine: Italian

The city's elite can be seen enjoying world-class fare at this elegant, family-run Italian restaurant, handy for anyone staying at the seafront hotels, and today considered the godfather of Santo Domingo restaurants. You can choose a romantic candlelit patio facing onto the Malecón (separated by a hedge from an ocean view and that of passing traffic), or opt for the sophisticated air-conditioned interior where three rooms offer distinct, albeit dated, decor. Shortly after being seated, a three-tiered antipasto cart is wheeled forth, offering tempting savory appetizers, such as grilled eggplant. The main menu is heavy on pastas, but ranges from oysters and crayfish *a la Vesuvio* (topped with garlic and bacon) to delicious risottos: A favorite is the calamari risotto

with squid ink. Another good, albeit pricey, bet is the lobster thermidor. And both the *asopao* (a thick flavorful soup of meat, rice, and vegetables) and the *pappardelle al Bosque* (noodles with porcini mushrooms, rosemary, and garlic) are winners. Leave room for dessert, or steel yourself to resist the scrumptious offerings that appear on a triple-tiered trolley. Tiramisu? Flan? Cheesecake. Mustard-keen service is a hallmark, and owner Enzo Bonarelli is often on hand to fuss over guests. Next door, the restaurant's Pizzeria Vesuvio offers wood-fired pizzas, including a unique 3-foot-wide pizza for the family. Open: Daily 11:30AM–1 AM. $$$–$$$$$.

YATOBA

809-562-4222

Avenida Abraham Lincoln 615

Cuisine: International

Tucked off Abraham Lincoln, this classy restaurant is lent a clubby feel by its hardwood floor and contemporary mahogany furnishings. Service isn't always on the ball, however. The eclectic menu suits all tastes and has plenty of pastas and nouvelle creations, plus international staples such as Angus steak are represented. Even the sushi is surprisingly good. Open: Daily noon–midnight. $$$–$$$$.

FOOD PURVEYORS

Bakeries/Coffee Shops

LA CAFETERÍA

809-682-7114

Calle El Conde 253

Celebrated by locals who swear by the fresh-ground coffees, espressos, cappuccinos, etc. Also makes blended juices (*batidos*) with water or milk, plus sandwiches and desserts. It's a favorite local hangout, good for catching the local gossip.

Colmados

These small local grocery stores often double as simple cafeteria-style diners selling local fare. They're favorites of the local working class, and even professionals at lunchtime. They're good for a quick snack or a filling *criolla* meal, and for a taste of the local lifestyle. You'll find them all over town. Two to know are **Chimmi** (809-835-8363; Calle Pina 206, Ciudad Nueva), a tiny outlet run by Yhoeny (pronounced |ohnny), who throws together great hot dogs, pork sandwiches, and burgers; and **Omeroliza D'Comer** (Calle Arzobispo Nouel 301, Zona Colonial), good for traditional Dominican dishes such as *mangu* and *bandera dominicana.*

SEGAFREDO CAFÉ BOUTIQUE AND LOUNGE BAR

809-685-9569
Calle El Conde 54, Zona Colonial

Romantic open-air setting just off Plaza Colón, enhanced by outdoor Ali Baba-style beds. Serves cocktails, coffees, and snack food, including pizzas. The redbrick interior has a hip industrial-style bar. Draws hip young professionals for the chic ambience and World Beat tunes. Live bands.

Burgers, Pizzas, Sandwiches, and Fast Food

ANDREA PANADERIA, CAFETERIA AND HELADERIA

809-221-7878

Calle Isabel La Catolica 251, Zona Colonial) Tremendous whole grain breads *(pan integrado),* croissants, and pastries. Also serves gourmet coffees, freshly made sandwiches, and pizzas by the slice. Leave room for an ice cream.

AUTO SANDWICH PAYANO'S

809-227-9330
Avenida Tiradentes, Plaza Naco)

Large selection of sandwiches, including tuna, plus the local *especial de cerdo* combining pork with turkey, ham, and cheese. Coffees, teas, and natural juices.

Sweets and Treats

Dominicans love ice cream. Ha, don't we all? When the heat gets to you, chill out with a few scoops of vanilla or tropical-flavored ice cream at **Helados Nevada** (809-687-6200; Calle El Conde 453, Zona Colonial), or **Helados Bon** (809-686-1580; Calle el Conde 310, Zona Colonial).

LA CASA DE LOS DULCES

809-685-0785
Calle Emiliano Tejera 106, Zona Colonial

Sells *dulces* (sweets, or desserts), plus cakes, cheeses, and all manner of confections. An Aladdin's Cave of treats! Ask for samples.

SURTIDORA PURA
809-687-8729
Calle Mercedes 377, Zona Colonial

All kinds of candies, beverages, and snacks.

Culture

Architecture

BANCO DE RESERVAS
809-960-2000
Calle Isabel la Católica 201, Zona Colonial

A magnificent exemplar of Art Deco, this bank dates from 1955 and features a facade of Belgian granite and bronze ornamentation. The interior astounds with its socialist-realistic mural, *Moneda,* by Spanish Vela Zanetti (1913–99).

CENTRO DE LOS HÉROES
Avenidas George Washington and Jiménez Moya

Centro de los Héroes, Santo Domingo

This complex—laid out in the 1950s for the Free World Fair for Peace and Fraternity, spon-sored by Trujillo—takes up a whopping 25 blocks and is the center of government. Several of the buildings here are fantastic exemplars of Modernist and postmodernist architecture. Let's start with the **Palacio de Justicia** (809-533-3191; www.suprema.gov.do; Calle Juan de Dios Ventura Simón and Calle Enrique Jiménez Moya). This futuristic seven-storey build-ing went up in 2006 to house the Supreme Court. Nip inside to admire the mural by Amable Sterling (1943–) in the lobby.

One block north, the **Palacio del Congreso Nacional** (809-532-5561; visitasguiadas @senado.gov.do; Jiménez Moya between Paul Harris and 4) is a magnificent five-storey Modernist structure where the National Congress sits. Guided tours are offered by appoint-ment. To the west, city father's hash out their differences in the **Palacio Municipal,** designed in Le Corbusier style in 1955 by Guillermo González (1900–70).

CIUDAD UNIVERSITARIA (UNIVERSIDAD AUTÓNOMA DE SANTO DOMINGO)
809-535-8273
www.uasd.edu.do
Avenida Paulo III and Avenida Alma Mater, Gazcue

This huge complex at the west end of the Gazcue district went up in the early 1960s and has several architectural sites of interest, including some fine Modernist buildings. Most notable is the **Biblioteca Pedro Mir**, the library—named for the Dominican Republic's poet laureate—with a planar facade bearing a spectacular ceramic mural by Dominican painter Amable Sterling (1943–). Avenida Paulo III is pinned by various busts of national heroes, including at its far west end a life-size bronze statue of Juan Pablo Duarte.

PALACIO DE BELLAS ARTES
809-682-1325
www.bellasartes.gov.do
Avenida Máximo Gómez at Avenida Independencia, Gazcue

The grandiose yet austere neo-classical Palace of Fine Arts, capped by a red dome, was completed in 1956 and serves as headquarters for the government's cultural institutions. It is the headquarters of the National Symphonic Orchestra, National Ballet, National Folk-loric Ballet, National School of Dance, and National School of Theater. The lavish Beaux Arts interior includes murals by José Vela Zanetti on the stairways. It hosts exhibitions and occasional concerts but otherwise is not open to the public.

A Date with Lady Luck

Barceló Gran Hotel Lina and Casino: 809-563-5000; Avenida Máximo Gómez, corner Avenida 27 de Febrero

Casino Diamante: 809-682-2102; Meliá Santo Domingo Hotel, Avenida George Washington 365

Hispaniola Hotel and Casino: 809-535-9292; Avenida Independencia 666, corner Avenida Abraham Lincoln

Occidental El Embajador Hotel and Casino: 809-533-2131; Avenida Sarasota 65, Santo Domingo, Dominican Republic

Renaissance Jaragua Hotel and Casino: 809-221-1453; Avenida George Washington 367

A Night at the Movies

Broadway Cinemas: 809-872-0272; Plaza central (3rd floor), Avenida 27 de Febrero, corner
  Avenida Winston Churchill
Cinema Centro: 809-685-2373; Avenida George Washington 457
Cinemateca: 809-685-9396; Nacional Museo de História y Geografía, Plaza de la Cultura
Malecón Center Cinemas: 809-412-7441; Plaza Malecón Center, Avenida Bolívar 832 at Avenida
  George Washington.
Mega Plex 10: 809-335-0007; Avenida San Vicente de Paul, Mandinga

PALACIO NACIONAL

698-695-8000
Calle Moisés García and Dr. Delgado Báez
By appointment only, Mon., Wed., and Fri., with 48 hours notice. A dress code applies.
Admission: Free.

This handsome neo-classical palace serves as the official presidential palace, housing the
offices of the president of the republic, plus other government ministries. Designed in
roseate Samaná marble by Italian architect Guido D'Alessandro, it was inaugurated in 1947
to serve as the official chambers of Dictator-President Rafael Trujillo. His ghost haunts the
sumptuous antique-filled hallways lined with gilt mirrors and ornate murals. Baccarat
crystal chandeliers hang overhead. A highlight is the Room of the Caryatids featuring 44
semi-clad caryatids. Bronze lions guard the entrance portico, which resembles the Capitol
building, in Washington, D.C., complete with dome.

TEATRO NACIONAL

809-687-3191
Avenida Máximo Gómez 35

Teofilo Carbonell designed this Modernist theater, inaugurated in 1973, with a travertine
facade supported by three arched tiers. Statues of early Spanish literati stand outside the
entrance. The interior is paneled with mahogany.

Art and Art Galleries

GALERÍA DE ARTE CANDIDO BIDÓ

809-685-5310
www.galeriacandidobido.com
Calle Dr. Baez 5, corner Calle Luisa Ozema Pellaramo, Gazcue
Mon. through Fri. 9:30–12:30 and 3:00–6:30

This gallery is in the gaudily painted 1950s-era home of Candido Bido, one of the Dominican Republic's most famous contemporary artists. His works, full of intense color and
naive, mystical symbolism, typically depict rural scenes.

MUSEO DE ARTE MODERNO

809-685-2153
www.museodeartemoderno.org.do

Plaza de la Cultura
Tues. through Sun. 10–6
Admission: RD$20

The country's preeminent art museum, with four floors of works by the nation's foremost artists and sculptors, as well as leading exponents from throughout the Hispanic world, such as Spanish exile artist José Vela Zanetti (1913–99). The country's best-known contemporary artists, including Elvis Aviles, Candido Bidó, Tony Capellan, and Jorge Severino, are well represented. One of the museum's strong suits is its large body of works representing the 1930s *costumbrismo* movement showing depictions of local everyday life and customs. Most sculptures are found on the lower level, which also houses temporary exhibits and shows multi-media presentations.

Historic Buildings, Plazas, and Religious Sites

ANTIGUO CEMENTERIO MUNICIPAL
(CEMENTERIO DE LA AVENIDA INDEPENDENCIA)
Avenida Independencia between Calle Las Carreras and Parque Independencia, Ciudad Nueva

As historic cemeteries go this one falls short of Paris's Père-Lachaise or Havana's remarkable Cementerio Colón. Although it dates back only to the Haitian occupation (1822–44), it has been declared a Patrimonio Cultural for its historic import. Many of the independent republic's men of import are buried here, most in unmarked graves, such as José Núñez de Cáceres (1772–1846). Notable tombs include those of the Italian Michellito Masturzzi, recognizable by its obelisk and Angel at Rest at its base. A Jewish section can be found in the extreme southwest corner.

CALLE LAS DAMAS
Between Calle Arzobispo Porutes and Calle Mercedes, Zona Colonial

This cobbled street, stretching just 400 yards between Fortaleza Ozama and Plaza de España, is the oldest colonial street in the New World. It is Santo Domingo at its most atmospheric, being lined with 16th- and 17th-century structures both grandiose and quaint. Street of the Ladies is named for María de Toledo (Diego Colón's wife, and King Ferdinand's niece) and her female retinue who walked the street daily.

The most important buildings are the Panteón Nacional (see below) and Ozama fortress (see Military Sites). The **Iglesia del Convento de Santa Clara** (corner Calle Padre Billini), opposite the fortress, was initiated in 1522 as the first Franciscan nunnery in the New World. Although sacked by Drake, it was rebuilt with an unadorned Renaissance-style wall. It's still in use as a convent. Note the bust of Santa Clara above the gable.

Adjoining the fortress on its north side, the **Casa Rodrigo de Bastidas** served as the treasury and home of the Royal tax collector, and today houses a children's museum (see the For the Children sidebar). Note the stone statue of Santa Bárbara above the door.

On the next block, the Gothic Casa de Francia (809-695-4300, Calle Las Damas 42) houses the French embassy in a house built in 1503. Hernán Cortés lived here briefly before sailing off to conquer the Aztec empire. To the north, across the street, the former fortified homes of Nicolás de Ovando, the island's first governor, and Francisco Dávila, are today combined as the Sofitel Nicolás de Ovando (see Hotels). The hotel faces Plazoleta de María

Toledo, a tiny and nondescript plaza occupying the site of a former monastery; visit on Sunday for the colorful *pulga* (flea market). It adjoins the Panteón Nacional, on the north side of which the stone and brick Casa de los Jesuitas, built in 1508 in Mudejar fashion, once served as a Jesuit university.

CAPILLA DE LA VIRGEN DEL ROSARIO
Avenida Olegario Vargas and Avenida España
Daily 10:30–4
Admission: Free

Reopened following a restoration completed in 2007, this small whitewashed chapel dates from the 19th century but stands atop the site of the first Christian chapel in the New World, established in 1496 by Bartolomé Colón. It stands in the grounds of Los Molinos Dominicano granary; the sentry at the gate will grant access.

CASA DEL CORDÓN
Calle Isabel la Católica, corner of Calle El Tejera, Zona Colonial

Dating to 1503 and ostensibly the city's oldest structure, this colonial mansion was built for conquistador Francisco de Garay, who sailed on Columbus's second voyage and became the island's notary public and later governor of Jamaica. Columbus's son Diego Colón later lived here. It is named for the sash-and-cord motif of the Franciscan order carved in stone above the door. The Banco Popular, a branch of which occupies the building today, restored it to pristine condition.

CASA DE LAS GÁRGOLAS
809-541-5652
Calle Las Mercedes 2, Zona Colonial

This 16th-century building, erected for Don José Fernández, is named for the six water drainage outlets shaped as gargoyles that guard the main entrance. It has since served as a seminary and a Masonic Lodge. It was here, too, that poet Emilio Prud'Homme and musician José Reyes wrote the song that later became the Dominican National Anthem. Today it houses the Fundación Dominicana de Desarrollo (Dominican Foundation of Development) and is closed to the public.

CASA DE LAS MONEDAS
Calle Arzobispo Meriño 358, Zona Colonial

Completed in 1540, this charming limestone mansion is named for the five medallions surrounding the Plateresque doorway. Each coin features a human face, including that of a young King Carlos V.

CATEDRAL PRIMADA DE AMÉRICA
809-541-5652
Parque Colón, Calle Arzobispo Nouel and Arzobispo Meriño, Zona Colonial
Daily 9 AM–4 PM
Admission: Free

Officially known as the Catedral Santa María de la Encarnación, the New World's oldest church dates back to 1510, when Christopher Columbus's son Diego Colón laid the foundation stone. Construction wasn't completed until 1546, during which time the design was radically altered (the original architect, Alonso de Rodríguez, left for Mexico with the drawings). In 1586, the pirate Francis Drake vandalized the church, destroying the belfry (which was never rebuilt) and bearing off with the stained-glass windows (the existing ones are reproductions by Dominican artist Rincón Mora). The unassuming northern entrance combines Gothic, Baroque, and classical elements. The Plateresque western (main) facade is more dramatic and features twin crenellated spires and fanciful friezes featuring cherubs and sea dragons that portray the arrival of the Spanish to Hispaniola. The south side opens onto the cobbled **Plazuela de los Curas** (Priests' Square) via the Puerta del Perdón (Portal of Clemency), which afforded sanctuary to renegades entering via this threshold: Access is via the narrow **Callejón de la Curas** (Alley of the Priests), lined with priests' homes.

Interior highlights include the ribbed-vault ceiling, 14 separate chapels containing elaborate friezes; Queen Isabella's emerald-encrusted crown (pawned, it is claimed, to pay for Columbus's first voyage); a Bishop's throne made of mahogany; and a bronze and marble sarcophagus—buttressed by four chiseled columns in the form of Royal palms—that Dominicans believe once contained the remains of Columbus.

The air-conditioned cathedral is sealed with glass doors on all three entrances. Dress respectfully: Shorts are not allowed for men, nor trousers or short skirts for women. Skirts can be rented.

CEIBA DE COLÓN
Avenida del Puerto, between Puerta de las Atarazanas and Calle Juan Parra Alba, Zona Colonial

Legend ascribes to this lowly and massive tree stump a larger-than-life import, for it was here, say locals, that Christopher Columbus moored his ship the Santa María. Truth is, of course, that Columbus arrived in 1492 on the island's *north* shore, where the *Santa María* had to be abandoned. The Genoese explorer *did* explore the southern shore, however, in August 1494, during his second voyage, although there was no settlement here until four years later. He berthed here during his third voyage, arriving on August 19, 1498.

IGLESIA NUESTRA SEÑORA DE LA ALTAGRACIA
Calle Las Mercedes and Luperón, Zona Colonial

Immediately north of the ruins of the Hospital San Nicolás de Bari, of which the original church formed a part, this is the Zona Colonial's most active church. Today's edifice dates from the 1930s and is strikingly Victorian Gothic in style, with an austere interior. Considered a place of healing, it draws a steady stream of supplicants come to beseech favors of a life-size statue to José Gregorio Hernández (1864–1919), a Venezuelan doctor whose spirit Dominicans believe is capable of performing miracles on the sick while they sleep.

IGLESIA DE NUESTRA SEÑORA DEL CARMEN
Calle Sánchez, corner of Arzobispo Nouel, Zona Colonial

This small church was initiated as a simple chapel in the early 16th century, and adjoined the Hospital San Andrés. Although vandalized in 1589 by Francis Drake's pirates, it was rebuilt and enlarged with an exquisite Isabelline brick portal that dates from 1729, and is topped by a niche containing a statue of the Virgin Mary. The life-size figure of the Nazarene, or Black Christ, above the elaborate mahogany altar in the Capilla de San Andrés is paraded through the streets of Santo Domingo each Ash Wednesday.

Following the Haitian occupation in 1844, the chapel was used as a secret meeting place for Juan Duarte's underground La Trinitaria independence movement.

IGLESIA DE NUESTRA SEÑORA DE LAS MERCEDES
Calle Las Mercedes, corner José Reyes, Zona Colonial

Completed in 1555, this small church dedicated to the Virgen de las Mercedes, was originally of Gothic style but has been remodeled several times. It is noteworthy for its baroque altar and its mahogany pulpit atop a serpent-demon base.

IGLESIA DE LA REGINA ANGELORUM
Calle Padre Billini, corner of Calle José Reyes, Zona Colonial
Mon. through Sat. 10–6 by permission

The first Queen of the Angels Church was built in 1537 as part of a convent for Dominican nuns. The current tiny building, however, dates from 1722 and is all that remains of the convent, demolished in 1941. The somber facade features weathered gargoyles, while the interior features Gothic ribbed vaults and 18th-century Baroque altar topped with the Spanish royal coat of arms. Father Padre Billini, an Italian priest revered for his charitable works on Hispaniola during the 19th century, is buried here. Nuns of the Sisters of Mercy order still reside here.

To the rear, a cobbled passageway is lined with quintessential colonial homes festooned with bougainvillea.

IGLESIA DE SANTA BÁRBARA
Calle Gabino Puello and Isabela la Católica, Zona Colonial

Completed in 1537, this delightful little church stands in the lee of Fuerte de Santa Bárbara, a small run-down fortress at the northern apex of the old city. It is actually attached to the fort, and was dedicated to the patron saint of the artillery. The facade is striking for its triple redbrick arches and uneven stone towers to each side. It was restored after depredation by Francis Drake's pirates. Juan Pablo Duarte (the Father of the Country) was baptized here in 1813.

PANTEÓN NACIONAL
Calle Las Damas, corner Plazoleta de María Toledo, Zona Colonial
Daily 9–4:30

This Rococo building was built in crucifix form between 1714 and 1743 as the Jesuit Convento de San Ignacio de Loyola, and later served various secular functions. Dictator-President Rafael Trujillo had the structure restored in 1958 as his own mausoleum, and to house the remains of La Trinitaria (Juan Pablo Duarte, Francisco del Rosario Sánchez, and Ramón Matías Mella). Instead, the multihued marble floor is inset with an eternal flame commemorating the three national heroes who led the fight for independence (the trio are actually buried in Parque Independencia; see below). Above, the dome features a magnificent fresco—The Apocalypse and Resurrection—by Rafael Pellicer (1906–63), and an elaborate bronze chandelier given to Trujillo by Spain's General Francisco Franco.

Note the Dominican Coat of Arms engraved above the entrance.

A uniformed soldier stands guard 24/7. No shorts or tank tops allowed.

PARQUE COLÓN
Calle El Conde and Calle Arzobispo Meriño, Zona Colonial

The core of the colonial city, this leafy and lively plaza is the setting for the Catedral Primada de América (see Historic Sites). The plaza was laid out in the early 1500s, when it was known as Plaza Mayor. It is pinned by a statue of Christopher Columbus pointing in the direction of Spain; cast by French sculptor Francé E. Gilbert in 1887, it features Taíno queen Anacaona at his feet.

To the east, the two-storey **Palacio de Borgellá** (Calle Isabel la Católica 103) was initiated in 1823 during the Haitian occupation of 1822–44. With its regal two-storey loggia, it served as the seat of government until 1875, and then as the president's residence until the 1930s. It was badly damaged by Hurricane Georges in 1998. Now repaired, it houses the office of the Patronato Cultural, a division of the tourism ministry. About 164 feet (50 m) to its south, on the southeast corner of the plaza, the **Casa del Sacramento** (Calle Isabela la Católica and Calle Arzobispo Nouel) was built in 1520 as the residence of Diego de Caballero, secretary of the Real Audiencia. It was added to in Spanish Revival-style during the Haitian occupation. Recently restored, today it is the archbishop's residence.

The 19th-century **Antiguo Palacio Consistorial** (Calle El Conde and Arzobispo Meriño), or former town hall, stands over the northwest corner. Its most striking feature is a half-moon tower, tiered and ornamented in stucco like a wedding cake.

PARQUE DUARTE
Padre Billini between Calles Hostos and Duarte, Zona Colonial

This delightful plaza is laid out in red brick beneath flame-red flamboyán trees, with a statue of national hero Juan Pablo Duarte atop a marble plinth. Gracious buildings line each side.

Rising over the south side, **Iglesia y Convento de los Padres Dominicos** (Calle Padre Billini corner Hostos) dates from 1649, replacing a predecessor initiated in 1510 (but later toppled by an earthquake) as the old Dominican monastery in the Americas. The first university of the New World was founded here in 1538 and it was here that Frey Bartolomé de las Casas chronicled Spanish atrocities: A contemporary statue of the benevolent friar stands one block east (between Calle Hostos and Arzobispo Moreño). The church's win-

Libraries
Biblioteca Juan Pablo Duarte (809-221-9111 ext. 3653; Avenida Dr. Pedro Henríquez Ureña and Avenida Leopoldo Navarro) Run by the Banco Central, this is part of the Museo Numismático y Filatélico. Specializes in finances and economics.

Biblioteca Nacional Pedro Henríquez Ureña (809-688-4086; www.bnrd.gov.do; César Nicolás Penson 91, Plaza de la Cultura). The National Library. The collection includes old documents, newspapers, and magazines pertaining to Dominican history and culture. Open Mon. through Fri. 8–10, Sat. and Sun. 8–4.

Biblioteca Pedro Mir (809-535-8273; www.uasd.edu.do; Avenida Paulo III and Avenida Alma Mater, Gazcue) The library of the Universidad Autónoma de Santo Domingo.

Biblioteca República Dominicana (809-686-0028; Avenida Dr. Delgado and Avenida Francia) Has 30,000 volumes.

Biblioteca Pedro Mir, Universidad Autónoma de Santo Domingo

dows are garlanded with Isabelline vine ornamentation and trimmed with Mudejar tiles. Its chapel displays a zodiac wheel guarded by pagan gods.

Immediately to the west stands the **Capilla de la Tercera Orden Dominicana** (Avenida Duarte corner Padre Billini; closed to the public), completed in 1729 with a baroque facade, replacing a predecessor vandalized by Francis Drake. To the rear is a delightful garden—a quiet place for contemplation.

PARQUE INDEPENDENCIA
Calle Palo Hincado between Avenidas Bolívar and Independencia, Ciudad Nueva
Daily 8:30–6

The major traffic hub marking the juncture of the Zona Colonial and Ciudad Nueva, Independence Plaza is hallowed ground. At its core rises the **Altar de la Patria** (Altar of the Homeland). The white marble mausoleum, also called Tumba de los Padres de la Patria (Tomb of the Patriarchs) was built in 1976 and contains the remains of Juan Pablo Duarte, Francisco del Rosario Sánchez, and Ramón Marias Mella—the republic's three founding fathers. Three life-size statues of the heroes stand over the tomb, in which an eternal flame flickers, guarded 24/7 by a soldier. Visitors are not permitted in shorts or hats.

The altar is surrounded by gardens containing various busts, and by reflecting pools that merge into a moat that formed part of the colonial city's defenses. You enter on the east side via the massive **Puerta del Conde**, the fortified main gate to the original city. It is named for the Governor Don Bernardino Meneses y Bracamonte, the Count of Peñalba, whose Spanish troops repulsed an English invasion in 1655. The Dominican flag was first raised here following independence on February 27, 1844. A ceremonial guard is present at all hours.

The plaza is also the official kilometer zero—the point from which all distances in the republic are calculated—marked by a 32-point brass star inset in the ground near the gate.

On its north side, the ruins of **Fuerte de la Concepción** are enclosed in their own park.

PLAZA DE LA BANDERA
Avenida 27 de Febrero and Avenida Luperón, Barrio Renacimiento

Don't bother driving all the way out to the west of the city, but if you happen to be passing, then this huge and, alas, run-down rotunda features a massive triumphal arc—the **Monumento a la Patria** (Monument to the Fatherland)—erected in 1997 and dedicated to the republic's slain soldiers. It supports a huge national flag draped below the apex. Beneath the arc stands *La Madre Patria* (The Motherland), a statue by Spanish sculptor Juan de Ávalos (1912–2006).

PLAZA DE LA CULTURA
Avenidas Máximo Gómez and Felix María del Monte, and Avenida Pedro Henríquez Ureña and César Nicolás Penson, Gazcue

This massive Modernist plaza spanning several blocks was laid out in the 1970s as a setting for the city's principal museums and cultural institutions. Although visually unexciting, the plaza is a must-visit for its four museums (see Museums and Monuments) and the Teatro Nacional (see Theater). The city's main library, the **Biblioteca Nacional** (809-688-4086; Cesar N. Pensón 164) is notable for its elegant Modernist facade.

PLAZA ESPAÑA
North end of Calle Las Damas, Zona Colonial

The largest of the colonial plazas, this sparse rectangular space is a lively venue at night, being framed on its west and north sides by restaurants and bars occupying former colonial mansions and warehouses. A **statue of Nicolás de Ovando** stands at its core.

In colonial days, access to the square from the harbor was via two gates—the **Puerta de La Atarazana** and **Puerta de San Diego**, to north and south, respectively. The most important building, standing all alone on the east side, is the **Alcázar de Colón** (see Museums), the former home of Diego Colón.

Redbrick former warehouses line the north side. Worth a peek is the **Escuela Taller de Orfebrería** (809-689-0132; Calle La Atarazana 7; Mon. through Fri. 9–8), where apprentice jewelers study the craft. Around the corner, the former Customs House today exhibits maritime relics in the **Museo de las Atarazanas Reales** (see Museums).

The sturdy colonial palace dominating the plaza's south side served for two centuries as the seat of Spanish authority in the New World. Today as the **Museo de las Casa Reales** (see Museums) it has superb historical exhibits. The pedestrian forecourt features a giant sundial—the **Reloj del Sol**—erected in 1753 to permit Spanish judges to check the time from their windows.

Reloj del Sol, Santo Domingo

PLAZOLETA PADRE BILLINI

Calle Arzobispo Meriño, corner of Padre Billini, Zona Colonial

This tiny plaza one block south of Parque Colón is pinned by a statue of the namesake philanthropist priest, Francisco Xavier Billini (1837–90). It was used for bullfights in early colonial days. The remodeled colonial homes that surround it host fancy restaurants, art galleries, and boutiques.

PLAZOLETA SAN ANTÓN

Calle Hostos and Restauración, Zona Colonial

This stepped plaza leads up to the tiny Fuerte San Antón and ruined old city wall. The ruins of the Monasterio de San Francisco are immediately south. The immediate surrounds are slightly run-down, including Avenida Mella, a narrow and congested thoroughfare immediately north of the fort.

PUERTA DE LA MISCERICORDIA

Calle Palo Hincado and Calle Arzobispo Portes, Zona Colonial

The Gate of Mercy, two blocks south of Parque Independencia, was one of the original entrance gates in the old city wall. It is named for the tent camp for the homeless that was

Whither Columbus?

Where are Columbus's bones? Even in death, the explorer was peripatetic.

In his will, he had asked to be buried in the Americas, but at the time of his death in Valladolid on May 20, 1506, the New World lacked a church of sufficient grandeur. Thus, he was laid to rest in a crypt of Valladolid's Francisco convent. In 1513, his remains were transferred to the Santa María de las Cuevas monastery, in Sevilla. Finally, in 1537 he was exhumed and transferred, supposedly along with the bones of his son Diego, to the newly built Catedral de Santa María, in Santo Domingo. When Francis Drake sacked the city in 1586 the bishop, fearful that Columbus's tomb would be desecrated, had the crypt inscriptions obliterated.

During two centuries the sepulcher was forgotten. Then, in 1795, after Spain ceded Santo Domingo to France, remains believed to be those of Columbus were removed and delivered with full military honors to Havana, where they were placed in the cathedral on June 15, 1796. Ever restless, Columbus was next transferred back to Seville following Cuba's independence from Spain in 1898. There, a lead box containing his bones was buried in the cathedral. To this day, Spaniards swear that the great explorer's bones are still preserved in the casket.

However, in 1877, back in Santo Domingo's cathedral, workers found a bone-filled lead urn inscribed with the words ILLUSTRIOUS DON CRISTÓBAL COLÓN.

"The real bones are here! The Spaniards have the wrong bones!"

In 1992, these relics were transferred to the massive Faro a Colón monument to commemorate the 500th anniversary of Columbus's discovery of the New World. To this day, Dominicans swear that his bones are preserved in their casket.

Sepulcher in the Faro a Colón, Santo Domingo

So who has the real bones? In 1960, a scientific study of the Santo Domingo remains determined that they were those of two people. Cristóbal and his son Diego, perhaps? Then, in 2003, DNA analysis of the Sevilla bones proved conclusively that they were those of Columbus. Meanwhile, Dominican authorities have steadfastly refused requests for a DNA analysis of the Faro a Colón bones, claiming that the wrong bones were removed to Havana in 1795 and that Columbus's ghost should finally be left in peace.

established here following a devastating earthquake in 1842. The arched gate is topped by a *baluarte*—a turreted sentry post. It was here that independence fighter Ramón Marias Mella fired the first shot against Haitian forces on February 27, 1844, leading to independence. A bust of Mella stands in the small redbrick plaza.

RUINAS DEL HOSPITAL DE SAN NICOLÁS DE BARÍ
Calle Hostos between Calles Mercedes and Luperón, Zona Colonial

Built of stone in the shape of a cross between 1519 and 1527 (and replacing a simple precursor founded in 1503), then expanded in 1556, the first hospital in the New World was funded entirely by contributions from the city's nobility. It was severely damaged by Francis Drake's pirates in 1589, and now lies in ruins.

RUINAS DE LA MONASTERIO DE SAN FRANCISCO
Calle Hostos between Emiliano Tejera and Restauración, Zona Colonial

These dramatic ruins stud a hillock and are all that remains of a monastery dating back to 1508. Drake's pirates pillaged the original monastery, which was twice rebuilt. Earthquakes toppled the latter two structures, the remains of which take up most of an entire city block. During the 19th century, the building was used as a lunatic asylum—you can still see chains bolted to the wall. If you visit the eerie ruins, illumined at night, ghosts of monks and maniacs will be your guides. Note the Cordón de la Orden Franciscana, the cord-belt coat of arms of the Franciscan order, carved above the main doorway.

Use caution here, as the homeless and destitute are often present in numbers begging for money.

Military Sites

FORTALEZA OZAMA
809-686-0222
Calle Las Damas between Arzobispo Portes and Arzobispo Nouel, Zona Colonial
Daily 9–5
Admission: RD$15; guides RD$200

Begun in 1502 at the mouth of the Río Ozama, this austere fortress contains the oldest colonial military structure in the New World. It was designed as a rectangle by military engineer Gómez García Varela and completed in 1508, although only the foundations of the original structure remain. The existing fortress evolved over the following two centuries and served as a fortress-prison until the 1960s.

The neoclassical 18th-century entrance gate features huge nail-studded doors of African ebony, studded too with bullet holes fired during the U.S. invasion of 1965. Beyond, the brick and grass esplanade has a bronze statue of Gonzalo Fernández de Oviedo (fortress commander 1533–57) cast in 1977 by Spanish sculptor Joaquín Vaquero Turcios. The sober, medieval-style **Torre del Homenaje** tower (all that remains of the early 16th-century complex) stands four-square above the river and served as the first home of Christopher Columbus's son Diego Colón, and his wife, Doña Maria of Toledo. The ground-floor courtyard has a hole-in-the-ground dungeon where Juan Pablo Duarte was imprisoned during the Haitian occupation.

In the center of the complex, the windowless **Armory Polvorín de Santa Bárbara** was built in 1787 as the armory. Note the statue of Saint Barbara, patron saint of the artillery,

Museo Alcázar de Colón, Santo Domingo

atop the door lintel. Nearby, rusting cannon point their muzzles over the river mouth from atop twin batteries.

The grounds also display various tanks, artillery pieces, and other 20th-century military hardware.

Multilingual guides lead tours (RD$200).

FUERTE DE SAN GIL
Avenida Paseo Padre Billini and Calle Palo Hincado, Zona Colonial

This small fortress stands atop a rocky promontory on the Caribbean shorefront. It marks the southernmost point of the city wall that ran south from Fuerte de la Concepción. Today, it is a venue for musical concerts on weekends.

FUERTE DE SAN JOSÉ
Avenida Paseo Padre Billini and Calle 19 de Marzo, Zona Colonial

One of the main bastions in the original city wall, this small fort and adjoining artillery platform was initiated in 1543 to guard the mouth of the Río Ozama. Now overgrown, yet in otherwise fine fettle, it offers a less than salubrious view over the dock and a larger-than-life **statue of Antón de Montecino**, a Franciscan friar who campaigned against the Spaniards ill-treatment of the Taíno.

Museums and Monuments

FARO A COLÓN

809-591-1492
Avenida Mirador del Este, Las Américas
Tues. through Sun. 9–5:30
Admission: US$1

What would Columbus make of his humongous, austere, cross-shaped pyramid-tomb? The imposing and, frankly, grotesque Columbus Lighthouse looks like something from an *Alien* movie. It was conceived in 1929, when a competition was held for a tomb to hold Columbus's remains. British architect Joseph Lea Gleave (1907–65) won with his design for a mega-monument of reinforced concrete rising 10 storeys and stretching 680 feet (207 m). Although Trujillo supported the project, construction proved beyond even his extravagant means. In 1966, President Balaguer resurrected the project. It was finished in 1992, just in time for the 500th anniversary of the explorer's discovery of the New World.

On October 11, 1992, Columbus's ashes were transferred from the Catedral Primada de América with full pomp. Pope John Paul II celebrated Mass here at the dedication. Columbus's remains (if, indeed, they're his) are preserved in a bronze urn inside an incongruously Gothic sepulcher in the core of the monument. This flamboyant 45-foot-tall (13.7 m), white marble tomb was designed by Spanish sculptor Pere Carbonell i Huguet (1854–1927) features four bronze lions and is topped by a bronze female figure. A uniformed soldier stands guard.

Running along the walls of the hollow interior are alcoves containing exhibits about Columbus. Together they form a museum that reopened in October 2008 after restoration.

Lighthouse? Well, the roof features 149 Xenon laser searchlights that can project a vertical cross-shaped sheet of light in the night sky. Rarely are they turned on, as they blow the fuses on most of the city's power supply!

LARIMAR MUSEUM

809-689-6605
www.larimarmuseum.com
Calle Isabel la Católica 54, Zona Colonial
Mon. through Sat. 8–6; Sun. 8–2
Admission: Free

In a colonial home a stone's throw south of Parque Colón, this museum has fabulous educational displays about larimar, the semi-precious stone found only in the Dominican Republic. The ground floor is a store selling amber and larimar jewelry.

MUSEO ALCÁZAR DE COLÓN

809-682-4750
Plaza de España, Zona Colonial
Tues. through Sat. 9–5; Sun. 9–4
Admission: RD$50, buy tickets from the office on the north side of the plaza

Built in 1511 as the Palacio Alcázar, or viceregal palace, this two-storey mansion was the principal home of Diego Colón and his wife Doña María de Toledo. On the east side of the plaza, the fortified rectangular Gothic palace is fronted by a two-tier loggia; note the arches engraved with vines in Isabelline style, and the gargoyles guarding the interior staircase.

The lobby exhibits a mounted knight in full armor. The rest of the 22 rooms are furnished in period fashion with more than 800 items, many of them actual possessions of the Columbus family, donated by Spain. Paintings. Tapestries. Leather chests. Porcelain and silver pieces. Domestic utensils. All arranged as if Don Diego were expected to arrive back home any minute.

MUSEO DE AMBAR

809-221-1333
Calle El Conde 107, Zona Colonial
Mon. through Sat. 9–6
Admission: Free

Although small, this museum attached to a private store selling amber supposedly has the world's largest collection of amber pieces, including extremely rare blue amber. The exhibits explain the geological processes and include many "inclusions" featuring trapped insects. The Victorian building, which faces onto Parque Colón, has an exquisite facade.

MUSEO DE LAS ATARAZANAS REALES

809-682-5834
Calle Colón 4, north side of Plaza España, Zona Colonial
Mon. through Tues. and Thurs. through Sat. 9–5, Sun. 9–1
Admission: RD$20.00

Also known as the Museo Marítimo (Maritime Museum), this is quite literally a treasure of a find. Today the 16th-century customs and port administrative headquarters is dedicated to colonial maritime history. Silver goblets, gold plates, Spanish doubloons, jewel-encrusted swords glitter under spotlights, while all manner of nautical miscellany are also displayed. Most pieces—from clay pipes to cannon—were salvaged from shipwrecks, notably the *Guadalupe* and *Conde de Tolosa* galleons, which foundered in a hurricane in 1724.

MUSEO BELLAPART

809-541-7721 ext. 296
www.museobellapart.com
Edificio Honda, Avenida John F. Kennedy between Los Framboyantes and Calle del Carmen
Mon. through Fri. 9–6, Sat. 9-noon
Admission: Free

Although this place (on the fifth floor of the Honda car showroom, in Naco) can be exasperating to find, the effort is amply rewarded for admirers of contemporary art. Juan José Bellapart's private art collection is world class and superbly displayed. Exhibits are arranged chronologically and feature works by the republic's leading contemporary masters from the mid-19th century onwards.

MUSEO DE LAS CASA REALES

809-682-4202
Calle las Damas, corner of Mercedes; south side of Plaza de España, Zona Colonial
Tues. through Sun. 9–5
Admission: RD$30

Amber specimens, Museo de Ambar, Santo Domingo

Once the most important building in all the Americas, this somber two-storey palace of solid limestone, completed in 1520, housed the Royal Houses *(casas reales)* that administered Spain's colonial New World possessions. Here were La Real Audiencia (the Supreme Court), the Contaduría General (the Treasury), and the Palacio de los Gobernadores y Capitanes Generales (the governors' palace). The functions were transferred to Cuba in 1799.

Today the Museum of the Royal Houses, on two levels, traces Spanish colonial history in the republic since Columbus's arrival. The splendid exhibits include a superb collection of ancient weaponry and armor, plus opulent period furnishings, and a wealth of other period treasures arranged by theme.

The building, which also serves as the principal archive for historic material, also displays contemporary art and sculptures in a series of inner courtyards and surrounding galleries.

MUSEO CASA JUAN PABLO DUARTE

809-687-1436
Calle Isabel la Católica 306, between Calle Restauración and Calle Vicente C. Duarte, Zona Colonial
Mon. through Fri. 9–5, Sat. 9–noon
Admission: RD$12

Independence fighter Juan Pablo Duarte—Father of the Country (see the sidebar, Juan Pablo Duarte and La Trinitaria, in the History chapter)—was born on January 26, 1813 in this modest home, one block northwest of Plaza de España. It displays period furnishings plus various busts, paintings, documents, and other mementos related to his life and to his underground independence organization, La Trinitaria.

MUSEO DE LA FAMILIA DOMINICANA DEL SIGLO XIX

809-689-5000
www.cultura.gov.do/dependencias/museos
Calle Arzobispo Meriño, corner of Padre Billini, Zona Colonial
Mon. through Sat. 9–5
Admission: RD$40

The Museum of the 19th-Century Dominican Family is housed in the Casa de Tostado, built in the early 16th century and once owned by president Buenaventura Báez. Today it replicates the home of a well-to-do 19th-century family with furnishings of the time. A spiral mahogany staircase leads to an airy tower-lookout with fine views over the city.

MUSEO DEL HOMBRE DOMINICANO

809-687-3622
Plaza de la Cultura, Gazcue
Tues. through Sun. 10–5
Admission: RD$50

What a pity the depressingly dowdy ambience of the Museum of the Dominican Man detracts from the fine exhibits spanning four levels. The collection of pre-Columbian artifacts, ranging from *duhos* (thrones used by caciques) to *zemis* (religious figurines), impresses. Other displays range through slavery and its impact on Dominican culture, to *Carnaval* costumes and masks. Alas, signage is in Spanish only.

MUSEO MUNDO DE AMBER

809-682-3309
www.amberworldmuseum.com
Calle Arzobispo Meriño 452, Zona Colonial
Mon. through Sat 9–4, Sun. 9–1
Admission: Free

This small museum is attached to a store selling amber and larimar jewelry. The superb educational displays give a great overview of how amber and larimar are formed, and the inclusions containing fossilized ants and other insects are especially fascinating.

MUSEO DE LA PORCELANA

809-688-4759
Calle José Reyes 6, Zona Colonial
Tues. through Sat. 10–6; Sun. 11–5
Admission: RD$15

Housed in an exquisite Moorish home modeled after the Alhambra Palace in Grenada, Spain, Santo Domingo's Porcelain Museum is the dream realized of Violeta Martínez, who was exiled during the Trujillo era. In four *salas* (rooms), the displays range from pre-Columbian ceramics through Chinese, English, French, and Dutch porcelain.

MUSEO NACIONAL DE HISTÓRIA Y GEOGRAFÍA
809-686-6668
Plaza de la Cultura
Tues. through Tues. Sun. 9:30–1 and 2–5
Admission: RD$100

Although musty and in need of an enlivening spruce up, this museum is principally given over to history and has excellent exhibits tracing the nation's past back to Taíno days. Its three wings are themed chronologically, with special focus given to pre-Columbian society; the early 19th-century Haitian-Dominican conflicts; the internecine wars of the late 19th century leading up to U.S. occupation; and the Trujillo era. The dictator's pancake makeup kit (used to lighten his skin) is here, as well as the bullet-riddled 1956 Oldsmobile 98 in which Trujillo was assassinated. Inexplicably, short shrift is given to the colonial period. Spanish signage only.

MUSEO NACIONAL DE HISTÓRIA NATURAL
809-689-0106
Plaza de la Cultura, Gazcue
Tues. through Sun. 10–5
Admission: RD$100

If you want to know what species of flora and fauna await in the Dominican wilds, then check out the dioramas here. It's not what one might call a world-class museum, but it's worth your perusal if the subject appeals. The whale exhibit is impressive. And it has a fine collection of amber, plus other exhibits spanning geology, zoology, and space. Signage is in Spanish only, alas.

MUSEO NUMISMÁTICO Y FILATÉLICO
809-221-9111 ext 3662
www.bancentral.gov.do/museo.asp
Avenida Pedro Henríquez Ureña, corner Calle Leopoldo Navarro, Gazcue
Mon. through Fri. 9–3
Admission: Free

Numismatists and stamp collectors will thrill to this excellent museum, housed in the 1947 neo-classical former headquarters of the Banco Central de la República Dominicana (the bank's new headquarters is a magnificent Modernist building across the street). There are three principal *salas* (rooms): one displays coins and notes dating from 1505 to the present day; the second exhibits gold and silver treasures recovered from colonial-era shipwrecks; the third displays stamps dating back to 1865.

OBELISCO DE SANTO DOMINGO
Avenida George Washington and Calle Vicinio Burgos, Zona Colonial

This classic Egyptian-style obelisk rises 39 feet (12 m) from a roundabout in the middle of the Malecóns. It was erected in 1937 by Trujillo to commemorate the city's rechristening as

Ciudad Trujillo. It was instantly rechristened as El Macho (the phallus). Even Vice President Jacinto Reynaldo—head of the Pro-Erection Committee—remarked that the obelisk was a fitting tribute to a man of "superior natural gifts." The obelisk is adorned with murals that change yearly, painted by a leading artist.

Music and Nightlife

Santo Domingo is abuzz by night, with something for every taste. Seeking a classical concert? Or perhaps a bohemian café as a prelude to letting your hair down in a dance-till-dawn disco? For laid-back bohemian venues, head to the Zona Colonial, chock-full of atmospheric bars, plus a vibrant gay scene. The more upscale nightclubs are mostly found in the Naco district, which gets in the groove on Wednesday and peaks on Friday night. The poshest nightclubs have strict admission policies—you need to look the part to get in. Unfortunately, many prefer white patrons only and openly flaunt the nation's anti-discrimination laws. In fact, in 2005 the U.S. Embassy banned its employees from patronizing The Loft due to racial discrimination against African American embassy staff.

Since 2006, a new regulation has imposed midnight closing Sunday to Thursday, and 2 AM closing on Friday and Saturday, on most venues. Hotel bars and clubs are exempt.

On weekend nights head to **Plaza España**, where live musicians and a folkloric troupe perform for free.

Here are a few of my favorite nightspots:

Aire (809-689-4163; Calle Mercedes 313, Zona Colonial) Caters mainly to gays, although everyone is welcome. Plays 1970s and 1980s classics and has theme parties, including a foam party on Wednesdays and drag shows on Sundays.

Atarazana 9 (809-688-0969; Calle Atarazana 9, Zona Colonial) One of the most popular bars in town. It packs in patrons like sardines—surely a fire hazard! Still, it's a great place to get your groove on, especially Thursday night for live music upstairs.

Beer House Café (809-566-2433; Avenida Winston Churchill, corner Gustavo Mejía Ricart, Naco) Serious sudsters congregate here on weekends to sample beers from around the world.

Bicicleta Café Bar and Lounge (809-687-3531; Calle Duarte and Arzobispo Nouel) Lounge bar themed with bicycle decor and serving tapas. Themed nights include DJ-spun electronica on Wednesday; 1970s and 1980s for classics; and karaoke on Tuesdays, Thursdays, and Saturdays.

Cacibajagua (809-670-6333; Calle Sánchez 201, Zona Colonial) One of the colonial district's hot spots, with an artsy bohemian ambience. Rock aficionados will love it, with the classics from Pink Floyd to Led Zeppelin. Ladies Night on Tuesday; two-for-the-price-of-one wines on Thursday.

Cibao Cigar Lounge-Bar (809-685-9955; Hotel Sofitel Nicolás de Ovando, Calle Las Damas, Zona Colonial) *The* place to savor a stogie in style. Often has live music, and you can choose either the air-conditioned cigar lounge or the cozy patio bar.

Cinema Café (809-221-7555; www.cinemacafe.com.do; Plaza de la Cultura, Zona Colonial) A meeting place for bohemians. Next to the National Film Library. Decorated with movie posters. Hosts poetry readings, and live music and theater performances.

Club 60 (809-685-6276; Avenida Máximo Gómez 60) A relatively mature crowd frequents this classy merengue club. Go on Sundays for Cuban *son* à la Buena Vista Social Club.

Club Abacus (809-221-4660; Calle Hostos 350, Zona Colonial). A chic bar for sophisticates, with four distinct rooms. Dress to impress. Ladies Night on Wednesday.

Coco's (809-687-9624; Calle Padre Billini 53, Zona Colonial) A good place to sip some suds, perhaps over some fish-n-chips or steak and kidney pie. Run by English expats Colin Hercock and Christopher Gwillym, this bar is made up to resemble a real English pub.

Encuentro Artesanal (809-955-1123; Arzobispo Meriño 407, Zona Colonial) Draws an eclectic and bohemian moneyed crowd. Favors electronic music.

Fantasy Disco (809-535-5581; Avenida Heroes de Luperón 29, La Feria) One of the city's top spots for *bachata*, merengue, and salsa. No cover. Dress code. Open daily 6 PM–4 AM.

Hollywood Café (809-566-3349; Avenida Gustavo Mejía Ricart 36, Naco) The name alone draws the city's moneyed crowd, who party until dawn in the café, while the upstairs tapas bar is more sedate.

Jet Set (809-535-4145; www.jetsetdisco.com; Centro Comercial El Portal, Avenida Independencia) Put on your hippest duds to make the most of this stylish nightclub, with seats arrayed in tiers overlooking the amphitheater-style dance floor. Couples only!

La Guácara Taína (809/533–1051; Avenida Mirador del Sur, in Parque Mirador del Sur) The top disco in town, this hot spot enjoys a sensational setting inside a real cave. Be prepared for Latin dancing hot enough to cook the pork. It has three bars and two dance floors. Open Wednesday through Sunday 9–until closing.

Loft Lounge and Dance Club (809-732-4016; Calle Tiradentes 44, Naco) Huge lounge and disco complete with smoke and confetti machines. Draws Santo Domingo's sexiest patrons—young, hip, moneyed, and dressed to kill. The velvet rope here isn't color-blind. Sounds run from 1980s classics to salsa.

Montecristo Café (809-542-5000; www.montecristocafe.com.do; Calle José Amado Soler, corner of Avenida Abraham Lincoln) An English-style pub with theme nights, including Monday-night big-screen music videos; free wine tastings on Tuesday evening (6–8); live music and dancing on Wednesday; and karaoke during Sunday Ladies Night.

Teleoferta Car Wash (Avenidas 27 de Febrero and Máximo Gómez) This car wash doubles as a disco by night. A DJ spins tunes, and live bands sometimes play. Gets packed with people.

What Do You Mean...It's a Car Wash?

Er, well, yes...car washes in the Dominican Republic are for washing cars. At least by day. The drinking and driving laws here aren't quite what they are in Europe or North America. Hence most car washes have small bars where you can enjoy a cool beer while your car gets its own suds. Come night many metamorphose into open-air bars-cum-dance clubs. Some *cah wah* have pool tables. They draw primarily relatively impecunious locals, and those in touristed areas usually have no shortage of *tigueres* and sankys. If you don't like *very loud* music (principally playing merengue and *bachata*) and a colorful local scene in which you'll likely be the only tourist, then pass. Otherwise, if you go with an open attitude, you'll have lots of fun with the locals. A true Dominican experience! Many have hostesses who function mostly to get you to buy drinks...and if at the end of the night you go home alone, at least you can do so with a clean car.

Nature and Gardens

JARDIN BOTÁNICO NACIONAL
809-385-2611
www.jbn-sdq.org
Avenida República de Colombia
Daily 9–5
Admission: US$1.50

Spanning a forested canyon on the northwest side of the city, the beautifully maintained National Botanical Garden sprawls over 440 acres (182 ha) and delights plant and nature lovers. Specialty gardens are given to aquatic plants, palms, succulents, bromeliads, ferns, medicinal, and toxic plants. A highlight, the orchid house displays more than 300 native species (visit in March for the annual orchid show). There's even a Japanese garden with a pagoda. And the **Museo de Ecología** has exhibits on Hispaniola's ecosystems. Birds abound.

An open-air trolley offers 30-minute tours every 30 minutes, but narration is in Spanish only. Rowboats can be rented on the lake.

PARQUE MIRADOR DEL ESTE
Between Avenida Boulevard del Faro and Avenida Iberoamerica, Las Américas

This pacific tree-shaded park, immediately east of Faro a Colón, on the east side of the Río Ozama, is principally given over to various sports stadiums and arenas. At its far eastern end, the **Cueva Los Tres Ojos** (809-788-7056)—three-eyes cave—is named for three sink-holes (cenotes), one filled with fresh water, one with salt water, and the last with sulphurous water. You can descend via steps to bathe in the first, and small-boat rides are available.

PARQUE MIRADOR DEL NORTE
809-926-9022
Avenida Máximo Gómez between Avenidas Hermanas Mirabal and Jacobo Majluta
Mon. through Fri. 8–5
Admission: RD$2

This huge 15 square-mile (40 sq km) forested park occupies the rolling hills north of town, to the north of the Río Isabela. It offers wetlands (great for birding), forest trails, plus man-made lakes. You can rent rowboats and paddleboats on Lago Artificial Yaguaza, and boat trips are offered on the river. There's horseback riding, and guides offer nature hikes (don't hike alone).

PARQUE MIRADOR DEL SUR
Avenida Mirador del Sur, between Avenidas Winston Churchill and Luperón

Running east-west for 3 miles (4.8 km), this pencil-thin park follows the contours of an ancient marine terrace raised from the sea eons ago. This limestone ridge is riddled with caves, such as **Cueva del Paseo de los Indios**, a roost for bats; and **Lago Subterraneo**, an underground lake. Though it has tree-shaded lawns studded with modern sculptures, drawing families for picnics on weekends, it's more a curiosity for tourists and wins no beauty prizes. Visit at night for a romantic meal in the Mesón de la Cava restaurant, followed by dancing in the Guácara Taina nightclub, both in caves. The cliff top Avenida Mirador del Sur is closed to vehicles daily 6–9 AM and 4–8 PM.

PARQUE ZOOLÓGICA NACIONAL

809-562-3149
Avenida Paseo de los Reyes Católicos
Tues. through Sun. 9–5
Admission: US$5

If you're curious to see the extremely rare hutia and solenodon, the republic's two principal (and critically endangered) mammals, then this is one place to see them. The zoo, in the hills on the north side of the city, also has American crocodile. And endemic bird species such as the Hispaniola parrot flit about a massive aviary. But most species here are African. Chimpanzees...elephants...lions...rhinos, etc. While many animals roam free in a spacious savanna-like park, others inhabit small cages. The zoo is badly managed and, frankly, depressing. Kids may like the petting zoo.

Theater

Café de Teatro (809-689-3430; www.casadeteatro.com; Avenida Arzobispo Meriño 110). This performing arts space hosts weekly events, from live jazz to poetry readings.

Centro Cultural Español (809-686-8212; www.ccesd.org; Avenida Arzobispo Meriño, corner Arzobispo Portes) The eclectic offerings here span cinema, live music, and theater, including puppet theater.

Teatro Eduardo Brito (809-682-7255; Avenida César Nicolás Penson and Avenida Máximo Gómez 35, Plaza de la Cultura) The former National Theater was renamed in 2005 for a famous Dominican-born baritone. A dress code includes no jeans, shorts, or tennis shoes for performances. It hosts classical and contemporary concerts, plus drama in the main theater, Sala Principal. The tiny Sala Ravelo hosts literary forums, etc.

Teatro Gayumba (809-682-3468; www.geocities.com/teatrogayumba; Calle Elvira de Mendoza 5) This theater group specializes in avant-garde productions.

Teatro Nacional (809-687-3191; www.teatronacional.com.do; Avenida Máximo Gómez 35) The nation's principal venue for theater, live music, etc.

Seasonal Events

Classical music fans will not want to miss the biennial **Santo Domingo Music Festival**, which draws leading orchestras and performers from around the world. Held in March, it's arranged by the Fundación Orquesta Sinfónica Nacional (809-532-6600; www.sinfonia .org.do). The symphony also performs individual concerts during its annual October through May symphony season. Its principal venue is the Teatro Nacional. Likewise, the **Santo Domingo Merengue Festival** is held on the Malecón each July, with both local performers and big-name bands. And the **Café de Teatro Jazz Festival** (809-689-3430; www.casadeteatro.com; Avenida Arzobispo Meriño 110) is hosted each June and July.

On February 27 in the afternoon head to the Malecón for the **Día de Independencia** celebration; the nation's military are on parade. The event culminates the city's *Carnaval*—a weeklong bash when male revelers dress up in outlandish devil costumes and masks, while women dress down, and everyone wines salaciously to merengue and salsa.

ATTRACTIONS, PARKS, AND RECREATION

Bird-Watching

The parklands bordering the city offer tremendous birding, particularly **Parque Mirador del Norte** and **Jardin Botánico Nacional** (see the Nature and Gardens section). To arrange guided birding, contact Kate Wallace at **Tody Tours** (809-686-0882; www.todytours.com; Calle José Gabriel García 105, Zona Colonial, Santo Domingo).

Boating

Despite its shorefront position, Santo Domingo has no marina. Yet! In 2007, plans were announced for the 550-slip Marina Puerto Bonito to be built fronting Avenida Paseo Presidente Billini, east of the Obelisko.

Meanwhile, if you have kids in tow, head to **Parque Mirador del Norte** (see the Nature and Gardens section), which has rowboats.

Bowling

The **Sebelén Bowling Center** (809-920-0202; www.sebelenbowlingcenter.com; Plaza Bolera, Avenida Abraham Lincoln, corner of Roberto Pastoriza) is the city's premier facility, with 48 lanes on two levels. Plus, there are pool tables, video arches, and even a kids' area. Open 10–2 Monday through Sunday.

Fitness Facilities

Most of the high-rise hotels along the Malecón have gyms that non-guests can use for a fee. Meanwhile, the nation's main sports facilities are found in **Parque Mirador del Este**; and at the **Centro Olímpico** (809-683-5985; between Avenida John F. Kennedy and Avenida 27

For the Children

Although Santo Domingo appeals more to adults, there's plenty to keep kids amused for a few days. In addition to the Parque Zoológico Nacional and Parque Mirador del Norte (see the Nature and Gardens section), here are three not-to-be-missed sites for the kids:

Acuario Nacional (809-766-1709 or 592-150; Avenida España 75, between Avenida 26 de Febrero and Calle de Cuarto) The open-air National Aquarium abuts the Caribbean Sea and exhibits more than 250 fishes and other marine species. A highlight is walking the plexiglass tunnel through a huge tank full of sharks, turtles, and rays. Guided tours. Open Tuesday through Sunday 9:30–5:30. Admission: US$2.

Agua Splash (809-766-1927; www.aguasplashcaribe.com; Avenida España 50, corner Avenida 26 de Febrero) This small theme park is the place to cool off and have fun. Dominican families flock for the water slides, wave pools, etc. Separate area for 2–8 year olds. Open Tuesday through Sunday 11–7. Admission: RD$200 Monday through Friday, RD$250 Saturday and Sunday.

Museo Infantil Trampolín (809-685-5551; www.trampolin.org.do; Calle Las Damas between Arzobispo Nouel and Calle El Conde) A fascinating children's museum housed in the Casa Rodrigo de Bastidas, dating from 1512. Educational interpretative exhibits span the sciences, history, and social sciences. Bilingual guides. Open Tuesday through Friday 9–5, Saturday and Sunday 9–7. Admission: RD$100 adults, RD$50 children.

de Febrero, and Avenida Máximo Gómez and Avenida José Ortega y Gasset), site of the Palacio de Deportes Olympic stadium and an Olympic swimming pool, plus basketball, baseball, and tennis facilities.

Hiking and Horseback Riding

There are hiking trails in **Parque Mirador del Norte** (see the Nature and Gardens section), which also has horseback riding facilities.

Running

The **Hash House Harriers** (www.sdh3dr.net; E-mail: info@sdh3dr.net), the world's most eccentric running club, has a Santo Domingo chapter that has runs, usually about 3 miles (5 km), every second Sunday afternoon. It welcomes visitors. You join the pack of hounds (runners) to chase a hare or hares (other runners) that set a trail. Afterwards, runners gather for social activity.

Otherwise, both the **Parque Mirador del Sur** and **Parque Mirador del Este** have running trails, and the latter has a formal running track.

SHOPPING

The capital city doesn't lack for opportunity, and shopaholics can fill days hunting out bargains. The best arts and crafts are to be found in the Zona Colonial. For more upscale galleries and clothes stores, head to Naco, where the major shopping malls are also located.

Art

You're spoilt for choice. If all you want is a cheap exemplar of native Haitian art, you'll find dozens of stores throughout the Zona Colonial. For the finest examples, though, head to **Galería Elín** (809-688-7100; Calle Arzobispo Meriño 203).

Seeking contemporary art? Check out these three places: **Arte Berri** (809-688-2073; www.arteberri.com; Calle Hostos 105); **Galería Bidó** (809-688-9370; www.galeriabido .com; Calle Dr. Báez 5, Gazcue); or **Galería de Arte Nader** (809-544-0878; Calle Rafael Sánchez, Gazcue), which represents many of the nation's top artists.

Books and Music

Looking for music? Avoid the roadside stalls selling DVDs and CDs. They're bootleg! Instead, head to **La Musicalia** (809-562-2878; Calle el Conde 464, Zona Tropical), which has an excellent selection of the Dominican Republic's hottest musicians and bands. Nearby **Karen CD Store** (809-686-0019; Calle El Conde 251) is a worthy alternative.

Also with a great music selection, **Librería Thesaurus** (809-508-1114; www.thesaurus.com.do; Avenida Abraham Lincoln, corner Avenida Sarasota) is the nation's top bookstore, with a café upstairs; open Monday through Saturday 9–9, and Sunday 10–3. Alternately, try **Librería Cuesta** (809-473-4020; www.cuestalibros.com; Avenida 27 de Febrero and Abraham Lincoln), also with an excellent collection of music and books. Most texts are in Spanish.

Clothing and Accessories

Stroll Calle Conde, west of Parque Colón, and you'll pass several outlets selling inexpensive

Hablas español?... Say what?

They say that the fastest way to learn a language is to take a lover who speaks no other. Failing that, you can live (even temporarily) in a place where that language is spoken, preferably immersing yourself in a language school for a week, month, or longer. No problem in the DR, which has several dozen language schools. Here are some to consider:

Hispaniola Academy (809-689-8350; Fax: 809-688-9192; www.hispaniola.org) Santo Domingo. Based in Zona Colonial, it has year-round classes for all levels, plus special Spanish classes as well as dance and cooking lessons.

Holiday Spanish School (809-571-1847; Fax: 809-571-4115; www.holiday-spanish-school.com) Sosuá. Based at the Hotel El Colibri, it offers individual and group classes; 20- and 40-hour packages. Prices depend on number of students.

Instituto Intercultural del Caribe (809-571-3185; Fax: 809-571-3174; www.edase.com) Santo Domingo and Sosuá. The Spanish section of the German-Dominican Language and Culture Institute (EDASE) is one of the largest institutions offering Spanish classes to foreigners in the Dominican Republic. Classes for beginners through advanced Spanish speakers. Weeklong courses from US$230.

Institute of Languages (809-571-1114; Fax: 809-571-1113; www.ilangdr.com) Sosuá. Teaches classes for everyone from beginners to advanced Spanish speakers seeking fluency. One-week, 10-lesson packages begin at US$195.

Mabraska (809-689-3617; www.mabraska.net) Santo Domingo. This small school also offers classes for all levels. Students make up their own schedule, from relaxed to intense, based on a one-week minimum, starting at US$200.

clothing. However, for fine duds and name-brand items, you're better off heading west to Naco. A good starting point is **Plaza Central** (809-541-5929; Avenida Winston Churchill, corner of Avenida 27 de Febrero), a mall with four storeys of boutique and shoe stores. Alternately, try **Acropolis** (809-225-2020; www.acropolisdr.com; Avenida Winston Churchill, corner of Avenida Julio A. Aybar), with more than 100 stores on five levels.

Crafts and Jewelry

The Zona Colonial is a veritable trove of stores selling island crafts. For the most complete collection under one roof, head to the **Mercado Modelo** (809-686-6772; Avenida Mella 50, between Calles Del Monte y Tejada and Santomé), a huge covered market that takes up an entire block. The sales pitch is aggressive, but competition is so fierce that you can bargain no less aggressively. If you're seeking Haitian art, cheap (fake) amber jewelry, wood carving, etc. you'll find it here. You can also buy *mamajuana* (see the special topic, Mamajuana ...It's Made of What!), herbal remedies, and icons related to the republic's Afro-based syncretic religion in the *botánicas* (herbalist stores) tucked in the northwest corner.

Also selling a little of everything, **Art Felipe & Co.** (809-689-581; Calle El Conde 105) is one of the better generic art and gift stores in the Zona Colonial. For quality *carnaval* masks, try **El Mamey** (809-689-0236; Calle Isabela 157).

If looking for amber and larimar jewelry, you can't beat the **Museo de Ambar** (809-221-1333; Calle El Conde 107); **Museo Larimar** (809-689-6605; Calle Isabel la Católica 54); and **Museo Mundo de Ambar** (809-682-3309; Calle Arzobispo Meriño 452). Most upscale tourist hotels also have jewelry and/or craft stores.

Gifts and Collectibles

Men...and perhaps even ladies! Surely you can't go home without a box of premium Dominican cigars. Whatever you do, avoid buying on the street: The sales pitch might convince you otherwise, but they're sure to be fakes or, at best, been sitting out in the sun for days on end. Two standout stores selling a wide choice of select smokes are **Cigar King** (809-686-4987; Calle El Conde 208) and **Boutique del Fumador** (809-685-6425; Calle El Conde 109), both on Parque Colón.

For the republic's famous faceless dolls porcelain, try **Artesanía Elisa** (809-682-9653; Calle Arzobispo Nouel).

4

THE SOUTH CENTRAL

Beaches Close at Hand

When weekends come around, *capitaleños* load up the family and head out of Santo Domingo for nearby beaches. Several beach zones lie within a one-hour's drive of the city. East of the capital, Boca Chica is the favored spot, with plenty of hotels, restaurants, and a night scene that borders on salacious. The scuba diving here is world class in the ship-wreck-littered, reef-protected cove betwixt Santo Domingo and Boca Chica. Farther east, Juan Dolio boasts better beaches and a string of all-inclusive hotels. The coastal plains hereabouts are carpeted in lime green sugarcane. The coastal town of San Pedro de Macorís is the nation's sugar central, as well as the epicenter of baseball. Nearby, you *must* visit the spectacular Cueva de las Maravillas!

The flatlands west of the capital were an important sugarcane production region during the colonial era. Today ruined plantations hide in the scrubby undergrowth. Carretera Sánchez (RD 2) connects Santo Domingo with San Cristóbal, a sprawling town with Trujillo associations, and gateway to a cave system containing the nation's most important galleries of pre-Columbian rupestrine art. Beyond San Cristóbal the eclectic attractions include salt pans (good for birding) and the largest sand dunes in the Caribbean.

BOCA CHICA

A 30-minute drive from Santo Domingo via the coast-hugging toll highway (Carretera 3), this beach town is just 19 miles (30 km) east of the capital. It evolved in the 1950s when the capital's middle classes built vacation homes at what was then a small fishing village overlooking the Bahía de Andrés. A decade later, the country's first beach resort was established. In ensuing years, this beach town became overdeveloped and dominated by single foreign males and Dominican hookers. Although since tempered, sex tourism is still a key *raison*. Today budget-oriented Boca Chica draws mainly budget-oriented package vacationers, and is thronged on weekends by Santo Domingo's music-loving, littering hoi polloi. If it's pristine sands and class you're seeking, give Boca Chica a miss. But it's great if you want to mingle with your average Dominican.

The soft white sands unspool along 2 miles (3 km) of reef-protected shoreline (actually, the barrier was man-made specifically to provide for safe snorkeling and swimming). Sapphire waters beyond the lagoon preserve several shipwrecks. The diving here is top-notch—perhaps the main reason to visit. And there's a reasonable choice of accommodations, and some great eating.

Playa Guayacanes, Juan Dolio

The town is accessed from the Autopista (freeway) by three boulevards: 24 de Junio, Bautista Vicini, and Caracol. In recent years, the town has witnessed a mad construction boom.

Getting There

Express Buses (no phone; no office; daily, 6 AM–8 PM; $2) to Boca Chica depart Santo Domingo every hour from Calle José Martí at Calle Henríquez y Carvajal, two blocks from Parque Enriquillo (in the Villa Francisca area north of Zona Colonial). Take care of your possessions, as thieves abound in this congested and chaotic commercial and transport district. In Boca Chica, buses pick-up and drop-off at Parque Central.

A taxi from Santo Domingo to Boca Chica should cost about $30. Boca Chica is only a few miles east of the airport; a taxi should cost about $15.

Lodging

DON JUAN BEACH RESORT

809-687-9157
fax: 809-688-5271
www.donjuanbeachresort.com
Avenida Abraham Nuñez 8

This handsome all-inclusive hotel is in the heart of town and faces onto one of the nicest parts of the beach, close to the main pier and just steps from shops, bars, and services. Palms soar over the two- and three-storey, pastel-painted structures. The beachfront free-

Restaurante Boca Chica at night

form pool is inviting, and there are plenty of water sports, including scuba diving clinics (the hotel has its own dive operation and dock), and tennis clinics, too A supervised kids' club and playground keeps the wee ones occupied. And the ice cream parlor is reason enough to check in. Shuttles will take you to Zona Colonial, and other organized excursions include a once-a-week guided bicycle tour. The 224 air-conditioned bedrooms in 5 room types vary considerably; some being older and a tad behind the times. But they're all spacious and have satellite TVs, direct-dial phones, and in-room safes. If you want soothing tones, pass on the gaudily decorated Garden View rooms; instead, opt for the more sober Captain's Club rooms with whirlpool tubs. $$–$$$.

HOTEL GARANT INTERNATIONAL
809-523-5544
fax: 809-523-6644
www.hotelgarant.com
Calle Sanchez 9

Clean. Modern. Canadian-run. You can't go wrong if all you're seeking is a bargain-priced spot with a pool, and rooms with basic essentials: ceiling fans, cable TVs, in-room safes, refrigerators, and functional bathrooms. Guests here range from families to *chica* chasers (yes, guests are allowed), but French Canadian owner Ghislain Garant runs a tight ship, and noise and security are usually never a problem. It's a 10-minute walk from the beach. $

HOTEL ZAPATA

809-523-4777
fax: 809-523-5534
www.hotelzapata.com
Calle Abraham Nuñez 27

If you shun large all-inclusives in favor of family atmosphere and intimacy, then this could be for you as an alternative to the Zapata. And it has a distinct advantage—it's directly on the beach. This small, charming hotel has 22 air-conditioned rooms, varying from standards to one- and two-bedroom apartments. Some have oceanfront balconies. All have cable TVs and in-room safes, and pleasant bamboo furnishings atop terra-cotta floors. It now has WiFi. You can savor international and Dominican *criolla* dishes in the airy restaurant, then cozy up at the thatched bar. $.

OASIS HAMACA BEACH RESORT, SPA, AND CASINO

809-523-4611
fax: 809-523-6767
www.hotelesoasis.com
Calle Duarte 26

By far the largest hotel in Boca Chica, this six-storey, Spanish-run all-inclusive at the east end of Boca Chica (yet just steps from downtown) has its own beach, with thatched umbrellas. Hence, no pestering from itinerant vendors. Hugging the shore, it rises in tiers, providing a serene countenance when seen from the beach. The lobby is a bit garish with its pea green walls and flamboyant artwork, but I shouldn't quibble. This is a nice hotel (despite the consistently slow and indifferent service I received from reception staff). I love the main restaurant with soaring thatched roof, and the thatched bar hanging over the waters, and the large free-form pool is a great place to be. The 587 rooms here are spacious and vary markedly. Some are gaily colored, with terra-cotta floors and rich floral fabrics. Suites are far more subdued, with contemporary styling and lots of calming whites. Still others have classical antique reproductions. As you'd expect, there's a choice of restaurants. And activities include non-motorized water sports, scuba diving, tennis, and *animaciones* laid on by entertainment staff. It has a small casino across the street. Still, it's not up to par with the all-inclusives of the Punta Cana region. $$–$$$.

NEPTUNO'S REFUGIO

809-523-9934
fax: 809-523-9863
www.dominicana.de
Calle Duarte, about 100 yards (100 m) east of the Oasis Hamaca

Independent-minded travelers should make a beeline for this small, eclectic, family-run offering, with a medley of accommodations in two 5-storey buildings boasting lots of glossy hardwoods. Furnishings here are pretty simple, and the cable TV delivers only a handful of channels, but on sunny days you'll be by the beach anyway. It has a plunge pool. Breakfasts are served in a garden gazebo. Although there's no restaurant here, the town's two premier restaurants are across the street. The door to my apartment was feeble, so security might be an issue, not least because there's no lobby to pass through at night (hopefully the security guard won't be snoozing). There are lots of stairs; this is one place definitely not suited to wheelchairs! $–$$.

Dining

Boca Chica is blessed with excellent restaurants, many of them Italian (and run by Italians). The large expatriate population here means no shortage of foreign-owned restaurants, from simple seaside cafés to beachfront grills serving genuine Dominican fare. Budget hounds can join locals who order fresh-cooked *lambi criolla* (conch) or whole fried fish with *casabe* (cassava bread) and *plátanos* (fried plantain) from the street stalls at the eastern end of Avenida Rafael, and at the western end of the beach. Here's my pick of the litter.

DI LUCIEN

809-523-5878
Calle Duarte 1
Cuisine: Italian

This casual beachfront shack does a bang-up job of fresh seafoods, including salads and complimentary appetizers. Of course, being Italian, this place serves fresh homemade raviolis, tortellinis, etc. You should be able to dine on grilled lobster or fish with salad and a glass of wine for less than $10. Open: Daily 9 PM–midnight. $–$$.

ITALY AND ITALY

809-523-4001
E-mail: italytaly@bocachicabeach.net
Calle Duarte 101
Cuisine: Italian.

Strange name, for sure, but here you get real Italian fare just like *mama* used to make (the owner is from Romagna). The charming decor is enhanced by trompe l'oeil murals. The pastas are homemade in the open kitchen, and the seafood dishes are always fresh. Leave room for the delicious tiramisu. It's right in the heart of town; choose the air-conditioned interior or the street-front patio. Open: daily 8:30 AM–midnight. $$.

NEPTUNO'S CLUB

809-523-4707
E-mail: neptunosclub2003@yahoo.es
Calle Duarte 12

Heaps of ambience at this open-air waterfront restaurant that plays up the pirate theme, and delivers seafood dishes spanning the spectrum from King Neptune's larder. The place actually replicates the inside of a Spanish galleon, a miniature of which floats off the dock and serves as a bar. And the wait staff is garbed in *"Agh...Jim laaaad!"* gear. My favorite dishes here are the sautéed shrimp and the lobster ravioli, and the seafood casserole will feed the family. *Do* hop aboard the ship to admire the aquarium, lit at night, when reservations are a good idea. Open: daily noon–midnight. $$–$$$.

PEQUEÑA SUIZA

809-523-4619
Calle Duarte 56
Cuisine: Fondues

Who on earth would have imagined a restaurant in Boca Chica that specializes in fondues?

Needless to say, the seafood fondue is a fave. The menu also includes lots of pasta dishes such as fettucini primavera, plus seafoods. You can pick from an extensive wine list. It's in a *pensión* of the same name and is easily missed due to its unassuming façade. Stefano, the owner, hails from the Swiss-Italian province of Ticinio and serves up a delicious cappuccino and espresso, best enjoyed early in the day when you can sit outside at street-side tables and take in the to-ing and fro-ing. Open: 9 AM–midnight. $$$.

RESTAURANTE BOCA MARINA
809-688-6810
bocamarina@hotmail.com
Calle Duarte 12-A
Cuisine: International.

The fancy sports cars and deluxe SUVs parked outside say it all. This is the top spot in town, and no wonder. The setting literally overhanging the beach is magnificent. And while the open-air, thatched restaurant architecturally plays on an indigenous theme, it does so with a classy travertine floor and glossy hardwood furnishings beneath a soaring Palenque roof. Candlelit tables, muslin curtains wrapping thick wooden columns, and Balinese beds on the deck add to the sense of sophistication. And at night the floodlit waters tempt diners to descend the metal steps for a preprandial swim (remember your mum's words never to swim on a full stomach). The globe-spanning menu includes pasta dishes, Thai shrimp, lobster with garlic and white wine, and a superb seafood risotto. Swallows nest in the thatch and pipe squeakily. Open: daily 10 AM–midnight. $$–$$$$.

Attractions, Parks, and Recreation

PLAYA BOCA CHICA
The palm-lined beach at Boca Chica is the republic's most popular beach with Dominicans, who flood from the capital on weekends and holidays. Tourist hotels fringe the handsome central beach section, with water-sports outlets and the lion's share of beachfront hotels, restaurants, and bars. The hoi polloi tend to flood the westerly patch, where the view is marred by an unsightly sugar refinery and dock cranes. The sands are never quiet by day, when hair-braiders, mariachis, the occasional hooker, and vendors selling jewelry and coconut water prowl in search of clients.

A man-made offshore barrier protects bathtub-warm waters comprising what is billed as the largest reef-protected lagoon in the Caribbean—great for wading out (the water is about 3 feet, 1 m, deep) to tiny, mangrove-lined **Isla La Matica**, a roost for herons and other waders; and farther out (the water is deeper) to larger **Isla Los Pinos**.

PARQUE NACIONAL SUBMARINO LA CALETA
Carretera Aeropuerto Luperón (Carr. 66) and Autopista A3, 12 miles (20 km) east of Santo Domingo
No telephone.
Open: Daily 9–6
Admission: Free

The ocean waters immediately west of La Caleta (5 miles/8 km west of Boca Chica), the peninsula hosting Santo Domingo's international airport, are a trove of littered shipwrecks. Here at a depth of 60 feet (18 m), lies the *Hickory*, a 130-feet-long (40 m) salvage vessel

Ostrich Heaven!

No, it's not a case of sunstroke or too much *mamajuana* messing with your head. Those really are ostriches to be seen at **Finca Vargas de Avestruces**, outside Bayaguana, 30 miles (18.6 km) due north of Boca Chica. The Ostrich Farm breeds these flightless birds, which hail from Africa (owner Jaime Vargas imported 100 ostriches from Zimbabwe) and can grow to a staggering 8 feet (2.4 m) in height and average about 250 pounds (114 kg). Although ostensibly an agro-ecotouristic project, the birds are intended for sale as meat, and their skins are used for Hermes handbags and the suede-like leather in Mercedes Benz cars. The facility also offers horseback riding and has a kids' play area. Even if the finca is closed, you can stand at the fence and the big birds will approach. The finca is 1.5 miles (2.4 km) along a dirt road that is signed about 1 mile (1.6 km) west of Bayaguana. **Colonial Tours** (809-523-6719 in Boca Chica; www.colonialtours.com.do) includes the farm on its Gran Safaris from Juan Dolio. Admission: RD$150, RD$250 with lunch.

scuttled in 1984 to create an artificial reef. Fishes stream in and around three other wrecks, including the *Capitán Alsina*. At least two dozen other dive sites are accessible in the bay.

Ashore, a narrow strip of beach is used by low-income families. And the tiny **Museo Ceremonial La Caleta** displays archaeological finds, including a Taíno grave with skeletons exposed in fetal position.

In Boca Chica, the following scuba outfitters offer trips: **Caribbean Divers** (809-854-3483; www.caribbeandivers.de; Avenida Duarte 28) and **Treasure Divers** (809-523-5320; www.treasuredivers.de), at Don Juan Beach Resort.

Nightlife

Narrow, traffic-thronged Calle Duarte (running parallel to and one block in from the beach) has the hog's banquet of nightspots, most of which are variants on a no-frills, crank-up-the-volume bar-disco theme. The street is closed off to traffic after sundown, when restaurants and bars set out their tables. The early evening atmosphere is pleasant. *Bachata* and merengue riffs fill the air. And families dine alfresco. Around 10 PM the sex workers rouse themselves from daytime slumber as the late-night crowd takes over and restaurants begin to shutter up. Calle Duarte begins to feel like a block party as the decibels crank up from the bars that suddenly seem as if they're shoulder to shoulder. The discos don't begin to get in the groove until midnight. By 1 AM local off-duty workers begin to filter in and the discos start to really warm up, reaching their zenith around 2 AM.

Venues change with remarkable frequency. What's hot one year may be gone the next, or enjoy nothing more than a season of popularity before the next-door neighbor gets hip.

Stick to the main streets at night. Even the beach is no place to be wandering after dark. Not least, local hookers have a habit of displaying their wares to tempt passing males.

Disco Hamaca (809-523-4611; Calle Duarte 26; admission US$10) In the Oasis Hamaca Beach Resort, this is the class act in town for those seeking a modern, no-hassles dance spot. It has a dress code. The entry fee includes all domestic drinks. In high season, entry is often restricted to hotel guests only.

Shopping

Calle Duarte has plenty of small stores selling the usual souvenirs, from batiks, wood carvings, and Haitian artwork, to rum and cigars. Itinerant jewelry vendors patrol the beach with large briefcases carried around their necks, like the old cinema cigarette salesgirls of old. Hair-braiders work the beach, too. You'll be expected to haggle: Prices are usually inflated to take the to-and-fro over pricing into account.

Food Purveyors

Punto Gourmet Italia (No telephone; Plaza Dareri, Calle Duarte 58) This gem—a *genuine* Italian deli—makes you do a double take, transporting you metaphorically to New York's Lower East Side. Delicious sandwiches are made to order from a superb selection of cheeses, sausages, deli meats, etc., plus savory ingredients you won't find in any other local *mercado*. Or sit down for a San Daniele ham roll with a glass of Chianti, or even a dry sparkling white wine from Valdobbiadene. Open: daily 8–5.

Supermercado Boca Chica (Calle Duarte at Juanico García) The largest supermarket in town, if it's not here you won't find it in Boca Chica (except perhaps at Punto Gourmet Italia). Open: Mon. through Sat. 9–8, Sun. 9–6.

Good to Know About

The Ministry of Tourism **tourist information office** (809-523-5106; between Calle Duarte and Calle San Rafael), upstairs in Plaza Boca Chica, is not much use; at last visit it had *no* literature whatsoever. But, hey, you never know! Open Mon. through Fri. 8–5.

    Politur (809-523-5120; bocachica@politur.gov.do), the tourist police, is in the same plaza; it's supposedly open 24/7.

JUAN DOLIO AND SAN PEDRO DE MACORÍS

About 12 miles (19 km) east of Boca Chica and spread out along 3 miles (4.8 km) of shoreline, the beach resort of Juan Dolio has never quite taken off. It was launched in the 1980s, when developers pumped in millions of dollars to create a Caribbean Riviera from scratch. Several resorts went up alongside towering condo units. Then the economic slump of 2001 knocked the wind out its sails, leaving many buildings unfinished. Despite an undeniable air of desuetude, Juan Dolio and the neighboring beach village of Guayacanes (immediately west) are slated for a deluxe pick-me-up if the proposed billion dollar Costa Blanca development announced in March 2008 comes to fruition (it includes a huge residential complex, an international tennis center, a conference center, a 100-berth mega-yacht marina, and the Greg Norman-designed Signatura Golf Course).

    For now, Juan Dolio is fine if all you want is a quiet, relaxing vacation and are not seeking heaps of nightlife or things to do. Most visitors, however, check into one of the four self-contained all-inclusive hotels.

    Much of the hinterland around Juan Dolio is smothered in lime green sugarcane fields. The port town of San Pedro de Macorís (population 195,000), about 6 miles (9.6 km) east of Juan Dolio, was founded in 1822 on the east bank of the Río Higuano and grew wealthy as a sugar-exporting center, with elegant mansions and wooden homes. It was ravaged by Hurricane Georges in 1998 but is still worth a half-day's visit for its buildings of architectural note, though many others are neglected and crumbling. Its biggest claim to fame, though, is as the birthplace for many of the republic's top baseball players. It's also an important industrial city, and the Universidad Central del Este has a renowned medical school. Entering town from the west, visitors are welcomed by a surrealist metal monument (Avenida Circunvalación and Avenida Francisco Domínguez Charro) by José Ignacio Morales—El Artístico—representing the town's four principal symbols: baseball players, *guloyas* (*carnaval* performers), a crab, and a steam train.

Getting There and Around

For budget travelers, **Expreso Covacha** buses (*guaguas*) depart Santo Domingo from Parque Enriquillo (Calles José Martí and Caracas) every 20 minutes, 6 AM—7 PM; in San Pedro, you can board at Parque Central. These buses (and those traveling between Santo Domingo and La Romana) pass by Juan Dolio; you can alight or flag down the bus on the Bulevár—you can stand pretty much anywhere and wave one down.

Taxis await custom outside the tourist hotels. You can also catch one in Guayacanes from the taxi stand on Carretera Vieja just east of Hotel Flor di Loto.

In Juan Dolio, the Carretera Vieja (Carretera Local farther east)—which slows traffic down with speed bumps—runs along the shore (in places it weaves around the all-inclusives) and has most of the hotels, shops, restaurants, etc., concentrated at the east end of Juan Dolio in the modern section known as Villas del Mar. Carretera 3 (colloquially called the Bulevar, or boulevard), the main street, runs parallel, inland. You can walk almost everywhere, and most hotels have bicycles for guest loan.

Lodging

The scene is dominated by four large all-inclusives, but smaller hotels and guest houses are scattered along the beachfront drive. (Hopefully the deluxe Maxim Bungalows—yes, of *Maxim* magazine fame—will finally open; the project was stalled as this book went to press; www.maximbungalows.com.). Meanwhile, in 2008 the former Playa Esmeralda Beach Resort, at Playa Guayacanes became an All Roses Club serving that company's Italian package vacationers.

BARCELÓ CAPELLA BEACH RESORT
809-526-1080
fax: 809-526-1088
www.barcelocapella.com
Carretera Nueva, Playa Juan Dolio

This huge Spanish-run, four-star all-inclusive sits in lush grounds studded with reflective pools where flamingoes strut their stuff, while peacocks patrol the lawns. It's a handsome property edging up to the beach and centered on a serpentine pool (one of two pools). You can soak in a Jacuzzi by night after a day playing tennis or minigolf or scuba diving. It has a choice of four restaurants, plus canned cabaret entertainment and a nightclub. A kids' club takes care of amusing the youngsters. The 497 rooms come in four types, including suites, all stocked with cable TVs, mini-bars, and in-room safes, and modestly gracious furnishings. It has its faults though, including rocky ocean waters. $$—$$$.

BARCELÓ TALANQUERA BEACH RESORT
809-526-1510

Swimming pool at Costa Cariba Coral, Juan Dolio

fax: 809-526-2408
www.barcelotalanquera.com
Carretera Local, Playa Juan Dolio

I prefer this four-star all-inclusive resort over the neighboring Barceló Capella. Partly because the rose-pink architecture and decor appeal, partly for the lush landscaping, and partly because with only 335 rooms, it's also more intimate. And the beach here is more attractive, with fewer rocks in the ocean. Facilities include three swimming pools, a gourmet French restaurant (one of five restaurants), disco, and lots of water sports and activities. While the Capella appeals to families, the Talanquera draws a younger, party-hearty crowd, including plenty of Dominicans who flood the place on weekends. $$–$$$.

COSTA CARIBE CORAL
809-526-2244
fax: 809-526-3141
www.coralhotels.com
Carretera Local, Juan Dolio

This handsome all-inclusive on Playa Juan Dolio has been through several incarnations, most recently as a Hilton. Newly renovated in 2006 and now non-smoking throughout, it's an appealing mid-priced option especially suited to families. Its elegant airy atrium lobby features a pink and black marble floor and columns, and contemporary mahogany furnishings. I like the vast sundeck of natural flagstone (landscaped with water cascades), thatched bar, open-air theater, and the Spanish-hacienda-style Ambar restaurant. And the 400 guest rooms on five levels are now graciously appointed and well equipped. Amenities include water sports, three swimming pools, and a casino. $$–$$$.

EMBASSY SUITES LOS MARLINS
809-688-9999
fax: 809-526-1130
http://embassysuites1.hilton.com
Autopista del Este, Juan Dolio

Set on the Metro Country Club, this country club hotel is about 1 mile (1.6 km) inland from the beach: A shuttle service delivers you to the hotel's beach club on a palm-shaded, man-made beach with its own swimming pool and restaurant. And the main hotel has its own large lagoon-shaped pool. Being an Embassy Suites it has an institutional hotel feel, but it's a good enough option if you're into tennis, or a round of golf at the club's Los Marlins Golf Course or the adjacent Guavaberry Golf Course. Accommodations are all two-bedroom suites with kitchenettes and regal contemporary furniture, plus Internet modems. It has a kids' club but is not really suited to families. $$–$$$.

HOTEL FIOR DI LOTO
809-526-1146
fax: 809-526-3332
www.fiordilotohotel.com
Calle Central 517, Playa Juan Dolio

A no-frills option for independent budget-minded travelers, this modern, rambling guest house inland of Playa Guayacanes has 23 rooms of varying sizes. Decor is very matter-of-fact and differs from room to room, but all have cable TV (some are air-conditioned; others have ceiling fans only). Mara, the Italian owner, is into Indian decor (found throughout the hotel) and offers yoga and martial arts classes in the third-floor gym. A tremendous bargain. $.

HOWARD JOHNSON SAN PEDRO DE MACORÍS
809-529-2100
fax: 809-529-9239
www.hojo.com
Avenida Gaston F. Deligne (Malecon), San Pedro de Macorís

Just what you expect a HoJo to be: Charmless yet with essential facilities, including a restaurant and swimming pool, plus amenities from cable TVs to irons and ironing boards in the soulless bedrooms. The seafront locale is a bonus. Take an upper-storey room for the best views. If you must stay in San Pedro de Macorís, one night at the HoJo is fine. But two nights? $–$$.

Dining

Pickings are slim! Once you leave the all-inclusive resorts (which sell day and/or night passes granting non-guests temporary access), your options are limited to a half dozen or so fairly simple options dispersed along the beachfront road. My favorites are:

DELI SWISS

809-526-1226
Carretera Vieja 338, Playa Guayacanes
Cuisine: Seafood.

This gourmet treat is hidden away off the beach road in the village of Guayacanes. It's not easy to find, but the effort is well rewarded as here the owner—a former White House chef, apparently—serves up gourmet daily specials, mostly seafoods using only the freshest ingredients. There's always a meat dish, and pasta too. The lobster with garlic is a favorite. The atmosphere is romantic and intimate, and wine lovers will appreciate the huge list of labels. Open: Daily 11–9. $–$$.

RESTAURANTE EL CONCÓN

809-562-2652
Carretera Nueva, Juan Dolio
Cuisine: Dominican.

I love this simple thatched open-air restaurant on Playa Real—actually a stone's throw from the sands, and lacking beach views, alas, from the main restaurant (but it does also have a funky beachfront patio under the shade of trees). Still, it's quite charming. The menu highlights Italian and Caribbean seafood dishes such as *filete de dorado al ajillo* (garlic mahi mahi), and fresh catch of the day in coconut sauce, both for about US$10. Great deal! Open: Daily 11–11. $–$$.

ROBBY MAR

809-529-4926
Avenida Francisco Domínguez Charro 35, San Pedro de Macorís
Cuisine: Seafood.

A stone's throw from Iglesia San Pedro Apóstol, this waterfront restaurant is a good value. Choose from lobster (served any of a half dozen ways) and other local seafood to filet mignon, including with mushroom sauce or wrapped in bacon. And Tony, the owner, offers a good choice of wines. On hot days you'll want to stay in the air-conditioned interior; otherwise opt for the waterfront patio. Open: Daily 9 AM–midnight. $–$$.

Attractions, Parks, and Recreation

The sands at Juan Dolio are a triptych—actually a series of beaches, dominated west to east by **Playa Guayacanes**, **Playa Juan Dolio**, and **Playa Real**, the latter running into the modern Villas del Mar section The sands aren't quite as attractive as at Boca Chica, nor the waters as conducive to wading due to a profligacy of rocks—neoprene booties are a good idea.

Still, farther out there's some great diving. **Neptuno Dive** (www.neptunodive.com) has outlets in the Barceló Capella (809-526-2005) and Barceló Talanquera (809-526-2923). It runs trips to 15 dive sites, including the wreck of the *Tanya V,* sank off Playa Juan Dolio in 1999.

Iglesia San Pedro Apóstol, San Pedro de Macoris

Golfers can take their pick of the **Guavaberry Golf Country Club** (809-333-4653; www.guavaberrygolf.com), a par 72, Gary Player-designed course with a golf academy; or the **Los Marlins Golf Course** (809-526-3315; www.metrocountry.com; Boulevard de Juan Dolio and Autovia del Este), designed by Charles Ankrom, and also with a golf academy.

The Guavaberry Golf Country Club has an equestrian center.

CATEDRAL SAN PEDRO APÓSTOL

Avenida Independencia, corner of Avenida Francisco Domínguez Charro, San Pedro de Macorís.
Open: Daily 9–5
Admission: Free

San Pedro de Macorís's neo-Gothic cathedral was erected in 1911 to replace a predecessor, and is the fifth in a series of ill-fated predecessors felled by fire or earthquake. Its gleaming whitewashed facade is topped by a crenellated bell tower with blood red steeple. The Romanesque doorway is guarded by gargoyles. Step inside to admire the exquisite stained-glass windows, two-tone marble floor, and lovely Gothic mahogany altar.

A monument to national heroes Juan Pablo Duarte and fellow compatriots pins the **Plazoleta Padres de la Patria**, to the fore.

CUEVA DE LAS MARAVILLAS

809-951-9009

Carretera 3, Ramón Santana, 10 miles (16 km) east of San Pedro de Macorís

Open: Tues. through Sun. 9–5

Admission: RD$200, including an obligatory guide

This underground cavern is a must-see on any visit to the DR. The complex comprises several huge grottoes and caverns dripping with limestone formations, as well as the Espejo de Agua—a stupendously beautiful pool overhung with sheets of stalactites. Most of the galleries are off-limits to visitors to protect them for posterity. But enough can be seen to more than impress thanks to a sensational recent rehab that has put in place 273 yards (250 m) of well-groomed concrete paths with motion-sensor lighting. Besides the beautiful stalagmites and stalactites, the highlights are the pre-Columbian galleries depicting human and animal figures. In all, 472 Taíno pictographs and 19 petroglyphs have been counted. Guides give enlightening spiels. And an elevator grants wheelchair access. Bats flit about overhead. Blind fish swim around in underground pools. And an endemic frog species inhabits the moist entrance passage. A museum was planned for a 2009 opening. No photographs permitted.

INGENIO PORVENIR

809-526-7311

Avenida Circunvalación and Calle Porvenir, San Pedro de Macorís.

Open: Mon. through Fri. 9–noon and 2–5:30, by appointment (24 hours notice required), January to August only.

Admission: Free

The largest *central* (sugar mill) in the region, this mill was built in 1879. Although partially modernized, it seems to ache with penury as the giant grinding wheels crush the cane (it processes up to 2,500 tons daily). Hurricane Georges did much damage, and the mill was upgraded and reopened in 2006. The tour provides a fascinating insight into how sugarcane stalks are processed into molasses and sugar.

An Architectural Tour of San Pedro de Macorís

Alas, the main sites of interest are fairly spread out. If you don't mind walking, no problem, as the city core has dozens of Victorian-era buildings of architectural note. Let serendipity be your guide. Begin at **Iglesia San Pedro Apóstol** (see main entry). On its south side, note the timeworn **Ayuntamiento**, the late-19th-century town hall, now the town library (*biblioteca*). About 109 yards (100 m) south on the waterfront stands the old Port Authority building: today it's the 1906 **Centro Cultural Fermoselle** (no telephone; Avenida Francisco Domínguez Charro at 10 de Septiembre; free), hosting musical and literary events and local art.

Heading east from Iglesia San Pedro Apóstol along Calle Ramón Duarte brings you to the **Benemerito Cuerpo de Bomberos** (Calle Duarte 46), the 1903 fire station in a most unlikely building topped by huge water tank and a polygonal belvedere with gingerbread decoration. Ask to climb the metal spiral staircase for a view over town. Two blocks north, **Parque Duarte**—the triangular main square at the junction with Avenida 27 de Febrero—is pinned by a bust of the national hero. The most remarkable building in town is the **Antiguo Edificio Morey** (corner of Calles Duarte and Sánchez) with a three-tiered rotunda turret graced by enormous vertical stained-glass windows.

Nightlife

Juan Dolio is not party-hearty central. Most of the nightlife happens in the all-inclusive hotels. No problem. Most sell night passes giving you access to the bars, cabarets, and discos—all-inclusive. Otherwise, head to the **Chocolate Bar** (Calle Central 127), especially on Friday, when the live singers put on quite a stage show and you can dance to merengue until you fall down with exhaustion; it also has pool tables.

The **Coral Costa Caribe Casino** (809-526-2244; www.coralhotels.com/costa_caribe/casino.htm) has video games plus blackjack, poker, roulette, and Texas Hold'em; it's open 8 PM–4 AM.

Food Purveyors

Juan Dolio locals do their shopping at **Naito Gift Shop Mini Mart** (Carretera Local at Entrada a Los Conucos; open 8:15–7), a mini-supermarket in Guayacanes. It has most staples plus fresh produce.

Weekly and Annual Events

Festival de San Pedro, held in September (formerly in late June), is San Pedro de Macorís's annual and highly unique *carnaval*. It's renowned islandwide for its representative figure, Dom Pacheco, who symbolizes a union of the various immigrant groups of the zone. The chief influence is that of *cocolos* (see the sidebar), English-speaking Afro-Caribbean immigrants who introduced their own music and dance styles.

San Pedro de Macorís also springs to life each October through February, baseball season, when *beísbol* fever sweeps town. Games are played at the 8,000-seat **Estadio Tetelo Vargas** (809-246-4077; www.estrellasorientales.com.do; Avenida Circunvalación at Carretera Mella), which hosts the home games of the Estrellas Orientales. Tickets (*taquillas*) cost RD$40 to RD$300.

Cocolos

During the late 19th century, migrants from the English-speaking islands of the Lesser Antilles were imported to work the canefields around San Pedro de Macorís, where they mixed with Haitian Francophone populations. They brought their own music and dance forms, as well as their surnames— Henderson, Simcox, Wilson, etc—and vernacular architecture. Their descendants are known as *cocolos*, a term apparently derived from the French *coco l'eau* (coconut water); originally considered a racial slur, it is today a term of endearment for the black Anglophone culture.

In the Dominican Republic, these Anglophone creoles evolved their own dance groups, performing to the music of bass drum, kettle drum, flute, and triangle. Performers don colorful African-derived costumes adorned with beads, ribbons, and mirrors. Most of the dances, such as *danza de padre invierno* (dance of Father Winter) and *danza el cocodril* (dance of the crocodile) are theatrical good-versus-evil masquerades—including the tale of David and Goliath (Goluya)—reminiscent of those once performed by English medieval roving troubadours.

The cocolos' Teatro Danzante Los Guloyas keeps the folkloric traditions alive. In 2005, the group was declared a UNESCO Living World Cultural Heritage, which honors Masterpieces of the Oral and Intangible Heritage of Humanity. They can be seen during the Festival de San Pedro, *carnaval*, and especially during the Christmas period culminating on January 6.

Good to Know About

Ilsa Internet Cafe Bar (809-526-2777; http://ilsainterprisesa.info; Carretera Local), in Plaza de la Luna, just east of the Costa Coral Caribe resort, is for multi-tasking. It has Internet and international phone service and acts as a general tour information center.

Plaza Turística Dr. Correa (Carretera Nueva, about 0.25 mile (400 m) east of Barceló Capella resort), in Villas del Mar, hosts a **Banco Popular** (809-526-2777) with an ATM.

There's a local tourism office in San Pedro de Macorís (809-529-2831; Calle Domínguez Charzo 8), and a **Politur** (1-200-3500; juandolio@politur.gov.do), tourist police, office in Juan Dolio.

SAN CRISTÓBAL AND VICINITY

Some 17 miles (28 km) west of Santo Domingo, this sprawling, chaotic, industrial city straddles the Río Haina. It was the headquarters of the first Congress following independence, and the first Dominican Constitution was signed here on November 6, 1844. However, the town is most famous as the birthplace of Dictator-President Rafael Trujillo, born here in 1891. He later renamed San Cristóbal after himself and built several edifices to his vainglory. The forested hills north of town are riddled with caverns containing the largest galleries of pre-Columbian pictographs in the Caribbean.

San Cristóbal lies about 8 miles (14 km) inland of the coast. On weekends, local families head to **Playa Najayo** and, farther west, **Playa Palenque**, two shingly beaches accessed by a convoluted lacework of roads. The beaches get noisy on weekends, when a series of bars pump out music to outcompete the neighbors.

Getting There

Buses depart Parque Enriquillo (Avenida José Martí and Calle Caracas), in Santo Domingo, every 30 minutes for Parque Central, in San Cristóbal.

Lodging

HOTEL NAJAYO BEACH
809-850-5508
Carretera Najayo-Palenque, Playa Najayo
E-mail: hotelnajayo@yahoo.com

This pleasant, no-frills, family-run hotel overlooks the sands and Caribbean waters. Don't expect any frills in the 18 sparsely furnished, air-conditioned rooms (some are Junior Suites), which are dark due to small windows; at least they have high ceilings and spacious bathrooms (but with tiny showers). Small cable TVs stand atop refrigerators. It has an air-conditioned restaurant, and has palm-shaded, 24-hour secure parking. $–$$.

HOTEL PLAYA PALENQUE
809-243-2525
fax: 809-243-2500
www.hotel-playa-palenque.net
E-mail: dra.elexia@hotmail.com
Carretera Najayo-Palenque, Playa Palenque

Beísbol Fever!

Beísbol (or *pelota*) is as much an obsession in the Dominican Republic as it is in the United States. More so, in fact. Baseball was introduced to the DR by Cubans (who learned it from U.S. sailors) fleeing the Ten Years War (1868–1878). The island's first professional team—the Tigres de Licey—was formed in 1906, and the first league was formed 15 years later.

In 1956, Ozzie Virgil became the first Dominican to play Major League baseball in the United States. He was followed by Juan Marichal and the three Alou brothers, Felipe, Jesús, and Mateo. Many aspiring young Dominicans have since fulfilled their dreams of making it to the big leagues. In 2007, the 30 big league teams signed 511 Dominicans (for an average bonus of $65,821). Many grew up around San Pedro de Macorís, where a sign on the outskirts of town welcomes visitors with the words: THE CITY WHICH HAS GIVEN THE MOST MAJOR LEAGUERS TO THE WORLD.

The City of Shortstops' most famous son is Sammy Sosa (1968–). Like many successful Dominican baseball stars, he started out life shining shoes and swinging at a makeshift ball with a makeshift bat. For poverty-stricken boys in the *bateys* (impoverished worker hamlets tied to the canefields), baseball is seen as about the only possible ticket to a better life. No wonder they practice with a passion unknown in North America. Lacking equipment, they make up for it in fierce determination . . . and talent. No wonder the countryside of the South Central DR is crawling with *buscones* (scouters) scouring canefields, city streets, and dusty sandlots in search of promising talent. The flow goes both ways. Twenty-five major league teams have training camps in the DR—the home of Winter Baseball.

Today the Dominican league (809-563-5085; www.lidom.com) consists of six teams: the Leones de Escojido and Tigres del Licey, from Santo Domingo; Estrellas Orientales (San Pedro de Macoris); Aguilas del Cibao and Gigantes del Cibao (Santiago de los Caballeros); and Azucareros del Este (La Romana). The teams play 50 games each, with the top four teams advancing to a round-robin playoff. The two top teams then meet in a best-of-five series to determine the league champion, which represents the country in the Caribbean World Series, involving the *campeones* of the Dominican Republic, Puerto Rico, Mexico, and Venezuela.

Run by an elderly Swiss gent, Peter Wegmüller and his Dominican wife Maria, this two-storey beachfront hotel has a lovely garden with a pool and thatched restaurant amid palms and fruit trees. The nine rooms are Spartan but spacious and spotlessly clean. Live jazz is hosted—a great addition! Alas, the website is in German only. $.

Dining

FELA'S PLACE
809-288-2124
Calle General Leger 55, San Cristóbal
Cuisine: Dominican.

No restaurants stand out in town, but this simple restaurant is a good bet for *comida criolla*—Dominican fare—such as fried chicken or roast pork with rice and beans. Just seeking snacks? They try a *pastelito en hoja* (pastry in paper)—empanadas stuffed with meat and veggies. Open: Daily 8 AM–midnight. $.

Attractions, Parks, and Recreation

San Cristóbal's downtown attractions concentrate on three squares. The main square is leafy, but **Parque Colón** (Avenida Constitución between Calles Padre Borbon and Mella), has a relatively unremarkable church on the north side; the **Palacio Municipal** (town hall) on the northwest; and the **Casa de la Cultura** (809-528-4929; Monday through Friday 9–noon) on the south side; the latter hosts *peñas* (literary and musical soirées). **Parque Piedra Viva** (Avenida Constitución between Calles Duarte and Doctor Baez), two blocks south of Parque Colón, hosts the mustard-colored, eclectic, almost Byzantine **Iglesia Nuestra Señora de la Consolación**, a fanciful church erected in 1946 by Trujillo and featuring fine interior murals by Spanish artist José Vela Zanetti. Note the winged angels on the steeple, and the empty tomb where Trujillo was briefly laid to rest following his death (his remains are now entombed in Paris).

Two blocks east of Parque Colón, circular and traffic-thronged **Plaza a los Constituyentes** (Carretera Sánchez and Avenida Libertad) features the **Monumento 6 de Noviembre** to honor the Congreso Constituyentes—Constituent Assembly—that met here in 1844 to formulate the nation's Constitution.

CASA DE CAOBA
Off Carretera a Hato Damas/La Toma, 0.9 mile (1.5 km) north of Autopista 6 de Noviembre

Another Trujillo creation, the House of Mahogany also sits atop a hill, this one on the north side of town. Built of concrete in 1938 in stark Modernist fashion, the three-storey mansion was lined virtually throughout with mahogany. Alas, it has lain in ruins for years and is in a sad state of disrepair (most of the wood has long gone). Termite-eaten wood lies in piles on the floor. For a tip, the *custodio* (guard) will let you roam. It's not signed: turn left at the rusting wrought-iron gates beside roadside water storage tanks at Urbanización Cerros de San Cristóbal.

CASTILLO DEL CERRO
Calle Luperón, off Calle Sánchez

Perched atop a hill on the southwest side of town, the Castle on the Hill was built in 1947 by

Iglesia Nuestra Señora de la Consolación, San Cristobal

Trujillo as a private mansion high above town. The semicircular, four-storey, concrete Art Deco mansion was lavishly adorned with black-and-white-checkered marble floors, carved mahogany doors, gold-leaf tile work, murals by Vela Zanetti, and numerous five-star decorations—a none-too-subtle reference to Trujillo's rank as five-star general. It stood abandoned and ruined for several decades. It was restored in 2006, and reopened as a school for prison guards—the **Escuela Nacional Penitenciaria**. It can be viewed from the outside only.

RESERVA ANTROPOLÓGICA EL POMIER
809-472-4204 ext. 223
Sector Villa Piedra, Los Cacaitos; 6 miles (10 km) north of San Cristóbal
Open: Daily 8–5
Admission: RD$50

I don't know whether to weep or to cry when my thoughts turn to these magnificent caverns, whose neglect by the government is a national disgrace. The complex of 55 caves in the hills north of town have earned El Pomier the title the Lascaux of the Caribbean. These caves were used as a ritual site by Taíno. With more than 6,000 pictographs and more than 500 petroglyphs dating back more than 2,000 years, no other cave system in the region comes close in archaeological import. In fact, Cueva Uno (the only cave currently open to

Pre-Columbian Cave Art

As a Stone Age people, it's easy to imagine the Taíno dwelling in caves à la Fred Flintstone. Wrong! The Taíno considered caves sacred portals to the spirit world, not humble abodes. Thus, only *behiques* (shamans) and other high-ranking community figures were allowed to enter. Depictions of fearsome gods guarded the entrances. In fact, the Taíno's creation myth centers on caves, where their *opia* (ancestor spirits) lived and emerged solely at night to eat *jobos*, a small plum-like fruit. One night, the spirits were so consumed eating the tasty *jobos* that they were still outside when the sun came up, turning them into human beings.

No wonder, then, that caves were used as centers of spiritual expression and as classrooms for spiritual training. Hispaniola boasts scores of caves containing pictographs (rock paintings) and petroglyphs (rock carvings) dating back more than 1,500 years and perhaps as far back as 5,000 years in some cases. A majority of the images represent *zemis*—spiritual beings—often shown 6.5 feet (2 m) tall alongside representations of shamans. Boiyanel, the rain god, is usually depicted with tears streaming down his face. Juracán, the mighty god of storms is here, too. And Yucahú, the god of cassava, the Taíno's main food crop.

Some caves, such as those of Reserva Antropológica El Pomier (with more than 6,000 images) and Cueva de Las Maravillas, have vast panels crowded with symbolic figures etched onto dripstones and limestone walls. Frogs and lizards are represented. So, too, bats and birds. Copulating dogs and images of women in childbirth are among the figures clearly representing fertility. Single human heads are also common, often depicted with two dots for eyes and a half circle mouth, like a Smiley Face. Other, more matter-of-fact images depict everyday items, such as the *cibucán* (the woven tube used to squeeze poisonous juices from yuca). Pictographs in Cueva Guacara Taína even show human slaves trussed to poles.

The crude pictographs were daubed with shredded-end sticks using paints made from charcoals, guano, and various clays mixed with animal fats. Like precious paintings in an air-conditioned gallery, they have been preserved through millennia thanks to the caverns' perfectly cool temperatures and humidity. A depiction of a Spanish galleon among the 1,200 pictographs in Cueva José María, in Parque Nacional del Este, presaged the extinction of a race.

Guide illuminating Taino pictographs, Parque Nacional Los Haitises

visit) has 590 paintings—more pictographs than all the other sites on the island combined. Lizards. Bats. Representations of the rain god. Copulating birds and other fertility symbols etched as if by Paul Klee or Wilfredo Lam. While all are naive, they're also remarkable, not least for having been painted eons ago with a mixture of animal fat and charcoal.

Alas, although declared a National Monument in 1969, later incorporated into the National Protected Areas System in 1993 as the Reserva Antropológica de las Cuevas de Borbón, the caves continue to be systematically abused by mining companies. Only 11 caves lie within the reserve; the others are within a huge, privately owned limestone quarry, where three companies have been granted concessions by the Dirección General de Minería (43 caves were later removed from the protected list). Explosive blasts have already destroyed several caves. Many others have been severely damaged.

Despite a campaign to elevate the caves to a unique status as Capital Prehistórica de las Antillas and as a UNESCO World Heritage Site, the destruction continues. The irreparable damage is unconscionable!

The caves also shelter seven species of bats. And a scientific study in 1995 revealed eight new endemic species of fauna.

Facilities: In 2003, Cuevo Uno was rehabilitated with concrete paths and sensor-powered spotlights, and modern toilets. However, development ceased in 2004 and the site—which remains virtually unvisited—still lacks a welcome center and other facilities adequate to its importance. Bring a flashlight.

Getting There: If driving, from downtown take Avenida Constitución north towards La Toma, where the caves are signed at a T-junction. Turn left. The road winds uphill to the mine; turn right and drive through the mining complex; the caves are not signed and you may need to ask to negotiate the maze of dirt tracks. Budget travelers with time on their hands can take a *guagua* pickup truck, departing when full from Calle Juanto María Montez

Drive to San José de Ocoa

To escape the heat of the lowlands, you can turn north off Carretera 2 at Las Carreras (13 miles—21 km—west of Baní) for a delightful drive into the foothills of the Cordillera Central. You'll arrive at the mountain village of San José de Ocoa, known for its *balnearios*—swimming complexes fed by natural springs. Several have simple hotels attached and draw Dominican families on weekends, when the *balnearios* are packed and noisy.

In San José you can turn left at the Y-fork in town and take the brutally challenging dirt road that leads to Parque Nacional Valle Nuevo and, eventually to Constanza, in the Cordillera Central. A 4WD is an absolute prerequisite! Less adventurous souls can turn right at the fork and follow the lovely valley of the Río Nizao. Gorgeous scenery unfolds.

You should aim for **Rancho Cascada** (809-890-2332; www.ranchocascada.com; Las Avispas, 15 miles (24 km) northeast of San José de Ocoa), an activity center on the far side of the river—you can ford or take a hand-hauled funicular! It has basic accommodations, serves filling meals under thatch, and offers guided hikes, mountain bike and motocross trips, horseback rides, and high-mountain hikes using hundreds of miles of mule trails (including Pico Duarte and Parque Nacional Valle Nuevo). Plus, it has canoeing and kayaking on the Río Nizao and Bahía de las Calderas. The slopes hereabouts are farmed in coffee, and Rancho Cascada arranges coffee-farm tours. Simple accommodations are offered in cabins made of river stone.

Guaguas operate to San José de Ocoa from Baní.

Dunas de Bani   The Dominican Republic Ministry of Tourism

and Calle Francisco Peynado, four blocks north and three blocks west of Parque Colón. **Tours, Treks, Trips & Travel** (809-867-8884; www.4tdomrep.com/education.html) offers tours.

Good to Know About

There's a **tourism bureau** (809-528-1844 or 528-3533, Avenida Constitución 25; open Mon. through Fri. 8–4) in the Gobernación, or town hall, on the corner of Calle Modesto. It's very meagerly stocked, so don't expect literature.

BANÍ AND VICINITY

Worth a stop while passing through, the town of Baní—straddling Carretera 2, about 20.5 miles (33 km) west of San Cristóbal and just 3 miles (5 km) inland of the coast—was founded in 1764 by immigrants from the Canary Islands. Later, it was the birthplace of Máximo Gómez, who rose through the ranks of the Spanish army before settling in Cuba, where he came out of retirement and led Cuba's insurgent rebels to victory in the Wars of Independence. The relatively prosperous town is surrounded by canefields.

Besides Gómez's birthplace and a quaint little church, Baní (supposedly a Taíno word meaning abundance of water) is gateway to Las Salinas and the Bahía de Las Calderas, with tantalizing sands that appeal.

Salt works at Las Salinas

Getting There and Getting Around

Guaguas (mini-buses) for Baní depart Santo Domingo from near Parque Enriquillo (Calle José Martí and Calle Caracas; every 20 minutes, 4 AM–8 PM; 90 minutes), and from Parque Colón in San Cristóbal, where they can also be flagged down on Autopista Sánchez or Autopista 6 de Noviembre.

Carretera Sánchez (the main highway to/from Santo Domingo) runs through the center of town and passes Parque Central (Avenida Presidente Billini and Avenida Favio Heredia) in Baní. *Guaguas* for San Cristóbal and Santo Domingo depart from here.

Lodging

HOTEL CARIBANI
809-522-3871
fax: 809-522-3872
Calle Sánchez 12, Baní

A reasonable, no-frills option for budget hounds, this hotel enjoys a handy location just one block west of Parque Central. The rooms are clean and quite comfortable, but try to see several before making a choice, as some get little light. All have cable TVs and hot water showers. It has a restaurant, and there's a pleasant pizzería next door. $.

HOTEL LAS SALINAS

809-346-8855
Calle Puerto Hermoso 7, Las Salinas
E-mail: salinas@hotelsalinas.com

The only show in town happens to be a pretty good choice for folks who prefer character over all else. Sitting over the waters of Bahía de Las Calderas, this informal, four-storey hotel draws sailors to its moorings, informal restaurant-bar (serving sandwiches, burgers, pastas, and delicious seafood), and huge free-form pool with a tiny palm island, beach walk-in, and thatched swim-up bar. The 16 air-conditioned rooms vary, although all are colorfully albeit simply appointed. A top-floor suite with metal spiral staircase and loft bedroom costs the same price as the smaller rooms (alas, it had only cold water in the small and slippery tub-shower during my stay). A better, albeit costlier, bet are the hotel's six villas across the street. The bar, which hosts occasional live music, operates on an honor system. Bring insect repellent. $–$$.

Attractions, Parks, and Recreation

BAHÍA DE LAS CALDERAS

17.4 miles (28 km) southwest of Baní

This deep, flask-shaped, jade-blue bay enclosed by a narrow hooked peninsula is lined by

Shoveling salt at Las Salinas

lovely but as-yet-undeveloped beaches with a lush mountain backdrop. The loveliest beach is white-sand **Playa Los Corbanitos**, on the north shore. It's set in a large cove hemmed in by mangroves and offers fine snorkeling in turquoise waters. A mega-resort (www.loscorbanitos.com) is slated to be built, with two golf courses and a marina. The turnoff to the beach is in the village of Salado Buey. If you continue straight, however, you'll arrive at **Playa Palmar de Ocoa**, another lovely beach where the nation's elite have vacation homes overlooking a deep-water bay—the **Bahía de Ocoa**.

The main draw is the off-the-beaten-track fishing village of **Las Salinas**, on the narrow isthmus that encloses the bay. To windward rise huge wind-sculpted sand dunes—**Las Dunas**. The taupe sands are supposedly the highest dunes in the Caribbean. It's hot work trudging across them. You'll have only lizards and goats for company as you traipse to the summit for superlative views. The entrance gate is opposite Maricultura Caribeña, o.6 mile (1 km) east of Las Salinas village. More interesting are the *salinas*—the salt pans—that spread out immediately west of the village; here coal black Haitians can be seen scooping up huge crystals, sparkling like diamonds from a Spanish treasure ship. Otherwise, Las Salinas is simply a great place to hang, sip chilled beers, and immerse yourself with the locals.

To reach Las Salinas, you'll pass through the Dominican Navy's main base. Be prepared to show I.D. to the sentry.

PARQUE CENTRAL MARCOS A. CABRAL
Avenida Sánchez and Avenida Favio Heredia, Baní

The town's main square, with a bandstand at its heart, is a pleasant spot to while away some time beneath shade trees. On its north side, the relatively modest **Catedral de Nuestra Señora de Regla**, erected in restrained neo-classical style in the 1950s, was restored in 2007–8. On the park's west side, the Modernist **Ayuntamiento** (town hall) hosts the **Museo**

Máximo Gómez

Máximo Gómez y Baez was born in Baní in 1836. In the early 1850s he fought to repel a series of Haitian invasions and in 1856 enlisted in the Spanish army. After training in Zaragoza, he was sent to Cuba as a cavalry commander, and returned to Hispaniola when Spain re-annexed the republic in 1861 (see the Invasion and Independence section, in the History chapter). After Spain lost the War of Restoration (1863–65), Gómez retired from the Spanish army and settled in Cuba, where he turned to farming.

Gómez became disillusioned with Spain's harsh treatment of its colonies. Thus, when Cuban nationalists initiated the first war for independence (the Ten Years War) in 1868, he joined the cause. A brilliant guerrilla strategist, he rose to be a general in the rebel *Mambises* army (he was shot through the neck but survived). After the war, Gómez returned to his homeland. He assisted other insurrectionist movements, including Puerto Rico, and remained active in the cause for Cuban independence.

In 1895 he was named Generalissimo (supreme commander) of the Cuban Mambises and on April 11, 1895, landed in Cuba alongside José Martí to lead the second War of Independence. U.S. intervention on the eve of victory for Gómez's Mambises was followed by Cuba's nominal independence in 1898. Gómez refused to be nominated as Cuba's president and retired to a villa in Havana where he died in 1905. He is buried in Havana's Cementerio Colón.

Sanctuario de San Martín de Porres, Las Tablas

Archivo Histórico de Baní (809-522-3314; Calle Sánchez 1; Monday through Friday 8 AM–4 PM; free), with rooms replicating a typical middle-class home of the mid-19th century, but also containing miscellany from pre-Columbian through the early 20th-century realms. Note the two-storey mural of Máximo Gómez adorning the town hall facade.

The park hosts the patron saint festival each November 21.

PARQUE MÁXIMO GÓMEZ
Avenida Máximo Gómez between Calle Nuestra Señora de Regla and Calle Inchaustegui, Baní

This lovely little landscaped park marks the site where once stood the house in which the hero of Cuban independence was born. The *banderas* (flags) of Cuba and the Dominican Republic hang above a marble bust of Generalissimo Gómez. In spring, the park is emblazoned with the blood-red blossoms of flame-of-the-forest.

SANCTUARIO DE SAN MARTÍN DE PORRES
Las Tablas, 9 miles (15 km) west of Baní

This enchanting hilltop hermitage, in the impoverished village of Las Tablas, is named for a 16th-century Peruvian saint who settled in Santo Domingo and dedicated his life to the

Five Fathoms Down!

Sure . . . the coral is fabulous. So too the fishes. But for many diving aficionados, the biggest rapture of the deep is the thrill of exploring the shipwrecks that litter the sandy bottoms of the Dominican Republic's shores. Many a Spanish galleon lies in a watery grave close to shore and just a few fathoms down. Plus, there is no end of latter-day vessels, many of them purposefully sank for divers' pleasure.

Ironically, the very first vessel to sail these waters—Christopher Columbus's *Santa María*—struck a reef and burst at the seams on Christmas Day, 1492, off Hispaniola (the wreck was later dismantled and its timbers used to build the first fort in the Americas).

The most famous wrecks in Dominican waters are *El Conde de Tolosa* and *Nuestra Señora de Guadalupe*—two Spanish treasure ships that foundered in a hurricane on August 25, 1724. Severely damaged while caught in the Mona Passage, they limped into Bahía de Samaná, where they sank, spilling their glittering treasures, cannons, and mercury (used to refine precious metals), and claiming the lives of almost 1,200 passengers. They were discovered in 1976. World-famous treasure hunter Tracy Bowden was hired to salvage the wrecks (much of the treasure retrieved is displayed in Santo Domingo's Museo de las Atarazanas Reales). In September 1641, a hurricane also thrashed the *Nuestra Señora de la Pura y Limpia Concepción*, another pregnant treasure ship that foundered on a shallow reef some 70 miles (112.6 km) north of Hispaniola. In 1686, a New England skipper called William Phipps managed to salvage a vast fortune in silver and gold (the English government, however, took a 10 percent cut before knighting Phipps), lending a name to the shallows—the Silver Bank. Although the wreck was subsequently picked at by various scavengers, during the 1990s Tracy Bowden went on to salvage large quantities of emeralds, lustrous metals, and precious pearls.

Many ships carrying more mundane cargo also went down. Notable among them is the Pipe Wreck, a merchant trader that foundered off Isla Cabra, near Monte Cristi, in the late 17th century. She is named for the large number of Dutch, long-stemmed clay smoking pipes that litter the seabed, just 13 feet (4 m) down.

Bowden's own salvage vessel, the 128-foot-long (39 m) *Hickory*, leans on its starboard side some 66 feet (20 m) down in Parque Nacional Submarino La Caleta, near Boca Chica. It was sank in 1984 to form an artificial reef. Here, too, is the *Limón*, a former tugboat. Nearby, the tugboat *Alto Velo* and the wreck of the *Tanya V* can be explored off Juan Dolio. At Bayahibes, divers can explore the *St. George*, a Norwegian cargo ship purposefully scuppered in 1999 to form a reef close to shore. At Bávaro, the rusting hulk of the *Astron* lies half-submerged in the turquoise shallows directly in front of the Gran Bahía Principe resort. And divers at Sosuá can join the resident moray eel as they admire the 148-foot-long (45 m) *Zingara* cargo ship at 115 feet (35 m) down.

poor. It was hand-built of rough limestone rocks cemented in place by local community members. Every November 3, the humble sanctuary draws pilgrims come to beseech imagined favors of the mulatto saint. The cactus-strewn base and stone steps are adorned with shrines and crevices full of mementoes left by pilgrims. Las Tablas is surrounded by a precious remnant of deciduous tropical dry forest—the church rises above a penurious plain of scrub and cactus.

Good to Know About

There is ostensibly a **Politur** (809-754-3100) tourist police bureau on Calle Principal, in Las Salinas. And Baní ostensibly has a **tourist information bureau** (809-522-6018, Avenida Sánchez at Calle Alejandro Acosta) in the Gobernación Provincial building.

Weekly and Annual Events

Every late June, Baní—the Capital del Mango—hosts **Expo Mango**, a festival celebrating the mango fruit—a major crop hereabouts. The festival is held in the main plaza. Various dishes featuring mangos are sold. Cultural exhibits are held. There's music, of course.

Baní holds its **Fiesta Patronal** in mid-June. A cultural highlight is *sarandunga,* a folkloric dance form unique to the town. And every November 21, an effigy of Nuestra Señora de Regla, the town's patron saint, is paraded.

Isla Catalina

5

Punta Cana and the Southeast

Sugary Sands

Ground zero in the DR's tourism, the southeast receives the lion's share of visitors. In fact, the region is the fifth most popular warm-weather destination in the world, according to a recent study by the American Society of Travel Agents. And no wonder! The beaches are unbelievable. Talk about picture-postcard perfect . . . with a seemingly endless strip of frost-white sands shelving into reef-protected lagoons of irresistible peacock blues and greens. Although there are several distinct beach resorts, best known is the Costa del Coco (Coconut Coast—a term that the tourism board for some reason dislikes, preferring the misleading term Punta Cana), featuring white, golden, and tangerine sands that unfurl virtually unbroken for some 40 miles (64 km). Add to that, sensational waters. Fabulous scuba diving. Great golfing. Marvelous water parks. Two national parks replete with wildlife, caves, fabulous natural formations, plus hiking trails. And the Caribbean's greatest concentration of bargain-priced, yet upscale all-inclusive resorts. Together they add up to a win-win scenario explaining this region's phenomenal growth, centered on the beach resort at Punta Cana.

Getting There

The region is served by **Aeropuerto Internacional de Punta Cana** (809-668-4749; www.puntacana.com), a privately owned airport that receives the bulk of tourist arrivals in the nation, with more than 1.8 million passengers in 2007. The smaller **Aeropuerto Internacional La Romana** (809-550-5088 or 813-9119) serves the La Romana area and Bayahibe. See the Planning Your Trip chapter for details.

See the regional sections, below, for information on bus service.

LA ROMANA AND VICINITY

A sprawling and horrendously congested town on the west bank of the Río Romana, some 80 miles (130 km) east of Santo Domingo, La Romana—a major sugar production center— has a pleasant colonial core full of pretty centenary houses. Sightseeing is concentrated around the central park. Other sites can be counted on one hand.

The town is dominated by **Central Romana** (809-802-0202; www.centralromana.com.do;

Avenida Libertad and Castillo Marquéz), the country's largest sugar mill, on the shore on the south side of town. The mill was initiated in 1917 by the U.S.-owned South Puerto Rico Sugar Company, which in 1967 was taken over by the multinational Gulf & Western Corporation. Gulf & Western invested huge sums in the town. It also built Casa de Campo, a deluxe resort that helped put tourism on the map some three decades ago, tempting serious golfers with some of the Caribbean's best courses plus a first-rate equestrian center and, today, a ritzy marina. The mill and Casa de Campo are now owned by the billionaire Cuban American Fanjul family-owned corporation. The highlight here, however, is Altos de Chavón—an incongruous faux Tuscan village that hosts some of the best restaurants around. And Isla Catalina, offshore, makes for a superb excursion.

In 2002, the Casa de Campo International Tourist Port (Muelle Turístico Internacional Casa de Campo) opened. It, too, was built by the Central Romana Corporation, and today welcomes several companies' cruise ships, including the 3,600-passenger *Freedom of the Seas,* the world's largest cruise ship.

Getting There

Aeropuerto Internacional La Romana (809-550-5088 or 813-9119) is 5 miles (8 km) east of town, on the coast highway. It is served by American Airlines, plus LTU and Thomas Cook charters from Europe. Casa de Campo is a 10-minute drive by taxi. Most passengers arrive on package tours. There is no bus service.

Expreso Macorís (809-687-2190) operates buses to La Romana, departing Santo Domingo from Calle Ravelo in front of Parque Enriquillo hourly, 5 AM–9 PM; and on the same schedule to Higüey, departing Calle Camino. In La Romana, *guaguas* depart and alight at Parque Central.

If driving, you'd be wise to take the *Circunvalación,* the ring road that skirts the city center, thus avoiding traffic-clogged Avenida Luperón (east-west) and Avenida Santa Rosa (north-south), the main in-town boulevards. Avenida Libertad, which leads east from town to Casa de Campo and Punta Cana becomes the Circunvalación westbound, linking directly to Carretera San Pedro de Macorís.

You can rent cars at La Romana International Airport through **Europcar** (809-813-9222; www.europcar.com).

Lodging

Most of the limited lodgings in La Romana itself are fairly matter-of-fact, even drab, affairs catering mostly to itinerant business folk. The yin to the in-town yang is Casa de Campo, well worth a splurge for anyone with a temptation to feel like a king . . . if only for a night.

CASA DE CAMPO
809-227-9494 or 800-877-3643
www.casadecampo.com.do
0.9 mile (1.5 km) east of La Romana

The original deluxe resort in the republic has been drawing the likes of the Bushes and Clintons since it opened in the 1970s as the republic's first getaway of the glamorous jet set. The millionaire celebrities tend to keep to themselves by renting one of the 150 exclusive villas, while the hoi polloi opt for the sophisticated digs in the 350-room hotel. The latter exude romantic good tastes—as they should, since haute-couture designer Oscar de la

Punta Cana Airport

Renta furnished them in plantation-style mahogany pieces. Plump duvets and down pillows, plus huge marble-clad bathrooms with Gilchrist & Soames toiletries are other draws. All guests get golf carts for whizzing around the sprawling grounds. Take your pick of gourmet restaurants on-site, plus several superb options are minutes away at Altos de Chavón. Sybarites can indulge in sumptuous treatments at the Cygalle Healing Spa, and there's no end of activities for epicurean tastes (see Attractions, Parks, and Recreation, below). $$$$.

FOUR SEASONS CASA DE CAMPO

Telephone to be announced
Casa de Campo, 0.9 mile (1.5 km) east of La Romana
www.fourseasons.com

This five-star resort is scheduled to open in winter of 2010 on 67 acres (27 ha) atop Punta Aguila, overlooking Playa Caletón, the main beach at Casa de Campo. It promises divine levels of luxe in its 200 rooms and five-bedroom Super Suites featuring their own wraparound pools. Plus, you'll feel like Dionysus in a 43,000-square-foot (3,995 sq m) spa. $$$$.

HOTEL FRANO

809-550-4744
Avenida Padre Abreu 9, La Romana

The best of the otherwise moribund offerings in town, this modern, three-storey hotel is on the north side of town—too far out to walk to the center. In the mode of a guest house, it offers 41 simply appointed air-conditioned rooms with cable TVs and small, somewhat disappointing bathrooms. The restaurant does a reasonable job of local fare. Secure parking is a bonus. $–$$.

Dining

BEACH CLUB BY LE CIRQUE
809-523-3333
Playa Minitas, Casa de Campo
Cuisine: Fusion

Gone is the El Pescador restaurant at Casa de Campo's beach, replaced by this chic new offering. Actually the old restaurant metamorphosed, overseen by Chef Pierre Schaedelin (who recently worked as Martha Stewart's private chef) of New York's world-famous Le Cirque restaurant, which now runs the place. New Executive Chef Paul Scordino and Chef Alfio Longo wave their magic wands in the kitchen, merging the French art of haute cuisine with fresh local ingredients. The result is exciting new dishes such as superlative foie gras ravioli; Chilean sea bass in champagne sauce, caviar, leeks, and hon shimeiji mushrooms; and prime dry aged strip steak with stuffed pearl tomatoes, and spring squash. I love the fact that you can reserve a private canopied beach cabana. Reservations are required for dinner. Open: Daily noon–3 and 6:30–11. $$$$.

LE BOULANGER
809-523-5359
Altos de Chavón

This little *boulangerie* (bakery and coffee shop) offers delicious fresh-baked croissants plus salads, pizza, and quality sandwiches. It also serves cocktails as well as cappuccinos, teas, and natural juices. Seating is outside on the tiny tree-shaded patio, where you can watch the to-ing and fro-ing of passersby on the cobbled alleyway. Open: 6–6. $.

CARIBBEAN COFFEE AND TEA
809-523-2273
Plaza Portofino 13, Marina Casa de Campo
Cuisine: Continental

An offshoot of the popular outlet in Santo Domingo, this classy café-bistro has a large menu featuring bruschettas, paninis, salads (including Caesar salad), wraps, crêpes, and desserts. The even longer drinks menu includes some tantalizing liqueur cafés, such as Café Bailey Gourmet, as well as Tazo chai teas, and fruit smoothies. Open 10AM–midnight. $–$$.

CHINOIS
809-523-2387
Plaza Portofino 2, Marina Casa de Campo
Cuisine: Pan-Asian

I guess marinas per se bespeak internationalism, which may explain why this Oriental-themed restaurant is tucked into a distinctly Italianate village reminiscent of Portofino. Whatever. Chinois is a treat, whether you're in a mood for Cantonese, sushi, or even pad thai. Start with the delicious Chinois Roll. The stylish contemporary decor features subtle hints of the Orient, including red walls, Chinese lanterns, plus waterfalls. The service here is eager to please. Reservations and dress code required for dinner only. Open: Daily noon–3 and 6–11. $$–$$$$.

DON QUIJOTE RESTAURANTE
809-556-2827
Calle Diego Ávila 44, La Romana
Cuisine: Continental

This small, homey restaurant on the west side of Parque Central is a surefire winner for simple Dominican and creative continental dishes. Surf and turf anyone? Try the Chateaubriand with shrimp in coconut sauce. I recommend the seafood paella, and lobster fans won't be disappointed with the lobster *criolla*. Open: Tues. through Fri. 11–4, Sat. and Sun. 11–11. $–$$.

LA PIAZZETTA
809-523-3333 ext 5339
Altos de Chavón
Cuisine: Italian

This marvelous Mediterranean restaurant in the heart of Altos de Chavón whisks you metaphorically back to Tuscany with its Italian country styling, including timber frame roof, and farm decor. It has a marvelous antipasto bar. Pastas are always freshly made under the fastidious attention of Chef Manuel Sánchez. Last visit, I enjoyed a Caprese salad with mozzarella, plus divine risotto with porcini mushrooms, and how could I resist the prof-iteroles? All washed down with a superb Chianti, although the wine list is expansive. Oh, and you can't go wrong with the gnocchi stuffed with three kinds of cheeses. And the for-mally liveried staff is friendly and mustard-keen in their duties. Musicians stroll and strum. Best yet, it has outdoor tables on a terrace with fabulous views down over the Chavón gorge. Reservations required. Dress code. Open: Daily 6–10 PM. $$$–$$$$.

ONNOS TAPAS BAR
809-523-5312
Altos de Chavón
Cuisine: Tapas

Opened in early 2008 with a perch beside the Amphitheater, this place is as much lively bar as a place to savor mouth-watering tapas—yes, even for breakfast, when omelets make the menu. You can also order burgers or sandwiches, while the dinner menu includes daily chef's specials and traditional Dominican dishes. And the cocktail list features more than 100 drinks, plus it's a great place to linger over a cappuccino or espresso. It has a tremen-dous and trendy (yet casual) ambience, with both indoor and outdoor seating. Hip music draws a young late-night crowd, which is encouraged to shove tables aside to dance. Open: 8 AM—until the last patron leaves. $$$.

SHISH KEBAB

809-556-2737
Calle Francisco del Castillo Marquéz 32, La Romana
Cuisine: Middle Eastern

When a taste for the Levant calls, this is the place. Unpretentious. Informal. And close to the heart of town. All good reasons to break the day while exploring downtown. It serves namesake shish kebabs and *dolmades* (grape leaves stuffed with rice), of course, but also delicacies such as *baba ganoush* (mashed eggplant with garlic, olive oil, and herbs), plus a delicious skewered shrimp and fresh grouper. Open: Tues. through Sun. 10 AM–11 PM. $–$$.

TRIGO DE ORO

809-550-5650
Calle Eugenio A. Miranda 9, La Romana
Cuisine: Baked goods, snacks

A great place to start the day, this charming café is tucked behind a wall one block northeast of the main plaza. It exudes all the charm of an upscale Parisian bistro, lent added ambience by its venue: a refurbished colonial home with verandas and a leafy, canopied patio with fountain and mosaic tables. Fresh-brewed coffee and cappuccinos complement fresh-baked baguettes, croissants, and other goodies. My favorite? The chocolate croissant. The afternoon menu expands to include sandwiches and cocktails. Open: Mon. 7 AM–6 PM. $–$$.

Attractions, Parks, and Recreation

Architecture
ALTOS DE CHAVÓN

809-523-8011
www.altosdechavon.com
Casa de Campo, 1.2 miles (2 km) east of La Romana

Conjectured in 1976 atop a cliff—the Heights of Chavón—overlooking the Río Chavón, this unlikely and irresistibly charming village recreates an idealized piece of Tuscany in the tropics. Made entirely of coral stone under direction of Roberto Copa, the Italian cine-matographer, it features cobbled streets swathed with bougainvillea and lined with cafés, restaurants, boutiques, and cultural draws. You could spend hours roaming (despite its small size) and lingering over cappuccino and wine.

Sites revolve around a main piazza, with a lion fountain, a colonnade of obelisks, and a fabulous view over the gorge. Here, peek inside tiny **St. Stanislaus Church**, which was blessed by Pope John Paul II and is a favored spot for weddings; Mass is held every Saturday and Sunday at 5 PM. Tucked behind it is the equally tiny yet marvelous **Regional Museum of Archaeology** (809-682-3111; Tues. through Sun. 8–8; free), which has excellent exhibits on pre-Colombian culture, with more than 3,000 artifacts, including an ancient canoe.

The village also functions as a thriving cultural center overseen by the Altos de Chavón Cultural Center Foundation (see the Culture section, below). And a spectacular 5,000-seat Roman-style open-air **amphitheater** hosts concerts, symphonies, theatrical events, and festivals featuring an international A-list of stars.

You can catch a free shuttle at Casa de Campo; supposedly it runs every 30 minutes.

Burro and St. Stanislaus Church, Altos de Chavon

MARINA CASA DE CAMPO
809-523-8646
www.marinacasadecampo.com

Designed by Italian resort architect Gianfranco Fini, this exclusive marina evokes images of Italy's Portofino—a fitting venue for the super-rich to berth their floating party palaces. The multicolored buildings form two semicircles around the harbor, replete with posh shops and fine-dining restaurants. Opened in 2001 with 350 slips, it is being expanded with 167 new slips capable of taking yachts up to 250 feet (76 m).

Baseball
ESTADIO FRANCÍSCO MICHELI
809-556-6188
www.lostorosdeleste.com
Avenida Padre Abreu, corner of Avenida Luperón, La Romana

This large modern baseball stadium hosts the La Romana Azucareros team. Games are played October through December. Tickets cost $50–150.

Beaches
MONUMENTO NATURAL ISLA CATALINA
5 miles (8 km) southwest of La Romana

One look at this gorgeous uninhabited cay—a tiny coral island—slung amid bathtub-warm turquoise shallows about 3 miles (5 km) south of the mainland and it will be love at first sight. With good reason, it's popular for day excursions on weekends, when it gets packed. The isle can also become thronged by cruise passengers of Costa Crociere, whose ships sometimes anchor offshore and unload scores of passengers.

The 20-minute boat ride from La Romana or Marina Casa de Campo delivers you to a wharf sheltered in the lee of a dog's-tooth cliff sheltering a magnificent white-sand beach, served by a bar-grill and souvenir stalls. Bring your snorkel gear, as there are plenty of corals and colorful fishes, especially at a shallow reef known as the Aquarium. And off the north shore, divers can thrill to a shallow reef flat, rich with pillar and boulder corals; and The Wall drops from 15 to 130 feet (5 to 40 m). In winter, humpback whales can sometimes be seen frolicking in the jade waters.

Major tour companies offer excursions, including **Colonial Tours & Travel** (809-688-5285 in Santo Domingo, 809-688-7802 in Bayahibe; www.colonialtours.com.do /catalina_Island.htm). You can also arrange trips through Casa de Campo.

PLAYA MINITAS

Other than the stupendous sands of Isla Catalina, your best bet for beach time is this lovely, reef-protected swath in Casa de Campo. Ostensibly open to resort guests only, non-guests are frequently permitted day-pass entry. It has cushy lounge chairs, plus huts for outdoor massage, and you can rent Hobie Cats, Aqua-Bikes, windsurfers, kayaks, and snorkel gear, or take an exhilarating ride on a banana boat (an inflatable banana-shaped raft towed by a speedboat). And a kids' camp takes care of wee ones.

Boating
Two charming old-world **paddleboats**, the *Empress Lily* and *River Princess*, take passengers on tours up the Río Chavón, departing Boca de Chavón each Wednesday at 8AM and 1 PM (5 hours; $45). The trips are narrated. You can book through most tour agencies and at Casa de Campo.

Nautic Terminal Romana (509-550-8156; http://nauticterminalromana.com) offers yacht charters, plus all-day catamaran excursions to Isla Catalina, departing La Romana. Yachts can also be chartered at Marina Casa de Campo through **Fraser Yachts** (809-523-2208; www.fraseryachts.com; Paseo del Mar 1) and **La Scuola Della Vela** (809-523-2379; www.scuolavela.com), an Italian sailing school offering tuition from beginner to competition level, including for children.

Casa de Campo Yacht Club (809-523-2247; www.casadecampoyachtclub.com) hosts sailing regattas and races throughout the year.

Equestrian Centers and Horseback Riding
Casa de Campo's world-class **Equestrian Center** (809-523-3333; www.casadecampo.com .do) has more than 100 horses—a perfect segue for one of my horsey sayings: "For people who love to ride, we have horses that love to be ridden; and for people who don't like to ride, we have horses that don't like to be ridden!" Excursions range from one-hour rides

for beginners to more advanced three-hour rides through canefields. The center offers tuition (English- or Western-style) in dressage and jumping. And three ponies—Anita, Juanito, and Miguelito—provide rides for children.

Casa de Campo is also the Caribbean's premier venue for the Sport of Kings—polo. It has three playing fields, a practice field, and the world's largest string of polo ponies. Even neophytes can partake of this princely sport by hiring ponies for stick and ball tourneys. Regular matches are played throughout the November through April polo season, when major tournaments are also hosted.

Fishing

The waters out of Marina Casa de Campo are world-renowned for superb marlin fishing. Several dozen sportfishing boats operate. It's cheaper to browse the docks and find yourself a skipper, although Casa de Campo can make arrangements (for a price). **Bi-Op-Sea Fishing Charters** (252-473-1138; http://biopsea.com/dr_marlin_main.asp) is based out of Marina Casa de Campo (809-523-2111) in springtime.

The Río Chavón offers a rod-bending challenge for snook.

Marina Casa de Campo hosts the annual **Torneo de Pesca Abierta** fishing tournament each March, and the **Marlin Masters Invitational** in April.

Golf

The Dominican Republic's golf revolution began here, at Casa de Campo, some four decades ago when golf architects Pete and Alice Dye fell in love with the area. They carved out an 18-hole course with rippling fairways suspended above the steep river gorge and named it for the sharp limestone terrain known to locals as *diente del perro*. Since the spectacular **Teeth of the Dog** course opened in 1971, it has been the *only* Caribbean course ranked in the world's top 50. (The Dog's fabled coral-fanged bite was sharpened in 2005 when Dye renovated and revamped the course.) Casa de Campo's **Links** course opened in 1976, followed in 2004 by the **Dye Fore** course. Tee times at all three public courses can be requested by fax (809-523-8800) or E-mail (t.times@ccampo.com.do). Rates: Links Course $150; Dye Course $200; Teeth of the Dog $225.

Parks and Plazas
PARQUE CENTRAL (DUARTE)
Calle Gonzalvo between Calles Duarte and Eugenio Miranda, La Romana

The town's leafy main square is a rare haven of peace in this bustling, hustling city. The park is notable for its surrealist wrought-iron sculptures of bulls, horses, and human figures, plus a statue of Juan Pablo Duarte at its southwest corner. It has a pergola at its heart and is surrounded by some intriguing buildings. Most notable, rising on the north side, is the Anglican-style **Iglesia Santa Rosa de Lima**, dating from 1924 and topped by a steeple. Immediately to its west, is the **Ayuntamiento** (Calle Eugenio Miranda, corner of Diego Ávila), the town hall erected in 1901 with an Art Deco clock tower. If you walk one block north along Gonzalvo you'll reach the outdoor **Mercado Municipal** (Calle Frey Juan de Utrera, corner Teofilo Ferry), the bustling market worth browsing for its trinkets and herbs sold at traditional *botánicas*.

Two blocks south along Calle Francisco del Castillo Marquéz brings you to Avenida Libertad and the town's most interesting feature: **El Obelisco**, pinning a tiny triangular plaza. This miniature replica of the George Washington Monument, in Washington, D.C., is painted with a beautiful mural depicting scenes in the nation's history.

Casa de Campo has guided two-hour excursions of La Romana daily at 9 AM and 4 PM ($25).

Spas

Cygalle Healing Spa (809-523-8529; www.cygallehealingspa.com/spa.html; Casa de Campo) Opened in 2006, Casa de Campo's new spa offers indulgent holistic pampering, from gentlemen's facials to soothing body wraps and sea salt exfoliations, in luxurious suites.

Tennis

La Terraza Tennis Center (809-523-3333 ext. 5940; www.casadecampo.com.do/en/sports /tennis.asp; E-mail: teniscasa@verizon.net.do). This world-class facility at Casa de Campo has 13 private har-tru courts (10 lit for night play). Pros are on hand for private lessons. It hosts the International Inter-Club Tennis Tournament in May. Open: 7 AM–10 PM.

Windsurfing, Kiteboarding, and Surfing

Non-motorized water sports are available at Casa de Campos' Minitas Beach, where options include Aqua-Bikes, Hobie Cats, kayaks, and windsurfers.

Culture

Cinema

Caribbean Cinemas Casa de Campo (809-523-2351; www.caribbeancinemasrd.com /cinema.php?cinema=15; Coconut Mall, Marina Casa de Campo). This three-screen cinema has lush leather recliner seats.

Hollywood Plaza (809-556-1616; Carretera Romana, San Pedro Km 2.5, La Romana).

Art and Art Galleries

ALTOS DE CHAVÓN SCHOOL OF DESIGN

809-523-8011
Fax: 809-523-8312
www.altosdechavon.com/fs_school.htm

A core component of Altos de Chavón from its inception has been this school run by the Altos de Chavon Cultural Center Foundation, a nonprofit educational and cultural institution founded in 1983 to promote excellence in art and design. It offers multifaceted classes encompassing two years of intensive professional training in fashion design, graphic design, interior design, and fine arts/illustration. Distinguished academics and design professionals serve as lecturers and artists in residence, who can be seen working alongside students in craft workshops producing paintings, lithographs, silk screens, ceramics, and weavings.

The Gallery (809-523-8470) showcases fine works by well-known and emerging Dominican and international artists in three distinct spaces—the Principal Gallery, the Rincón Gallery, and the Loggia. Exhibits change on a regular basis. Many of the works are for sale in the gallery's consignment space. Open: Tues. through Sun. 10–10.

Cabaret dancer, Playa Bavaro

Music and Nightlife
ALTOS DE CHAVÓN AMPHITHEATER
809-523-8011
www.altosdechavon.com

What a venue! This huge, open-air amphitheater would do ancient Greece proud with its 5,000 seats in a steeply tiered limestone seating in a massive half-moon. Since its inauguration in 1982 by Frank Sinatra and Carlos Santana, the amphitheater has hosted a Who's Who of stellar international performers. Recent acts have included Sting, Gloria Estefan, Shakira, Diego Torres, and Julio Iglesias. Placido Domingo performed in June 2008, when rumors swirled that Andrea Bocelli would soon perform.

CLUB ONNO'S
809-523-5341
Altos de Chavón

A serious place for postprandial partying, Onno's (in the old Discoteca Génesis) offers relatively quiet evenings over cocktails and half price pitchers during Happy Hour (5–7) and before the late-night crowd kicks it up a notch on the dance floor. Music tends to salsa, merengue, and techno, courtesy house DJs. Open: 8 AM–3 AM.

Altos de Chavon Amphitheater The Dominican Republic Ministry of Tourism

KANDELÁ: THE SHOW
809-523-2424
www.kandela.com.do
Altos de Chavón Amphitheater

Rumbling drums...Trilling trumpets...Whirling spotlights...The lights go down...and a troupe of near-naked showgirls swarm onto the stage, announcing the beginning of a spectacular two-hour, open-air musical extravaganza showcasing the island's sensuous Afro-Caribbean dance, music, and culture. A story line is discernible amid the gratuitous skin and erotic gyrations highlighted by a never-ending parade of *mulata* (mixed race) show-girls sashaying and shaking in sequined bikinis, ruffled frills, sensational headdresses, and feathers more ostentatious than a peacock's. Solo singers also perform everything from *boleros* to romantic opera. Dominican couples delight in these razzmatazz spectacles of Las Vegas-style paganism—girls! girls! girls!—and shake their head at any puritanical concept that they're not quite PC. The *cabaret espectáculo* (show) is performed January through mid-April, at 9:30 PM; $35.

CASA DE CAMPO YACHT CLUB

809-523-2247
www.casadecampoyachtclub.com
Marina Casa de Campo

The exclusive members-only yacht club hosts regular concerts, from jazz and Cuban bebop to classical (in 2007 it even hosted a tango concert with members of the National Symphony Orchestra).

POT BUNKER SPORTS BAR

809-227-9494
Casa de Campo

The Casa de Campo resort's liveliest bar features contemporary decor, pool tables, and large screen TV sets with satellite transmission so you follow your favorite sport live. Open: 3 PM–1 AM.

VICTORY CLUB

809-523-2264
Paseo del Mar 10, Marina Casa de Campo

This dressy bar is the place to be when the sun goes down, not least for its three-hour-long

Aerial view of Casa de Campo Marina   The Dominican Republic Ministry of Tourism

two-for-one Happy Hour (6–9). Live DJ's spin on weekends. It serves a limited menu. A shuttle runs from the marina plaza to the club, at the end of the pier. Open: noon–midnight.

Shopping

La Romana's **Mercado Municipal** (Calles Teófilo Ferry and Fray Juan de Utera) is a trove of colorful stalls selling fresh crafts, fresh produce, flowers, and medicinal herbs and *mama-juana* (the republic's home-brewed aphrodisiacal alcoholic cure-all).

The yin to the *mercado's* yang is Marina Casa de Campo, lined with posh boutiques and shops—a sort of Rodeo Drive by the sea. Here you'll find, among others: **Art' Arena** (809-523-2271; Calle Barlovento 21), for quality artwork; **Bibi León-Jenny Polanco** (809-523-2304; Plaza Portofino 5), selling women's high fashion; **Club del Cigarro** (809-523-2275; Pórtico de Sotavento 1), for the best of Cuban and Dominican smokes; **Conchita Llach Fine Jewels** (809-523-2268; Plaza Portofino 8), for designer watches and jewelry plus local amber and larimar pieces; **Conchita Llach Logo and Gifts** (809-523-2317; Plaza Portofino 4), selling upscale decorative items and crafts; and **Varelli Arte Contemporáneo** (809-523-2501; Calle Barlovento 5), exhibiting premium artworks and crafts.

Golfers can outfit themselves at the **Dye Fore Golf Pro Shop,** in Altos de Chavón. Here, the fabulous creations of the art and craft ateliers are sold at **The Gallery** (809-523-8011), the Altos de Chavón Foundation store. And the original handcrafted fine jewelry at **Everett Designs** (809-523-8554) is produced on site.

Food Purveyors

Supermercado Nacional (809-523-2344; Avenida de la Marina 3, Marina Casa de Campo).

Good to Know About

La Romana-Bayahíbe Hotel Association (809-472-9565 or 1-866-588-6856; www.explorelaromana.com; Avenida 27 de Febrero, La Romana).
Hospital Arístides F. Cabral (809-556-2344; Avenida Teniente A. García, La Romana).
Politur (Tourism Police; 809-550-7112, 556-2848, or 754-3033; Avenida Libertad and Calle Francisco Ducoudrey, La Romana).
Tourism Office—Oficina de la Secretaría de Turismo (809-550-6922; Calle Teniente Amado García 22, La Romana). The minimally stocked tourism office is in the Gobernación Municipal, open Mon. through Fri. 8–6.

Weekly and Annual Events

Carnaval **de La Romana** (Late February to mid March). Two weeks of warm-up events build up to the colorful and vivacious finale with locals in masquerade.
Fiesta Patronal de La Romana (Mid- to late August). This is one of the liveliest regional patron saint day festivals in the country, with folkloric and contemporary music, and a colorful parade.

GRAN FERIA DE ANDALUCÍA
809-523-8734
www.feriaandaluciaenelcaribe.com
Casa de Campo

Initiated in 2006, this annual four-day festival—an extension of the century-old festival of the City of Seville—celebrates everything Spanish. It's hosted at the Casa de Campo Equestrian Center, a fitting venue given the presence of traditional Spanish horse carriages, an equestrian parade; and a show of purebred Cartujano horses. The Fair replicates the City of Sevilla, with its streets of *albero* (sand traditionally used in bullfighting arenas), and men, women, and children dressed in traditional flamenco garb. Events include folkloric dancing, a fashion parade, and Spanish dance and music lessons and demonstrations. And of course, there are plenty of *casetas* (stalls) selling tapas and Spanish wines. Children will enjoy a petting zoo, kids' theme park, and Casa de Campo's famous donkey polo matches. Reservations are essential. Book well in advance. February.

BAYAHIBE AND VICINITY

Formerly a sleepy fishing village, the erstwhile hamlet of Bayahibe, about 15 miles (25 km) southeast of La Romana, has exploded with development in recent years. This, due to the lovely beaches that extend south of the village to adjoining Playa Dominicus (aka Dominicus Americanus), where several ritzy all-inclusive resorts now line the white sands. And a casino opened in April 2008. The place is burgeoning so quickly it's dizzying! Alas, the helter-skelter development doesn't seem very well planned, and away from the actual sands, much of the former charm is already lost. Still, there's no denying the beauty of the actual beaches, and the village clings by its fingernails to a laid-back, offbeat charm lent by its colorful wooden shacks now converted to little cafés, etc. The turquoise waters are lovely and the snorkeling exquisite, although care must be taken with razorlike limestone outcrops. Bayahibe is also renowned for fantastic diving: Ancient wrecks lie a few fathoms down. Nearby Isla Saona makes for a sensational day trip. And Bayahibe is gateway to Parque Nacional del Este, a rugged region of jagged limestone and semi-deciduous forest pitted with caves, and also a fabulous venue for birding.

Lodging
Small inns proliferate in Bayahibe. Dominicus is dominated by large all-inclusive hotels.

CATALONIA GRAN DOMINICUS
809-221-6767
fax: 809-221-5894
www.hoteles-catalonia.com
Playa Dominicus

The setting of this modest all-inclusive hotel is lovely. And so is the main pool, roughly shaped like a grand piano edging up to the sands. The 404 rooms are divided among 16 two-storey blocks and are adorned with turquoise, pastels, and blue-and-white-striped fabrics. Rooms here have the advantage of WiFi access and ceiling fans (plus air-conditioning). And Catalonia competes with neighboring all-inclusives with a choice of restaurants, a full range of non-motorized water sports, organized activities, spa treatments, tennis, and nightly entertainment. $$$

DREAMS LA ROMANA

809-221-8880
fax: 809-221-2776
www.dreamsresorts.com/drelr
Playa Bayahibe

This is my favorite among the all-inclusives as it matches my taste for contemporary styling and effusive use of thatch, since being upgraded in its new guise: The handsome, albeit huge, 563-room property was formerly the Sunscape Casa del Mar. I also like its lush, broad palm-shaded lawns and low-key architecture, topped by turquoise roofs to match the brilliant ocean. The rooms boast a gorgeous aesthetic combining whites, chocolates, and robin's-egg blue. The furnishings are 21st-century chic, with crisp white lines and duvets atop beds, some of which are four-posters. Huge picture windows open to balconies. And bathrooms are clad in marble. You can enjoy an open-air massage under thatch. Seven restaurants here include Japanese and Italian, and there's a wide choice of bars. The entertainment includes the usual roster of nightly cabaret shows and a disco. All in all, the most deluxe (actually, the *only* deluxe) offering in the area. $$–$$$

HOTEL BAYAHIBE

809-833-0159
Calle Principal, Bayahibe

Two blocks from the beach, this small, clean guest house offers simply appointed, no-frills rooms perfect for travelers on a budget or not too fussed about amenities. At least you have a fan, plus cable TV for rainy days, and the modern bathrooms are spacious. Avoid rooms on the first floor if possible; rooms on the upper levels are more spacious, get more light, and have small balconies. The room rates include breakfast. It has Internet service in the lobby, but no room safes. $

IBEROSTAR HACIENDA DOMINICUS

809-688-3600 or 888-923-2722
www.iberostar.com
Bulevar Dominicus Americanus, Playa Dominicus

This eye-pleasing all-inclusive commands a lovely slice of Playa Dominicus, here pinned by the hotel's signature black-and-white hooped lighthouse bar. The architecture is loosely Spanish-colonial in inspiration, although many of the structures are thatched. The 498 colorful bedrooms are done up in yellow and blue pastels throughout, with wrought-iron headboards and sponge-washed furnishings. All the mod-cons you might want are included, not least ceiling fans and hair dryers, although in-room safes cost extra. Every room has a balcony or terrace. A plus here is the dive center, offering certification courses. Facilities include three swimming pools plus a kiddy's pool; five restaurants; and a theater with nightly entertainment. $$$

OASIS CANOA LA ROMANA

809-682-2662
fax: 809-688-6371
www.hotelesoasis.com
Playa Dominicus

Star feature at this sprawling all-inclusive is the gorgeous free-form pool with palm-studded islands surrounded by thatched beachfront structures. Dining options include a Mexican beachfront grill. A Japanese restaurant was added in 2008, and the 532 rooms (in 12 three-storey blocks) were being remodeled on my last visit. Gone are the colorful exteriors, replaced with more upscale white facades. Inside the rooms, the eclectic, halfhearted result isn't quite to my taste: The new look incongruously mixes rattan, stainless steel, and antique reproduction fixtures, and the old and slightly weary terra-cotta floors remain. Modern bathrooms now gleam afresh and feature square (!) tubs. You won't get bored here. Amenities include tennis and badminton courts, a nine-hole golf course, plus heaps of water sports, and live entertainment nightly. $$–$$$

VIVA WYNDHAM DOMINICUS PALACE
809-686-5658 or 800-WYNDHAM
fax: 809-687-8583
www.wyndham.com/hotels/PUJDP/main.wnt
Playa Dominicus

This family-focused all-inclusive resort-hotel features a dramatic, soaring atrium, thatched lobby draped with white curtains, and flanked by three-storey accommodation blocks enfolding lush landscaped grounds. The gorgeous lobby sets the tone with its polished travertine floor and contemporary furnishings. The travertine floors extend to the 330 bedrooms (choose either superior rooms or Junior Suites, which have king beds), featuring two-tone blues and yellow pastels. Certainly not chic or sophisticated, but perfectly satisfying decor. Dining spans the globe here with five restaurants that include Mexican, Italian, and Chinese. Among the amenity highlights: a climbing wall, tennis, and full-service spa. $$–$$$

Dining
Several simple thatch-fringed bar-restaurants overlook Playa Bayahibe—a lovely setting for watching the fishing boats to-ing and fro-ing. Dominicus is booming as foreigners with a certain sensibility open mom-and-pop businesses.

BAMBOO BEACH
829-410-1326
Playa Bayahibe

This French-run thatched restaurant hangs over Playa Bayahibe. Open-air, hewn of simple timbers with a stone floor and dark-glazed bamboo furnishings, it is cooled by breezes and has a lovely laid-back ambience. The eclectic menu spans the spectrum, from crêpes and spaghettis to curry chicken, plus a delicious lobster. Leave room for crème brûlée. No credit cards. Open Thurs. through Tues. 11 AM–10 PM. $.

MARE NOSTRUM
809-833-0055
Calle Principe, Playa Bayahibe

This upscale Italian restaurant, also on the peninsula overlooking Playa Bayahibe, doesn't look like much from the outside, at least from the street. Pop inside this two-storey, thatched structure and you soon change your tune. I love the fabulous vistas from the upper deck. Celebrities often pop in (Ben Affleck and Steven Seagal were recent patrons) to savor the seafood and Italian dishes featuring homemade pastas prepared by the Italian-Spanish owners. My favorite dish here is the *risotto mare* (seafood risotto). Open: Mon. through Sat. 6:30 PM–10 PM. $$$.

RISTORANTE BARCO BAR
809-972-5708
Playa Bayahibe

Adorable pretty well describes this charming open-air beachfront bar-restaurant, painted robin's-eggshell-blue and white with gingerbread trim, and facing onto the waters of Playa Bayahibe. The bar, decorated with seashells, is shaped like a boat. The roof is of tin. And yellow curtains add a touch of romance, enhanced at night by lanterns of dangling seashells. It even has a tree house. Roberto, the Italian owner, dishes up some fancy fusion food. I enjoyed a fish tartar followed by salmon fettuccine in vodka, but I was equally tempted by the homemade pasta with ravioli and ricotta. Carnivores might opt for the traditional Argentinian *churrasco*. Open Fri. through Wed. noon–3 and 7–2 AM. $–$$.

VESUVIO
809-833-0510
www.vesuvio.com.do
Casino Dominicus, Avenida Dominicus Americano corner of Wayne Fuller, Playa Dominicus

I was fortunate to be at the opening night of this sensational newcomer in April 2008, which has since catapulted the Bayahibe dining scene into the stratosphere. In fact, it could well be the chicest eatery east of Santo Domingo. This circular restaurant has a classy and chic ambience, not least thanks to a travertine floor and wall of glass, its white leather chairs, and clinically white walls graced by contemporary art and vases stuffed with twirled twigs.

The restaurant is an offshoot of the popular Vesuvio Malecón, in Santo Domingo. Owner-Chef Maria Bonarelli studied at the Italiana Culinary Academy of New York, then worked in Italy for two years before bringing her skills to bear here. How about these Italian-fusion treats? Lobster bisque... carpaccio de bresaola (cured beef)... porcini mushroom risotto... filet mignon of tuna à la siciliana with butter, anchovies, and capers... all followed with a super chocolaty tiramisu or a superb cuatro leches (four creams) dessert? The service is top-notch. Open: noon–midnight. $$$$.

Attractions, Parks, and Recreation

Beaches
Fishing boats still bob at anchor on **Playa Bayahibe**, immediately north of Punta Bayahibe. Many fishers have turned to a livelihood ferrying tourists to and from Isla Saona and Isla Catalina, but enough remain to add color to the local scene. You can watch them scaling and preparing their fresh catch, still dripping with brine from the sea, beneath the shade trees to each end of the beach. The sand here is thin and hard and not really conducive to sunning, and the pack of fishing boats precludes wading and snorkeling. Vendors sell *mama-juana*, including bottles with labels imprinted with your photo. And there are craft stalls and a sprinkling of rustic restaurants in the village. The place thrums with activity mid-

morning and late afternoon when tour buses drop off and collect island-bound cargo and the vendors' sales pitches get heavy. Alas, many of the quaint wooden homes in tropical ice cream pastels have now been subsumed by a wave of less tasteful concrete development, diluting the agreeable ambience.

For sheer beauty, **Playa Dominicus** far surpasses Playa Bayahibe. The beach runs south for several miles, broken in places by craggy headlands. With the maze of new development and the all-inclusives taking up so much space, finding access to the beach can be difficult. Easiest access is via the sandy track that runs between the Viva Wyndham and Iberostar hotels. A crafts village is set up at this point, and there are lovely albeit rustic restaurants and food stalls, plus water sports outlets. Bring your snorkel gear for exploring the fish-packed shallows. Parasailing is a great option. And you can rent beach loungers and umbrellas.

Wildlife and Wilderness Parks
PARQUE NACIONAL DEL ESTE
809-833-0022
Open: Daily 8–5, RD$100

Covering 162 square miles (420 sq km), this huge park protects tropical humid and seasonally dry deciduous forests covering, and ocean waters surrounding, a trapezoidal peninsula of craggy limestone marine terraces jutting into the Caribbean south and east of Bayahibe. The park also encompasses Isla Saona and the submerged continental plate extending approximately 1 mile (1.6 km) from the park's coastline (certain sections are closed to the public). It is famed for fantastic birding, and for its many caverns replete with Taíno rupestrine art.

Four species of marine turtles consider the creamy sands clean enough in which to lay their eggs. Manatees inhabit the coastal lagoons. Ashore, rhinoceros iguanas scurry about amid the leaf litter, while critically endangered hutias and solenodon would be a rare sight indeed for lucky hikers. And bird life abounds. The endemic ashy-faced owl, the Hispaniolan lizard-cuckoo, and the Hispaniolan parrot are among the park's 112 bird species. The mangrove bushes are roosts for frigate birds and red-footed boobies. And flamingoes are a highlight of any visit to Isla Saona.

The park office—in the main parking lot at Bayahibe—displays maps, and you can hire ranger-guides here (RD$500–750). Dominican entomologist Kevin Guerrero (www.geocities.com/strateagus; E-mail: kaguerrero@hotmail.com) is recommended for a more educational excursion. The park entrance is at Guaraguao, 3 miles (5 km) south of Bayahibe. Take plenty of water and insect repellent for hiking. No overnights are allowed.

The park can also be entered on its east side from the hamlet of Boca de Yuma (see the Higüey and Vicinity section, later this chapter).
Caves: A relatively flat self-guided trail (one hour each way) leads inland from Guaraguao to **Cueva del Puente**, one of more than 200 known caves here; this one features dramatic dripstone formations and Taíno pictographs; there are three caverns here, and most of the pictographs are off-limits to visitors. You'll need a flashlight to go beyond the collapsed entrance to the first cavern.

The track to Cueva del Puente bifurcates, with an offshoot leading to **Cueva José María**. Although a guide is not obligatory, it's a wise investment so as not to get lost. This cave is renowned for its more than 1,200 Taíno pictographs—most famously the only known such depiction of a Spanish galleon.

You can hire a boat in Bayahibe to take you about 5 miles (8 km) south to a ranger station at **Playa La Palmilla**, a lovely white-sand beach from where a trail leads inland about 1.2 miles (2 km) to **Cueva de Panchito** (also known as Peñon Gordo). It has 28 petroglyphs in the first cavern, but most remarkable is the Taíno figure with arms raised above his head that guards the slippery entrance. A guide is compulsory. The trail loops around to **Playa Tortuga**.

Wear sturdy shoes to protect against sharp rocks, thorns, and scorpions. Take a flash-light. And be cautious entering the caves, where the ground may be slippery due to bat guano and mosses.

Sendero Ecológico y Arqueológico de Padre Nuestro: The Padre Nuestro Ecological and Archaeological Trail is a triptych delight, leading through tropical semi-dry forest and con-necting a series of *manantiales* (underground caverns with natural cisterns) displaying pre-Hispanic rupestrine art that honored Atabey, the Taíno Goddess of Water. This section of the park was adjoined to the already extant Parque Nacional del Este in 2003, when the trail opened.

Giant cactus claw the sky, adding to the drama of this splendid hike, beginning at the **Interpretive Center**, at Padre Nuestro, 2 miles (3 km) east of Bayahibe. The loop trail climbs to **Mirador del Farallon**, offering views over the park. Among the manantiales you'll pass are Chicho I and Chicho II, the latter with an astonishing underground lake, plus a Taíno spiritual site with 26 ancient pictographs; and Manantial de la Lechuza (Owl Spring), named for the petroglyph of an owl sculpted in bas-relief on a stalagmite.

The **Asociación de Guías de Padre Nuestro** (866-588-6856), the local guides' associa-tion, offers interpretive tours.

Isla Saona: A boat excursion to this 45-square-mile (115 sq km) island, part of Parque Nacional del Este, is a treat... but be warned: On most days in high season, the place can become crowded with day-trippers. You're whisked from Bayahibe by high-speed boat (a 30-minute journey), but slower-paced party boats idle along so as not to spill the rum. Some boats call in at **Piscina Natural**, a lagoon enclosed by a sandbar; starfish populate the shallows—look, but don't touch!

You're deposited on the south coast (the north coast is mostly cliffs) at **Mano Juan** (also known as Adamanay), a palm-thatched village backing a gorgeous white-sand beach; Mano Juan was created by Dictator Rafael Trujillo as a village to house political dissidents. There's a visitors center where individuals must register upon arrival. Vendors ply cold drinks, tourist trinkets, and hair-braiding. There's usually music blaring. A far cry from September 14, 1494, when Christopher Columbus anchored here, noting a lunar eclipse the next day.

Immediately west of Mano Juan, **Laguna de los Flamencos** is named for the flamingoes, looking like feathered roses atop carnation stems. The interpretive trail continues past the lake some 8 miles (13 km) to Punta Catuano, at the western tip of the island; about 546 yards (500 m) before the trail-end is **Cueva Cotubanamá**, a cave with pre-Columbian pic-tographs etched on the walls. A second trail leads east 8 miles (13 km) along the shore to **Laguna Canto de la Playa**, another jade-colored watering hole with flamingoes and other stilt-legged waders.

All the major hotels sell excursion packages, as do tour agencies such as **Colonial Tours** (809-688-7802; fax 809-688-7802; www.colonialtours.com.do/Englishsaona.htm; Plaza El Castillo, Bayahibe). Or you can book with the **Asociación de Lanchero de Bayahibe** (809-952-4450), the local boatman's association, at Playa Bayahibe. Tours cost about $40, including drinks.

La Aleta: A Site to Behold... or Not

In 1981, Dominican archaeologist José Guerrero, carrying out a reconnaissance for the Museo del Hombre Dominicano, unearthed a *bateye* (ceremonial plaza) and a vast hoard of Taíno artifacts, including war clubs, *duhos* (curved stools), canoe paddle blades, and intact vases. In 1998, a team of archaeologists from Indiana University peeled away the vegetation to reveal three additional *bateyes* with stone pillars surrounding a cenote, or flooded underground cavern—the Manantial de la Aleta (Spring of the Fin)—some 131 feet (40 m) in diameter. Seven holes in the surface rock were used as wells by Taíno, who drew water in woven baskets. The water attains a depth of 262 feet (80 m) and is pure on top and at its base, but between 36 and 59 feet (11 and 18 m) depth it is impure and milky.

The site, today known as La Aleta, was one of the most important Taíno ceremonial sites of its day. Evidence suggests that natives came from hundreds of miles away to worship at Manantial, which may have been seen by the Taíno as a portal to the watery underworld known as Coaybay (abode place of the dead). Many Taíno artifacts litter the base of the cenote and were presumably made as offering to Atabey.

Archaeologists believe that this may have been the site of the massacre of Taíno by Spaniards that Friar Bartolomé de las Casas famously recorded.

La Aletas—3 miles (5 km) inland of La Palmilla—is off-limits to visitors.

Punta Bayahibe

The charming village of Bayahibe sits atop a craggy limestone headland. The name is Taíno (*baya* was a native word for mollusks), and a huge quantity of pre-Columbian artifacts have been found atop the point, including middens of seashells. The Museo del Hombre Dominicano has been conducting excavations since 1998.

The **Ruta Cultural La Punta de Bayahíbe** follows the sole road (dirt) along the peninsula, passing traditional wooden houses; the quaint bottle green wooden church dating from 1925; the archaeological exhibition; traditional fishing boats; and the Bosque de Pereskya Quisqueyana, where grows an endemic woody plant known as Rosa de Bayahíbe (Rose of Bayahibe).

Scuba Diving

Some of the finest diving in the republic awaits offshore of Bayahibe, where teal-blue waters support superb coral reefs sheltering more than 120 species of tropical fish. Some 20 dive sites beckon. Most notable (and for advanced divers only) is the wreck of the *St. George*, a 240-foot-(73 m) long cargo freighter built in 1962 and scuttled in 1999 (after being severely damaged by Hurricane Georges) in front of the Viva Wyndham Dominicus Beach, where she slumbers in her sloping watery grave beginning just 50 feet (15 m) down: www.indiana.edu/~e370/bayahibe/stgeoslate_eng.pdf.

Initiated in 2002 by the Indiana University Underwater Science Project, the **1724 Guadalupe Underwater Archaeological Preserve** is billed as the world's first underwater shipwreck museum. An anchor, cannon, cannonballs, and other artifacts recovered from the wrecks of the Spanish galleons *Guadalupe* and *Tolosa,* which sank in Samaná bay in 1724, have been laid in 12 feet (4 m) of water in front of the Viva Wyndham Dominicus Beach—at a depth perfect for snorkelers to enjoy, too. And IU team members are creating a replica shipwreck site in front of the Oasis Canoa La Romana.

Off the southeast coast of Isla Saona, the **Caballo Blanco** reef ensnared 16th and 18th-century Spanish galleons: various cannon, plus anchors and eclectic ceramics can still be seen.

Tiny **Isla Catalinita**, studding the Canal de Catauno channel off the southeast side of the park, is a great place for snorkeling.

Humpback whales are often seen in these waters in winter months.

Cave Dives: Several of the *manantiales* (subterranean lakes) at Padre Nuestro are accessible to divers. Permits and guides can be obtained from the Parque Nacional del Este offices in Bayahibe or Mano Juan, but it's far easier and safer to book through one of the local dive operators. Strict regulations are enforced for cave dives. The crystal clear fresh waters are a constant 78 degrees F (26 degrees C), although thermoclines define alternating layers of salty seawater and fresh water.

Manantial del Chicho is 230 feet (70 m) deep and features pre-Columbian ceramics at its base. Nearby, **Manantial de la Lechuza** is equally grand, but lacks Taíno detritus. Most spectacular is **Manantial de Padre Nuestro**, dripping with stalagmites.

Dive Outfitters: The following scuba operators offer organized dives: **Casa Daniel** (809-833-0050, www.casa-daniel.com; Calle Principal 1) and **Scubafun** (809-833-0003; www.scubafun.info; Calle Principal 28), both on the waterfront in the center of Bayahibe; and **Pelicano Water Sport** (809-947-0894; www.pelicanosport.com), with six outlets in Punta Cana.

Culture

Casinos
CASINO DOMINICUS
809-685-1717
www.casinodominicus.com
Carretera Dominicus Americanus, corner of Wayne Fuller, Playa Dominicus
Open: Daily 3 PM–3 AM

The republic's only stand-alone casino is a 45,000-square-foot mega-casino with 150 video slots, 25 tables including roulette and blackjack, plus a small poker room, an exclusive players' club, and both the lowest minimum bets and the highest limits in the nation. It also has a Race and Sports Book for sports and racing fans, including live simulcasts. Free hotel shuttles.

Music and Nightlife
BIG SUR DISCOTEQUE
No telephone
Playa Bayahibe
Open: 8 PM–4 AM

When you tire of the all-inclusive hotel's in-house discos, head to this open-air disco and nightclub at the north end of Bayahibe beach. Although open nightly, it's pretty dead except on Friday and Saturday nights, when locals pack in. Nothing fancy here, and the music—a mix of *bachata*, merengue, and salsa—is DEAFENING! Don't even think about arriving before 10 PM.

CASINO DOMINICUS

809-685-1717

www.casinodominicus.com

Carretera Dominicus Americanus, corner of Wayne Fuller, Playa Dominicus

Open: Daily 3 PM–3 AM

The casino is the happening place in Bayahibe with its chic disco bar featuring live bands playing *bachata* and merengue. And there's also a 1,000-seat theatre hosting big-name entertainers.

Shopping

The Casino Dominicus shopping plaza includes top-end boutiques, including Conchita Llach Joyería (jewelry), Kalipsos (women's fashions), La Cigua Gift Shop (arts and crafts), and Tabaco & Ron (cigars).

There are craft markets in the parking lot at Bayahibe, and on Playa Dominicus.

Good to Know About

Asociación de Hoteles Romana Bayahíbe (809-472-9565; www.explorelaromana.com; Avenida 27 de Febrero, La Romana).

Santa Rosa Taxi (809-556-5313) and **Taxis Service of Bayahibe** (809-833-0059).

Politur (Tourism Police; 809-833-0019 or 754-3012; Calle Juan Brito 1, Bayahibe).

Weekly and Annual Events

You'd hardly expect a tiny place like Bayahibe to slug it out with the big boys in terms of annual events. But you'd be wrong. Let's start with the **Fiesta Patronal de Bayahibe** (April 26 to May 2), which includes folkloric musical shows, a *guloya* parade (see the Cocolos sidebar, in the South Central chapter), a children's model fishing-boat regatta, and the *Procesión de la Divina Pastora* (Procession of the Divine Shepherd), when the parishioners parade a painting of their patron saint along the coast by boat to bring good luck to the fishermen.

An annual competition of traditional handmade fishing boats is held during Holy Saturday, Easter, when the simple sail craft with graceful lines are raced between Bayahibe and Isla Catalina. The dinghies are about 12 feet (3.6 m) long and carry only a mainsail. Remarkably flexible yet strong, they're built without blueprints, guided only by rule of thumb, and plumbed by eye alone.

At the time of writing, two new festivals were in the planning stage: the **Festival del Merengue de Bayahibe** and **Feria Artesanal de Dominicus**. Contact the Asociación de Hoteles Romana Bayahíbe for information.

HIGÜEY AND VICINITY

Capital of La Altagracia province, this sprawling and bustling city (population 105,000) abuzz with *motoconchos* serves as the gateway to the beach resort of Punta Cana. Officially known as Salvaleón de Higüey, it was founded in 1502 by conquistador Juan Ponce de León. It is the nation's preeminent pilgrimage center: Its statuesque cathedral—an astonishing exemplar of modern religious architecture—is known for its magnificent altar and an elaborate shrine of the Virgin Mary. And the basilica's tiny 16th-century predecessor is also worth a visit.

Nearby attractions include the fishing village of Boca de Yuma, gateway to the eastern half of Parque Nacional del Este. And nearby is one of the republic's unsung gems: the Casa Juan Ponce de León, the explorer's former fortified home. This is prime sugarcane growing country.

Getting There

Expreso Bávaro (809-682-9670; 7 AM, 10 AM, 2 PM, and 4 PM, or when they fill up, whichever comes earlier; four hours; RD$250) buses bound for Bávaro/Punta Cana depart Santo Domingo from Avenida Máximo Gómez, at either Plaza Los Girasoles or at Avenida Juan Sanchez Ramirez 31 (near Supermercado Nacional). Slower *guaguas* (operated by Sichoprole) depart Santo Domingo from Parque Enriquillo every 15 minutes 8 AM–6 PM, and every 30 minutes 6–8 AM and 6–8 PM (RD$150; three hours).

All buses stop in Higüey at Avenida Laguna Llana and Calle Colón, across the street from the Sitrabapu Terminal (in front of the basilica), serving Bávaro/Punta Cana. Sitrabapu buses run between Bávaro and Higüey about every 15 minutes, 6 AM–10 PM, then hourly (RD$1, one hour); these buses can get packed and you may have to stand; air-conditioned express buses leave at the top of the hour. The Friusa (Sitrabapu) bus station in Bávaro is next to the Politur police station, across from the Texaco gas station.

From Bayahibe, you can take *guaguas* to the Carretera 3 intersection and catch a passing Santo Domingo-Higüey bus in front of the gas station. Return *guaguas* depart Higüey from Avenida La Altagracia, on the south side of the basilica.

Lodging

HOTEL DON CARLOS
809-554-2344
fax: 809-554-1942
Calle Juan Ponce de León, corner of Avenida Sánchez, Higüey

A second-rate hotel, in the event that the much better Hotel Restaurant Mira Cielo is full. Its simply decorated rooms are clean and have cable TV. The best thing here is the restaurant (popular with locals), and its central location just southwest of the basilica. $.

HOTEL RESTAURANT CASA CLUB
809-853-1283
0.75 miles (1 km) north of Boca de Yuma

I love this relative newcomer built and run by an Italian couple, in old plantation style of coral stone. Set in lush gardens, it boasts a beautiful aesthetic enhanced by bamboo furnishings and wrought-iron chandeliers. A spiral staircase coils up to the six air-conditioned guest rooms, with modest contemporary furnishings and loft bedrooms. Some have king beds; three have half-moon balconies with ocean views; and one is a suite with lounge. There's a swimming pool and separate kiddy's pool. And the owners offer horseback rides, plus boat rides to a private little beach. The elegant open-air restaurant has a travertine floor plus ceiling fans. The menu here ranges from carpaccios, lobster, calamari, and shrimp, to tagliatelle tenderloin! No credit cards. $–$$.

HOTEL RESTAURANT MIRA CIELO

809-554-1736
http://hotelmiracielo.net
Calle 4, corner of Carretera 3 (Carretera de Yuma), Higüey

There's not much reason to overnight in Higüey, but if you do then this ostentatious (did you say gaudy?) hotel rising four storeys over the main Santo Domingo highway is the best bet. Its 12 clean, air-conditioned rooms are pleasantly furnished with eclectic pieces and they differ markedly; check several to see what you like. All have cable TVs and modern bathrooms. Some have king beds. The no-frills restaurant serves *criolla* and continental fare. It also has live music and a small and sexy cabaret show. $$.

HOTEL RESTAURANTE EL VIEJO PIRATA

809-355-3365
E-mail: nancy.felix@hotmail.com
0.5 miles (1 km) west of Boca de Yuma

A delightful little canary-yellow hotel sitting atop the breeze-swept cliffs. A patio restaurant with vine-clad ceiling occupies a little walled garden with a small swimming pool. Its 10 air-conditioned rooms are on the small side but are pleasantly, albeit simply, furnished with rattan foldout sofa beds. All have ceiling fans and modern bathrooms with showers, but storage space is minimal. Take the cross-ventilated large room. No credit cards. $.

Dining

MESÓN DE CERVANTES

809-554-2506
Arzobispo Nouel 79, Higüey

You can't miss this friendly, no-frills hole-in-the-wall restaurant, one block east of the basilica (perfect if you get hungry after exploring the cathedral), thanks to the little windmill atop the roof. It's a great place to sample *criolla* fare, including *camarones rellenos* (stuffed shrimp). A pianist tickles the ivories at night. Open: 10AM–midnight. $.

Attractions, Parks, and Recreation

BASILICA DE NUESTRA SEÑORA DE LA ALTAGRACIA

809-554-4541
Avenida Laguna Llana between Avenida La Altagracia and Avenida de la Libertad, Higüey.
Open: Mon. through Sat. 8–6, Sun. 8–8

A staggering, almost bombastic, cathedral made entirely of poured concrete, this massive avant-garde building causes an immediate double take. Serving as the nation's most important pilgrimage venue, Our Lady of High Grace was designed in 1950 by French architects André Dunoyer de Segonzac and Pierre Dupré, and inaugurated on January 21, 1971, on the anniversary of a Dominican victory over the French on that day in 1691. Pilgrims flock each January 21 to pay homage to the Virgin, venerated in a painting brought to Higüey from Spain in the early 16th century; superstitious people believe that it grants miracles.

The brash exterior—spectacularly lit at night, as if for a son-et-lumière—is remarkable for its facade like an upturned ship's prow. The motif is repeated throughout, including a

Basilica de Nuestra Señora de la Altagracia, Higüey

246-foot-tall (75 m) twin-arched spire representing hands cusped in prayer. The interior, also of poured concrete, is graced by a spectacular stained-glass wall framing the altar, again in the upturned-prow form. Note the murals by José Vela Zanetti to each side.

A dress code supposedly applies (no shorts for men, or trousers or bare shoulders for women), but is rarely enforced. Expect to be hit upon by beggars and rosary vendors as you approach and depart.

BOCA DE YUMA
21 miles (36 km) south of Higüey

The fishing village of Mouth of Yuma sits over the mouth of the Yuma river. Poised atop limestone cliffs, the village clings fast to its fleet of simple homemade fishing boats, which still set out to bring in fresh catch daily. The sheltered little harbor here was of great import during early colonial days; Juan Ponce de León supposedly set sail from here in 1508 to conquer the isle of Puerto Rico. Today villagers earn added income taking visitors on boat trips up the Yuma River, with a stop at a lovely grotto. **Malecón Tours** (809-902-2696; two hours; $100 for up to eight people) offers tours

A few rusting cannon stand over the harbor mouth, where colorful fishing smacks are hauled out on the sands below. Boatmen will also ferry you to **Playa Borinquen**, a small beach nearby.

CASA PONCE DE LEÓN
No telephone
Calle Los Jobitos, San Rafael del Yuma, 14 miles (24 km) southeast of Higüey
Open: Tues. through Sun. 9–3:30
Admission: RD$30

Standing four-square in the midst of the *campo* (countryside), the former home of Spanish conquistador Ponce de León is well worth the detour if you're passing anywhere near Higüey. The sturdy two-storey fortress-home was built of thick limestone in 1505, with gun slits and minimal windows, all on the upper level. It sits in a garden of mangoes and palms. León accompanied Columbus on his second voyage in 1494, and later participated in the massacre of Taíno inhabitants nearby in 1502. Here he lived with his wife and three daughters while serving as provincial governor. In 1508 he set out to colonize Puerto Rico (León was killed by Native Americans while searching for the fabled fountain of youth in Florida). The perfectly preserved house contains his suit of armor, plus weaponry, and various furnishings and other artifacts pertaining to León and his epoch. Alas, signs are solely in Spanish.

The house is kept locked. Be patient until the *custodio* (guard), who happens to be a local farmer, spots you and comes to open up.

IGLESIA SAN DIONISIO
Calle Agustín Guerrero and Pedro Livio

Completed in 1572, this is one of the oldest and the loveliest colonial churches in the nation. Its simple yet sturdy facade with a rippling roofline boasts a lovely purity characteristic of the Mediterranean renaissance style. Within, you can marvel at the exquisite mahogany altar beneath an elaborately frescoed dome. The church is the original sanctuary of the Virgin of Altagracia, now honored in the Basilica de Nuestra Señora de la Altagracia.

Wildlife and Wilderness Parks

PARQUE NACIONAL DEL ESTE (EASTERN SECTION)
1.5 miles (2.5 km) west of Boca de Yuma
Open: Variable hours
Admission: RD$100

The eastern half of this park (see Parque Nacional del Este, in the Bayahibe and Vicinity section, above) can be accessed from just west of Boca de Yuma. There's a ranger station (no telephone), from where a 0.6-mile (1 km) trail leads to **Cueva de Bienve**; a guide is obligatory (don't forget to tip); the cave has about three dozen pre-Hispanic motifs, most quite tiny. You can also visit **Cueva de Berna**, outside the park, about 0.6 mile (1 km) before the ranger station. This cave features more than 300 pictographs and petroglyphs, most of them very deteriorated and hard to discern. A stalagmite just inside the entrance (where bats and swallows swoop about) is engraved with a human face looking out. Bring a flashlight.

Good to Know About

Tourism Office (809-554-2672; Fax: 809-746-0702; Avenida Altagracia 85, Higüey).

Weekly and Annual Events

Fiesta de los Toros (August 14) Known as the Festival of the Bulls, Higuey's *fiesta patronal* is renowned for its *topes* (horse parades) and cattle fair.

Fiesta de la Virgen de la Altagracia (January 21) The 45 bells of the Basilica de Nuestra Señora de la Altagracia ring day and night each January 21 as pilgrims pour into town from throughout the republic to beseech favors and pay tribute to a small framed picture of the Virgin of Altagracia—the patron saint of all Dominicans—kept in effigy within a glass case. The pilgrimage, the most important religious day in the Dominican calendar, lasts several days.

PUNTA CANA AND VICINITY

Served by Aeropuerto Internacional de Punta Cana, the extreme southeast of the country receives the lion's share of visitors to the republic, with more than 1.8 million passengers in 2007. In fact, the Punta Cana region is the fifth most popular warm-weather destination in the world. And no wonder! Picture postcard perfect in every regard, the so-called Coconut Coast (a term that the republic's Ministry of Tourism downplays) boasts miles of impossibly frost-white sands shelving into ocean lagoons of irresistible peacock blues and greens. The larimar-blue waters are still as a millpond thanks to a coral reef a quarter-mile out.

The Punta Cana region also boasts a remarkable assemblage of all-inclusive resorts for every budget (the trend is to ever-greater levels of luxe). Plus, there are marine-based theme parks, and Jeep safaris, plus horseback rides and no end of other attractions and recreation. And the water sports here—from parasailing to speedboat safaris—are unrivaled.

Getting There

By Air

Almost 2 million visitors a year arrive at the Aeropuerto Internacional de Punta Cana (see the introduction) on more than 20 airlines, including American Airlines, Continental, Delta, and Spirit Airlines. Others land in La Romana, about a two-hour drive away. Most folks arrive on a prepaid package that includes airport transfers by air-conditioned bus. Otherwise, there are plenty of taxis outside baggage claim. Independent travelers can also

Punta Cana and Vicinity

reserve airport transfers through **Dominican Airport Transfers** (809-330-1262; www.dominicanairporttransfers.com).

Santo Domingo's airport is about four hours away; very few prepaid air-hotel packages use this option. However, independent travelers already in Santo Domingo can fly to Punta Cana with **Punta Cana Express** (809-552-1333; http://takeoffweb.com), operated by Destination Service Take-Off Travel Agency, which uses 10-passenger Cessna Grand Caravans. It flies twice daily between Punta Cana and Santo Domingo's Las Américas International Airport ($99); and twice daily between Punta Cana and Samaná ($99), and once daily between Punta Cana and La Romana ($29) and Puerto Plata ($129).

Punta Cana—What's in a Name?

In 1969, a group of American investors led by entrepreneur Theodore W. Kheel acquired a 6-mile (10-km) strip of coastal land south of Punta Borrachón (Drunken Point, but better known as Cabo Engaño, Deception Cape) remarkable for white-sand beaches fringed by thousands of coconut palms. Kheel teamed with Dominican entrepreneur Frank R. Rainieri and in 1971 launched development of the virgin territory with a small hotel—the Punta Cana Club. In 1978, Club Mediterrané added a 350-room hotel. And in 1984, Punta Cana International Airport (owned and developed by Kheel and Rainieri's Grupo Puntacana S.A. corporation) opened as the first private international airport in the country, birthing the region's tourism boom.

The term Punta Cana is misleading. Many hotels use the name Punta Cana although they may not be located near Punta Cana. Upon arrival at Punta Cana International Airport, many visitors are surprised to find themselves bussed to hotels located up to one hour away in the relatively remote areas of Macao and Uvero Alto, with relatively few services. It pays to know where you're heading!

Punta Cana

Punta Cana proper, and the Punta Cana International Airport, lies south of Cabo Engaño, the nation's easternmost naze thumbing into the Mona Passage. Most hotels, however, are north of Cabo Engaño, where high winds whip up whitecaps and ferocious tides preclude swimming. The three hotels at Punta Cana proper are the Puntacana Hotel and sibling Tortuga Bay Villas, and Club Med.

Cap Cana

A few miles south of Punta Cana, heretofore virginal Cap Cana is the setting for the largest residential tourism project in the Caribbean, and one intended to be the crown jewel of the region's deluxe developments. The multifaceted project targets wealthy travelers with the Caribbean's largest inland mega-yacht marina, three Jack Nicklaus Signature golf courses, five deluxe hotels, to include a Ritz-Carlton, the NH Soto Grande, and a Trump Ocean Club, plus 5,000 private villas. Meanwhile, in 2008 the $2.5 billion Punta Perla Tourist Complex was launched.

By Bus

You can also hop a bus from other venues in the republic. See Getting There, in the Higüey section, for information on bus service.

In Bávaro, the bus station (known as Friusa) is on Carretera Coco Loco Riu, next to the Texaco station. You can also catch infrequent local buses here for Punta Cana or Cabeza del Toro (see the sidebar, Punta Cana—What's in a Name?); these *guaguas* can be waved down anywhere along their route, as most pass by the major hotels. Alternately, you can catch a bus from Higüey direct to Punta Cana or Cabeza del Toro (see Getting There, in the Higüey section).

Touring in Punta Cana and Beyond

The three main regions are linked by a half-completed highway—Bulevar Turística del Este highway—that runs north from the airport to Bávaro and Cabeza del Toro. Eventually the highway will also link the Macao and Uvero Alto regions, currently accessible by a winding and dangerously narrow rural road.

Alas, the Bávaro area has been totally unplanned and seemingly unregulated, with zero thought for pedestrians. Besides the grotesque ugliness of the place away from the beach,

CABEZA DEL TORO

Immediately north of Cabo Engaño, this compact resort region features five hotels along lovely sands backed by a sleepy village where fishermen still haul in their boats; and by a huge lagoon—Laguna Bávaro —and wetlands that extend north to a craggy headland called Punta de los Nidos. It is isolated from Punta Cana and Bávaro (see below), which can be accessed by the Bulevár Turística del Este highway.

BÁVARO

The lion's share of the region's all-inclusive resorts are concentrated north of Cabeza del Toro and Punta de los Nidos along three contiguous beaches—(south to north) Playa Bibijagua, Playa El Cortecito, and Playa Arena Gordo—that run unbroken for almost 10 miles (16 km). This rapidly booming district began as a village for local hotel workers at Punta Cana. Today it's the center of shops, restaurants, and other services, concentrated in the region of El Cortecito. Alas, development has been haphazard and poorly regulated and the place is an eyesore inland of the sensational sands.

MACAO

North of Playa Arena Gordo, the beaches along the pristine white-sand shores of the Macao district were virginal until 2006, when ground was broken on the Roco Ki mega-resort. Seven deluxe hotels and four championship golf courses were in evolution at last visit, when the first hotel, the Westin Roco Ki Beach and Golf Resort was almost ready. It's a 30-minute drive from Punta Cana International Airport.

UVERO ALTO

This newly emerging resort region north of Macao likes to bill itself as part of Punta Cana, but it's a 50-minute drive away and too remote to be accurately billed as such. Although it has several resorts, from mid-priced to super deluxe, facilities here are thus far relatively meager.

walking the roadways is *not* an option. It's too dangerous! You can walk the beach all the way from Punta de los Nidos to Arena Gorda—a distance of some 10 miles (16 km).

Also for reasons of safety, I do *not* recommend hiring a scooter or light motorcycle; nor *motoconchos*—the local staple of getting around. Foreign government advisories are full of horror stories of tourists maimed in accidents while riding *motoconchos*, but who otherwise never make the news. Stick to local buses or taxis. Taxis have stands at most hotels, where your concierge can also call one. Local buses (*guaguas*) ply the two main roads that connect all the hotels and services. Service is fairly regular (RD$30 for local rides). Buses are often crowded. And they're usually driven in an unsafe manner.

Most major hotels have car rental concessionaires on site.

Lodging

There are so many hotels in the Punta Cana region, and good ones at that, it's hard to decide which ones to recommend here. Boutique hotels, bed-and-breakfasts, and budget hotels are very slim pickings and the few that exist are, with rare exception, inland of the beach. The vast majority of hotels are large-scale all-inclusive resorts. Many are quite ritzy, with deluxe being the current trend. A decade ago the first wave of all-inclusive resorts transformed Bávaro into the Caribbean's trendsetter in value-priced mass-market chic. Today, a new crop of super-chic resorts is boosting the Punta Cana region into the rarified air of deluxe Caribbean retreats. Heretofore untrammeled sands are being tapped for swank new resorts in the making. And existing resorts have been invigorated by sensational facelifts, with soul-satisfying spas, fine-dining restaurants, and Frette linens.

Reservations are advisable during midwinter high season, December through April.

I've included here accommodations that span the budget and styles. Think about location before making your choice (see the sidebar, Punta Cana—What's in a Name?).

BARCELÓ BÁVARO RESORT
809-686-5797 or 800-277-2356
www.barcelo.com
Playa El Cortecito

This gigantic resort combines five contiguous all-inclusive hotels in one, totaling 2,300 rooms. The individual hotels run the gamut of price brackets, from the budget-oriented (but nonetheless three-star) Bávaro Beach to the not-quite-five-star Barceló Palace. Together they stretch along 3 miles (4.8 km) of beachfront. Two hotels—the Barceló Casino and Barceló Golf—are inland of the beach. A shuttle connects the hotels, and most of the facilities (such as the 14 restaurants and 16 bars) at individual hotels are open to guests in the others; however, guests in the budget properties cannot access the Bávaro Palace. Together they offer as complete a vacation experience as you can muster in the region—the complete package, as it were. The facility initiated a major four-year-long upgrade in 2008. The Bávaro Palace now has gorgeous rooms with a sophisticated 21st-century look, and just in time, as the old rooms were beat-up and dated. $$–$$$.

BARCELÓ PREMIUM PUNTA CANA RESORT
809-476-7777
fax: 809-412-2288
www.barcelopuntacana.com
Playa Arena Gorda, Bávaro

Barceló's latest edition—fresh from a multi-million dollar renovation in 2008—is this Mediterranean-inspired all-inclusive high-rise (at least by local standards), towering six storeys over lagoon-like swimming pools in a vast beachfront sundeck. With its multiple peaked red-tiled roofline, it's not the prettiest architecture. The 798 guest rooms come in six types, including two Presidential Suites for the super-well-heeled. It's worth dropping a little extra money for one of the 300 deluxe oceanfront suites furnished in high design, with flat-screen TVs. No conceivable facility has been omitted. Spa...Disco...Kids' disco ...etc? All here. There are better hotels around for the price, but this one should satisfy most tastes. $$–$$$$

BLAU NATURAPARK BEACH ECORESORT AND SPA
809-221-2626
fax: 809-221-6060
www.blau-hotels.com
Cabeza de Toro, Punta Cana

This 510-room resort makes the most of its surrounds, being tucked betwixt a gorgeous

Giant chess game at Barcelo Bavaro

white beach and a huge wetland with lagoon, mangroves, and dense forest. The resort itself has its own lake, and a surfeit of log-and-thatch structures, plus lavish bamboo furnishings in the reception that add to the ecological, almost Balinese, mood. This is a gorgeous all-inclusive beach resort. I love the bedroom decor: a combination of chic contemporary styling with earthy rattan and glazed hardwood pieces atop travertine floors. A complete resort, its facilities range from children's club to a full-service spa and all the water sports you would expect. $$$.

CORTECITO INN
809-552-0639
Cortecito, Bávaro

One of the few options for independent-minded budget travelers, the main advantage here is its location close to the beach and adjoining a shopping complex with restaurant (however, the latter can also be a bane, thanks to the ear-shattering music from the complex's pool-hall/bar—and the early morning roosters). The air-conditioned guest rooms are in five separate structures surrounding a pool. Nothing fancy here. Simple furnishings include a small TV, large refrigerator, ceilings fan, and modest sized bathroom (but you'll need to bring your own facecloth and toiletries). Some rooms have a balcony with rocker. Take a look at several rooms; one I saw had no toilet seat, many fixtures don't work, and the hotel has clearly seen better days. Secure parking is a bonus. But multiple online reports of surly and unethical reception staff are a concern. $$.

EDENH REAL ARENA

809-221-4646 or 888-726-0528
www.edenh-realarena.com
Playa Arena Gorda, Bávaro

It was love at first sight when I attended the opening night at this gorgeous property in April 2008. Everything here is city slicker contemporary with not a hint of the tropics (notwithstanding Edenh's sales pitch: "inspired by the beauty of the natural surroundings"), except by the beach, of course. But that's fine. Let's start with the cavernous lobby, oozing modernist attitude with its glossy travertine floor and sexily chic minimalist furnishings. Its 658 rooms—170 of them Paradise Rooms with their own VIP lobby, lounge, and swimming pool—similarly cater to the retro-hip culture with sophisticated top-dollar pieces and tasteful contemporary art. Four swimming pools, six restaurants, casino, spa, shopping plaza, kids' club, and the to-be-expected fare of nightly entertainment, disco, and six bars round things out. $$$$.

Speedboat, palm trees, and green ocean at Playa Bavaro

THE GOLF SUITES

809-552-8888
fax: 809-552-8989
www.thegolfsuites.com
Avenida Real, Bávaro

Golfers will appreciate this upscale apartment-suite complex within the Cocotal Golf and Country Club. Its 58 one-, two- and three-bedroom suites feature private Jacuzzis. The best thing here though is the superb Opio restaurant. And there's a small but top-notch spa. $$$$.

GRAND PALLADIUM PALACE RESORT SPA AND CASINO

809-221-0719
fax 809-221-0819
www.fiestahotelgroup.com
Playa El Cortecito, Bávaro

One of four Palladium hotels in the Bávaro, this luxury option has gracious neo-colonial styling, and its 504 guest rooms have king beds (68 have queen beds, and 140 are Royal Suites), sparkling travertine floors, and free-standing whirlpool tubs in the bedroom. For something different, take a Loft Suite, intended for families. Badminton, basketball, and tennis courts will keep you on your toes. Facilities include a casino, 11 restaurants, four swimming pools, and a kids' club. $$$$.

IBEROSTAR BÁVARO

809-221-6500
fax: 809-688-6186
www.iberostar.com
Playa Arena Gorda, Bávaro

An airy open-walled atrium lobby provides an inviting introduction to this sophisticated, low-slung all-inclusive resort, with 590 junior suites with mezzanine bedrooms and lively blue-and-red-striped fabrics. This is a great family option, as the rooms are family sized. The adjoining 346-room Iberostar Dominicana and 346-room Iberostar Punta Cana comprise a triptych, with all facilities available to guests of each hotel. Together they compete with nearby all-inclusives with tennis, a state-of-the-art spa, complete water sports, a dive center, nightly entertainment that includes a casino and nightclub, and globe-spanning restaurants that include Mexican and Japanese. $$$.

LA POSADA DE PIEDRA

809-221-0754
fax: 809-221-0754
www.laposadadepiedra.com
Playa Cortecito, Bávaro

This little family-run hotel may suit frugal travelers. It has three very tiny beachfront cabañas, plus two rooms upstairs in the main lodge. All are simply appointed. The latter have terra-cotta floors, rattan and wrought-iron furnishings, ceiling fans, and colonial touches. Try to get Cabin 3—it has a tree growing up through the center! One of the two rooms has its own bathroom; the other, slightly larger room, shares an outside bathroom.

And these rooms share an ocean-view balcony. There's no air-conditioning. The Argentinian owners cook up simple yet tasty foods. You can't beat the exceptional price for beachfront digs, although maintenance is clearly an issue. Guests have use of Internet, and there are plenty of services nearby. $–$$.

MAJESTIC ELEGANCE PUNTA CANA
809-221-9898
fax: 809-552-9995
www.majesticcolonial.com
Playa Arena Blanca, Bávaro.

Raising the bar on its own equally adorable twin, the Majestic Colonial Punta Cana, next door, this lavish newcomer opened in October 2008 with 600 spacious suites. The remarkable feature here is a snake-like swimming pool extending the length of the property. The lavish guest rooms sparkle with polished travertine floors and feature mahogany furnishings that include romantic draped four-poster king beds, and sophisticated white, orange, and chocolate color schemes. Flat-screen TVs and two-person Jacuzzi tubs in the bedrooms are adorable touches. An Argentinian-style steak house and Italian and sushi restaurants provide the dining options, plus the resort has its own spa and casino. $$$$.

MELIÁ CARIBE TROPICAL
809-221-1290
fax: 809-221-0809
www.solmelia.com
Playa Bávaro

Spain's Sol Meliá group's budget-level all-inclusive here is still a four-star winner. Mammoth-scaled, with 1,244 rooms, it has pretty much all the facilities you could want, including 13 restaurants, seven swimming pools, two spas, a casino, and even a climbing wall. Strongly family focused, its Flintstone-themed kids' facilities will keep youngsters amused while mom and pop enjoy activities that are more adult. Guest rooms are elegantly furnished with white, beige, and peach color schemes. Bonus points for the ceiling fans, but I don't like that guests are charged extra for use of in-room safes. $$–$$$.

PARADISUS PALMA REAL
809-688-5000 or 888-956-3542
fax: 809-688-5800
www.solmelia.com
Playa Arena Gorda, Bávaro

Opened in December 2005, this sumptuous all-suite all-inclusive is one of Sol Meliá's most prestigious properties. I love its magnificent Moorish-inspired architecture. And thankfully, Meliá's slightly overdone trademark pastels here give way to a much more sophisticated contemporary aesthetic that makes bold use of whites. Travertine gleams underfoot, including in the 554 oversized suites with their stylish and modish furnishings, and two-person Jacuzzi tubs conducive to romance. It has all the facilities you would expect, including nine eclectic but top-notch restaurants, a lagoon-size swimming pool overhung with canopied day beds, plus a casino. The nearby 500-room Paradisus Punta Cana is a tad less deluxe. $$$$.

PUNTACANA HOTEL

888-442-2262
http://puntacana.com
Puntacana Resort and Club, Punta Cana

The original hotel that kick-started tourism to the region in 1971, this lovely property—one of my favorites here—began life with just 10 two-room villas. It still has those (along with three-room villas), although they are affectionately now called beach casitas, in tropical ice cream pastels, along with Junior Suites and Deluxe Rooms in a handsome, thatch-fringed three-storey block that faces directly onto the hotel's private beach. The hotel is set in 105 acres (43 ha) of lush gardens. The open-air lobby is a study in elegance, thanks to Oscar de la Renta furnishings, including lots of oversize rattan chairs. Coral stone floors throughout add to the sense of refinement. Guest rooms are also furnished by de la Renta (a major investor here) in plantation style. The resort has its own stable, marina, and dive center. The kids' club has a carousel. Mom and dad get to enjoy the sensational Six Senses Spa and superlative dining at eight restaurants, including the gourmet Bamboo and Cocoloba restaurants, decorated by de la Renta. And this hotel is ground zero for golf in the area, with three P. B. Dye- and Tom Fazio-designed courses. $$$$.

RITZ-CARLTON

800-542-8680
www.ritzcarlton.com/en/Properties/CapCana
Cap Cana

Promising to blow the competition out of the water when it opens in early 2010 within the exclusive Cap Cana development, this 220-room resort is guaranteed to wow. Occupying a 2-mile (3 km) slice of talcum-white, talcum-fine Playa Juanillo, this sumptuous resort will feature five restaurants, a spa, private beach club, and conference facilities, and the guest rooms promise all the divine comforts you could wish for.

SANCTUARY CAP CANA GOLF AND SPA

809-955-9501 or 800-785-2198
www.altabellahotels.com
Cap Cana, 3 miles (4.8 km) S of the airport

The first hotel to open at Cap Cana (in April 2008), this deluxe 176-suite resort was designed as a faux medieval castle—an architectural faux pas in my eyes. Still, once inside the gates the colonial theme and traditional European luxury overwhelm. Gorgeous use of coral-stone walls, glossy hardwood floors, sumptuous fabrics, and state-of-the-art amenities such as WiFi connectivity and 37-inch plasma TV prove irresistible lures in the guest rooms, where bathrooms have slippers and robes. It has 12 room categories. The setting is stunning. The saltwater swimming pool is divine. So, too, the Mandara Spa. And you have access to the marina and the Jack Nicklaus Signature golf courses. $$$$.

TORTUGA BAY VILLAS

809-959-2262 or 1-888-442-2262
www.puntacana.com.
Puntacana Resort and Club, 0.6 mile (1 km) SE of the airport, Punta Cana.

Tortuga Bay Hotel, Punta Cana

Penelope Cruz, Uma Thurman, and Barbara Walters count among recent guests, reflecting this boutique inn's reputation as an en-vogue retreat for the rich and famous. Opened in 2006, this sumptuous option is the first Dominican hotel to be accepted as a member of The Leading Hotels of the World. It puts a 21st-century twist on the plantation house theme, courtesy of world-famous Dominican couturier Oscar de la Renta's impeccably refined styling (he's part owner, along with Spanish crooner, Julio Iglesias, both of whom are often seen here). It has 50 airy suites in 15 four-bedroom villas. All come with gorgeous calming whites, beiges, and soft yellow color schemes, plus mahogany, rattan, gleaming white plantation-style furnishings, and cozy comforts from 400-count Egyptian cotton sheets to slippers and L'Occitane en Provence toiletries in the marble-clad bathrooms. World-class dining, water sports, a serene spa, and two championship golf courses are added draws. Guests have full use of the facilities at the sibling Puntacana Hotel, next door, but not vice versa. This is one romantic pin-drop-quiet venue guaranteed to melt your sweetie's heart. $$$$.

VIK HOTEL ARENA BLANCA
809-221-6640
fax: 809-221-4658
www.vikhotels.com
Carretera Arena Gorda, Bávaro

Formerly the LTI Beach Resort, and still catering predominantly to a European clientele, this 447-room all-inclusive serves the mid-price crowd. The heart of affairs is the huge meandering swimming pool flanked by thatched restaurants overlooking the beach. Although lacking pizzazz, the guest rooms in three-storey blocks are spacious enough, have most desired amenities, and feature two features I always like—ceiling fans and cool terra-cotta tile underfoot. The VIK has three restaurants, four bars, plus a spa, tennis, and dive center. Guests in the hotel's 47 Cayena Beach Club Junior Suites have exclusive access to their own restaurant and pool. $$–$$$.

Dining

BLU II

809-552-1793
Plaza Brisas de Bávaro 103, Cortecito

This chic Spanish-run restaurant in a nondescript plaza in Cortecito is themed to its name with blue-and-white decor throughout, and is a tremendous option for a more dressy, off-the-beach dining experience. Jazz, bossa nova, and World music add to the hip vibe, enhanced by halogen lighting. It serves Mediterranean fusion cuisine with Caribbean flavors. My favorite dish? Sea bass with puree of capers, anchovies, and olives in sherry wine and cream over pasta. Open: noon–11 PM. $$$.

Catch of the day, Playa Bavaro

CAPITÁN COOK

809-552-0645
Playa El Cortecito, Bávaro.

Giving Jellyfish a run for its money as the coolest place to eat on the beach, Captain Cook is known for its excellent seafood. Complimentary appetizers include homemade potato chips and veggies with vinaigrette dressing. Famous for its lobster thermidor and charbroiled fish, prepared at a series of outdoor *planchas* (grills). Enormous *parrillada mixta* seafood platters include mussels, baby lobsters, fresh fish, squid, and shrimp. Thatched tables on the sands. Free hotel and water-taxi transfers. Open: Daily noon–1 AM. $–$$$.

COCOLOBA

809-959-2262
www.puntacana.com
Puntacana Resort and Club, Punta Cana

Elegance defines this magnificent restaurant furnished in plantation style by designer Oscar de la Renta. The mood is romantic. The ambience is classy and chic. And the world-class Dominican nouvelle cuisine is enhanced by artful crockery. A typical dinner might include crabmeat cakes with mango chutney followed by lobster tempura over glazed pumpkin with spinach sauce. Shuttered French doors open to an airy veranda for in or out dining. Reservations required. Dress code. Open: Tues. through Sun. 7–11 PM. $$$$.

JELLYFISH

809-868-3040 or 840-7684
www.jellyfishrestaurant.com
Playa Bávaro

When you want to escape the all-inclusives but still dine in flip-flops and shorts, head to this fantastic restaurant right on the sands at the east end of Playa Bávaro, between the Meliá Caribe and Barceló Bávaro hotels. Rising two storeys, hewn of coral stone, and open-walled on the oceanside, this half-moon thatched bar-restaurant is a marvelous venue to chill over a great meal and cold beer. Winners here include the spicy lobster bisque, Greek salads, tempura shrimp, and langostina in brandy. I love settling into a deep-cushion bamboo and rattan sofa on the mezzanine, shaded by canopies, and lighting up a stogie (sold here). It has occasional live music and events. Free hotel transfers. Open: Daily 11–11. $$–$$$$.

EL PULPO COJO

809-272-8875
Playa Cabeza del Toro

This simple yet atmospheric, open-air thatched seafood restaurant is built around a beached ship with the prow sticking into the road. Maritime decor (coral, turtle shells, etc.) plays up the theme. Ever tried cuttlefish in ink? Do . . . it's delicious. Garlic shrimp and grilled fresh catch of the day are other options. Open: Tues. through Sun. 11 AM–11 PM. $–$$.

La Palapa restaurant at Caleton Beach Club, Cap Cana

LA PALAPA
809-688-5587
www.capcana.com/gastronomy/en/beach-club/palapa.html
Caletón Beach Club, Cap Cana

Perfect after a round of golf or when you want to partake of the sumptuous facilities at Caletón Beach Club, this small but elegant thatched boutique restaurant sits atop a lime-stone bluff between a quaint cove and the Punta Blanca golf course. Chef Jacinto A. Romero uses only the freshest of seafoods. Start with ceviche, then follow with fish fillet à la Ricardo. Open: Daily noon–6. $$$.

LA TASCA
809-350-0239
Palma Real Shopping Plaza, Carretera El Cortecito 57, Bávaro

Decked out in minimalist fashion, this sophisticated tapas and wine bar could have been transported from Beverly Hills or Manhattan. Faux-wood floor. Black and charcoal decor. Frosted glass. Brushed-steel furnishings. All very chic! Take a sweater, as the air-condi-tioning is sometimes cranked up full bore. Open: Daily 10 AM–midnight. $$$$.

MITRE BAR AND RESTAURANT
809-469-7010
www.capcana.com/gastronomy/en/marina/mitre.html
Cap Can Marina, Cap Cana

This super chic restaurant lit up local dining when it opened in 2008, with sensational views over the marina and equally exciting contemporary decor in its three dining rooms. Polished cement floors and oh-so-today chocolates and charcoals beneath ice-blue lighting. Nice! Chefs Miguel Roques and Giancarlo Bonarelli deliver consistently divine signature fusion dishes such as *risotto a la valenciana,* meticulously prepared and presented. Put on your finest duds to fully enjoy the experience. Open: Daily 11 AM–11 PM. $$$$.

OPIO
809-552-6371
www.grupoanthuriun.com/opio/web.php
Cocotal Golf and Country Club, Avenida Real, Bávaro

I adore the decor and ambience at Spanish Chef Kiko Casals's upscale fusion restaurant with a part Indian, part Moroccan decor. You can choose air-conditioned indoor dining, but the place to be is on the upstairs terrace, with sensual drapes overhanging concrete bench seats with plump cushions. I like to start off with an appetizer of salmon ravioli stuffed with maize (corn) mousse and vanilla with smoked vinaigrette, followed by smoked turkey rolls with cognac. Delicious! Open: Daily 1–5 and 8:30–midnight. $$$$

LA YOLA
809-959-2262
www.puntacana.com
Puntacana Marina, Punta Cana

Another of the Puntacana Resort's several posh world-class venues, this thatched open-air restaurant hangs over the Caribbean. The experience is romantic to a tee. The Mediterranean-pan-Latin menu makes the most of local seafoods and fresh organic vegetables grown on-site. Start with arugula and grilled squid salad, or crunchy shrimp tempura, or tangy fish ceviche. You can't go wrong with the grilled lobster in buttery garlic sauce, being sure to leave room for the divine tiramisu. The classy place is in demand. Book well ahead. Daily noon–3:30 PM; Dinner daily 7 PM–11 PM

Attractions, Parks, and Recreation

Aerial Tours
Soaring over the Coconut Coast is a spectacular way to appreciate the beauty of the region and is an experience you won't quickly forget. Parasail vendors can be found on the beach at Playa El Cortecito and at several major all-inclusive resorts.

HELIDOSA
809-688-0744
Fax: 809-552-6162
http://helidosa.com/excursiones.html
Carretera Arena Gorda, adjoining Manati Park, Bávaro

Take to the air in a three-passenger R-44 Raven or a four- to six-passenger Bell helicopter for 10- to 30-minute sightseeing tours of the Punta Cana coastline, including zipping down for close-ups of shipwrecks ($60–130).

CARIBBEAN OCEAN ADVENTURES
809-586-1239
www.caribbeanoceanadventures.com/parasailing.htm

To see things as a seagull sees things, strap on a harness, attach yourself to a parasail, and let a speedboat tow you 150 feet (46 m) up into the air. The first few moments are pure adrenaline rush as you soar upwards. Then you settle into a smile-inducing calm as you're towed along the coast, the warm rushing wind caressing your face, and the entire coast passing slowly by far below. Trips typically last 12 minutes and cost $45 single, $80 tandem.

Aquatic Tours
At least half a dozen catamarans offer scheduled sailing trips along the coast. Most are variants on a party theme, with lots of rum swizzles and a stop for snorkeling. Hotel tour excursion desks can make reservations for all the aquatic excursions listed here.

The two-storey **Kontiki** is a dedicated party boat with a live steel-drum reggae band and lots of free-flowing booze at the open bar. It sails at 1:30 to Buccaneers Reef for snorkeling (four hours, $69 adults, $34.50 children).

Mike's Marina (809-729-5164; www.mikesmarina.info) offers four-hour trips aboard the 10-passenger *Patatatu* catamaran, departing Bibijagua beach market on Playa Bávaro at 9 AM ($65 per person).

You can rent sailboats at **Cap Cana Marina** (809-785-2198 or 959-2262; www.capcana .com), and at **Puntacana Marina** (809-959-2262), at Puntacana Resort and Club.

BÁVARO SPLASH
809-688-1615 or 350-3896
bavarosplash@hotmail.com

Many a vacationer in Punta Cana will swear that piloting their own two-seater speedboat James Bond-style was the most fun they had. This three-hour adventure involves zipping along in convoy to a snorkeling platform, where you don masks, snorkels, and fins for a plunge in the waters before buzzing back across the turquoise oceans. Pilots must be 18 years of age. Hotel transfers are included. Departures daily at 9 AM, 11 AM, and 10 PM. $69.

DOLPHIN WORLD
954-525-4441 (Florida office)
www.dolphinislandpark.com or www.dolphinworld.org/punta_cana_dolphin_swim.htm

Want to play tag with Flipper? Your day begins with a short boat ride to Dolphin Island, a floating platform where you can swim in ocean waters with bottlenose dolphins, which respond to food and verbal signals to perform trained behaviors such as acrobatics. The cute and intelligent animals swim around you and let you touch them. They even kiss you. A bit hokey, but who can resist their cute smiles. Sea lions are an added bonus, plus you spend time on a private beach. I think the price ($175 adult or child participant; $20 non-participant) is crazy . . . but the experience *is* memorable. Offered daily at 11:15 AM and 4:15 PM. Book online, or through hotel excursions desks and local travel agents.

MARINARIUM MARINE PARK AND AQUARIUM/REEF EXPLORER

809-689-5183

www.marinarium.com

A variant on Dolphin World, this half-day excursion features a glass-bottom catamaran ride to an offshore lagoon for snorkeling with stingrays and harmless nurse sharks; then your sightseeing cruise continues along the coast to a private lagoon for wallowing with cocktail in hand. $83 adults, $41.40 children.

SEAQUARIUM

809-688-9525

www.sea-aquarium.com

This outfit gives you yet another option for discovering the beauty of the undersea world. First option is to use Snuba, a cross between snorkeling and scuba diving, but with your oxygen tank floating on an inflatable raft, leaving you unencumbered; your air line is of course attached to the tank. Second choice is the Sea-trek, in which you don a state-of-the-art diver's helmet (also with a life line attached to a floating tank) for a walk along the sea bed.

Bowling
PUNTA CANA LANES

809-959-4444

http://pclanes.com

Plaza Bolera, Bávaro.

Two huge pins outside beckon you inside this bowling alley with 20 lanes, plus pool tables, video golf, and a sports bar grill. Open: Mon. through Thurs. 4 PM–midnight, Fri. 4 PM–2 AM, Sat. 1 PM–2 AM, Sun. 1 PM–midnight. Admission: $10 per hour.

Golf
The Punta Cana region is renowned for its superb courses. Three new courses debuted in 2007.

COCOTAL GOLF AND COUNTRY CLUB

809-687-4653

www.cocotalgolf.com

Avenida Real, Bávaro

Six-time Spanish Champion Jose "Pepe" Gancedo designed this gently rolling, 7,285-yard (6,661-m) course, carving it out of a former coconut plantation. Clubhouse. Pro shop. Tee-off times 7 AM–2:30 PM. $112.

LA CANA GOLF CLUB

809-959-4653

www.puntacana.com

Puntacana Resort and Club, Punta Cana

Teeing off the local golf trend when it opened in 2000, this 7,152-yard (6,539 m) P. B. Dye-designed course is a well-rounded favorite of President Bill Clinton. It's laid out with spectacular ocean vistas (four holes play along the shore) and a new hybrid grass called Seashore Paspalum, which tolerates seawater irrigation. Golf pro Kim Jensen runs the PuntaCana Golf Academy. $156 non-guest, $115 hotel guest.

The first nine holes of P. B. Dye's **Hacienda Course**, also at Puntacana Resort and Club, are scheduled to open in winter 2009. And Tom Fazio has designed the members-only **Corales Golf Course**, also currently being laid out at the Puntacana Resort and Club.

PUNTA BLANCA COURSE

809-468-4734
www.punta-blanca.com
Carretera Arena Gorda, Punta Cana

Designed by South African Nick Price and opened in 2007, this relatively flat course features natural wetlands in play on the 13th and 15th holes. Several holes edge up to coconut-white sands. Nearby hotels such as the Majestic Colonial Beach Resort offer discounts. $150.

PUNTA ESPADA

809-472-2525
www.capcana.com
Cap Cana

The first of three Jack Nicklaus Signature Courses slated to open within the next few years at Cap Cana, this sensational championship course opened for play in August 2006 with ocean views from every hole. The design makes the most of the natural bluffs and gorgeous sands, and accommodates golfers of all levels, including those playing at world championship ranking. There's a pro shop and fabulous restaurant as befits this super-chic development.

Las Iguanas, the second course, will open in 2010, followed by the **Farallon Golf Course**. Two additional courses—the **Mountain Golf Course** and the **Marina Golf Course**—will eventually open here.

Miscellaneous Attractions and Recreation

FARALLON ZIP LINE ADVENTURE

809-455-1135
www.bavarorunners.com

It had to happen! Following the explosion in popularity of ziplining in Costa Rica, Bávaro Runners' founders wisely hired one of Costa Rica's most experienced canopy tour builders to erect 11 platforms and 10 ziplines stretching along about 1 mile (1.6 km) of the Taíno Anamuya mountain range. Your five-hour adventure includes a 45-minute drive aboard a safari truck. After a safety briefing and demo, you're put in harness to face the challenge of flying from one platform to another via a secure traversing system using steel cables. The longest zipline is 820 feet (250 m). Pure exhilaration, and well worth $89.

SEGWAY TOURS

829-707-1469
www.segwaycaribedominicano.com or www.segwayguided-tours.com/segwaytour.cfm?State=BAVARO

Segway Caribe Dominicano, inside the Barceló Bávaro hotel complex, offers Segway rental ($30 per hour) and tours ($70). It's a fun way to explore the huge Barceló complex and along remote sections of beach.

Safaris
BÁVARO RUNNERS

809-455-1135
www.bavarorunners.com

You're forgiven for thinking yourself on an African safari, what with a zebra-striped open-top safari truck as your transport. The half- ($55 adult, $21 child) and full-day ($85 adult, $43 child) tours travel deep into the countryside for a taste of the local lifestyle at farms, a sugarcane plantation, tobacco farm, and cigar factory, and even local schools. Horseback riding is included and there's beach time, of course. Giving back to the community is an important part of the company's philosophy. A portion of the proceeds go to local rural schools and Lagunas de Nisibón Rural Hospital.

FUN-BUGGY

809-221-1359
www.fun-buggy.com/eng.html

Coastal track near Cabo Engano, Punta Cana

Like to drive? Then consider a 75-mile (121-km) group tour using dune buggies with manual shifts and a capacity for five people. The full-day tours (8–5) stop every 30 minutes or so, including at a rural school, a cigar factory, and Playa Macao. Offered Tues., Thurs., and Sat.; $90 adult, $45 children. Advance reservations essential.

SAFARIS PUNTA CANA EXPRESS
809-686-9290
http://safaripuntacanaexpress.com

If you prefer a drive-yourself copycat version to the highly successful Bávaro Runners' safari, sign up for this trip. Driving your own ragtop Suzuki jeep, you'll travel in convoy through the countryside of the eastern provinces with stops at fruit farms, a tobacco factory, and for hiking.

Sportfishing
The fabulous sportfishing around Punta Cana has barely been tapped. Talk about a rod-bending challenge! The streaming waters of the Mona Passage are a veritable pelagic highway for dorado, marlin, and tuna. The billfish season here runs seven months a year, with March through July peak time for white marlin and July through September bounty time for blue marlin. During calmer winter months, barracuda, dorado (mahi-mahi), and sailfish are fish of choice. Few outfitters here operate catch-and-release; the low-paid crews get to sell off your catch.

Many crews and touts drum up business on the beach. However, there are relatively few truly professional crews currently operating out of Punta Cana (that should soon change as the new Cap Cana and Roco Ki marinas kick into gear). Stick with a reputable outfitter with a sizeable boat—you don't want to be tossed around all day in a flimsy little boat that will have you puking your lunch (take sea-sickness tablets well in advance).

I recommend **Mike's Marina** (809-729-5164; www.mikesmarina.info) which, despite its lousy website, operates top-class vessels out of Punta Cana Marina; or **Punta Cana Sport Fishing** (809-867-0381; www.firstclassfishing.com), which operates from El Cortecito. Expect to pay $640–695 for a private half-day charter for up to six people, or $1,240–1,295 full day. Punta Cana Sport Fishing also charges $99 per person for split-charter walk-ons.

Wildlife and Wilderness Parks
ANIMAL ADVENTURE PARK
809-221-7275
www.animalpark.com.do
Cabeza del Toro

Fabulous! Grab the kids and head off to this beachfront animal park where the displays include Bengal tigers, monkeys, and macaws. Animal shows include sea lion acrobatics four times daily—you even get to swim with these adorable mammals ($80 adults, $65 children). And you can swim with nurse sharks and rays in a lagoon enclosed by a natural coral reef ($80 adults, $65 children). There's a touch pool for kids to learn about starfish, etc. Admission: $40 adults, $25 children, including hotel transfers.

BÁVARO LAGOON NATIONAL WILDLIFE REFUGE
Cabeza del Toro

The Refugio Nacional de Vida Silvestre Laguna Bávaro protects a mangrove and Sisal palm swamp forest reserve measuring 5.8 square miles (15 sq km) and centered on a lagoon to which ducks and other migratory waterfowl flock by the gazillions. The lagoon (and the smaller Laguna del Cuerno, adjacent) is separated from the ocean by a 328-yard-wide (300 m) isthmus. Four species of mangroves provide shelter to juvenile fishes, crabs, and other tiny critters, including a fish species—*Cyprinodon higuey*—found only here. In 2008, plans were announced to build a visitors center and ecological trails.

MANATÍ PARK
809-221-9444
www.manatipark.com
Carretera Manatí, Bávaro

On a grander scale than Animal Adventure Park, this park offers a day's worth of family entertainment and education that includes equestrian shows plus dolphin and sea lion shows. Even the parrots perform amusing pirouettes. Nine shows are hosted daily, including folkloric performances that recreate aspects of indigenous life in a reconstruction of a Taíno village. A museum displays pre-Columbian relics, and artisans make indigenous-style pottery and other crafts on site. Plus you can swim with dolphins (9 AM, 2 PM, and 5:15 PM, $85 by reservation), touch snakes and iguanas, admire flamingoes strutting their stuff, and get eye-to-eye with American crocodiles. Open daily 9–6. Admission: $30 adults, $14 children, including hotel transfers.

PUNTA CANA ECOLOGICAL PARK
809-959-9208 or 959-9221
www.puntacana.com
Puntacana Resort and Club, Punta Cana

If you're hankering for a bit of hiking, this 45-acre (15 ha) nature sanctuary offers short trails through native lowland subtropical forest pitted with freshwater lagoons. Open to the public, this park is but a small portion of the 1,500-acre (607 ha) Indigenous Eyes Ecological Reserve (open only to locals and to guests of the Puntacana Resort and Club), owned and managed by the Puntacana Ecological Foundation, established in 1999 to fund research and education into sustainable development of the Caribbean. More than 500 species of plants, plus endangered rhinoceros iguana, numerous bat species, snakes, and more than 100 bird species can be seen while hiking. It has an experimental botanical garden and traditional Dominican farm that includes a petting zoo for kids. Guided tours and horseback riding ($$$) are available. Admission: free.

Water Sports
There's no shortage of water sports to be enjoyed. All the all-inclusive resorts include use of non-motorized water sports in their rates. This usually includes Aqua-Bikes, Hobie Cats, kayaks, and windsurfing gear. Private concessionaires offer motorized action; they have outlets on all the beaches, but are concentrated at El Cortecito. The main outfitter is **Pelicano Water Sports** (809-947-0894; www.pelicanosport.com), with outlets on the beach at six hotels; it offers a range of water sports, from banana-boat rides and Hobie Cat sailing to scuba diving and even whale-watching trips.

Ban Those Jet Skis!

I'm all in favor of banning Jet Skis . . . I consider them a dangerous and noisy intrusion on the peace and quiet. Fortunately, they *are* banned in many tourist beaches such as those at Punta Cana. Meanwhile, so is *every* form of water sport during the annual Holy Week Water Sports Ban. It's a safety measure to cut down on the frightening levels of injuries and deaths among drunken Easter revelers.

Culture

Cinema

The only cinema is the three-screen **Palacio del Cine Bávaro** (www.palaciodelcine.com.do /cine_Bavaro.htm; Carretera El Cortecito 57, Bávaro), in the Palma Real Shopping Village.

Nightlife

Most of the nightlife occurs inside the all-inclusive resorts, where patrons can choose from suave piano bars and cozy pubs to live merengue to (relatively dull) discos. Independent travelers can buy night-passes to most all-inclusive resorts, which may prove a good deal if you want to dine and enjoy the cabarets.

However, there's plenty to do when you tire of the cabaret shows and guests-only discos, from sand-floored sunset bars amid the palms, to discos that don't even open their doors till most vacationers are asleep. The main hot spots are close together, so you easily hop between them. And the current building boom has graced Bávaro with ritzy shopping plazas—surprising venues for lively lounges and sports bars that crank into disco mode come midnight.

Bars

HARD ROCK CAFÉ

809-552-0594
Palma Real Shopping Village, Carretera El Cortecito 57, Bávaro
www.hardrock.com

You know exactly what you're getting at this lively chain lounge-bar-café full of pure Americana, including an authentic rock atmosphere, thanks to guitars and other rock music memorabilia on the walls. And you get to listen to some great oldies music. Open: 11:30 AM—2 AM.

HIGH WAVE

809-309-0500
Bávaro Shopping Center, Avenida Italia, Cortecito.

High-definition, big-screen TVs (including on the terrace) and an ultra-chic lounge combine to bring smiles to sports-loving sophisticates' faces. A great place to kick start the evening, this upbeat sports bar also serves American-style food, and a mix of lively Latin tunes and retro 1970s and 1980s R and B, etc. are spun by night. Opposite the Bávaro Princess resort.

HURACAN CAFÉ BAR

809-221-6643

Hotel Tropical Alisios, Avenida Alemania, Cortecito.

This simple thatched beach bar, unassuming by day, becomes a classic Caribbean chill-out spot by night, when tourists and locals gather to down killer cocktails and dance right on the sand. It has live merengue and occasional fun theme nights when the music is cranked up to way beyond respectable levels.

SOLES CHILL OUT BAR

809-729-4371

Playa de Los Corales, Bávaro

The name says it all. Throw away the sandals and feel the sand between your toes at this simple yet lively thatched beach bar and restaurant (next to Ocean Bávaro Hotel), with lounge chairs and dining right on the sands. The place packs in the crowds at night. Outdoor movies on Sunday nights; live music Monday nights; and DJ Taro spins tunes the rest of the week.

Cabarets

Sexy cabaret routines are a staple of all-inclusive resort hotel entertainment. But the Punta Cana region also has a dedicated cabaret for the public. (Meanwhile, the former Caribe Caliente open-air show—to my mind, far superior to the indoor Tropicalissimo—is no more.)

TROPICALISSIMO

809-686-5797

Barceló Bávaro Casino Hotel, Bávaro

This musical extravaganza is staged in an air-conditioned (but usually crowded and not all-that-comfortable) theater at Barceló Bávaro Casino Hotel, six nights weekly. Rainbow-hued searchlights sweep over hordes of gaudily feathered, mocha-skinned voluptuous showgirls (and guys in tights) who perform amid a frenzied melee of horns, drums, and maracas in a show full of sinister and sexual content. Guests at the Barceló resort get free admission. Open: Mon. through Sat.

Night Clubs

Most all-inclusives have disco/nightclubs for their patrons only. However, there *are* a few that have discos open to the public This being the DR, the hot nightspots draw their fair share of sankys (young males pimping themselves to female tourists under the guise of romance) and none-too-subtle hookers, who often seize the arm of single males to gain entrance as a couple. The nightclubs don't get into their groove until well past midnight.

AREITO

809-687-7788 ext. 4044

Bávaro Princess, Avenida Italia, Cortecito.

Decorated with a mix of state-of-the-art lighting and giant pre-Columbian Taíno sculptures, this air-conditioned disco-bar permits the public and draws a mix of locals and tourists. National drinks included for guests of the Bávaro Princess. Open: 11 PM–2:30 AM. Admission: free.

THE CAVE
809-552-6262
Carretera Friusa, Bávaro

This venue has had more makeovers than Madonna, as the owners try to settle on a winning formula. It should be a no-brainer given the sensational venue—a medieval castle facade fronting a massive underground cavern. Most recently hosting the defunct Tropicana Garden Show (earlier known as Caribe Caliente) cabaret, it now hosts a disco. Naturally air-conditioned and comfortably cool, it's a spectacular venue. Its two dance floors play *bachata*, hip-hop, merengue, and reggaeton, plus house and rave, respectively. Free shuttles to/from hotels. Open: Nightly 11 PM–4 AM. Admission: $30 all-inclusive of drinks.

JAZZY'S
809-435-5502
Carretera Veron-Bávaro, Bávaro.

Have you driven by this Arabian-style roadside palace lit up at night like a Christmas tree and wondered "what on earth is that?" Well, curiosity killed the cat! A ritzy gentleman's club befitting Las Vegas's finest, this strip club offers high-octane adult entertainment, with women in go-go dance cages on two levels and X-rated antics behind the velvet curtains. The decor is straight out of the *Arabian Nights,* with its minarets and sparkling marble. You're expected to spend money here. Bring a *very* fat wallet. (A far less expensive and ritzy alternative is **La Punta**, Avenida Estados Unidos, outside the Gran Paradise Bávaro, at Playa Arena Gorda.) Open: 8 PM–4 AM.

MANGÚ DISCO BAR
809-221-8787
www.mangudiscobar.com
Gran Flamenco Punta Cana, Avenida Italia, Cortecito

Considered the hottest nightclub around, this place—at the entrance to the Gran Flamenco hotel—has been a sophisticated local institution since it opened in 2001. Take your choice of two floors: one upstairs playing techno and house, and the other catering to those who prefer top 40, disco, hip-hop, etc. Five bars keep the libations flowing, plus there's a snack bar to fuel up for the dance floor. It hosts special theme events, including foam parties. Open: 9 PM–4 AM. Admission: $6 including one drink.

PACHA
809-221-7515
Hotel Riu Naiboa, Arena Gorda

At the entrance to the Hotel Riu Naiboa resort, this disco is larger (but less active) than Mangú and the DJs here spin hip-swiveling Latin tunes—merengue, salsa, even *bachata*. Hence, it draws plenty of locals. Ironically, the patrons tend to drift away by around 2 AM and head over to nearby Mangú, where the party extends to 4 AM. Open: 10 PM–2 AM. Admission: Free.

Casinos

The Punta Cana region has half a dozen major wagering spots associated with the all-inclusive hotels but open for public play. Most offer a combination of blackjack, craps, roulette, three-card poker, and Texas Hold'em, plus Caribbean stud poker and mini-baccarat.

Bahía Principe Casino (809-552-1444; Gran Bahía Principe Bávaro, Playa Arena Gorda).

Barceló Bávaro Casino (809-686-5797; Barceló Bávaro Casino, Bávaro). Open 24 hours.

Carabela Casino (809-552-0144 or 221-2728; Carabel Beach Resort and Casino, Playa El Cortecito).

Iberostar Punta Cana Casino (809-688-3210 or 221-6500; Playa Arena Gorda). Open 4 PM–3 AM.

Palma Real Casino (809-688-6625 or 221-1290; Meliá Caribe Tropical, Playa Bávaro). Open 8 PM–3 AM.

Paradisus Punta Cana Casino (809-687-0903 or 687-9923; Paradisus Punta Cana, Playa El Cortecito).

Princess Tower Casino (809-552-1111), Bávaro Princess, Playa El Cortecito). Free hotel transfers.

Riu Palace Casino (809-221-7121; Riu Palace, Playa Arena Gorda). Open 4 PM–3 AM.

Shopping

All the all-inclusive hotels have souvenir stores and boutiques, but prices are usually significantly higher than you'll pay for similar products at beach stalls and local markets. Several markets line the sands. These each host dozens of local stall-holders who compete to hustle colorful but mostly tacky Haitian paintings, coral jewelry, cigars (usually cheap varieties), T-shirts, wood carvings, batik sarongs, *mamajuana*, and the like. Competition is fierce and the sales tactics often annoyingly aggressive. Bartering over the price is expected, and adds to the fun of a purchase. Rest assured that you'll initially be quoted a ridiculously high price. Aim to bargain the price down by 30 percent. *Do not buy animal products, such as the seashells, tortoise shell products, or grotesque stuffed frogs.* Itinerant vendors also wander the beach with their fold-down oversize trays full of trinkets.

You can't always trust the amber and larimar jewelry sold at the beach stalls. Much of it is fake (see Arts and Crafts, in the What to Buy section in the Planning Your Trip chapter). You can have faith, however, in the **Museo de Ambar** (809-552-6332, daily 8:30–5:30), a store-cum-museum on the sands at Cortecito.

Shopping malls are sprouting like mushrooms on a damp log. The largest and most impressive is the **Palma Real Shopping Village** (809-552-8725; www.palmarealshoppingvillage.com; Carretera El Cortecito 57, Bávaro), with more than 30 upscale boutiques and stores including **Cig's Aficionado** (809-552-8754) for fine cigars; **La Maraka** (809-552-8744) or **Marea** (809-552-8742) for quality souvenirs; **Prota-Rolex** (809-552-8798) for Rolex watches and similar super-fine jewelry; **Verganti** (809-552-8770) for international high fashion; and **Allure Lencery** (809-552-6159) for super-sexy lingerie. For the best of amber and larimar jewelry, head to **Museo de Ambar y Larimar Bávaro** (809-552-9710) or **Harrison's** (809-552-8721), also here.

Lacava (809-552-9000; www.palmarealshoppingvillage.com; Carretera El Cortecito 57, Bávaro), a snazzy cigar lounge, sells quality stogies.

Good to Know About

Centro Médico Punta Cana (809-552-1506; Sección El Salado, Bávaro) Multilingual staff. Has an in-house pharmacy. Open: 9–9 for doctor visits, 24 hours for emergencies.

Farmacia el Manglar (809-552-1533; Plaza Punta Cana, Bávaro) Delivers to hotels. Open: 8 AM–midnight.

Hospiten Bavaro (809-686-1414; bavaro@hospiten.com; Galería Punta Cana, Carretera Higüey-Punta Cana, Punta Cana) Fully equipped medical facility for emergency treatment. Open: 24 hours.

Pharma Cana (809-959-0025; Galería Punta Cana, Carretera Higüey-Punta Cana, Punta Cana)

Open: 9 AM–10 PM.

Politur (809-688-8727) Tourism police with 24-hour stations next to the Sitrabapu bus terminal in Cortecito, and at Galerías Punta Cana near the airport.

Tourism Office (809-552-1237; Plaza El Tronco, Carretera Friusa, Bávaro).

MACAO, UVERO ALTO, AND VICINITY

North of Playa Arena Gorda, a white-sand beach unspools for miles to the headland of Punta Macao, a rocky headland thrashed by crashing surf. Astonishingly this beach, which equals in length those of Bávaro, Cortecito, and Arena Gorda combined, has until now been virgin terrain. The heretofore untrammeled and inaccessible sands are being tapped for swank new resorts in the making; the project—**Roco Ki**—promises to finally put these sands on the map.

North of the headland, undeveloped and silvery **Playa Macao**, about 8 miles (13 km) north of Bávaro, is a popular destination for ATV, Jeep, and horseback excursions. Colorful wooden fishing boats haul out here, and vendors prepare simple seafood. The beach extends 1 mile (1.6 km) to the mouth of the Río Anamuya, beyond which tangerine and golden sands of the **Uvero Alto** district are evolving as a new resort destination (although they're a one-hour drive north of Punta Cana, they capitalize on the Punta Cana name). The sands of Uvero Alto extend to **Boca de Maimón**, the mouth of the eponymous river backed by a lagoon and mangrove marshes framed by the Cordillera Oriental.

The next 30 miles (48 km) or so is the **Costa del Coco** proper (but also known as Costa Esmeralda). It's named for the coconut palm plantation that extends the length of this coast. Vestal gold- and white-sand beaches—**Playa Lavacama**, then **Playa del Muerte** and **Playa Nisibón** among them—follow one upon the other in sweeping scallops. With a 4WD vehicle you can follow the sandy tack (strewn with palm leaves and coconuts) that parallels the shore just a few yards inland. Otherwise, only marine turtles crawl ashore to nest on this virginal shore. Falling coconuts are a hazard! It's a fantastic shore for exploring à la Indiana Jones. Ironshore ledges good for tidepooling are exposed at low tide; fishermen cast nets to haul in their silvery catch. An irregular reef keeps wave action to a minimum, but not sufficient for snorkeling. Surf crashes ashore in stormy weather. A freighter clasped on reefs at Del Muerte, farther north, is testament to the tricky tides here.

Roco Ki cliffside Golf The Faldo Legacy at Roco Ki Golf Club The Dominican Republic Ministry of Tourism

Lodging

AGUA RESORT AND SPA

809-468-0000 or 866-757-2482
www.aguaresort.com
Uvero Alto

This upscale resort tries to distinguish itself from the local competition with its superb indigenous Taíno-inspired architecture featuring dramatic thatched roofs. First the good points, starting with the gorgeous breeze-swept open-air lounge with its lavish travertine floors and sumptuous bamboo and rattan furnishings, conducive to relaxing with a cigar and cocktail. And the 18 villas and 53 suites (fringing a lazily serpentine pool) are gorgeous: Highlights include glamorous hardwood floors, flat-screen TVs, king beds with throw pillows and cloud-soft duvets, plus massive bathrooms. And the full-service Varari Spa earns raves. Two glaring weak links are the ho-hum restaurant, and the truly rough-hewn wooden boardwalk linking upper-level rooms—a faux pas you'll understand the first time you trip while negotiating this unlevel walkway at night. $$$$.

DREAMS PUNTA CANA RESORT AND SPA

809-682-0404
fax: 809-468-0183
www.dreamsresorts.com/drepc
Playa Uvero Alto

Anyone who knew this hotel as the Sunscape the Beach Punta Cana simply won't recognize it now. Metamorphosed like a caterpillar into a butterfly, in December 2007 this 620-room all-inclusive resort reopened after a ritzy multi-million dollar makeover. The stunning highlight remains the enormous free-form pool snaking 437 yards (400 m) from the lobby to the beach. Meanwhile, the bedrooms shine with new tile floors and plantation-style furnishings in golds, creams, and whites. $$$.

EXCELLENCE PUNTA CANA
809-685-9880
fax: 809-688-4657
www.excellence-resorts.com
Uvero Alto

This adults-only all-inclusive resort has a singular advantage over competitors: it runs parallel to the beach so that all rooms are oceanfront. Fresh from an 8 million dollar refurbishment, the now-stunning hotel has upgraded all 452 suites in a soothing mélange of eggshells and whites. For an even more extraordinary level of luxury, check in to the resort's Excellence Club, granting access to a private Club beach and lounge, plus swim-up *cabaña* suites with personal concierge service and Bulgari toiletries. The resort boasts all the facilities you could want, including eight restaurants. $$$.

FAIRMONT ROCO KI
1-800-441-1414
www.fairmont.com or www.rocoki.com/fairmont.html
Punta Macao

The Westin Roco Ki (see below) will be followed in 2010 by this equally sumptuous rival, to include a 255-room hotel and the Fairmont Residences—a collection of condominiums, villas, and estate homes to be placed in a rental pool. It will also offer a 15,000-square-foot Willow Stream Spa sure to have Hollywood stars and other sybarites flocking. $$$$.

HOTEL RANCHO LA CUEVA
809-470-0876
www.lacuevalimon.com
Playa Limón

This simple, German-run hotel about 400 yards (365 m) inland of Playa Limón might appeal to independent travelers searching for offbeat adventure. It has six large rooms with ceramic floors, queen beds, ceiling fans, and modern bathrooms with tub showers. The rooms I viewed smelled of damp cement. The thatched restaurant serves *criolla* and continental fare. The place is popular with day-trippers here for horseback rides. $.

SIVORY PUNTA CANA
809-333-0500
fax: 809-334-0500
www.sivorypuntacana.com
Uvero Alto

The posh, all-suite Sivory Punta Cana—a member of the Small Luxury Hotels of the World—fuses 21st-century styling with a serene Asiatic motif. Its holistic Aquarea Spa and Wellness

Center is an oasis of pampering and pleasure that extends to the 55 suites, some right on the beach with their own private plunge pools. Decor is ultra contemporary, combining clinical whites, chocolaty hardwoods, and splashes of romantic color. I love the sumptuous double-vanity bathrooms with their deep whirlpool tubs and separate all-glass showers big enough for a *Playboy* party. Sivory's holistic Aquarea Spa and Wellness Center is an oasis of pampering and pleasure. The Spanish-run hotel emphasizes fine dining with three gourmet restaurants, one Asian fusion, one contemporary Mediterranean, the third French. $$$$.

WESTIN ROCO KI BEACH AND GOLF RESORT
954-624-1771 or 914-640-8100
www.starwoodhotels.com
Punta Macao

Planning a late-2009 opening, this divine resort will kick off the greater Roco Ki project. Perched atop cliffs overlooking a 2-mile-long (3.2 km) strip of powder-fine sands, the lavish hotel promises to exude luxury beyond the dreams of Croesus. Its 337 cavernous accommodations include 56 condominium hotel suites, plus 20 thatched, beachfront Westin Jungle Luxe Bungalows with tropically inspired architecture, glistening hardwood floors, him-and-her Jacuzzi tubs, and a retractable wall for that full-on beachfront experience. Highlights will include the 18,000-square foot (1,672 sq m) spa, four spectacular swimming pools, complete water sports, six lighted tennis courts, plus the Nick Faldo Championship Golf Course. $$$$.

Dining
There are very few options for now outside the resort hotels, most of which are closed to non-guests. The scenario should take an exciting turn when the restaurants at the Roco Ki hotels open their doors.

An exception is **El Navegante** (809-552-6166), a delightfully rustic hut sitting on the sands at Uvero Alto. It serves simple seafoods, such as fish fillet and octopus ($10), and a mixed seafood grill ($40). And meals can be had at **Hotel Rancho La Cueva** at Playa Limón; it specializes in lobster and roast suckling pig, prepared mainly for groups; daily 7:30 AM–11 PM (see Lodging, above).

SIVORY PUNTA CANA
809-333-0500
Uvero Alto

Punta Cana residents make the 45-minute drive to dine at the resort's air-conditioned **Gourmond Restaurant**, a member of the Chaine de Rotisseurs. Famed Executive Chef Denis Jaricot conjures up mouthwatering sophisticated nouvelle French dishes, supported by a wine cellar with 8,000 bottles presided over by Sommelier Juan Pierre. Chef Jaricot offers free cooking demonstrations each Monday (3–4 PM); plus a lunch with Jaricot himself every Friday at noon ($40), for 10 people only. Open Mon. through Sat. 7–10 PM.

The minimalist **Tau Restaurant** exudes urban hip and is guaranteed to satisfy a craving for sushi or other pan-Asian dishes. Open Tues. through Sun. 7–10:00 PM. Meanwhile, the poolside **Laveranda Restaurant** serves Mediterranean dishes. Open daily 7–10 AM, noon–3 PM, and 7–10 PM.

Cordillera Oriental

Attractions, Parks, and Recreation

Golf

The massive Roco Ki development plans to up the ante on Punta Cana with a sensational Nick Faldo-designed course, to open in winter 2009. Faldo's 7,118-yard (6,509-m) par-73 **Legacy Course** (www.rocoki.com/golf.html)—the first of *four* Faldo courses to be built at Roco Ki—will feature some of the most dramatic golf holes in the Caribbean: The 18th hole is destined to become one of golf's most thrilling finishes, requiring finite precision over two ocean inlets to land on the small patch of green perched atop a rocky, windblown peninsula battered by waves.

Horseback Rides
RANCHO MAR TAÍNO

809-390-4790
Playa Lavacama

Enjoying a to-die-for setting on a magnificent swatch of wind-sculpted, blindingly white sand, this is the perfect spot to saddle up and gallop down the sands, fling yourself into a game of volleyball, or snooze in a hammock slung between palms. It has a thatched restaurant, a swimming pool, a small and dispiriting zoo (with ostriches, monkeys, crocodiles, etc.), and simple cabins (rented out by the hour).

RANCHO EL DIFERENTE

809-552-6322
E-mail: ranchoeldiferente@hotmail.de

The tourist hotels sell tour packages for this horseback ranch, about 2 miles (3 km) along the dirt road to Boca de Maimón. You'll ride through sugarcane fiends and gallop down the sands. Or you can ride into the nearby mountains.

Scuba Diving

Pelicano Water Sport (809-947-0894; www.pelicanosport.com) offers dive trips in cenotes—flooded underground caverns full of stalactites and stalagmites and exotic crystal formations. The first, Cueva Taína Macao, is at Macao. Cueva La Sirena is considered an excellent grotto for cave-dive training.

Wildlife and Wilderness Parks
RESERVA CIENTÍFICA LAGUNAS REDONDA Y LIMÓN

c/o 809-472-4204 ext. 223
Carretera 104
Los Icacos (Laguna Redonda); Las Lisas (Laguna Limón)

These natural freshwater lagoons framed by swampy bayous are sustained by rivers washing down from the Cordillera Oriental. The twin lagoons are the foci of Round and Lemon Lagoons National Park, which supports profuse bird life and extends out to sea to protect a precious marine habitat. Birders will delight to spot roseate spoonbills ladling the ink-black tannin-stained waters. Black-crowned night heron, pied-billed grebe, common gallinule, and northern pintail are among the dozens of other waterfowl and wading species that are here most numerously in winter months, when migratory birds flock. With luck you might spot manatees chomping the lake-bed vegetation, while marine turtles can also be seen during the spring-summer nesting season. Then, females haul themselves up the beach under cover of night to lay their eggs in the soft sands above the high water mark.

The two lagoons, about 3 miles (4.8 km) apart, lie at either end of palm-shaded, golden **Playa Limón**, at the eastern end of which a shallow river connects Laguna Limón to the sea at **Boca de Limón**. Boats can be hired here to explore the lake. Playa Limón can be accessed from Carretera 104 via a dirt track that begins 2 miles (3 km) north of the hamlet of Las Lisas and leads past Hotel Rancho La Cueva, which offers guided tours by horseback ($10 per hour) and flat-bottom boat (advance notice required). You can also reach the lagoon by 4WD via a track that begins in Las Lisas.

Laguna Redonda can be reached by 4WD from the community of Los Icacos, 4 miles (6.4 km) west of Las Lisas. However, it has no facilities.

SABANA-DE-LA-MAR AND VICINITY

The slightly desultory town of Sabana-de-la-Mar, on the southern shores of the Bahía de Samaná, is a place to pass through en route to nearby Parque Nacional Los Haitise, or to catch a ferry to Samaná. Carretera 104 connects Sabana to Punta Cana via the equally undistinguished town of **Miches**, set in a bay good for bonefishing. The Sierra del Seibo mountains rise south of Miches, just 5 miles (8 km) west of the turn-off for Laguna Redonda.

Valley in the Cordillera Central, west of Miches

Lodging and Dining

COCO LOCO

809-886-8278
www.puntaelrey.com
Playa Miches

This little beachfront Swiss-run gem is a perfect retreat for the backpacker and independent explorer. Set amid palm-shaded lawns, its 10 simply appointed cabins have cold water only, yet are comfy enough for all but demanding epicureans. And the handsome thatched restaurant of stone and timber serves snacks and hearty meals and has an upstairs lounge. It's open to day visits. $.

HOTEL LA LOMA

809-553-5562
fax: 809-553-5564
www.puntaelrey.com
Miches

On the west side of Miches, you can climb the hill (you'll need to ask directions) to this no-frills yet friendly hotel (owned by the same folks who run Coco Loco) with a lofty perch high over town. Its eight airy air-conditioned rooms and one 3-bedroom suite have ceiling fans, but simple decor and bare furnishings. Come for the spectacular views over the mountains and bay, to be enjoyed from the small bar or the kidney-shaped pool studding a coral stone deck. No credit cards. $.

PARAÍSO CAÑO HONDO

809-248-5995
www.paraisocanohondo.com
Los Haitises, 8 miles (12.8 km) W of Sabana de la Mar

A cliffside Tolkeinsian fantasy made of river stones and rough timbers, this nature lodge and activity center straddling a tumbling stream is a gateway to Parque Nacional Los Haitises. The lodgings—in standards, junior suites, or villas—are no-frills and verge on ascetic; my room had cold water only. But the place has undeniable charm. The staff is super friendly. And the open-air restaurant with diced-log tables serves hearty Dominican fare. It offers hikes, horseback rides, plus guided ecotours into the park.

Attractions, Parks, and Recreation

PARQUE NACIONAL LOS HAITISES

809-556-7333
Paseo Elupina Cordero 5, Sabana de la Mar (national park office)

Protecting the most rugged and dramatic terrain in the country, this wild and isolated 316 square-mile (826 sq km) park encompassing the southwest quarter of Samaná Bay is a trove of delights. First, the beguiling scenery. The rugged terrain comprises dramatically eroded *mogotes* (sheer-faced hillocks) and soaring cliffs and offshore islands fit for a Hollywood epic. The craggy formations are overgrown with luxuriant subtropical humid forest and riddled with caves, many of which contain Taíno pictographs, notably to be seen in

Cueva Arena and **Cueva Linea**.

The park is rich in biodiversity. Hutia and solenodon grub out an existence, protected by the wild terrain. Los Haitises was named a national park in 1976 partly to save the critically endangered endemic Ridgway's hawk, found only here. And the park's 112 other bird species include many seabirds. **Isla de los Pájaros** is a rare roost for roseate terns. Swallows swarm around **Cueva de las Golondrinas**. And pelicans, frigate birds, and double-crested cormorants nest atop the dense mangrove forests that provide protection for manatees in shoreline lagoons and creeks along 15 miles (24 km) of rugged shoreline.

Boat trips can be arranged from **Embarcadero Caño Hondo** pier, 7 miles (11 km) west of Sabana; and with **Paraíso Caño Hondo** (see Lodgings); **Sabana Tours** (809-868-4301; Avenida de los Héroes) in Sabana-de-la-Mar; **Prieto Tours** (809-221-1335; www.prieto-tours.com) in Punta Cana; and tour operators in Samaná.

CUEVA FUN FÚN
809-553-2812
http://cuevafunfun.com
c/o Calle Duarte 12, Hato Mayor

Rancho Capote, at Yerba Buena (14 miles (22.4 km) west of Hato Mayor), is the setting for this well-named adventure. Arriving at the ranch, you'll hop in the saddle for a horseback ride to a huge underground cave. Then, rappel down to explore the chambers full of dripstone formations and gawk in awe at the underground river and sacred Taíno art. You can book online, and trips are sold in most tourist hotels in Punta Cana. $120 including hotel transfers.

Salto El Limon Waterfall   The Dominican Republic Ministry of Tourism

6

SAMANÁ

A Whale of a Time

The mountainous, tendril-thin Península de Samaná probes east 30 miles (48 km) into the clear blue Atlantic with the oblong Bahía de Samaná beneath. The bathtub-warm waters of Samaná bay are a breeding and birthing ground for humpback whales, which gather in early winter in large numbers and seemingly so close to shore you feel you can swim out to touch them. The slender peninsula boasts stupendous beaches, notably along the north shore and fringing Cayo Levantado, a small cay that levitates in the bay south of the main town, Santa Bárbara de Samaná. Fishing villages cling to old ways in the face of booming tourism that is bringing deluxe hotels and fine dining. Cooling trade winds bear down on the north shore beaches—fabulous strips of white sand that are also excellent kiteboarding sites. Waterfalls cascade down from the rugged and deeply forested Cordillera Samaná—the peninsula's mountainous spine. At least one cascade, El Salto de Limón, makes for a popular horseback excursion. Meanwhile, the Bahía de Samaná is a graveyard for treasure-laden Spanish galleons that lure divers, although the best diving is off the north coast.

The government is investing heavily in the region, most noticeably with the opening in 2006 of El Catey International Airport and, in July 2008, of a new highway that finally offers direct connection from Santo Domingo to this heretofore off-the-beaten-track region. A new wharf capable of accepting large cruise ships is finally putting the peninsula on the map as a destination for day-tripping visitors arriving by sea. And a convention center is planned, along with a ferry that will link the peninsula to Punta Cana.

Getting There

By Air
A fistful of international flights touch down at **El Catey International Airport** (809-338-5888 ext. 100), 5 miles (8 km) west of Sánchez, a sultry and once-prosperous port town that derives much of its income from shrimping. Sunwing and Skyservice have charter flights from Canada. LTU International and Condor offer charter flights from Germany.

Charter flights land at **El Portillo Airport**, a small strip in Las Terrenas; and at **Arroyo Barril International Airport**, a few miles west of the town of Samaná. **Aero Domca** (809-826-4141 in Santo Domingo, 809-240-6571 in Las Terrenas, www.aerodomca.com) flies three times daily to El Portillo from Santo Domingo's La Isabela airport ($90).

By Bus

Caribe Tours (809-221-4422; www.caribetours.com.do) offers daily service to Samaná from Santo Domingo at 7, 8:30, and 10 AM, and 1:30, 2:30 and 4 PM. And **Sánchez** (809-552-7434, Spanish only) operates buses to Las Terrenas.

At press time, **Metro Expreso** (809-227-0101) had canceled its service connecting Samaná with Santiago de los Caballeros and Puerto Plata; check to see if it's been reinstated. **Transporte Pepe** (809-582-2134, or 582-5709, Spanish only) serves Samaná from Santiago de los Caballeros, departing Calle Pedro Francisco Bonó at 8 AM, 9:30 AM, 1:15 PM and 2:30 PM, and to Las Terrenas at 3 PM.

Transporte Papagayo (809-749-6415, Spanish only) departs from outside the hospital in Puerto Plata at 6:45 AM. You can catch it in Sosuá at 7 AM outside Playero Supermarket, from where **Transporte El Canario** (809-291-5594, Spanish only) also serves Samaná on an irregular schedule.

All buses pass through Sánchez, where you can catch local *guaguas* to Las Terrenas and Las Galeras.

By Car and Ferry

Getting to the Samaná peninsula from the Punta Cana region is more problematic. A **Transporte Maritimo** (809-538-2556) passenger-only ferry operates between Samaná and Sabana-de-la-Mar, departing Samaná at 7 AM, 9 AM, 11 AM, 3 PM, and 5 PM (RD$140). They can get seriously overloaded! A car ferry has been planned for a while, but at press time had not materialized.

If the ferry isn't working, the quickest route (believe it or not) is to return to Santo Domingo by road and turn north on the new highway. If you try to drive via what appears the shortest route on a map, via the road shown as running west-east via Hato Rey and Monte Plata, you're in for a true Indiana Jones-style adventure. Believe me, I've done it . . . with my 4WD bottoming out on the rocks in sections designed to stump anything that doesn't have hooves.

SANTA BÁRBARA DE SAMANÁ

This orderly little port town enjoys a fabulous setting overlooking a beautiful natural harbor opening to the Bahía de Samaná. Lush mountains loom behind. Columbus named the bay the Golfo de Flechas (Gulf of Arrows) for the unwelcome reception Taíno people gave him on January 12, 1493. A few inhabitants still set out to earn their keep off the sea. However, when winter comes around the boat business is all about whale-watching—a major business.

The town was founded in 1756 by Spanish Governor Francisco Rubio Peñaranda (1700—73). Settlers from the Canary Islands were encouraged and were joined in 1824 by two shiploads of freed American slaves. A few town elders still speak *inglés del muelle* (dock English)—a form of Spanglish. The American free-slaves also introduced their own distinct culture and cuisine, typified by *pescado con coco* (fish in coconut sauce) and *yaniqueques* (Johnny cakes), and by parochial dances (some quite erotic) such as *bambulá, chivo florete,* and the *olí-olí,* which are performed during Samaná's patronal festivals.

Alas, a fire in 1946 destroyed many of the historic buildings, which were replaced by concrete buildings in nondescript style during the 1970s. But the recently built waterfront Pueblo Principe commercial plaza attempts to resurrect the Caribbean vernacular style.

Gran Bahia Principe Cayo Levantado

The broad seafront boulevard, Avenida La Marina—colloquially called the **Malecón**—makes for pleasant strolling (if you discard the smell of sewage and the revoltingly littered beach).

Lodging
There's a modicum of options for all budgets, but caveat emptor when it comes to budget options.

GRAN BAHÍA PRINCIPE CAYO LEVANTADO
809-538-3232
fax: 538-2425
www.bahia-principe.com
Cayo Levantado

Now here's a class act. The Principe hotel group has spent millions in 2006–7 upgrading its three local hotels, but this entirely new offering raised the ante when it opened as the only hotel on Cayo Levantado. Talk about an exclusive locale! It takes up the eastern half of the island, with the rest left to the public. The hotel's own water taxis run you to and from the gracious plantation-style reception on the mainland, about 5 miles (8 km) east of Samaná town. The beaches are gorgeous, as is the massive pool complex. Decor throughout is done to refined European classical taste. There are heaps of facilities, inlcuding water sports, tennis, and even a jogging trail. And the 195 rooms, suites, and villas feature state-of-the-art amenities, plantation furnishings, plus marble-clad bathrooms with Jacuzzi tubs. $$$$.

GRAN BAHÍA PRINCIPE CAYACOA

809-538-3135
fax: 809-538-3135
www.bahia-principe.com
Loma Puerto Escondido, Samaná

Fresh from a recent remake, this all-inclusive hotel also shines. Its hilltop position high above Samaná town guarantees spectacular views. A dramatic highlight is the sundeck with free-form pool suspended atop a ledge pinned by palms. An elevator whisks you down to the resort's private beach, with water sports. It has a disco and a choice of restaurants. The decor is classically elegant, with lots of coral stone, green marble, and gleaming mahogany panels. $$$$

GRAN BAHÍA PRINCIPE SAMANÁ

809-538-3434
www.bahia-principe.com
Carretera Samaná-las Galeras, 7 miles (11 km) east of Samaná

Not to be outdone by its sibling competitors, this gracious Victorian-style, four-storey property studs a lush promontory overlooking turquoise and azure ocean waters and its own beach—Playa La Petrona. It reminds me of a hotel you'd expect to find in Monte Carlo,

Beach, Gran Bahia Principe Cayacoa hotel, Samana

except with an even more sensational setting. It copies its siblings' theme, combing elegant yesteryear plantation decor with thoroughly contemporary amenities, including in the 110 guest rooms and suites. $$$$.

HOTEL BAHÍA VIEW
809-538-2186
Calle Francisco de Rosario Sánchez 15

It's not saying much that this is the nicest budget property in town. My room had a broken toilet, no showerhead, and not even bedsheets! Still, rooms are clean enough if all you need is a bed for the night, and it does have ceiling fans and hot water. Some rooms have balconies. The best thing is its location—close enough to everything to walk, yet far enough away from the booming music on weekend nights. $.

Dining

CLUB DE PLAYA CAYENAS DEL MAR
809-538-3114
www.cayenasdelmar.com
Playa Anadel, 2 Miles (3 km) E of Samaná

What a delight! This thatched, open-air beach restaurant is nestled in its own palm-shaded cove just 1 mile (1.6 km) east of town. French-owned, it oozes Mediterranean ambience. The dining area is raised above the beach and has chic navy-blue-and-white contemporary furnishings. Below, a wooden deck invites you to relax in orange lounge chairs. Start with a Mediterranean salad or eggplant rolls. The grilled sea bass ($10) or coconut shrimp ($21) are tempting entrées. Open: Daily 8–6. $$.

LA MATA ROSADA
809-538-2388
Avenida La Marina 5, corner Rubio Peñaranda

A favorite of local expats, this French restaurant has a pleasant open-air patio enclosed by a trellised grill. Ceiling fans whir overhead. White bamboo furnishings. French-Caribbean fusion cuisine features crab and shrimp omelette, lobster flamed with rum, and coconut chicken. Open: Thurs. through Tues. 10–3 and 6–midnight. $$.

MI RESTAURANTE TERRAZA BAR
809-779-4345
Calle Francisco del Rosario Sánchez 39

At the west end of the Malecón, I like this thatch-fringed place for its open-air ambience. Eye-pleasing decor includes wrought-iron tables atop a washed-cement floor. The simple menu offers burgers, sandwiches, salads, and entrées such as chicken cordon bleu. Open: Daily 8 AM–10 PM. $.

RESTAURANTE XAMANA
809-538-2129
Avenida La Marina 1

Facing the bay at the west end of the Malecón, this sensational Italian-run restaurant upped the ante considerably when it opened in 2007, bringing chic minimalist styling to town. The bay views can be enjoyed through a wall of glass. Halogens beam down from the ceiling, while candles float in frosted bowls on the tables. I listened to Roberta Flack followed by Mozart then Ol' Blue Eyes. Cool! And the nouvelle cuisine ain't half bad. I started with a delicious cream of black bean soup, followed by hand-cut tagliatelle, then a divine risotto with porcini mushrooms, and ended with a *grappa,* on the house. No credit cards. The only negative here was that only one red wine was served by the glass (fortunately, it was a delicious Chilean). Casually elegant dining at its best. Open: Daily noon–3 and 7–midnight. $$$.

Attractions, Parks, and Recreation

A brief downtown walking tour reveals a handful of architectural curiosities, most notably **La Churcha** (Calle Desereaux and Rubio Peñarada), a small non-Conformist church—today serving as the Dominican Evangelical Church—prefabricated in England in 1823 and that originally ministered to the freed African American slaves.

Out in the bay, the small island of **Cayo Vigia** is linked to the mainland by the **Bridge to Nowhere**, a multi-arch bridge accessible solely to guests at the Gran Bahía Principe Cayacoa hotel, which owns the cay.

Cayo Levantado

Garlanded with spectacular sands, this postcard-perfect coral cay about 4 miles (7 km) offshore of Samaná pokes up from turquoise waters. Supposedly, early Bacardi rum company ads were filmed here. No wonder. It's everything you imagine a quintessential tropical isle

Cayo Levantado 3 The Dominican Republic Ministry of Tourism

La Churcha, Santa Barbara de Samana

could be, with tousled palms leaning over sugar-fine sands dissolving into bathtub-warm, electric-blue waters. The eastern half is the private terrain of the Gran Bahía Principe Cayo Levantado hotel. The western half is taken up by **Playa Pública** (Public Beach), a gorgeous sliver of sand with shallow turquoise ocean good for snorkeling. It has gift shacks and a bar-restaurant, and gets crowded with locals on weekends. Water taxis depart the Malecón and you can hire private boats at **Caranero**, 5 miles (8 km) east of Samaná.

MUSEO DE LA BALLENA

809-538-2042

Avenida La Marina

This small museum run by the Center for Conservation and Eco-Development Samaná, is hidden away by the old dock at the west end of the Malecón, where it's signed. Its exhibits include a full skeleton of a humpback whale, and it shows videos. You can even listen to the humpbacks' haunting songs. Open: Mon. through Fri. 9–11 and 2–5. RD$50

Culture

Music and Nightlife

At night, the Malecón throbs to the *boom-boom-boom* of warring music as the bars that

Whales Ahoy!

Benign behemoths of the deep, humpback whales (*ballenas jorobadas*) are warm-blooded, air-breathing mammals that can reach up to 50 feet (15 m) long and weigh up to 50 tons. Although not actually humped, when diving they appear so from the way they arch their backs sharply. Pewter colored above, they are easily identified from other whale species by their speckled white underbellies, long white flippers, long jaws, and the knob-like bumps atop their snouts.

The species was hunted for two centuries for its precious oils and meat, and was driven to the point of extinction by commercial hunters. Although it was granted protection in 1962, it is still considered endangered. The current population of North Atlantic humpbacks is around 12,000 individuals and is divided into three main populations: around Greenland and Iceland; in the Gulf of Maine and Nova Scotia; and off Labrador and Newfoundland.

Humpbacks are baleen whales. Instead of teeth, they have pendulous bristles (baleen) through which they filter their food, which is swallowed whole. Spring, summer, and autumn are spent feeding on krill and small schooling fish in the relatively shallow waters over the continental shelves. When winter months darken, virtually the entire Atlantic population of humpback whales migrates to the warm shallow waters of the Caribbean, with by far the greatest number concentrating around the Silver Bank and Samaná Bay. Together the twin zones are protected as the Sanctuary for the Marine Mammals of the Dominican Republic, which includes the eastern third of the bay. Females give birth in the calm inner bay, where newborn calves frolic alongside their mothers while aggressive males compete for the favors of willing females in the rough, deep cobalt outer bay. Here, they can be seen engaged in vigorous and solicitous foreplay that often involves stimulating the cows with bubbles blown from below.

The male leviathans sing haunting and elaborate arias to woo the females. While singing, the bulls hang motionless in a head-down posture, flippers outstretched like true Pavarottis. Like any good sex, a bit of wild action is called for. Males jockey for position next to females and strive hard to protect them from jealous suitors, including ramming each other, swatting at each other with their massive pectoral fins, and dramatic leaps clear of the water (breaching) thought to be acts of territorial intimidation. Females give birth every other year. Gestation takes 12 months, and the 15-foot (4.5 m) calves are weaned throughout their first year.

Individuals from the three distinct Atlantic populations interbreed in these waters before returning to their respective feeding areas.

EYEBALL TO EYEBALL ENCOUNTERS

Few places in the world offer premier whale-watching with so much ease. The 25-mile-long (40 km) by 13-mile-wide (20 km) bay is like Grand Central Station January through March, the mating and calving season, when as many as 300 individual whales may be in the bay at any given time. Whales often come within 100 yards (100 m) or so of the shore of Samaná. Still, for real eyeball-to-eyeball encounters, sign up for a whale-watching excursion. Take your pick from inflatable dinghies to flat-hulled vessels with viewing platforms and shaded decks. It's worth going with a specialist operator that uses larger vessels: some, for example, lower hydrophones into the water so you can listen to the haunting and elaborate courting songs of male humpbacks. Strict regulations are in effect, including a ban on swimming with whales.

Whale Samana (809-539-2494; www.whalesamana.com; Calle Mella and Avenida La Marina) offers twice-daily trips, mid-January through mid-March, from both Samaná and Cayo Levantado. It also has multi-day trips to the Silver Banks. **Samaná Tourist Service**, (809-538-2740; Avenida La Marina 6, corner of Rubio Peñaranda) and **MotoMarina** (809-538-2302; Avenida de la Marina 3) also offer trips.

stand shoulder to shoulder compete by pounding out merengue and *bachata* at eardrum-shattering levels. And it's made worse by the local youth who park their cars along the boulevard and crank up their own sound systems till the cars themselves are bouncing. *Awful!*

Alternately you can sup beers at a fistful of unremarkable bars farther along the Malecón prior to working up a sweat on the dance floor of **Naomi's** (Avenida La Marina and Avenida 27 de Febrero), a disco and local institution that crowds 'em in for merengue and the like on Friday and Saturday nights.

Shopping
Shopaholics will fare better in Las Terrenas, but the **Pueblo Principe** commercial plaza at the west end of Avenida La Marina offers possibilities, as does **Harrison's Fine Caribbean Jewelers** (809-538-3933; Carretera Samaná-El Valle 1, Samaná).

Good to Know About
Centro para la Conservación de la Bahía de Samaná (809-538-2042, www.samana.org.do; Calle Julio Lavandier). This organization promotes ecotourism and environmental awareness among locals.

Politur (Tourism Police; 809-754-3066; Calle Francisco del Rosario Sánchez 27).

Samaná Tourist Service (809-538-2740; Avenida La Marina 5). Open Mon. through Sat. 8:30 AM–12:30 PM and Mon. through Fri. 2:30–6.

Secretaría de Turismo (Tourism Office; 809-538-2332; Calle Santa Barbara 4) Open Mon. through Fri. 8:30–3. Limited amount of literature and maps.

LAS GALERAS

At the far eastern end of the peninsula, the fishing village of Las Galeras enjoys a spectacular position, with snow-white sands and gorgeous gin-clear waters against a mountainous coastline sculpted with deep bays and tiny coves. The village is tucked into the southern end of **Bahía del Rincón**, a gentle miles-long scimitar that is slowly evolving as a tourist destination, but not at the frenetic pace of Las Terrenas. It is still old-world Dominican Republic, where fishermen play dominoes beneath the shade of coconut palms—the parochial scene being enhanced by their colorful fishing boats drawn up on the sands.

Lodging

CASA MARINA BAY BEACH RESORT
809-538-0020
fax: 809-538-0040
www.amhsamarina.com
1.5 miles (2.4 km) W of Las Galeras

I give this all-inclusive barely a pass but undiscerning budget hounds may appreciate it, and indeed many seem to. The majority of guests here are Canadians and Europeans. The location is a boon: The palm-studded resort has its own curvaceous beach with water sports. But it was an aged property urgently in need of upgrading when I recently stayed there. It has 284 rooms and 50 bungalows. $$–$$$.

Palms at Playa Las Galeras, Samana Peninsula

LABELLAVENTURA
809-538-0206
www.labellaventura.com

A perfect self-catering option, this European-run charmer offers a choice of a two-bedroom house and a one-bedroom, thatch-fringed bungalow, both with delightful tropical color schemes and furnishings plus full kitchen. The rates are an absolute bargain. $.

PLAZA LUSITANIA HOTEL
809-538-0093
www.plazalusitania.com
Plaza Lusitania

Right in the center of Las Galeras, this little family-run hotel has charming decor in its 10 otherwise modestly furnished air-conditioned rooms and apartments, with ceiling fans and terraces or balconies opening to a calming tropical courtyard. There's an Italian restaurant and an Internet café in the plaza. $$.

VILLA SERENA
809-538-0000

www.villaserena.com
400 yards (366 m) E of Plaza Lusitania

Now here's a gem! And just a five-minute walk from the village center. Take a magnificent plantation-style mansion. Place it atop a craggy limestone platform with manicured lawns and coconut palms and its own tiny white sandy cove. All 21 rooms are decorated in their own stylish fashion, some in Victorian vogue with chintz. Several have king-size beds, and all have terra-cotta balconies. A cross-ventilated gourmet garden restaurant has ocean views and a nightly three-course menu. *Nice!* $$$.

Dining

You can buy fresh-fried seafood and local fare from the simple beach shacks at the far west end of Playa Rincón.

CHEZ DENISE

809-538-0219
Calle Principal, Las Galeras

This French Restaurant run by Denise, from Marseille, is a local institution drawing tourists and locals alike for divine dishes. Nothing too fancy, mind you. Call it Gallic meets Galeras. Her specialty is delicious crêpes, stuffed with seafood, but she also does a mean curried fish, which you can enjoy while dining on the beachfront terrace. Open: Daily 9 AM–10 PM. $$

Villa Serena, at Playa Las Galeras, Samana Peninsula

Sunset over Bahia de Rincon, Las Galeras, Samana Peninsula

LA YUCA CALIENTE
809-240-6634
E-mail: yucacaliente@hotmail.com
Calle Libertad

This small beachfront restaurant specializes in tapas and Spanish dishes, but it also has pizzas. You'll love the chic ambience enhanced by gauzy drapes wrapped around the palms. $$.

RISTORANTE PIZZERÍA
809-538-0093
Plaza Lusitania, Calle Principal

You can dine under thatch at this lively Italian restaurant in the center of Las Galeras. Bamboo furnishings add tropical airs. The menu includes tasty pizzas and nightly specials, such as *spaghetti al pulpo* (with octopus) on Tuesday nights.

Attractions, Parks, and Recreation

Beaches
Although Las Galeras' own beach is attractive and made more so by the colorful fishing

boats drawn up on the sands, the most appealing beach is **Playa Rincón**, on the west side of the bay, about 5 miles (8 km) west of Las Galeras. It requires a 4WD to access via the hamlet of Manuel Chiquito. Backed by swaying coconut palms and bottle green mountains, this great scimitar of platinum sands draws locals, who prefer to cool off in the Río Frío, a small river that spills onto the sands at its far west end, where makeshift kitchens grill seafoods. You can hire boats in Las Galeras to reach Playa Rincón (RD$1,400).

Alternately, you can hike to virginal **Playa Playita**, a tiny cove just west of Hotel Villa Serena. It's great for snorkeling. Another trail that begins at the far east end of the Casa Marina Bay Beach Resort beach (a lovely, but crowded sliver of white sand) leads along the craggy shore to **Playa Cala Blanca**, popular with local families for its reef-protected swimming; then **Playa Madama**, surrounded by crags; and finally **Playa Frontón**, a gorgeous beach at the tip of Cabo Samaná, with a huge rock face soaring behind. You can rent horses and boats (RD$1,700) in town.

Miscellaneous
You can rent ATVs from **R-Azor Tours** (809-538-0218), in the center of Las Galeras. And **Labellaventura** (809-538-0206; www.labellaventura.com) offers mountain biking excursions.

GARGANTA DEL DIABLO
6 miles (9.6 km) W of Las Galeras

This blowhole—Devil's Throat—in wave-battered limestone cliffs is worth the visit as much for the dramatic backdrop as for the spout of hissing spray that blasts up through the gaping yaw. It's signed off Carretera 5. The dirt road hemmed in by a glade of dense vegetation passes beneath towering *mogotes*. The limestone surface is knife-sharp. Use caution!

The easy, level, and well-marked 3-mile-long (4.8 km) **Sendero Ecológico de Playa Frontón** trail leads past the **Cueva del Agua** (a cavern enshrining a brackish lake) to Playa Frontón. This area is being developed as the **Monumento Natural Cabo Samaná**.

PROYECTO GUARIQUÉN
809-932-1624
www.guariquen.org
Arroyo el Cabo 13, Las Galeras

This community ecotourism project is centered on the hamlet of Los Tocones, midway between Las Galeras and Playa Rincón. Here, the **Iguanario** breeds rhinoceros iguanas for release to the wild. Local guides lead birding and hiking excursions to **Laguna Salada** (Salt Lake), ironically a freshwater habitat for waterfowl, frogs, and freshwater turtles; and to **Laguna del Diablo**, another vital habitat for endemic species.

Scuba Diving and Water Sports
The waters off the eastern tip of Samaná spell Nirvana to snorkelers and divers. Trips are offered by the **Casa Marina Bay Dive Center** (809-538-0020). The top site is **Cabo Cabrón**, which has it all: fabulous reefs, walls, a cave, and The Tower—150-foot-tall (45.7 m), sponge-laden pinnacle rising almost to the ocean surface.

You can buy a day pass to the Casa Marina Bay Beach Resort, which has water sports. And **R-Azor Tours** (809-538-0218) offers whale-watching trips ($75) and catamaran excursions to Cayo Levantado ($78, including lunch).

Good to Know About

Plaza Lusitania (Calle Principal; open Mon. through Sat. 8:30–1 and 2–8) has an Internet café ($4 per hour), telephone call center, and money exchange.

If you get caught short, **Hermanos Cruz Casa de Cambio** (809-341-4574; Calle Principal) can change money for a stiff commission. The **Farmacia Joven** (809-538-0103), nearby, is open Mon. through Sat. 8 AM–9:30 PM.

LAS TERRENAS

This sensational beach resort, midway along the north shore of the peninsula, is a laid-back place that in many ways is the most appealing of *all* the Dominican Republic's beach resorts. The setting is simply magnificent, with several blindingly white-sand beaches in scalloped bays framed by rugged headlands. There's plenty to do off the beach, from wind-surfing to horseback rides to nearby waterfalls deep in the mountains. The mood is laid-back, even down to the selection of guesthouses and boutique hotels and gourmet yet casual restaurants and bakeries (many run by savvy French, Germans, English, and Italians) set back from the beach. You can actually *breathe* here, which is a pleasant change from Playa Bávaro, Cabarete, and even Sosuá...all thanks to the fact that the beach road actually runs along the shore with all the buildings on the inland side. Still, the place is booming and growth is unregulated, threatening to spoil the mood.

Lodging

ALISEI HOTEL, RESTAURANT AND SPA
809-240-5555
www.aliseihotel.com
Calle Francisco Camaaño Deño

Facing the beach at Punta Francisco Frances, this boutique hotel has an enviable setting. The Italian owners have created a bargain-priced winner offering 48 apartments (in four-storey blocks), six suites, and a penthouse tucked in lovely gardens with a free-form pool. The air-conditioned units are tastefully and richly furnished in colorful contemporary fashion, and all come with satellite TV, phone, DVD and MP3 player, WiFi internet, and in-room safe. The main draw here, though, is the stylish bar, which would look right at home in L.A. The circular restaurant with log supports and glass walls also gets two thumbs up. It also has a full-service spa. $$$.

CACAO BEACH RESORT SPA AND CASINO
809-240-6000
fax: 809-240-6197
www.cacaobeachresort.com
Calle Coronel Francisco

A neighbor to the Alisei Hotel, this brightly colored all-inclusive resort has 204 air-conditioned rooms with white walls, modest furnishings (some with wicker), plus cable TV, phone, and fridge. The hotel structures are set back from the beach, with palm-studded lawns betwixt. You can choose from five restaurants, and there's even a casino, and a disco opened in 2008. If you're not looking for snazzy sophistication, this could well suit you. $$.

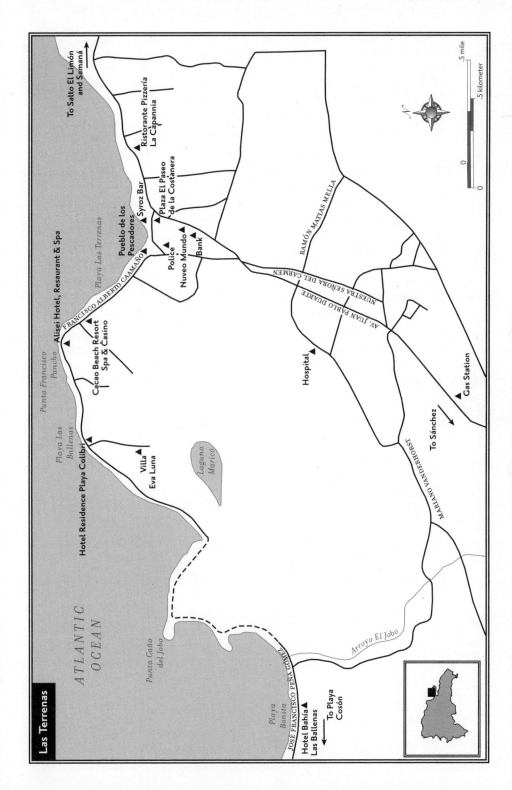

Las Terrenas

ATLANTIC OCEAN

To Salto El Limón and Samaná

Ristorante Pizzería La Capannia

Syroz Bar

Pueblo de los Pescadores

Plaza El Paseo de la Costanera

Aliisei Hotel, Resaurant & Spa

Playa Las Terrenas

F FRANCISCO ALBERTO CAAMAÑO

Police

Nuveo Mundo

Bank

Punta Francisco Pancho

Cacao Beach Resort Spa & Casino

Playa Las Ballenas

Hotel Residence Playa Colibrí

Villa Eva Luna

Laguna Maricó

Hospital

RAMÓN MATÍAS MELLA

NUESTRA SEÑORA DEL CARMEN

AV. JUAN PABLO DUARTE

MARIANO VANDERHORST

To Sánchez

Gas Station

Punta Caño del Jobo

Arroyo El Jobo

JOSÉ FRANCISCO PEÑA GÓMEZ

Playa Bonita

Hotel Bahía Las Ballenas

To Playa Cosón

.5 mile
.5 kilometer
0
0

GRAN BAHÍA PRINCIPE EL PORTILLO

809-240-6100
fax: 809-240-6104
www.bahia-principe.com
Carretera Las Terrenas-el Limón Km 4

I really like this handsome low-rise all-inclusive resort on its own gorgeous white-sand beach east of town. The sprawling resort has an airy and regal lobby with gray and black marble sparkling underfoot. Of the 204 rooms and 192 junior suites, only a few have ocean views. Still, they're stylish enough and feature subdued pink and ochre color schemes, ceiling fans, and most expected mod-cons, plus a choice of king-size beds. Alas, you pay extra to use the in-room safes—a miserly negative touch. There's tennis, a gym, water sports, four restaurants, theme entertainment, a disco, and stores. $$$

HOTEL BAHÍA LAS BALLENAS

809-240-6066
fax: 809-240-6107
www.samana.net/bahia-lasballenas.html
Calle José Francisco Peña, Playa Bonita

Set in spacious palm-shaded lawns, this beachfront hotel makes a grand tropical statement with its thatched structures and bright tropical color schemes. Its 32 rooms in eight buildings are a jumble of eye-catching pinks, greens, and yellows. Each room differs. I particularly love the canary yellow room with purple throw pillows and mushy pea green louvered doors and windows. The down-to-earth rusticity is enhanced by simple furnishings and open-air showers in your own private garden with burbling fountain. There's a free-form pool, a whirlpool spa, and a thatched restaurant serving local and international dishes. $$.

HOTEL RESIDENCE PLAYA COLIBRI

809-240-6434
fax: 809-240-6917
www.playacolibri.com
Calle Francisco Camaaño Deño, Playa Bonita

Wow! That's how I feel about the sensational location of this lovely hotel overlooking Playa Las Ballenas. You're far enough out of the village on a dead-end beachfront road for peace and quiet, yet close enough to walk to the restaurants and nocturnal action. The three-storey units amid palm-studded lawns are a bit somber, but the 45 self-catering apartments, studios, and suites come as a surprising delight for their charming and colorful Caribbean-style interiors. All have ceiling fans, rather high-speed Internet, cable TVs, in-room safes, and some have air-conditioning. A simple open-air thatched restaurant-bar serves seafoods and Italian dishes. $$–$$$

VILLA EVA LUNA

809-978-5611
fax: 809-240-6600
www.villa-evaluna.com
Calle Marica

Fishing boats at Playa Las Terrenas, Samana Peninsula

This chicly simple and simply chic boutique hotel appeals to discerning sybarites who like to hang in flip-flops by day and night. A little beyond a stone's throw inland of Playa Las Ballenas, it offers five Mexican-style adobe villas in lush landscaped grounds. Each comes in tropical ice cream pastels. Papaya. Mango. Kiwi fruit. Furnishings are kept to a bare minimum, and include gauzy mosquito nets draping platform king-size beds with quality linens. All have small kitchens and outside terraces. The thatched Le Table de l'Oly restaurant is a gourmand's delight and even serves sushi. $$$.

VIVA WYNDHAM SAMANÁ
809-240-5050 or 800-WYNDHAM
fax: 809-240-5536
www.vivawyndhamresorts.com
Playa Cosón

Approached via a narrow, winding, roller-coaster road, this family-focused all-inclusive commands a tremendous position on Playa Cosón, a 10-minute drive from Las Terrenas. Once beyond the ungainly entrance facing a sparse parking lot, things improve. The airy lobby in Caribbean style is the node of daytime activities away from the beach, and opens to the noisy pool, with bars, shops, and an open-air buffet restaurant (food quality is merely average) to the flanks. The sprawling property is framed by three-storey accommodation blocks perpendicular to the beach, with bungalows filling the grassy space between. A Chinese restaurant, water sports, a kids' camp, and nightly entertainment rounds things out. The 218 rooms are spacious enough, but the modest furnishings in my room were ho-hum, and I wrote up a long list of physical faults. The resort closed for a much-needed and complete renovation in mid-2008 and was slated to reopen in December 2009. $$$.

Dining

The dining scene in Las Terrenas is worldly wise, with more European-run fine-dining outlets per square meter than any other resort in the nation. It's also highly fluid, with new restaurants blooming while others fade away just as quickly.

BARAONDA

809-240-5555
http://baraonda.aliseihotel.com
Hotel Alisei

When you want to feel like a city slicker enjoying the tropics, put on a nice shirt (you can keep the shorts and sandals) and start out with a martini or rum punch at the chic bar. Then opt for the daily seafood special or a fresh homemade pasta or hearty salad. End with an espresso or cappuccino drawn on a genuine Italian machine. Also has excellent breakfasts and lunches. Open: Daily 8 AM–10 PM (bar until 2 AM). $$$.

PACO CABANA BAR RESTAURANT BEACH CLUB

809-240-5301

Playa Las Ballenas, Las Terrenas, Samana Peninsula

www.pacocabana.c.la
Paseo de la Costanera, Playa Las Terrenas

I love the vibe at this thoroughly tropical yet hip thatched restaurant, which spills its tables onto the sands. You can also opt for the deck-bar, with its scalloped henequen-rope chairs and poured-concrete sofas with plump cushions. This is the place for gourmet seafood, such as delicious ceviche. By day, stick to something light, then relax with cocktails on your bamboo-framed lounge chairs laid out on the sands. Late at night, DJs crank up the Latin tunes. Open: Daily 11 AM–11 PM (bar until 2 AM). $$.

RISTORANTE PIZZERÍA LA CAPANNINA
809-886-2122
Calle 27 de Febrero

On the east side of the village, this laid-back oceanfront restaurant is where locals come for pizza (30 types) and fresh pasta and risotto dishes prepared by Paola, the Italian cook, who even conjures up local favorites, such as tripe, with Mediterranean flair. Yummy! Open: Daily noon–2 PM and 7–11 PM. $$$.

SANTI RANCHO
809-343-0716
El Limón, 8 miles (12.8 km) E of Las Terrenas

This thatched roadside restaurant in the village of El Limón serves tasty *criollo* dishes (I enjoyed fish in coconut milk with rice and beans and *tostones*), but also has burgers and sandwiches. *Do* try a delicious *batidos* (fruit shake). $.

TIKI SNACK
809-705-5190
Paseo de la Costanera.

This heart-of-town family-run kitchen is a great option for good value pancakes, breakfasts, and inexpensive exotic salads, sandwiches, burgers, paninis, and even crêpes. Natural fruit juices. Take-out available. Open: Daily 7:30 AM–8:30 PM. $

Attractions, Parks, and Recreation

ATV and Jeep Safaris
Fancy whizzing around the countryside on an ATV? **Safari Quads** (809-240-6056; www.safari-quads.com), at Hotel Eva Luna, offers four distinct excursions, including the thrilling Indiana Jones. And you can rent ATVs from **Fun Rental** (809-240-6784; E-mail: funrental@hotmail.com; Calle Principal 258), which also rents small motorcycles.

Beaches
Reason enough to visit! Las Terrenas boasts sensational beaches, beginning with coral-colored **Playa Las Terrenas**, directly in front of the village. It has water sports outlets and any number of bars and restaurants, concentrated in palm-shaded **Pueblo de los Pescadores** (Fishermen's Village), right on the sands. It's a perfect venue where I love lazing in a hammock while sipping a chilled Presidente and watching the lissome local lasses, tall and tan and young and lovely, dripping with brine from the sea.

Playa Las Terrenas extends east to **Playa Punta Popy**, a lonesome beach of wind-whipped white sand where kite-surfers scud across reef-protected teal-colored waters. Playa Las Terrenas curls west around Punta Francisco Pancho and arcs for 1.2 miles (2 km) of palm-lined shore. Here, **Playa Las Ballenas** is indisputably the most gorgeous beach, with the craggy forest headland of Punta Caño del Jobo as a backdrop. The headland, and the swampy Laguna Marico (great for birding) at its base, separate Playa Las Ballenas from **Playa Bonita**—well-named Pretty Beach—accessed by heading *south* out of Las Terrenas then following Calle Fabio Abreu west to the Y-fork at Colmado León. Here, turn right for Playa Bonita, lined by a fistful of boutique hotels (alternately you can hike a narrow, marshy trail via the mangroves of Laguna Marico); turn left for **Playa Cosón**, a broad scimitar arcing west for miles like a scallop shell edged by a peacock blue sea. The snorkeling here is superb, thanks to a nearshore coral reef patrolled by a kaleidoscope of tropical fish.

Boat Excursions, Sportfishing, and Water Sports

Playa Punta Popy competes with Cabarete for kiteboarding and surfing thrills, notably January to September. **Pura Vida** (809-964-7051; www.puravidacaraibes.com; Calle Libertad 2) offers lessons and rentals.

Cap Ocean (809-803-5595; www.capocean-lasterrenas.com) will take you sportfishing ($400 for three hours, $600, six hours) and on boat excursions to your own private beach.

Azulaventura (809-240-6349), at Playa Bonita, offers excursions aboard a sea kayak with sail.

Miscellaneous

Floratours (809-240-5482; Calle Juan Pablo Duarte 262) offers excursions to Parque Nacional Los Haitises, as does **Enmanuel Tours** (809-240-6069; www.enmanuel-f-tour .fr.tc; Calle Principal 211A), which also has a Jeep safari to El Salto de Limón.

El Salto de Limón

A horseback ride to the Lemon Waterfall is a must-do while in Las Terrenas. This cascade pours from the rugged Sierra de Samaná and falls 130 feet (52 m) into a jade-colored pool. Although less than 2 miles (3 km) from the trailhead, on the edge of El Limón hamlet, the muddy trail ascends sharply, fording a river en route. It's rugged going. You make a steep descent by foot to reach the pool.

Wise travelers take horseback excursions. Roadside *boscones* (touts) or *paradas* (the word means stop, but is also used for these freelance guides) wave you down to solicit your business. Not all are trustworthy. Ensure that you only use a guide licensed with the Association of Community Ecotourism of Salto del Limón (ASECAL), which has stewardship of the falls and the Arroyo Chico, the river that feeds the falls. I recommend **Santí Rancho** (809-343-0716 or 829-343-9976; www.santirancho.com; depart at 9 AM, three hours), which offers both horseback and hiking options.

Scuba Diving

The three islands that rise from the aquamarine ocean about 0.6 mile (1 km) from shore are the **Islas las Ballenas**, named for their whaleback shape. Below the sea, these triplets enthrall divers with their fabulous corals, sponges, and caves. The isles are also roosts for brown boobies and white-tailed tropic birds. **Stellina Diving** (829-887-5503; www.stellinadiving.com), at Hotel Las Cayenas, offers trips.

Culture

Casinos
No luck with the ladies? Then head to **Las Terrenas Casino** (809-240-6000), at Cacao Beach Resort Spa and Casino. However, your date with Lady Luck is heavily stacked in the house's favor. Open 4 PM–4 AM.

Dance
To learn the right dance moves, sign up for a class (from 1 to 15 days) with **Escuela de Baile Salsa Caribe** (809-977-1795; www.salsacaribevent.com), where national salsa Champion Pipo Alcalá teaches *bachata*, merengue, salsa, and the hot new bachatango, a dance so sexy it's a surprise the birthrate isn't higher.

Music and Nightlife
Las Terrenas is hopping at night and competes with Cabarete as the *in* spot for party hounds. You'd need at least a week to do the place justice, especially on Friday through Sunday nights when impromptu bars and bands set up on the sands for a night market-cum-party.

If you're merely seeking a mellow cocktail scene, check out the **Baraonda** bar at the Hotel Alisei (see Dining), or the beachfront **El Mosquito Art Bar** (809-877-2844), at Pueblo de Los Pescadores, and serving great piña coladas and mojitos.

You can kick it up a notch at **El Mambo Social Club** (809-884-9971; Avenida 27 Febrero), an upscale lounge bar with huge sofas, pool and poker tables, and board games. Spanish owner Alex Rodríguez serves sushi and Caribbean appetizers and hosts live dance shows and music. For a Latin vibe, head to **El Toro Sobre el Techo** (809-240-6337; Pueblo de los Pescadores), open Wednesday through Monday 6 PM–2 AM, and which also serves tapas and gets in the groove late at night with theme parties on the beach. Nearby, the thatched seaside **Syroz Bar** (809-866-557) tempts R and B and jazz lovers, but also has theme nights.

Now you're warmed up, it's time to get serious at **Nuevo Mundo** (809-240-6414; Calle Duarte 250), the town's main disco, popular with the locals for its merengue and Latin music. Open 9 PM–3 AM. Free except night with live bands. There are plenty of sanky-pankys here eager to hit on foreign females (and no shortage of local lasses offering love beneath the palms for a price).

Shopping
The large resident population of artsy Europeans has given rise to some tremendous shops here. Several of the best are concentrated in **Paseo de la Costanera**, a modern two-storey complex in the heart of town at the junction of Calle Libertad and Duarte. It has more than 40 boutiques, bars, and restaurants, with **Terrenas En Plata** (809-240-5359) and **Blue Corazón** (809-240-6284) for fashion jewelry, including amber and larimar. Across the street, Plaza Taíno hosts **La Cueva de los Indios** (809-240-5168) and **Nativ'Art** (809-240-6412), both also selling amber and larimar jewelry plus Taíno-inspired art. The best selection of art, however, is at **Haitian Caraibes Art Gallery** (809-240-6250; Calle Principal 233), run by connoisseur, Claude Lachamp. He loves his smokes, too, so cigar lovers should make a beeline here.

For beachwear and casually elegant clothing, check out **Tu Closet**, in Plaza Rosada (Calle Duarte and Ramón Mella).

All the lazing around you'll do requires good reading matter. Try **Prensa Internacional** (809-240-6744), in Plaza El Paseo; it sells international magazines, newspapers, and books.

Food Purveyors

The best-stocked store is **Supermercado Lindo** (809-240-6003; Plaza Rosada, Calle Juan Pablo Duarte), selling everything from fresh fruit to your favorite imported products.

El Pan de Antes Boulangerie (809-994-3282; Calle Carmen) sells fresh-baked croissants, brioches, breads, etc.

Good to Know About

Domrescue (809-240-5533; Calle Duarte 131). Ambulance.

Hospital Pablo A. Paulino (809-274-6474; Calle Ramón Mella).

Politur (809-754-3017; Calle Libertad). Tourist police. 24 hours. Immediately west of Plaza El Paseo.

Post Office (Plaza El Paseo). Open Mon. through Fri 9 AM–1 PM and 3–5 PM.

Tourism Office (809-240-6363; Calle La Ceiba 6 at Calle Principal).

Cable car at Pico Isabel del Torres, Puerto Plata

7

NORTH COAST

A Little of Everything

The original ground zero of tourism in the republic, the Costa Ambar (Amber Coast) is a broad-based resort region. Silvering almost 100 miles (160 km) of shore, it has dozens of beaches, although hotels are currently concentrated in three distinct regions: Cabarete, Sosuá, and Playa Dorada outside Puerto Plata. Atlantic trade winds take the edge off the sun while whipping up whitecaps year-round. Wind-whipped Cabarete is the Caribbean capital of extreme water sports and tourism here revolves around surfing, windsurfing, and kite-boarding. Hence, the crowd is predominantly young and party focused, with dozens of bars and restaurants standing shoulder to shoulder along the beach. Sosuá, by contrast, is a hill-top village that can't quite shake its reputation as a center for sex tourism. Playa Dorada is the domain of all-inclusive package vacations (elsewhere tourism is, for the most part, focused on independent travelers seeking small boutique and budget hotels, most run by Europeans and North Americans).

Farther west and as yet virtually undeveloped for tourism, the gorgeous beaches around Luquillo and Punta Rucia butt up to coastal lagoons, such as Estero Hondo, that shelter manatees and enthrall birders. Vast mangrove systems are also a signature of the far west around Monte Cristi, the scorchingly hot and dry westernmost town in the republic. Here, the delta of the Río Yaque forms a soggy floodplain that is a vital staging and wintering site for waterfowl, shorebirds, and waders such as flamingoes. Offshore, coral reefs protect turquoise seas that are a graveyard for Spanish galleons.

The coastal plain is buttressed its entire length by the Cordillera Septentrional, a rugged and lushly clad mountain chain that rises to 4,098 feet (1,249 m) atop Pico Diego de Acampo and offers Indiana Jones-style diversions, such as canyoning and waterfall cascading. There's history here, too. Parque Nacional La Isabela preserves (albeit barely) the scant ruins of the first permanent settlement in the Americas, founded by Columbus in 1493. And the main town, Puerto Plata, boasts a colonial core teeming with gingerbread vernacular buildings—a legacy of a tobacco boom in the mid-1800s.

Getting There and Getting Around

By Air
The region is served by **Gregorio Luperón International Airport** (809-586-0408 or 586-0107), 11 miles (17.6 km) east of Puerto Plata. **American Airlines** (800-433-7300; www.aa.com) flies to Puerto Plata from New York and Miami, and **American Eagle** (same

contact) flies from San Juan. **Continental** flies from Newark, and **Ryan International** flies from Minneapolis. Puerto Plata is also served by **Air Canada** and **Air Transat** from Canada; and by **Martinair** (Amsterdam), and **Condor** (Frankfurt), **LTU** (Frankfurt, Düsseldorf, Munich).

If you plan on basing yourself around Río San Juan, consider flying into **El Catey International Airport** (809-338-5888 ext. 100), near Nagua; see the Samaná chapter.

If you fly into Santo Domingo, the drive to Puerto Plata takes at least four hours. Santiago's **Cibao International Airport**, about one hour south, is second best.

By Bus
Caribe Tours (809-221-4422 in Santo Domingo, 586-4544 in Puerto Plata, and 531-3808 in Sosuá; www.caribetours.com.do) has hourly departures between Santo Domingo and Puerto Plata and Sosuá, on the hour, 6 AM–7 PM (RD$250); from Santo Domingo to Cabrera/Río San Juan at 7:30 and 9 AM and 1, 2, and 3 PM (return departures are at 7, 8:15, and 9:50 AM and 2:15 and 3:50 PM); and from Santo Domingo to Monte Cristi at 6:30, 8 and 9:30 AM and 1, 2, and 3:45 PM (return departures are at 7 and 9 AM and 1:45, 2:45, and 4 PM).

Metro Expreso (809-227-0101) offers bus service between Santo Domingo and Puerto Plata at 7, 9, and 11 AM and 2, 4, and 7 PM (return buses depart Puerto Plata at 6:30, 7:30, and 11 AM, and 2, 4, and 6:30 PM).

Bring a jacket to guard against the excessive air-conditioning on the buses.

Local *guaguas* and *motoconchos* (not recommended) provide service between Sosuá and Cabarete

By Car
Puerto Plata is linked to Santo Domingo by the Autopista Duarte via Santiago de los Caballeros (four hours), from where you cut over the mountains on Carretera 25.

The quickest route to reach the Río San Juan area from Santo Domingo is via the new highway to Sánchez and Samaná; it links up with the coast highway (Carretera 5) just south of Nagua. Carretera 5 runs along the shore for the entire way between Nagua and Puerto Plata, west of which it curls south and transcends the mountains to link up with Highway 1 (RD 1).

At last visit I was able to drive west from Puerto Plata as far as Parque Nacional La Isabela, beyond which even in 4WD it was real tricky, and storms had torn down the bridge over the Río Bajabon, necessitating a return to Carretera 5, then west on Carretera 1, then north via dirt road to Punta Rucia. Carretera 1 continues west, ruler-straight and in good condition all the way to Monte Cristi, with offshoot dirt roads probing north to lonesome white beaches. In 2009, a new coast highway was planned to link Puerto Plata with Luperón and Monte Cristi.

Alamo, Avis, Budget, Europcar, and Hertz all have car rental offices at airport Gregorio Luperón International Airport.

PUERTO PLATA AND VICINITY
Known for its lovely historic center, this port city—the largest on the North Coast—evolved in the 18th and 19th centuries and boasts a huge portfolio of Victorian clapboard vernacular architecture. The name Silver Port was given by Christopher Columbus, who anchored here on January 11, 1493, although the settlement was actually founded in 1502 by Nicolás de

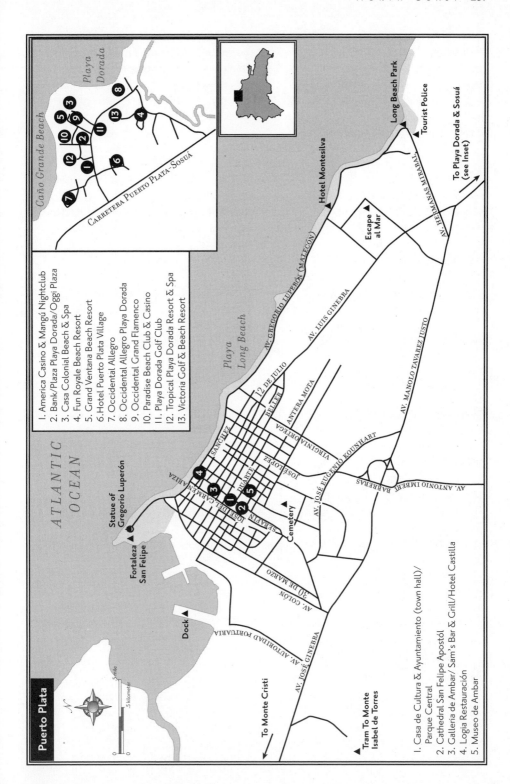

Puerto Plata

ATLANTIC OCEAN

Playa Dorada

Caño Grande Beach

CARRETERA PUERTO PLATA-SOSUÁ

1. America Casino & Mangú Nightclub
2. Bank/Plaza Playa Dorada/Oggi Plaza
3. Casa Colonial Beach & Spa
4. Fun Royale Beach Resort
5. Grand Ventana Beach Resort
6. Hotel Puerto Plata Village
7. Occidental Allegro
8. Occidental Allegro Playa Dorada
9. Occidental Grand Flamenco
10. Paradise Beach Club & Casino
11. Playa Dorada Golf Club
12. Tropical Playa Dorada Resort & Spa
13. Victoria Golf & Beach Resort

Long Beach Park

Tourist Police

To Playa Dorada & Sosuá (see Inset)

Hotel Montesilva

AV. HERMANAS MIRABAL

Escape al Mar

AV. GREGORIO LUPERÓN (MALECÓN)

AV. LUIS GINEBRA

AV. MANOLO TAVAREZ JUSTO

Playa Long Beach

12 DE JULIO

BELLER

ANTERA MOTA

VIRGINIA ORTEGA

JOSÉ LÓPEZ

AV. JOSÉ EUGENIO KOUNHART

AV. ANTONIO IMBERT BARRERAS

SÁNCHEZ

JOSEF IDL DEL CARMEN ARIZA

DUARTE

SERAFÍN

Statue of Gregorio Luperón

Fortaleza San Felipe

Dock

AV. AUTORIDAD PORTUARIA

AV. COLÓN

30 DE MARZO

AV. JOSÉ GINEBRA

To Monte Cristi

Cemetery

Tram To Monte Isabel de Torres

1. Casa de Cultura & Ayuntamiento (town hall)/ Parque Central
2. Cathedral San Felipe Apostól
3. Galleria de Ambar/ Sam's Bar & Grill/Hotel Castilla
4. Logia Restauración
5. Museo de Ambar

0 .5 mile
0 .5 kilometer

Ovando. It lay beyond the pale of Spanish authority and thrived as a smuggling center until 1605 when the authorities burned the town to the ground as punishment. Refounded in 1737, it grew to wealth throughout the 19th century as a port city during the tobacco boom.

A few miles east of town, Playa Dorada has the largest concentration of hotels in the region. This purpose-built complex includes more than 15 all-inclusive and boutique hotels for all budgets. They share a gold sand beach (hence, Playa Dorada) plus an 18-hole Robert Trent Jones-designed golf course.

Puerto Plata is hemmed close to the shore by Mount Isabel de Torres, a soaring mountain whose often-mist-shrouded summit is accessed by the Caribbean's only cable-car ride. There are heaps of other activities and excursions, too. The mountains are a base for mountain biking, waterfall canyoning and cascading, and Jeep safaris. Ocean World Adventure Park is a first-rate facility where you and the kids can swim with dolphins. And there's plenty of whirligig nightlife, from a Las Vegas review to casinos.

Getting Around

Puerto Plata is a large city, although most sites of interest are concentrated around the main square in the eminently walkable historic center. Most hotels, however, are out of town, necessitating a taxi into town; cabs are not metered, so agree with the driver on the fare before your trip starts. Alternately, *guaguas* pass along the main east-west highway and congregate around the central plaza for journeys farther afield. *Motoconchos* and scooter rentals are not safe in Puerto Plata, with its badly potholed roads.

Lodging

BLACKBEARD'S ADULT RESORT
809-970-3268
www.blackbeardsadultresort.com
Costambar

I always do a double take when I see adult resort. Often it merely means no kids. But this elegant resort hotel (known to locals at Hotel Barba Negra) on the beach is the real thing, catering to mature travelers, including couples seeking an erotic vacation. It has a lovely pool and Jacuzzi, plus a thatched bar and restaurant. And the 22 room are comfy enough. Classy it is not. But then, most patrons visit to match up with one (or more) of the Dominican and Haitian ladies who work there as escorts. $$

BLUE BAY VILLAS DORADAS
809-320-3000
fax: 809-320-4790
www.bluebayresorts.com
Playa Dorada

This contemporary adults-only stunner is supremely stylish, appealing to a young-at-heart clientele with its vaguely minimalist furnishings in its 245 rooms. The gorgeous open-walled lobby sets the tone with its rattan sofas. Facilities include three swimming pools, three tennis courts, and a beach club, plus four restaurants, five bars, and live shows in a lounge-theater. $$$–$$$$

Bust of Antonio Maceo, Fortaleza San Felipe, Puerto Plata

CASA COLONIAL BEACH AND SPA

809-320-3232
fax: 809-320-3131
www.casacolonialhotel.com
Playa Dorada

Squeezed incongruously betwixt two all-inclusive resorts, this class act draws society figures to savor a contemporary chic ambience and gourmet cuisine at the nation's preeminent boutique hotel. Hewn of coral stone, its stylish plantation design combines graciously
timeless elegance with hip styling. Wide, breeze-swept hallways double as an art gallery-
museum. A stream trickles through the lovely orchid-filled beachfront garden. Its 50 cavernous guest rooms are impeccably furnished with custom-designed Caribbean pieces
(including mahogany four-poster beds), coral stone floors cool underfoot, and sumptuous
bathrooms. Two gourmet restaurants, a sleek lounge bar, a world-class spa, a lap pool, and
four whirlpool tubs that stud the wooden rooftop deck add to the allure. You'll soon understand why it's a member of the Small Luxury Hotels of the World and why the likes of Grace
Jones, Jonathan Silverman, and Donatella Versace have been seen here. I love it! $$$$

THE BUNGALOWS

809-200-3364 or 866-970-3377
www.thebungalows.com
1 Paradise Drive, Cofresí
Price: Very Expensive.

Aiming for young sophisticates, this ultra-sexy resort opened in 2007 as Maxim Bungalows with an over-the-top party that set the ongoing mood as a society hotel. Although associated with the racy *Maxim* magazine, in 2008, Maxim was dropped from the name and the hotel has been rebranded as an all-inclusive. Spilling down a hillside to a somewhat narrow sliver of beach, its 108 bungalows-rooms spell deluxe with their gorgeous contemporary decor and up-to-the-minute amenities, including 42-inch flat-panel TVs. Its 17,000-square-foot (1,579 sq m) spa has a men-only section and the sumptuous Social restaurant (opened by prolific society restaurateur Jeffrey Chodorow) is a minimalist eye-pleasure with a sensational bar. The resort is renowned for its VIP services, and the sleek 54-foot (16 m) yacht *Independence* available for hire. Sure it's adults only, but don't expect busty babes in g-strings serving at the bar. This is far tamer and classier than the Maxim association suggests. $$$$

FUN ROYALE BEACH RESORT

809-320-4054
fax: 809-320-5301
www.funroyale-tropicale.com
Playa Dorada

Intended for the fun-loving family with kids to keep entertained, this all-inclusive shares facilities with its budget sibling, the adjoining Fun Royal Tropical. Colorful guest rooms (352 in total) play on a quasi-tropical theme with bamboo highlights. It has a kids' club. $$-$$$

HOTEL CASTILLA

809-586-7267
www.samsbar.tk
Calle José del Carmen Ariza 34

The place for budget hounds to rest their heads, this hotel above Sam's Bar and Grill exudes creaky yesteryear atmosphere. Its 12 rooms are no-frills and Spartan, but kept spic-and-span. Best yet, you get the awesome restaurant downstairs, and the steps-to-everywhere downtown locale. $

HOTEL MONTESILVA

809-320-0205
Calle La Estancia

There aren't many budget options around, but this small, no-frills hotel is fine for a night or two. It has few amenities, so consider it as merely a place to lay your head. The 12 small-ish rooms have ceiling fans and cable TVs, but no meals are served. $-$$

IBEROSTAR COSTA DORADA

809-320-1000
fax: 809-320-2023
www.iberostar.com
Carretera Luperón Km. 4, 1 mile (1.6 km) W of Playa Dorada

Among the more attractive all-inclusives, this colonial-themed resort hotel has lively and colorful decor throughout, including in the 498 rooms and 18 suites. Completely self-contained, it features three restaurants, separate adult and children's pools, plus water sports, entertainment, nightclub, and spa. $$$–$$$$

SUN VILLAGE RESORT AND SPA

809-970-3364 or 888-446-4695
fax: 809-970-3156
www.sunvillageresorts.com
1 Paradise Drive, Cofresí

An upscale result with a lovely hillside locale, it makes a huge first impression with its magnificent open lobby fringed by thatch. Seven swimming pools stair-step the hill, and there are five restaurants and a huge spa. The 420 guest rooms are furnished with modern amenities and bamboo furniture, but they don't get me excited. It's a short walk to Ocean World Marine Park. $$$–$$$$

Statue of Gregorio Luperon, Fortaleza San Felipe, Puerto Plata

VALLE TRANQUILO

829-359-7406, in North America 702-818-5007, in the U.K. 01226-726078
www.drcamping.com or www.milet-design.com
El Puerto, 4 miles (6.4 km) E of Imbert

What a gem! This intimate mountain retreat, amid lush gardens at the hamlet of El Puerto, 20 minutes west of Puerto Plata, started life as the eccentric home-away-from home (Rancho Nazdrowie) of Milet Delmé-Radcliffe, an English blue blood who forsook her country-house estate for a more genuine country life in the tropics. In 2008, the eco-sensitive mountain retreat was bought by an English couple, Peter and Sharon, and is now rented out. The setting, the colorful eclectic decor, the ambience are divine. The Plantation Guest House has four romantic guest rooms. And campers are welcome (US$10 per person)—bring your own tent, which you can pitch wherever you wish. A café-bar serves meals throughout the day, and there's a communal kitchen, plus a swimming pool enclosed by lush foliage. Totally irresistible! $$

VICTORIA GOLF AND BEACH RESORT

809-320-1200
fax: 809-320-3862
www.vhhr.com
Playa Dorada

Yet another beautiful contemporary-themed hotel graced by a surfeit of coral stone and travertine. This low-rise resort fringes the golf course, a 10-minute walk from the beach. The 190 rooms and suites are airy and romantic, with gleaming clinical whites and soft tropical pastels—nice! I like that they all have ceilings fans, too. It has three restaurants on site, and Tex-Mex dishes at its own beach club. $$$$

Dining

CAFÉCITO CARIBBEAN BAR AND AMERICAN GRILL

809-586-7923
www.popreport.com/CC2
Plaza Isabela, Carretera 5, 2 miles (3 km) E of Puerto Plata
Cuisine: International

A great breakfast spot, this legendary expatriate hangout is a laid-back, bohemian café-restaurant with fantastic music and an eclectic menu ranging from burgers and wraps to escargots in garlic butter, plus surf-and-turf and lobster dinners. It also serves fresh-cooked daily specials, such as meat loaf with mashed potatoes, peas, and gravy. I enjoyed a delicious sea bass in sherry followed by a Swiss chocolate mousse. With free WiFi, it's a cool spot to hang while checking your E-mail. Free hotel transfers. Open: Sat. through Fri., noon–midnight, Sun. 6 PM–midnight. $$.

ESCAPE AL MAR

809-261-4990
Malecón, 600 yards (549 m) W of Avenida Hermanas Mirabal
Cuisine: Seafood

The only restaurant on the beach in Puerto Plata town, this elegant restaurant has a deck right next to Playa Long Beach. It specializes in *parilladas* (BBQ) but the menu also features crêpes, sandwiches, and sirloins, and I enjoyed a delicious sea bass with ginger, soy, and leek sauce, with prompt and courteous service. The restaurant was due to relocate at press time. Open: Daily 11 AM–9 PM. $$

HEMINGWAY BAR AND GRILL
890-320-2230
Playa Dorada
Cuisine: American

A classic, over-air-conditioned, nautical-themed sports bar serving the tourist trade. It serves salads, sandwiches, burgers, steaks, and seafoods, plus Tex-Mex. Busy on weekends, with live music. Karaoke kicks in most evenings. Open: Daily noon–2 AM. $$.

RISTORANTE STEFY AND NATALE
809-970-7630
Las Rocas, 1 mile (1.6 km) E of Ocean World, Cofresí
Cuisine: Italian

Unknown to most tourists but a favorite among local expats, this thatched Italian restaurant is enhanced by rock walls festooned with fishing nets and Italian decor. Homemade pasta dishes and fabulous thin-crust pizzas highlight the menu. I recommend the penne with vodka. Bargain prices. Open: Tues. through Sat. 4:30–11 PM and Sun. 11:30–11:30. $$.

SAM'S BAR AND GRILL
809-586-7267
www.samsbar.tk
Calle José del Carmen Ariza 34
Cuisine: American

When you hanker for a pancake breakfast, Mexican scramble, or Philly cheese steak, then this unlikely venue in a Victorian building in the heart of Puerto Plata will fill the bill. The decor is down-home friendly, like a piece of the Midwest transplanted. And the menu ranges to chicken cordon bleu and seafood. On Sunday, make a beeline with the local expats for traditional roast beef with Yorkshire pudding and roasted potatoes. Open: Daily 8 AM–10 PM. $$.

VERANDA RESTAURANT
809-320-3232
Casa Colonial, Playa Dorada
Cuisine: Fusion

I love this beachfront restaurant at the chic Casa Colonial boutique hotel. On super-hot days you can dine inside behind a soaring wall of glass, enjoying the gorgeous minimalist decor, while on cooler days and evenings I opt for the wooden deck overhanging the sands. Its fusion menu ranges from health-conscious salads and sandwiches to pasta of the day. For more elegant dining, opt for the indoor Lucia restaurant, serving Dominican-born Chef Rafael Vásquez's Caribbean-Asian fusion. Open: Daily 11:30 AM–6 PM. $$$.

Attractions, Parks, and Recreation

Beaches

The town center slopes gently to the sea and is fringed by **Playa Long Beach**. This broad, 3-mile-long (4.8 km) swath was recently expanded and spruced up by the City Fathers and is now a lovely spot for families, who prefer to hang at the far east end, where there's a small park and shade trees. The Malecón boulevard runs its length, making for a lovely walk. Note the small monument of the Roman god Neptune that pins a small island offshore.

Most tourist action centers on **Playa Dorada** (www.playadorada.com.do), a sinuous beach that begins east of Playa Long Beach. It is backed by a mega-resort complex with 15 hotels in a half-moon around the championship Playa Dorada Golf Club. Non-guests are granted access to the beach, and some hotels sell day and/or night passes for you to use their facilities.

The locals' favorite gathering spots are two west of Puerto Plata: **Costámbar** and, farther west, the slightly more touristy **Playa Cofresí**, backed by hills studded with villas and upscale hotels. Farther west, and virtually the exclusive domain of two all-inclusive hotels (the Riu Meringue and Riu Bachata), is **Playa Maimón**.

Sportfishing

The **Ocean World Marina** (809-970-3373; www.oceanworldmarina.com) is the only full-service marina on the north coast of the Dominican Republic.

Gone Fishing (809-589-1239) offers two sportfishing trips daily out of Puerto Plata; $99 per person, or $690 for a half-day boat charter. **Puerto Plata Fishing** (809-261-4773; www.puertoplatafishing.com), at Playa Dorada, also offers trips. Note that the ocean swells can be mighty rough in winter off the north coast.

Beach in Costa Dorada The Dominican Republic Ministry of Tourism

Cascading at 27 Charcos de Damajagua Falls The Dominican Republic Ministry of Tourism

Golf

The Robert Trent Jones-designed **Playa Dorada Golf Course** (809-320-3472; www.playadoradagolf.com) is open to public play; $45 in summer, $75 in winter. A golf academy includes beginner lessons.

Miscellaneous Attractions and Recreation

If you get bored and need to kill time, the **Brugal rum bottling plant** (809-586-2531; Avenida Louis Ginebra; Monday through Friday 9–noon and 2–5, free) offers short tours following a blink-and-you'll-miss-it video primer on Dominican rums. It's all a prelude to being hustled into the gift store for a meager cocktail and the temptation to purchase.

You can whiz around a track on high-speed go-karts at **Fun City Action Park** (809-320-1031; Calle Sousa), 1 mile (1.6 km) east of Puerto Plata. Open: daily 10–8.

Using its trademark tiger-stripe trucks, **Outback Safari** (809-244-4886; www.outbacksafari.com.do; Calle Aldo Moro 6) offers a daylong excursion that includes community visits, a plantation tour, hiking, swimming, etc. $79 adults, $39.50 children.

And **Aligatours** (809-261-4773; www.aligatour.net) offers adrenaline-packed country-side tours by ATV, Fun Buggy, and six-wheeler amphibious vehicles.

Statue of Christ atop Pico Isabel de Torres, Puerto Plata

Aligatours also offers half-day guided motor coach tours of Puerto Plata, including the Brugal rum factory, Museo de Ambar, San Felipe fortress, and the cable car to Monte Isabel de Torres.

27 CHARCOS DE DEMAJAGUA NATURAL MONUMENT
No telephone
www.27charcos.com
2 miles (3 km) S of Imbert; 16 miles (25.6 km) SE of Puerto Plata
Open: Daily 8:30–4
Admission: RD$250–460 depending on number of falls visited

Making for a great half-day excursion, this park protects 27 waterfalls that fall in a stair-step cascade through the Cordillera Septentrional. Together they form a natural water slide. It's fun to wade along and through the riverbed (which can be thigh-deep in rainy season) as you ascend the cascades one by one, then plunge back down into a series of jade-colored pools. Wear appropriate footwear with good grip and that you don't mind getting soaked. You're outfitted with a life jacket and helmet at the well-organized entrance, which has a restaurant. The falls can get crowded.

You can book a group excursion with **Iguana Mama** (809-571-0908; www.iguanamama.com; $79).

MONTE ISABEL DE TORRES

809-970-0501
E-mail: teleferico.pp@verizon.net.do
Camino a Los Domínguez
Open: Every 10 minutes, Thurs. through Tues. 8:30–5
Admission: RD$200

Towering over Puerto Plata, this flat-topped mountain (2,565 feet/781 m) beckons invit-
ingly. Fortunately, a *teleférico* (cable car) departs every 10 minutes. Unfortunately, when I
was there, the tram operators crammed as many people as would fit in the tram, with no
regard for load limits; and the tram sometimes doesn't operate in bad weather. You ascend
from the sultry coast to step out into a much cooler clime. Go in early morning, before
clouds form. The views are quite breathtaking. At the top, you can stroll a huge botanical
garden and forest reserve spanning 334 acres (135 ha) that are great for birding. There are
snack bars and souvenir stalls beneath a statue of Jesus Christ inspired by the far larger
statue in Rio de Janeiro, Brazil.

No guides are required. Don't fall for the freelance guides who tout their services as you
arrive at the tram station.

Iguana Mama (see above) offers a daylong guided hike from sea level into the montane
rain forest ($75).

Museums
GALERÍA DE AMBAR

809-586-6467
www.ambercollection.itgo.com
Calles 12 de Julio and Carmen Ariza
Open: Mon. through Fri. 8:30 AM–6 PM
Admission: US$1

Competing with the far more well known Museo del Ambar, this has a similarly astounding

Juan Pena looks for inclusions in amber, La Cumbre

A Walking Tour of Puerto Plata

Puerto Plata's Zona Victoriana—the historic core—is replete with gingerbread buildings, many of which were recently restored. Laid out in a tight grid, the zone is easily navigated, with most sights of interest concentrated within a few blocks of Parque Central. A three-hour walking tour reveals the main sights.

Pick up a map at the **Secretario del Estado de Turismo** (809-586-3676; Calle José del Arizo 45), then walk north half a block past the gingerbread-trimmed **Casa Curial** (Bishop's House), adjoining **Catedral San Felipe Apostól**. After roaming the church, head east along Calle Duarte two blocks to the **Museo del Ambar**. Then return along Calle Duarte to explore **Parque Central** in a counter-clockwise direction.

Exit the square west along Calle Beller. At the corner of Calle San Felipe, pop in the tiny **Museo de Arte Taíno** (809-586-7601; Calle Beller 25), a private jewelry store displaying Taíno relics. Exiting, turn north along Calle San Felipe. At the third junction, turn right on Calle Mella. After two blocks, turn left on Calle Separación to admire the two remarkable buildings at the junction with Avenida Gregorio Luperón (Malecón). That one on the right is the **Logia Restauración** (809-586-2717; Calle Separación 11), or Mason's hall. It's normally closed to the public, but I was let in and given a fascinating tour when I asked. The interior features of this lovely mansion in Caribbean vernacular include a spiral wooden staircase and a barrel-vaulted wooden ceiling with sky mural.

Finally turn left onto the Malecón and follow it 400 yards (366 m) to the end, where a bronze **statue of Gregorio Luperón**—the Dominican general who led resistance to Spanish rule in the 1860s—stands in the traffic circle. A small landscaped storefront park features a **granite monument** to the 189 passengers killed when a German commercial aircraft crashed into the sea nearby on February 6, 1996.

Finally enter **Fortaleza San Felipe** (open Thursday through Tuesday 9–5; RD$40). This ancient fortress is the oldest in the New World and was erected in 1577 to guard the harbor entrance. The meager exhibits include a few rusting cannon and a small display of colonial-era weaponry.

collection of amber pieces, but broadens its appeal with educational exhibits on other Dominican products, such as sugar, tobacco, and rum.

MUSEO DEL AMBAR
809-586-2848
www.ambermuseum.com
Calle Duarte 61
Open: Mon. through Sat. 9–6
Admission: RD$40

This superb little museum is housed in the pink and white Villa Bentz, a beautiful Beaux Arts Victorian wooden mansion (perhaps the city's finest) dating from 1919 and fronted by columns and balustrades. The ground floor is a jewelry store selling amber and larimar pieces. The museum, on the second floor, displays a magnificent collection of amber exhibits, including inclusions—most notably a 17-inch-long (43 cm) piece of amber containing a lizard trapped millions of years ago, and the famous mosquito inclusion that inspired *Jurassic Park*.

Parks and Plazas
PARQUE CENTRAL (INDEPENDENCIA)
Calle Duarte between Calles Ariza and Separación

The town's tree-shaded main square was restored in 2007 and is a charming place to relax and soak in the local atmosphere. At its heart is **La Glorieta**, a gingerbread bandstand that is a reconstruction of the original made in Belgium in 1872; musical ensembles still play on weekends.

Looming to the south, the twin-steepled **Catedral San Felipe Apostól** (Monday through Saturday 8–noon, Sunday 7 AM–8 PM) also emerged from a restoration in 2008. It combines various architectural elements, including Art Deco plus exquisite Italianate stained-glass windows.

On the park's west side, the gleaming white Victorian mansion at the corner of Calle Ariza and Beller now hosts the Pentecostal **Iglesia Cristiana El Buen Samaritano** church (Calle José del Ariza 29). Facing it, on the east side, are the **Casa de la Cultura** (809-261-2731; Calles Separación and Duarte; Monday through Friday 9–noon and 3–5; free), which has an art gallery upstairs and hosts cultural performances; and, adjoining, the yellow and white neo-classical **Ayuntamiento** (town hall).

Water Sports and Sailing
Several concessionaires offer motorized water sports at Playa Dorada, where hotels have their own non-motorized water sports for guests. Many hotels have dive shops on-site.

Scuba Caribe (www.scubacaribe.com/puerto_plata_en.htm) offers a wide range of fun

Banana boat ride at Punta Rucia

Marine Mammal Sanctuary of the Dominican Republic

During winter months, as many as 5,000 Atlantic humpbacks gather to procreate in the warm waters off the north and east coast of Hispaniola. The breeding and calving grounds extend from the Banco de Plata or Silver Bank—a shallow submerged limestone plateau located 50 miles (80 km) northeast of Puerto Plata—to Samaná Bay. This vitally important marine habitat is protected in entirety as the Santuario de Mamíferos Marinos de la República Dominicana.

Although the easily accessible Samaná Bay gets the lion's share of tourist attention, the hard-to-reach Silver Bank gets the lion's share of whales. In fact, it's the most important breeding site in the world for humpback whales. For this reason, access is strictly regulated, by permit only. You can sign up with **Aquatic Adventures** (954-382-0042; www.aquaticadventures.com) or **Conscious Breath Adventures** (305-753-1732; www.consciousbreathadventures.com), both of which have weeklong whale-watching trips to the Silver Bank from Puerto Plata, January through April. Trips include swimming with the whales.

activities, from banana-boat rides to scuba dive certification and trips.

Caribbean Ocean Adventures (809-586-1239; http://freestylecatamarans.com) offers half-day trips aboard 55-foot-long (17 m) catamarans departing Playa Dorada for Sosuá, with time for snorkeling ($79 adults, $40 children).

Wildlife and Wilderness Parks
OCEAN WORLD ADVENTURE PARK

809-291-1000
www.oceanworldadventurepark.com
Cofresí, 3 miles (5 km) W of Puerto Plata
Open: Daily 9:30–5:30
Admission: $55 adult, $40 children

This fabulous facility has enough to keep you enthralled all day. The big draw is the chance to swim with dolphins in a huge lagoon (at 12 million gallons, it's supposedly the largest such marine habitat in the world). In all, there are 52 scheduled events daily, including sea lion and dolphin shows, plus acrobatic parrots and macaws. There's even a tiger grotto. Kids can snorkel a coral reef and swim with harmless nurse sharks and rays.

Culture

Casinos
Ocean World Marina and Casino (809-291-1000; www.oceanworldcasino.com). At Ocean World Marina, Cofresí. Video slots plus blackjack, Caribbean poker, craps, roulette, and no limit Texas Hold'em (Texas Hold'em tournaments every Tuesday and Saturday at 7 PM). Open: Daily 2 PM–4 AM.

Cinemas
Cine Roma (809-320-7010; Calle Beller 35). Twice-daily showings.
Cinemar (809-320-1400; Plaza Playa Dorada). Modern cinema with multiple screens.

Music and Nightlife
The Playa Dorada complex has four discos. The most popular are **Crazy Moon**, in the Paradise Beach Resort and Casino (809-320-3663); and **Mangú** (890-320-3800; 8 PM–2 AM), in the Occidental Allegro Village. Mangú is the liveliest, with a broad mix of locals and tourists (many of the former looking to score off the latter) and music hot enough to cook the pork. No cover charge.

Bravissimo (809-291-1111; www.oceanworldcasino.com). Inspired by Havana's renowned Tropicana, this Las Vegas-style cabaret exudes sensuality with its exorbitantly yet scantily clad performers, electrifying music, and sensational dance routines. Open: Wednesday through Sunday 9:30 PM. $35 show only, or $69 for Ocean World Magical Nights (includes round-trip transfers, a dinner buffet, dolphin and sea lion show, plus the cabaret).

Café Cito Caribbean Bar and American Grill leads a pub crawl every Wednesday and Saturday night taking in a car wash bar, Sosuá's main street, and the party scene at Cabarete ($55 per person, including dinner). Café Cito is also cigar-friendly, and a great place to kick back with a wine or cocktail and enjoy the tunes.

Lighthouse Lounge and Disco (809-291-1000; www.oceanworldcasino.com). This stylish nightclub on the top floor of the Ocean World Casino building, in Cofresí, draws a moneyed crowd and has dance shows on Friday and Saturday, plus themed parties. Open: Daily 8 PM–4 AM.

Octopus Bar and Grill (809-291-1000; www.oceanworldcasino.com) Also at Ocean World Casino, this huge bar includes sweeping waterfront views and a swim-up bar. It hosts live bands and occasional special theme events that have included the Miss Dominican Universe pageant.

Shopping
The Playa Dorada complex has boutiques and gift stores, as do several of the individual hotels. In town, the **Galería de Ambar** and the **Museo de Ambar** (see Museums, this section) are *the* places to go for amber and larimar jewelry. Giving them a run for their money is **Joyería y Artesanía La Canoa** (809-586-3604 Calle Beller 15), which gives you a free sample of *mamajuana*—the local aphrodisiacal liquor.

Good to Know About
Centro Médico Bournigal (809-586-2342; www.bournigal-hospital.com; Calle Antera Mota) This private hospital offers emergency service.

Politur (809-320-0365 or 754-3101; Malecón and Calle Manolo Taverns). The tourist police are at the east end of Playa Long Beach.

Tourism Office (809-586-3676 or 586-5059; Calle José del Arizo 45). Open: Mon. through Fri. 8–3.

Weekly and Annual Events
Brugal Rum sponsors the annual three-day **Puerto Plata Merengue Festival** (809-221-4660) each September, with non-stop live events on the Malecón seafront boulevard.

Sun Village Resort and Spa (see Lodgings, this section) hosts the four-day **International Film Festival** (212-627-3439 ext. 409; www.dominicaninternationalfilmfestival.com) each December.

Sosuá

This coastal resort town, 15 miles (24 km) east of Puerto Plata, is unique in several regards. First, its position atop twin headlands straddling a broad cove adds character to an already colorful town. On the west side of the bay is the humble and nondescript Dominican community of Los Charramícos. On the east is the far more interesting community of El Batey, the heart of the tourist section, with some intriguing architecture and all the restaurants, hotels, and salacious night scenes. Sosuá has a dubious distinction of sharing with Boca Chica the title of sex tourism capital in the republic. The scene is a lot tamer than prior years following several police crackdowns but there's still a sleazy nocturnal edge, most noticeable along Calle Pedro Clisante. Plenty of expats (notably Germans) live here and run a majority of the bars and restaurants.

Still, Sosuá has plenty of pluses, not least a lovely and lively beach that gets packed with Dominicans on weekends. It's also the diving capital of the north coast. And there are some intriguing architectural highlights. El Batey was founded by German Jews given refuge here by Rafael Trujillo in the 1940s. Prior to that it had been a headquarters for the United Fruit Company and a major shipping center for bananas (the company closed shop here in the 1920s).

Getting There and Getting Around

Guaguas (RD$45-RD$60; 6 AM–9 PM) run between Puerto Plata and Sosúa, as do *motoconchos*. Expect to pay about RD$600 (US$20) for up to four occupants each way in a taxi.

Sosuá's narrow and convoluted one-way streets are best negotiated on foot.

Playa Sosua

Lodging

CASA VALERIA
809-571-3565
www.hotelcasavaleria.com
Calle Dr. Rosen 28

My favorite place to rest in Sosuá, this charming, no-frills, family-run, Mexican hacienda style hotel is perfectly situated in the heart of town. It has colorful sponge-washed walls and heaps of potted plants. Its nine rooms open to a small swimming pool and have lively fabrics and relatively simple furnishings, including rough-hewn beds, plus kitchenettes in two studios. Meals are served in a rustic open-air thatched restaurant. $–$$

PIERGIORGIO PALACE HOTEL
809-571-2626
fax: 809-571-2786
www.piergiorgiopalace.com
Calle La Puntilla

A gleaming white cliff top hotel with colonial gingerbread trim, it looks over landscaped grounds and deep-blue ocean. I like the restaurant with its cliff-edge dining patios. Its 56 air-conditioned rooms and suites are cozy and furnished with white rattan furniture and pink floral chintz fabrics. $$–$$$

SEAHORSE RANCH
809-571-3880
www.sea-horse-ranch.com
Carretera 5, 2 miles (3 km) E of Sosúa

Twelve privately owned, three- to five-bedroom luxury villas in a reclusive setting amid 250 acres (101 ha) of dramatic shorefront. Features include a private beach, equestrian center, and tennis, and brand-new seaside pools at a beach club with water sports. Concierge service. $$$–$$$$

SOSUA BAY RESORT
809-571-4000
fax: 809-571-4545
www.sosuabayresort.com
Calle Dr. Alejo Martínez 1

The setting overlooking the bay is fantastic and the impressive Spanish-hacienda-themed atrium lobby gets things off to a great start at this all-inclusive hillside resort. Alas, decor in the 193 spacious, air-conditioned guest rooms is insipid, due to the overdone turquoise and orange color schemes and fabrics. Still, it might be to your taste, and rooms do have balconies and most modern amenities. The resort has six restaurants, casino, gym, squash court, and water sports. $$–$$$

SOSUA BY THE SEA BEACH RESORT
809-571-3222
fax: 809-571-3020

www.sosuabythesea.com
Calle David Stern

Appealing to the budget-package vacation crowd, this cliff top hotel overlooks its own broad beach right in the heart of town. The 58 spacious air-conditioned studios and 33 suites all have cable TV, telephone, in-room safe, and mini refrigerator, plus cool tile floors and handsome mahogany furnishings that include an option for king beds. It has a dive center. $$$

VICTORIAN HOUSE BOUTIQUE HOTEL

809-571-4000
fax: 809-571-4545
www.sosuabayresort.com
Calle Dr. Alejo Martínez 1

Affiliated with the adjoining Sosuá Bay Resort, this more upscale boutique hotel is designed in Victorian fashion and done up in elegant plantation style. The main draw, however, is the magnificent vistas from the 50 guest rooms with broad balconies, many of which have four-poster mahogany beds. Suites have loft bedrooms with king beds and en-suite Jacuzzi. You can make use of the Sosuá Bay Resort's six restaurants and other facilities. $$$–$$$$

Dining

The dining options are excellent thanks to the large number of North American and European expatriates, for which reason there's something for every taste. The competition keeps restaurateurs on their toes. Just about the only thing you won't find here is sushi. The many simple *colmados* and grills down at Playa Sosuá serve local dishes for a pittance.

JOSEPH'S GRILL AND GRAPE

809-571-3222
Calle David Stern

A local institution inside the Sosuá by the Sea Beach Resort, this small, elegant cliff top restaurant serves a mean steak, plus inventive fusion dishes and ever-changing prix fixe dinners. Service is attentive and proficient. Reservations required. Open: Thurs. through Sun. 7–11 PM. $$.

LA ROCA

809-571-3893
Calle Pedro Clisante 1, corner Calle Arzeno

A fun venue for its eclectic decor (tabletops, for example, are decorated with movie posters), this old wooden building offers a choice of dining on the street-side veranda or beneath whirling ceiling fans inside. Its no-less-eclectic menu spans the globe. I enjoyed a shrimp cocktail followed by a tasty Mexican baked fish. Other good bets include a seafood fettuccine, and you can even get a wiener schnitzel. Daily specials are listed on a board, and Friday night features all-you-can-eat barbecue (6–10 PM). Leave room for the calorie bomb crêpe with chocolate sauce and whipped cream! It has pool tables. Open: 8 AM–midnight. $$

MORUA MAI

809-571-2966
http://moruamai.com
Calle Pedro Clisante 5, corner Calle Arzeno

This large, airy, and highly respected two-tier restaurant, opposite La Roca, delivers consistently good burgers, and the international menu also features club sandwich, and Chef's special such as paella, Chateaubriand with Béarnaise sauce, and Mario's seafood casserole. The lobster dishes here are renowned, as are its sea bass specials. It's also a good place to breakfast. Pancakes and syrup, anyone? A pianist tickles the ivories at night. Ceiling fans help keep things cool. Upholstered banquettes and wicker furniture. Open: Daily 8 AM–midnight. $$$.

ROCKY'S

809-571-2951
www.rockysbar.com
Calle Rosen 22

A local institution run by a Canadian, Marco, this is where expats gather for breakfast in bare-bones surrounds that could do with a good spruce up. We're talking filling pancakes and omelettes. For lunch, try a BLT sandwich or chicken 'n' fries. And dinner includes

Playing dominoes at Playa Sosua

An Excursion into the Cordillera Septentrional

At Monte Llano, midway between Puerto Plata and Sosúa, you can turn south and follow badly potholed Carretera 25—the Carretera Turística—as it snakes into the Cordillera Septentrional (Northern Mountains). The area is developing rapidly as a center for ecotourism, and new entities are popping up all the time. Enjoy it for the beautiful drive, and make a day of it.

ATTRACTIONS, PARKS, AND RECREATION

The following are in order southbound . . .

Tropical Plantation (809-656-1210; open Monday through Saturday 7:30 AM–4 PM by appointment) At Tubugua stop at this 30-acre (12 ha) flower farm with sensational views back down the mountain. It gives half-day guided tours (US$15) that include a netted butterfly garden, two free-flight aviaries, a petting zoo, a huge pond stocked with koi, plus fruit orchards and grounds bursting with heliconias, gingers, etc. . A trail leads to a spectacular waterfall where you can bathe in a cool pool at its base. Alas, at last visit it was beginning to deteriorate, with the French owner away long-term. **Tours, Trips, Treks & Travels** (809-867-8884; www.4tdomrep.com) offers excursions.

Yasika Zipline Adventures (809-650-2323; www.yasikaadventures.com; 2 miles (3 km) south of Yasika) The first zipline in Puerto Plata opened in 2008 after being built by Costa Ricans—the world experts in zipline construction. It features eight sturdy metal cables slung between 10 treetop platforms at varying elevations. You're secured in harness to the cable, then you step off the platform, and gravity does the rest as you fly through the air, suspended at up to 100 feet (30 m) above the ground. What an adrenaline kick! Children 8 through 18 must be accompanied. Allow three hours for the circuit. Open: Monday through Saturday 8 AM–5 PM. US$79. Hotel transfers cost additional.

Jasmine Spa and Wellness Centre (see Lodging) Why not treat yourself to a day-spa treatment, such as facials, mud treatment, and/or massage, from shiatsu to hot stones . . . all following a peaceful walk to waterfalls and freshwater pools. It also offers meditation, yoga, and *bachata* dance classes, plus hikes and horseback rides. It also has a day package ($125) including lunch, spa treatment(s), and transfers from Puerto Plata, Sosúa, and Cabarete.

Parque Ecológico del Café La Cumbre (809-580-0710; free) In the village of La Cumbre, 10 miles (16 km) south of Tabagua, is a coffee *finca* run by the Consejo Dominicano del Café (Dominican Coffee Council). It has a tiny museum of meager interest, and trails of varying difficulty through native forest. Some lead to *miradores* (lookouts) with fabulous views. An old mansion—La Mansion del Café—and the *beneficio* (coffee mill) across the road comprise a training school for the coffee industry.

Factory Ambar La Cumbre (809-656-1499) is the best of several roadside museums and stores in La

steak filets, lemon chicken, and spaghetti. The great music is another reason to eat here, plus you have use of free Internet. It also has bare-bones, run-down, rooms. Open: 7 AM–10 PM. $.

Attractions, Parks, and Recreation

Beaches

Sosúa has two beaches, both right in the heart of town. All the action centers on slender **Playa Sosúa**, a tree-shaded beach tucked by headlands, and unfurling for almost a mile beneath a cliff face. It's great for mingling with locals. You can hang at any of two dozen

Cumbre, the center of amber mining in the republic. There are at least 15 mine sites in the area. For the easiest to reach, turn east at the police station and follow the dirt road 0.6 mile (1 km) to **La Toca**, a tiny hamlet where there are some 20 mine pits known for producing yellow gold amber with some of the world's finest inclusions (see the special topic, Liquid Gold) hewn from strata of sedimentary rock. Ask for the house of Juan Peña (no telephone); he's a friendly fellow and will guide you to narrow tunnels bored into the hills. The primary source for blue amber is a short distance southeast of La Toca, at **Los Cacaos**. Note: The tunnels and pits are narrow, unlit, and very unsafe. Entering is not recommended!

LODGING AND DINING

JASMINE SPA AND WELLNESS CENTRE
829-970-5272, in North America 877-461-2004
http://jasmine-spa-wellness.com
Carretera Turística km 24, Tubagua

Nestled amongst 40 acres (16 ha) of lush rain forest, this gorgeous health-focused mountain retreat is as beautiful as it is calming. The setting—think fresh air and fabulous vistas—is its own cure for the moody blues, but I particularly love the enlivening decor, such as the bright-painted cement floors in the eight rooms. It specializes in spa packages, so reservations are essential. Don't just arrive and expect to book a room!

The dining room tantalizes with three- or four-course organic meals using produce fresh from the estate's own garden—choose from Dominican, Indian, Italian, and Thai menus.

TUBAGUA PLANTATION VILLAGE
809-586-5761 or 696-6932
www.popreport.com/tubagua
Carretera Turística km 18, Tubagua

This place is fantastic! Perhaps the most true-to-life, simple and enriching eco-hotel experience to be had in the republic, I highly recommend an overnight at this Taíno-style ranch integrated into the community life of Tubagua. And you get sensational views to boot! You'll sleep under mosquito nets on rough-hewn beds beneath simple, open-air thatched huts. Be prepared to be awakened early by crowing roosters. Authentic Dominican meals are prepared on a wood-fired grill and stove, and served in an open-air thatched restaurant hanging over the edge of the mountain. It has a tiny plunge pool and makes a great base for mountain hikes that include visits to farmsteads. $$

funky beach bars and grills, and private concessionaires tout banana-boat and glass-bottom boat rides plus water sports. It gets packed (and disgustingly littered) on weekends. A path that runs the length of the beach is lined with bars and art galleries.

Smaller and far quieter, the pretty, cliff-enclosed, half-moon **Playita Alicia** is a virtual private domain of the Casa Marina Reef Resort. The all-inclusive hotel generally lets non-guests pass through the property to access the beach, or you can hire a boat at Playa Sosúa. It has no facilities.

Scuba Diving
Sosúa is renowned for its spectacular diving, with walls, reefs, and wrecks all within a few

minutes of shore. Premium sites include the wreck of the *Zingara*, a freighter scuttled in 1993 to form an artificial reef and beginning at 90 feet (27 m) down; and **Airport Wall**, beginning at 40 feet (12 m) and renowned for its swim-through caves and fine elkhorn, although slightly devoid of pelagics.

Dolphin Dive Center (809-571-3589; www.dolphindivecenter.com) and **Merlin Dive Center** (809-545-0538; www.tauchschule-merlin.com) have outlets at the entrance to Playa Sosúa, and **Northern Coast Diving** (809-671-1028; www.northerncoastdiving.com) is at Calle Pedro Clisante 8.

Miscellaneous
Columbus Aquapark (809-571-2642; www.aguasosua.com) This theme park features raft rides, spiraling slides, a lazy river, and other attractions. Open: Thurs. through Sun. 8 AM–6 PM.

Sea Horse Ranch Equestrian Center (809-571-4462; www.sea-horse-ranch.com; Carretera 5) This English-style stable, 3 miles (4.8 km) east of Sosúa, offers beach and mountain rides.

Museums
MUSEO JUDÍA DE SOSÚA
809-571-1386
Calle Dr. Alejo Martínez at Calle Dr. Rosén
Open: Mon. through Fri. 9–1 and 2–4
Admission: RD$75

This tiny circular museum, lit through skylights shaped like Magen Davids, honors Sosúa's Jewish community with poignant exhibits that tell the story of how in July 1938, brutal Dominican Dictator Rafael Trujillo attended a conference on Jewish refugees and opened his nation to Jews fleeing Nazi persecution. Some 600 suitable immigrants were selected by the newly formed Dominican Republic Settlement Association. They were each granted 80 acres (32 ha) (plus cattle and a mule) on 26,000 acres (10,530 ha) that Trujillo's government purchased from the United Fruit Company. Sosúa became their base, and the settlers' original Productos Sosúa (a dairy and meat producer) is still going strong, albeit now foreign owned. Twelve families from the original settlers still live in the town. The entire tale is regaled in photographs, documents, and artifacts.

The wooden **synagogue** next door bears a Star of David above the door.

Music and Nightlife
Sosúa throbs after dark with a sizzling and mostly salacious night scene. Party bars and discos pack shoulder to shoulder along Calle Pedro Clisante. Most bars are run by expats and are open to the street; the predominant clientele comprises foreign males and young Dominican and Haitian female *putas* (hookers). Meanwhile, in the discos foreign females will be beset by sanky pankys whose approach might seem romantically harmless (they'll whisk you onto the dance floor) but is usually also intended to bilk you for money. The scene is very fluid. Most places keep the same hours and close up at 2 AM.

There's not much to choose between the dance clubs. The hot places are **Classico's** (the disco is above its street-front **Merengue Bar**), the **Latino Club**, the high-tech **Club X** and, across the street, **Club 59**. The **Calypso Disco** (11 PM–4 AM) at the Casa Marina Beach Resort is open to non-guests, as is **After One**—the class act in town—at Sosúa Bay Resort; the latter

Liquid Gold

Thar's gold in them there hills! Liquid gold. Or rather, solidified liquid gold, otherwise known as amber. Popular as an item of jewelry, amber is a fossilized resin from the prehistoric *Hymenaea protera* tree, which became extinct about 15 million years ago. The tarlike resin, oozing from tree trunks as long ago as 40 million years, hardened over eons into a transparent rocklike polymer considered a semi-precious gemstone.

Although most amber comes from the Baltic (it was traded as jewelry as far back as ancient Egyptian and Roman times), the Dominican Republic has the world's second largest amber reserves. The pre-Columbian Taíno also traded amber jewelry and burned amber as an incense to keep mosquitoes away.

Most amber is found in sedimentary rock strata. Nuggets typically measure less than 2 inches (5 cm) wide, but occasionally massive pieces are found. Hispaniola has three main mine sites, with the greatest concentration around La Cumbre, in the Cordillera Septentrional, and secondary sites at Bayaguana and near Sabana de la Mar, in the southeast. It is mined by bell pitting—crude shafts, tunnels, and pits that are unlit, unsafe, and so narrow that miners are forced to crawl around on their knees using flickering candles for light. Many miners earn a reasonable living, although they sell the amber they extract to the actual landowners. Entire communities exist on the income from amber.

The amber found at particular sites varies in color (grading from golden yellow to red, claret, blue, purple, and black), with darker ambers usually the oldest. The most valuable is blue amber, found mainly at Los Cacaos. Even yellow amber can shimmer with a blue sheen when light reflects through it at certain angles. Most precious of all are inclusions, amber pieces containing leaves, insects, and even lizards and frogs that were trapped in the oozing resin, which hardened to form a translucent tomb. The largest-known inclusion is one containing a 16-inch-long (40 cm) lizard, displayed in Puerto Plata's Museo de Ambar. (An inclusion containing a mosquito inspired Michael Crichton's best-selling novel *Jurassic Park*. Much of the 1993 blockbuster movie was filmed in the republic, whose amber sales were given a significant boost.) Inclusions are protected by law and may not be exported without a license from the National Museum of Natural History.

Dominican amber displays the largest concentration of inclusions, the greatest variety of colors, and the highest quality (determined by degree of transparency). Nonetheless, much of the so-called amber sold in markets is fake. How to tell a plastic counterfeit? Real amber floats in salt water, becomes statically charged when rubbed against cotton, and emits a pine scent when held over a flame.

resembles a New York club, charges a cover, and is open until 5 AM.

Ruby's is an elegant Tuscan-style bar that has karaoke. And Canadian-run **Jolly Roger** also has karaoke and is relatively hooker free.

Watch for **Batissa El Mago**, a magician who cruises Calle Pedro Clisante looking for business. You'll recognize him by his funky hairdo!

The Sosuá **Bay Grand Casino** was slated to open in June 2008 at Sosuá Bay Resort but was still not open at last visit.

Good to Know About

Tourism Office (809-571-3433; Calle Duarte 1) Minimally stocked with literature.
Police (809-571-2475).

CABARETE

Party central on the north coast, this burgeoning yet laid-back beach resort 10 miles (16 km) east of Sosuá is as different from the latter as chalk to cheese. Take the setting: Stretching along the shore highway for several miles, the hotels, restaurants, and bars are pretty much all beachfront. And what a beach! Stretching for 3 miles (4.8 km), the silvery sands are broad and spacious—the main beach was extended out to sea by 100 feet (30 m) in 2006—and whipped by constant trade winds, drawing windsurfers and kiteboarders to the Caribbean's capital of wind-and-wave action. The après-surf night scene is off the hook, and pleases the young college crowd that predominates in Cabarete. And the restaurant scene is also fantastic, with more than a dozen casual gourmet restaurants spilling onto the sands.

Getting There and Getting Around

Guaguas run between Sosuá and Cabarete every 10 minutes or so; you can wave them down anywhere in either town. And the coast highway is abuzz with *motoconchos*, although I do not recommend them for safety reasons.

You can pretty much walk anywhere in town—I prefer to walk along the beaches. Alas, the sole main drag gets jammed with traffic, worsened by the local habit of double parking, which entirely blocks the flow.

Lodging

If boy-meets-girl (or vice versa) is part of your plan, be aware that many hotels won't accept non-registered guests.

Watch for the ultra-sexy **Nikki Beach Resort and Spa** (www.nikkibeachhotels.com) to open in 2010, and aiming to draw Hollywood's finest with its international jet set partying style.

AGUALINA
809-571-0787
fax: 809-571-0383
www.agualina.com
Kite Beach

For my mind, the best bargain in town, this lovely little modern hotel is where I lay my head in Cabarete. Attractive and well run, it is also bargain priced. It has secure parking, free Internet, a lawn studded with a small half-moon pool, plus there's a delightful restaurant and a kitesurfing school. Its 22 beachfront guest rooms on three levels include nicely furnished studios, junior suites, suites, apartments, plus a penthouse. $$

ALI'S SURF CAMP
809-571-9748
www.alissurfcamp.com
Kite Beach

A totally cool place appealing to kiteboarders and surfers, it's set in lush grounds and offers thatched studios, bungalows, apartments, and Tarzan's Treehouse, all delightfully furnished with lively color schemes plus ceiling fans and high-speed WiFi connections. The budget Surfcamp Cottage shares a washroom. Kite Club Cabarete offers tuition. And Chichiguas Surf Side Grill is a popular place to dine. $–$$

BLUE MOON RETREAT
809-757-0614
fax: 809-571-0964
www.bluemoonretreat.net
Los Brazos, 8 miles (12.8 km) S of Cabarete via Sabaneta de Yásica

Set in 48 acres (19.4 ha) of lush mountain terrain in the heart of the Cordillera Septentrional, this country retreat is often booked in entirety for events. It has eight suites (two for families), sparsely yet nicely furnished, and splashed with tropical pastels. A thatched poolside restaurant serves gourmet East Indian fare; at dinner you sit on cushions and eat with your hands. $$

CELUISMA PARAÍSO TROPICAL BEACH HOTEL
809-517-0342
fax: 809-571-0651
www.cabareteparaisotropical.com
1.5 miles (2.4 km) E of Cabarete

This sprawling neo-colonial-themed all-inclusive is done up with rattan furnishings and gold and cream fabrics in its 170 air-conditioned rooms, all with ceiling fans and cable TVs. It has three restaurants, tennis court, beach volleyball, and a disco. Nothing exciting here, but a reasonable bargain for anyone shunning sophistication. $$$

HOTEL MAGNIFICO CONDOMINIUMS
809-571-0868
fax: 809-571-0868
www.hotelmagnifico.com
La Punta, Carretera 5

Seeking self-catering digs? These 30 gorgeous condos, in six separate buildings in lush and lovely grounds, are themed with beautiful contemporary decor and come in a choice of crisp whites or more colorful Caribbean Art. Also choose from studios to penthouse suites. There's free WiFi, a whirlpool spa, and a kidney-shaped pool. All in all, quite stunning and a great value. $$$

HOTEL VILLA TAINA
809-571-0722
Fax: 809-571-0883
www.villataina.com
Playa Encuentro

I consider this three-storey hotel in the heart of Cabarete overpriced, although it's handsome enough. The mode is that of a contemporary European-style pension. It offers 57 spacious rooms in eight categories; each has a distinct style. Facilities include a small spa and gym, a kiteboarding center, and oceanfront restaurant and lounge-bar. $$

NATURA CABAÑAS

809-571-1507
fax: 809-571-1056
www.naturacabana.com
E-mail: reservations@naturacabana.com
Paseo del Sol 5, Perla Marina, Cabarete

As close as you can get to a jungle lodge hereabouts, this delightful place makes the most of indigenous elements: natural stone, thatch, and even palm trunks for building supports. The focus at this oceanfront retreat is on ecotourism. The 11 one-, two- and three-bedroom bungalows were designed with feng shui concepts in mind. The stonework throughout, including floors, helps keep things cool, assisted by ceiling fans. Walls are graced by batiks. There's a swimming pool, and a high-tech albeit small spa, plus two thatched open-air restaurants: one serves health-conscious breakfasts, the other serves gourmet international dinners. $$–$$$

VIVA WYNDHAM TANGERINE

809-571-0402 or 800-WYNDHAM
fax: 809-571-9550
www.vivawyndhamresorts.com
Playa Encuentro

Squeezed between the beach and noisy main highway (the noise reverberates through the small road-front lobby), this mid-priced, family-oriented all-inclusive improves in the palm-shaded grounds centered on a free-form pool. Lively color schemes extend to the 221 guest rooms with tasteful furnishings. The entertainment staff in sexy red-and-white hot pants keeps the activities going day and night, and there's a kids' camp, a full-service spa, and three restaurants. $$$

Dining

CASANOVA

809-571-0806
Playa Cabarete
Cuisine: International

Yet another thatched beachfront restaurant on Playa Encuentro, this one is popular for its breakfast and light-dining meals, which include salads (my favorite is the grilled goat cheese), wraps, and pizzas, which are half price during happy hour (5–7 PM). It also features a few fusion dishes, plus Thai spring rolls and even Tandooris. The moodily Moroccan decor includes colorful velvet pillows and huge bamboo sofas—a perfect setting for enjoying a house specialty drink such as Champagne Foreplay. Open: 11:30 AM–10 PM. $$

CASITA DE DON ALFREDO

809-986-3750
Playa Cabarete
Cuisine: Fusion

Affectionately called Chez Papy, this beachfront restaurant is actually run by a Frenchman. You can kick off your shoes and literally dine with sand between your toes. The delicious seafood temptations include anise-infused, shell-on prawns sautéed in coconut-cream sauce, and langostinos di Papy—a huge platter of mini lobsters drenched in garlic, onions, and butter sauce. And the drinks are strong (do try their caiparinhas). Get there early for a table on the veranda. Open: noon–11 pm. $$

CASTLE CLUB

809-223-0601
www.activecabarete.com/castleclub
Jamao del Norte, 10 miles (16 km) S of Cabarete
Cuisine: Caribbean fusion

Wondering why you packed long pants? Here's the reason. This classy hilltop restaurant, in the mountains 20 minutes south of Cabarete, offers tablecloth dining along with breathtaking views. You do a double take as you draw up to the Mediterranean-style villa home of expat Americans Doug and Marguerite Beers. The gregarious gourmand couple throw their digs open to small groups of diners (minimum six persons), by reservation only. They also grow their own produce and even raise their own chickens and goats, so you know the food is fresh! Your five-course prix fixe meal might include a pesto with goat cheese in pastry, carrot soup, then coconut sea bass with cilantro-jalapeno rice, and Thai-style cabbage salad, followed by a cold lemon mousse. It's quite a steal at $25 (drinks extra). Reservations essential! $$$$

LAX

809-710-0569
www.lax-cabarete.com
Playa Cabarete
Cuisine: International

Although known more as *the* nightspot on the beach, Lax—a German-run bar-restaurant—also serves tasty food ranging from pastas and pizzas (two-for-one during happy hour, 6–7 PM) to seafood and sushi. I head here on Saturday nights for Thai specials (although the chicken pineapple curry is always tempting) and to sink into a sumptuous deep-cushion sofa to enjoy their killer cocktails. Service is enthusiastic, but can be slow. An outrageous 25 percent surcharge applies if you pay by Visa. Open: 9 AM–1 AM. $$

MARABÚ RESTAURANT AND CLUB

809-781-6095
Playa Bozo
Cuisine: Italian

At the Ocean Dream condominiums, this chic contemporary beach bar and restaurant is unique in Cabarete for its urban sophistication. Think of walls of glass, a tent roof, and white leather sofa beds atop a coral stone floor. Chef-owner Antonello waves a wizard's wand in the kitchen, which produces amazing pizza (I recommend the vegetable pizza with eggplant), plus pastas and Italian specials such as stuffed calamari and linguini with baby lobster. It has a vegetarian salad bar with cold pasta salads and roasted vegetables. Open: Thurs. through Mon. noon–11 PM. $$$$.

WABI SABI / MIRÓ ON THE BEACH
809-853-6848
Playa Cabarete

Moroccan owner Lydia Wabana has created a loveably eclectic winner in her thatched open-air beachfront restaurant, with its wonderful North African and Balinese decor and live music later at night. A Peruvian-Japanese chef serves up a delicious spicy ceviche, plus mouth-watering sashimi and sushi. The menu also has some Moroccan dishes. Open: 3 PM–midnight. $$$

Attractions, Parks, and Recreation

Beaches

Arranged in an S-curve around a broad, shallow crescent-shaped bay, the beaches spread to either side of town, which is fronted by the main beach, **Playa Cabarete**, enclosed to the east by Punta de Cabarete. Crowded with lively beach bars and intimate hotels, Playa Cabarete is the mode for windsurfing action. It curls west to become **Playa Bozo** (Fool's Beach), so-named because its downwind and beginner windsurfers who don't know how to tack usually wash up here. Bozo curls around Punta Goleta and merges into **Kite Beach**, the main beach for kiteboarding. Together these beaches are protected from Atlantic swells by a coral reef. Farther west, however, the coral reef breaks up and waves pound ashore at **Playa Encuentro**—the focus of surfing action.

To the east of Punta de Cabarete, sands stretch along 2 miles (3 km) of shore to La Boca de Yasica, literally the mouth of the Río Yasica.

Water Sports

Trade winds brush Cabarete obliquely creating ideal conditions for windsurfing, kite-boarding, and surfing. Enthusiasts of all three sports agree that nowhere else in the republic quite rivals Cabarete, especially February through August, when conditions are at their best (June is best of all). More than a dozen outfitters have outlets on the three main beaches.

Kiteboarding: This is *the* hot new water sport. Imagine strapping yourself onto a modified surfboard and into a harness attached to a giant kite, or wind foil, then skimming over the ocean at a helluva speed. Talk about an adrenaline rush! Experienced kiteboarders are capable of performing spectacular leaps 30 feet (9 m) above the water. Yes, the sport is potentially dangerous. But like every sport, you learn to walk before you try to run. Novices should aim to be out early morning, when winds rarely exceed 10 knots. By late morning the winds crank up to 30 knots before subsiding towards late afternoon.

Most kiteboarding takes place on Kite Beach, where the majority of schools are located. Two premium schools to consider are **Kite Club Cabarete** (809-571-9748; www.kiteclubcabarete.com), **Kite Excite** (829-962-4556; www.kitexcite.com), and **Laurel Eastman Kiteboarding** (809-571-0564; www.laureleastman.com).

Windsurfing: Cabarete has been a hotbed of windsurfing for two decades and every June hosts the Cabarete Race Week international windsurfing competition. The action concentrates at Playa Cabarete. Rentals and tuition are offered by half a dozen outlets, including **Cabarete Windsports Club** (809-571-0784; www.cabaretewindsportsclub.com), at Hotel Villa Taina, and **Carib Wind Center** (809-571-0640; www.caribwind.com), on Calle Principal.

Kiteboarders at Kite Beach, Cabarete

Surfing: Most surfing takes place at Playa Encuentro, between Cabarete and Sosuá. Conditions are perfect for everyone from beginners to experienced surf dudes seeking the next Hawaiian wave. Well-respected surf schools include **Cabarete Surf Camp** (809-571-0733; www.cabaretesurfcamp.com), **No Work Team** (809-571-0820; www.noworkteam cabarete.com), and **Take Off** (809-963-7873; www.321takeoff.com).

Wildlife and Wilderness Parks
PARQUE NACIONAL EL CHOCO
809-541-5652
Callejón de la Loma, Caberete
Open: Daily 9–4:30

You can literally walk from the beach to this national park (actually, it's privately owned), about 1 mile (1.6 km) inland of the shore. Spanning 48 square miles (124 sq km) of wetlands at the base of Cordillera Septentrional, it's centered on two lagoons—**Laguna Punta Galeta** and **Laguna Cabarete**. A sign points the way from the Tigermart on the main street in Cabarete; the lane—Callejón de la Loma—passes through the Dominican community of El Choco. Trails lead through forest and lagoons. And three underground caverns feature fabulous dripstone formations and pre-Columbian Taíno pictographs—one cave has its own crystal-clear lagoon, so bring a swimsuit. Tours at the Callejón entrance are operated by the

Balneario at Playa La Entrada, near Cabrera

Cabarete Caves Company. You can also sign up with **Iguana Mama** (809-571-0908; www.iguanamama.com; Calle Principal 74), a reputable adventure tour specialist.

You can also enter the park just east of the village of Islabon, about 3 miles (4.8 km) east of Cabarete (look for the sign reading ÁREA PROTEGIDA CABARETE Y GOLETA). **Islabon Jungle** (809-248-2818) has a trail into El Choco, plus a mini-zoo and rain forest riverboat tour.

Miscellaneous
Rancho Montana (809-739-0733; www.ranchomontana.com) This ranch in the Cordillera Septentrional south of Gaspar Hernández offers half- and full-day horseback excursions, Sunday and Tuesday through Friday.

Culture

Music and Nightlife
Many vacationers return year after year to party at Cabarete. It's quite the scene, although an effort in 2007 to reduce crime and drunk driving by closing bars at midnight knocked the wind from Cabarete's sails. Action centers on Playa Cabarete and the 400-yard-long (366 m) strip of restaurants and bars spilling on to the sands. Typically, the party crowd moves from one bar to the other throughout the night. Hookers work the crowd, patrolling

up and down the beach, but it's nowhere near as pervasive as in Sosuá.

The hot venue is **Lax** (809-571-00421 www.lax-cabarete.com), which packs 'em in with great lounge music and killer cocktails. Bartenders sometimes blow fire! Nearby, at **Bambú** (809-982-4549), you can sink into a deep sofa and watch big-screen movies on the sands. Later, everybody heads next door to **Onno's** (809-383-1448), a pirate-themed beach club that pounds out reggaeton and techno so loud only the dead can sleep. It hosts a foam party on Saturday nights.

There's even **José O'Shay's Irish Beach Pub** (809-571-0775; www.joseoshays.com), a Latino-Irish bar good for if you really must watch football or basketball on a wide-screen satellite TV. It has live music most nights, courtesy rock guitarist Russell White.

When the bars begin to wind down after midnight, the sophisticated air-conditioned **Ocean Club Disco** (809-571-0000), upstairs at Ocean Sands Casino, picks up the slack until 4 AM. Downstairs, the casino (8 PM–3 AM) has blackjack, roulette tables, Caribbean poker, and Texas Hold'em tables, plus slots.

Food Purveyors

Eze Bar and Restaurant (809-880-8779; Playa Cabarete) An around-the-clock hangout for kiteboarders come to sup banana smoothies, wheatgrass juice, and the like. Come sundown it's time to switch to killer cocktails.

Panadería Repositera Dick (809-571-0612; http://panytortadick.com/panaderia.en.html; Playa Cabarete) My preferred spot for a breakfast of spicy omelette or granola, fresh fruit, and yoghurt, it's also the best bakery in town, with breads and pastries fresh from the oven every day. The decor is cozy. Open: Thursday through Tuesday 7 AM–6 PM.

Good to Know About

Tourism Office (809-571-0962; Plaza Tricom, Calle Principal) Minimally stocked.
Police (809-571-0810).

Weekly and Annual Events

Cabarete hosts several premier water sports championships every year, including the **Cabarete Classic** windsurfing regatta (www.cabarete-classic.com; July), the **Kiteboard World Cup** championship (www.kiteworldtour.com; June), and the **Master of the Ocean** (www.masteroftheocean.com; February), combining windsurfing, kitesurfing, and surfing.

RÍO SAN JUAN AND VICINITY

At the far northeast of the Dominican Republic, the small town of Río San Juan and the coastal hinterland is relatively undeveloped for tourism. The town itself, tucked in a small bay, retains a functioning fishing harbor. There are some fantastic beaches nearby, including Playa Grande (site of a world-class golf course), as well as some of the island's finest diving. However, you'll need to look elsewhere if you're seeking nightlife, as there is no resort center as such. That may soon change though. In 2008, multi-millionaire money manager Boykin Curry and well-heeled buddies (including eco-activist musician Moby and talk-show host Charlie Rose) partnered with Aman Resorts to build two super-deluxe hotels hooked to the Robert Trent Jones-designed Playa Grande Golf Course, near the town of Cabrera.

East of Río San Juan, the coast highway curls around Cabo Francés (the island's north-easterly point) and passes through the quaint town of Cabrera, south of which the shore is lined with a long string of palm-fringed, wave-washed beaches just waiting for developers to harness them. The beaches stretch south for 20 miles (32 km) to the nondescript town of Nagua, gateway to the Samaná peninsula.

In winter months, humpback whales can sometimes be seen close to shore.

Lodging

Accommodations tend to be dispersed along the shore. This region is known for its many private rental villas and there are some lovely hotels. It's also the setting for **Vikings Exotic Resort** (www.cat69.com), a male fantasy resort.

At press time, the former Occidental Allegro Playa Grande, a large all-inclusive at Playa Grande, stood vacant and awaited new investment.

BAHÍA PRINCIPE SAN JUAN
809-226-1590
Fax: 809-226-1994
www.bahia-principe.com
5 miles (8 km) W of Río San Juan

One of the nation's largest all-inclusive resorts, this splendid hotel enjoys a lovely beach setting. Golf-cart shuttles run you around the vast property, divided into two sections, with one for private club members. It has all the amenities you could wish for, from multiple restaurants and a huge pool complex, to tennis courts, mini-golf, gym, spa, water sports, a

Caliente Caribe, Cabrera

theater for nightly entertainment, plus a casino and disco open to the public. The 941 rooms are in two-storey blocks and feature ceramic floors, lovely tropical fabrics, and well-stocked bathrooms. $$$

CALIENTE CARIBE
809-589-7750 or 866-333-6229
www.calienteresorts.com
Cabrera, 1.5 miles (2.4 km) E of Playa Grande

This all-inclusive clothing-optional resort, professionally managed by a U.S.-Vietnamese couple, has a fabulous location within its own cliff-enclosed cove and is a tremendous option for liberal-minded vacationers seeking an all-over tan. The beautiful landscaping and handsome redbrick lobby with tropical decor set a welcoming tone. The open dining room where meals are family-style (yes, most folks dine in the buff) overlooks a lovely free-form pool and Jacuzzi. During my stay, a fabulous jazz duo performed at night, plus there's a soulless TV lounge, and a disco with a stripper's pole. A thatched beach bar has pool, darts, and a grill, and there's beach volleyball and a second pool by the beach, which has water sports. Choose from Seacliff apartments or beach bungalows. Furnishings and decor win no prizes, but the former are spacious and the latter have full kitchens and king beds (in slightly cramped bedrooms). You can even rent Casa Grande, a huge villa once owned by Rafael Trujillo, whose estate this once was. The Dominican staff, dressed in black-and-white uniforms, is courteous and respectful. $$$

HOTEL BAHÍA BLANCA
809-589-2563
Calle G F Deligne, Río San Juan

A slightly deteriorated hotel with a lovely beachfront situation in town. It has a pleasant balcony restaurant over the sands. Suitable for travelers not too fussy about their digs, which are clean and have simple furnishings and private bathrooms. $

HOTEL LA CATALINA
809-589-7700
fax: 809-589-7550
www.lacatalina.com
3 miles (4.8 km) W of Cabrera

Amid lovely gardens atop a forested hillside, this breeze-swept hotel is a great option if you don't need to be by the beach. The views alone are worth a stay here. And the decor is nice. The 30 air-conditioned guest rooms and apartments, cross-ventilated through louvered windows, feature white rattan furnishings with yellow and salmon highlights, and clean modern bathrooms with step-in showers. The restaurant—open to the public (8–10 AM, noon–2, and 7–8:30 PM)—serves French-inspired delights such as foie gras mousse and grilled lobster. It has a pool and Jacuzzi, plus tennis court, billiard room, and horseback excursions. $–$$

HOTEL RESTAURANT SINAI
809-584-2284
www.hotelsinai.com.do
Calle Sánchez 97, Nagua

Playa Breton, near Cabrera

Dating from 1942, this historic hotel has wraparound balconies on two levels. Old-world furnishings. It has 38 clean, modestly appointed rooms with ceiling fans and cable TV, plus the best restaurant in town. $

LOS GRINGOS BEACH BAR, GRILL, AND CABAÑAS

809-841-5601

www.losgringosdr.com

Playa Magante, 6 miles (9.6 km) W of Río San Juan

Rootsy and rustic, this delightful place exudes charm and will appeal to anyone seeking a romantic, unpretentious escape that is true to its tropical roots. It has three thatched wooden cabins raised on platforms atop the sands. Each has a bamboo four-poster bed slung with mosquito nets, plus ceiling fan and oodles of jungle ambience. And can you believe you get a fabulous restaurant to boot (see Dining). It doesn't have water sports, but there are lounge chairs and Patrick, the Belgian owner, arranges horseback rides, snorkeling, and boating excursions. It's backed by a mangrove forest—take insect repellent. $$

Dining

Playa Grande is lined with simple food shacks selling fresh-grilled seafood and local dishes.

Chef Diomedea, at the **Hotel La Catalina** (see Lodging, above), produces delicious fare enjoyed alfresco with a fabulous view. And the **Hotel Restaurant Sinai** (see Lodging, above) is a good bet when passing through Nagua.

LOS GRINGOS BEACH BAR, GRILL, AND CABAÑAS
809-841-5601
www.losgringosdr.com
Playa Magante, 6 miles (9.6 km) W of Río San Juan

Peter, the Belgian owner, whips up a mean breakfast omelette, and delicious seafood specials such as plump river shrimp, lobster thermidor, and conch creole. And how about Belgium beer stew? Or a seafood paella? His burgers are also first rate, and you can choose various salads. The ambience is lovely at this thatched bar-restaurant where you can munch with your toes on the sand. Open: Daily 11 AM–10 PM.

Attractions, Parks, and Recreation

Beaches
In Río San Juan, a sandy trail beside the Hotel Bahia Blanca leads to **Playa Caletón**, a narrow mile-long sliver of white sand edging up to teal-colored waters good for snorkeling.

The most popular beach, at least with locals, is **Playa Grande**, 10 miles (16 km) east of Río San Juan. This wind-whipped gold-sand beach has food shacks and you can rent boogie boards and beach chairs. It merges east into wave-pounded **Playa Preciosa**. Surfers in the know rave about the ride, but swimming is not advised due to dangerous riptides.

South of Cabo Frances Viejo, lonesome **Playa Breton** has tangerine sands enclosed by chalk-white cliffs; a staircase leads down to the beach from the roadside hamlet of Breton.

My favorite beach by far is **Playa Diamante**, enclosed in a flask-shaped bay 5 miles (8 km) south of Cabrera. Its snow-white sands shelve into turquoise shallows that extend for 200 yards (183 m) to the reef-fringed, cliff-clasped mouth of the cove. A ramshackle hut serves simple meals.

Farther south, at the village of La Entrada, the coast highway (Carretera 5) swings inland for 10 miles (16 km) and hits the coast again at the village of Boba, about 5 miles (8 km) north of Nagua. There are some lovely beaches between La Entrada and Boba, accessible by a sandy track. It's a gorgeous shoreline. Locals gather at **Playa La Entrada**, where there are food shacks. Riptides make swimming unsafe.

Miscellaneous
Cueva El Dudú (809-298-4590), 7 miles (11 km) south of Cabrera and 2 miles (3 km) north of La Entrada, is a perfectly circular, cliff-bound cenote (blue hole) filled with a refreshingly cool jade-colored lake. Local kids plunge in off a rope swing. Take care on the slippery and dangerously sloping steps that lead down to the water. Entrance costs RD$30—buy your ticket at Restaurante Parador Dudú, on the coast highway 200 yards (183 m) south of the entrance to the cenote.

Hotel/Restaurante La Catalina (see Lodging) offers horseback excursions, including to a tobacco and coffee farm on Wednesday.

Playa Grande Golf Course (809-582-0860; www.playagrande.com) This Robert Trent Jones-designed championship course is considered one of the finest in the Caribbean. At press time, it was slated to close in 2009 and reopen after being refurbished as a private course for the Aman project.

Sanctuario La Virgen de la Piedra, 2 miles (3 km) north of La Entrada, is a roadside reli-gious shrine where a chapel is built against giant boulders entwined by the roots of a strangler fig. Worshipers gather to make offerings to a figure of Nuestra Señora de Lour-des carved into the rock face inside a chapel.

Wildlife and Wilderness Parks

Laguna Gri Gri The town of Río San Juan wraps around this tannin-stained freshwater lagoon framed to north and east sides by thick mangrove forest great for birding. White egrets are numerous, as are herons, and thousands of swallows nest in **Cueva de las Golondrinas** (Swallows' Cave). The lagoon is fed by subterranean waters. Crocodiles are said to lurk leery-eyed in the mangroves. Boats compete for your custom at the end of Calle Duarte, the town's unremarkable main street. **Northern Coast Diving** (809-571-1028; www.northerncoastdiving.com), in Sosuá, offers excursions that combine a trip on the lake with snorkeling at nearby coral reefs.

Parque Nacional Cabo Frances Viejo (no telephone) covers the craggy limestone headland betwixt Playa Grande and Playa Breton. Although totally undeveloped for tourism, you can follow goat trails through scrubby humid subtropical forest. The tip of the headland is pinned by a concrete tower that serves as a lighthouse.

Reserva Científica Loma Guaconejo (c/o Sociedad Ecológica del Cibao, 809-247-3833, or Sociedad para el Desarrollo Integral del Nordeste, 809-584-2747) This wildlife reserve, 3 miles (4.8 km) southwest of Nagua, protects 5,900 acres (2,390 ha) of humid submon-tane rain forest and mangroves at the easternmost base of the Cordillera Septentrional. Drained by the Boba and Nagua rivers, it's a great site for birding, with 51 species. There's a visitor center at **Centro Ecoturístico Cuesta Colorada** at the hamlet of Cuesta Colorada; trails lead into the reserve from here. The center has campsites and rustic accommodation, and guided hikes and horseback rides are offered.

Good to Know About

Tourism Office (809-589-2831 or 589-8034 Calle Mella 25, Río San Juan).

LUPERÓN AND VICINITY

West of Puerto Plata, the coast highway (Carretera 5) swings inland and over the Cordillera Septentrional. At Imbert, 13 miles (20.8 km) west of Puerto Plata, Carretera 30 leads west and back to the coast at Luperón, a small and somewhat somnolent town with a hit-and-miss recent history of tourism development. Luperón is popular with international yachters for its marina within a natural deepwater hurricane harbor wrapped by forested hills (many boaters have dropped anchor and never sailed away; there's an active gringo community). Alas, a long-touted $1.8 billion, 10-year tourism development project—Atlantica—has been on again, off again, and although ground has been broken, it was unknown at press time whether it would ever *really* get off the ground. If so, it promises to result in its own airstrip, a marina, cruise-ship terminal, multiple hotels, 3,000 residential condos and villas, and three signature golf courses. For now it's you and the goats ambling down the street. You're welcomed by a life-size statue of Gregorio Luperón—the nation's hero of independence from Spain—at the entrance to town.

Meanwhile, Luperón has a lovely beach, although most current tourist activity centers on lonesome Punta Rucia, farther west. Luperón is gateway, too, to Parque National La

Isabela, preserving what little remains of the New World's oldest colonial settlement, founded by Christopher Columbus in 1493. And if you've ever wanted to see a manatee in the wild, nowhere in Hispaniola are your chances better than in the lagoons of Estero Hondo.

Getting There and Getting Around

Unless you're arriving by boat, you'll need to take a *guagua* (bus, RD$35) from Puerto Plata (or Santiago de los Caballeros) and change in Imbert for Luperón (RD$40).

Motoconchos await business outside Letty's, in the village center at Calle Duarte and Calle 27 de Febrero. And Humberto Balbuena hires out as driver-with-van; he's trustworthy.

Lodging

There are a handful of simple budget hotels in Luperón, in addition to those listed here.

At Punta Rucia, several budget options include **Hotel Tortuga** (809-647-1344), with clean and comfortable rooms with window screens but cold water only; and the nearly identical **Punta Rucia Sol** (809-471-0173).

CAYO ARENA DIVERS

809-757-2252
www.cayoarenadivers.com
Punta Rucia

This German-run dive company rents out two options. The Tuscan-style **Villa Nadine** sleeps six people and is available for weekly rental (US$2,000). It includes a large master suite with private balcony, plus a gourmet kitchen and lounge with flat screen TV and surround-sound system. Or you can choose **Casa Libre**, with simple picturesque cottages on a hillock above the beach; they share a bathroom (US$20 single, US$30 double). The friendly French-German owners, Guertie and Marc, make dinner and cocktails.

LUPERÓN BEACH RESORT

809-571-8303
fax: 809-571-8180
www.besthotels.es
Ciudad Marina, Playa Grande, Luperón

Appealing to a budget European package-vacation crowd, this all-inclusive is a two-star property in my eyes. Despite its gorgeous beach, there's little that's inspiring here, including the desultory decor. Still, it has plenty of facilities, including three restaurants, tennis courts, water sports, and entertainment (which I thought very ho-hum during my stay). It shares facilities with its twin sister, the adjoining Luperón Beach Hotel. $$

PEQUEÑO MUNDO

809-264-3511
Calle 27 de Febrero, Luperón

This small hilltop hotel, about 500 yards (457 m) inland of the shore, is run by Willi and Inez Freud, a German-Dominican couple who offer five spacious yet sparsely furnished rooms with refrigerators and cold-water bathrooms. Some are air-conditioned. It's OK for budget travelers. $

Dining

At Punta Rucia, **El Paraíso** (809-612-8499; daily 8 AM–3:30 PM) caters to its excursion groups with a buffet lunch served at its beach bar and restaurant. I was able to buy lunch also as a call-in visitor (RD$300). If that fails try **El Buzo**, next door; the only restaurant in the village, this rustic thatched restaurant festooned with maritime miscellany serves great seafood and local dishes, as do the food shacks at Playa Ensenada.

RESTAURANT LUPERÓN LOBSTER HOUSE
809-571-8606
http://luperonmarina.com
Marina Luperón Yacht Club

Overlooking the harbor, this no-frills open-air restaurant specializes in lobsters, but also has burgers and seafood such as coconut grouper fillet. The restaurant sometimes runs at half-mast (and is in an interminable state of disrepair) but usually comes alive for the nightly Happy Hour, followed by darts and karaoke, and even dancing on Saturday night when a local eight-piece band plays. Open: Daily 7:30 AM–10 PM.

THE UPPER DECK
No telephone
Calle Duarte and Calle 27 de Febrero, Luperón

Renowned among sailors, this rustic upstairs eatery (formerly known as Gina's) with plastic chairs and thatch-and-tin roof is run by Gina (from Holland) and her hubby Max. They serve excellent burgers, sandwiches, nachos, etc., plus filet mignon au Roquefort, and lobster and seafoods of surprisingly gourmet quality. Pool table and lively ambience. It began life as a brothel, apparently, but today there are no tarts on the menu. Open: 11 AM–11 PM Mon. through Thurs. and Sat.; 6–11 PM Sun.

Attractions, Parks, and Recreation

Take care for spiny sea urchins when wading and swimming off Playa Grande.

PARQUE NACIONAL LA ISABELA
El Castillo, 9 miles (14.4 km) W of Luperón
Open: Daily 9 AM–5:30 PM
Admission: RD$50

Site of the first permanent Spanish settlement in the Americas, La Isabela was founded by Christopher Columbus and 1,500 followers during his second voyage of discovery. The first mass in the New World was held here on January 6, 1494. The site named in honor of the Spanish queen is a promontory on the east bank of the Río Bajabónico and overlooking a placid bay. Famine and disease soon overtook the settlers, who relocated to present-day Santo Domingo in 1498. Nonetheless, the abandoned buildings (including a church and Columbus's own home, which he occupied for five months before sailing off) stood the test of time fairly well. Alas, in 1952, an archaeological work crew misinterpreted Rafael Trujillo's instructions to tidy up the site. They bulldozed the site! Today there are scant remains. The foundations of Columbus's house of rammed earth (*tápia*) and cut limestone can be seen, along with those of a plaza and fortified wall. And a Taíno skeleton drawn up in

Templo de las Américas, Parque Nacional La Isabela

Shells for sale at Punta Rucia

fetal position slumbers in an early cemetery. A **museum** that's barely standing displays a motley collection of Taíno artifacts, cannonballs, etc. It's all rather sad.

More uplifting is the **Templo de las Américas**, a handsome early-colonial-style church built in 1990 and featuring exquisite stained-glass windows by Dominican artist José Rincón Mora (1938–). Pope John Paul II said Mass here in 1992 on the 500th anniversary of Columbus's arrival. It's half-a-mile east of La Isabela.

PUNTA RUCIA
15 miles (24 km) W of Luperón (as the crow flies)

Utilized mainly by day-trippers on fun-filled excursions from Puerto Plata, the bay at Punta Rucia is a real beauty. Cusped in a wide bay, the beach is backed by a rustic but welcoming fishing village where you can immerse yourself in the local lifestyle. But the big draw is the talcum white sands of **Playa Punta Rucia**...oh, and the stunning turquoise waters...and the dramatic scenery...and the banana-boat rides and other water sports that add to the fun. **El Paraíso Tours** (809-612-8499 in Punta Rucia, 809-320-7606 in Puerta Plata; http://201.229.190.45/cayo) offers boat excursions, as does **Alf's Tours** (809-571-9904; www.alftour.com/prE.html) in Sosuá. Most trips include a speedboat trip to **Cayo Arena** (aka Cayo Paraíso), a tiny and idyllic circular coral cay ringed by sun-bleached sands and teal waters. You can also hire boats in Punta Rucia to take you out to the cay, 6 miles (9.6

km) from shore (about US$75 per person). Tour operators in Puerto Plata, Sosuá, and Cabarete offer excursions to Punta Rucia.

While Playa Punta Rucia is used mostly by day-trippers, Dominicans gather in droves at **Playa Ensenada**, 2 miles (3 km) east. Food shacks and open-air restaurants line the sands, and on weekends the place is hopping with *bachata* and merengue music, often blaring at ear-shattering volume. Alas, in the Dominicans' usual manner, they also trash the place with garbage!

Getting There: If you're driving, the quickest way is via Carretera 1, then turn north at Villa Elsa—the partially paved road leads directly to Punta Rucia via El Papayo. Coming from Puerto Plata, Carretera 29 via El Castillo and the village of La Isabela necessitates two river fordings and can be impassable at times, and a 4WD is required. If you can't get through, backtrack to Imbert, turn south on Carretera 5, turn west for Guananico and follow the scenic dip-and-rise dirt road to reconnect with Carretera 29 at Los Hidalgos; turn right (north) for La Isabela, then turn west (this route requires a 4WD) for Punta Rucia via Las Lagunas and Estero Hondo (see below).

You can also catch a bus to Monte Cristi and get off at Villa Elisa, from where *motoconchos* (RD$150) will take you to Punta Rucia.

SANTUARIO DE MAMÍFEROS MARINOS ESTERO HONDO
No telephone
2 miles (3 km) E of Playa Enseñada
Open: Daily 6 AM–6:30 PM
Admission: Free

This refuge serves to protect a precious mangrove and dry forest system centered on the lagoon of Caño Estero Hondo—an invaluable habitat for manatees. At least 15 of these critically endangered, herbivorous marine mammals live in the T-shaped lagoon, measuring 8.5 square miles (22 sq km) and fed by the Ríos Paso Seco and Solimán. The manatee population has suffered gravely from illegal hunting (for meat) and destruction of habitat. Individuals can be seen swimming at the estuary mouth by the ranger station around dawn and dusk, and the ranger told me that dolphins are sometimes seen leaping around the river mouth, too. The teeming bird life will thrill ornithologists. And *careyes* (hawksbill turtles) nest on Playa Marisa, where the visitors center is located. You can hire the rangers as guides for boat trips (when scientists aren't using the boat).

Is That a Bee or a Flower?
Hispaniella henekenii (or *orquídea cacatica* to locals, and colloquially as the bumble bee orchid) is an endemic black orchid that grows only in a rare remnant patch of subtropical dry forest in the northwest corner of the Dominican Republic. This gorgeous plant relies on a tiny black bee for pollination. To do so, the flower (dark purple fringed with yellow) mimics the form of the bee. Amazingly, it actually looks like a bee with wings abuzz gathering pollen at a tiny green flower.

The forest is protected within the 17-acre (7 ha) **Reserva Científica Villa Elisa** (no telephone), 5 miles (8 km) north of Villa Elisa.

Miscellaneous

Cayo Arena Divers (809-757-2252; www.cayoarenadivers.com), at Punta Rucia, offers scuba excursions and open-water PADI certification. Beside spectacular coral reefs, sites include the *Manzanillo* freighter.

Caribbean Marine Watersports (809-261-4773; www.caribbeanmarine.net) offers half-day sportfishing charters out of Marina Luperón.

Good to Know About

Tourism Office (809-571-8020; Ayuntamiento, Luperón) In the town hall, this office is meagerly stocked with literature.

MONTE CRISTI AND VICINITY

At the extreme northwest of the republic, the remote town of San Fernando de Monte Cristi gets very few visitors, despite an intriguing history, superlative diving, one of the nation's premier national parks, and nearby sites of historical import. The original settlement dates to 1501, evolved as a smuggling center, and was razed by Spanish authorities in 1606. The current town dates from the 18th century, when it was settled by migrants from the Canary Islands, and grew to be an important port. Although ravaged during the 1860s War of Restoration, plenty remains of the town's intriguing and eclectic 19th-century Victorian architecture. Monte Cristi also draws throngs each last week of February for its unique *carnaval*.

The region is in a rain shadow and, thereby, relatively dry. The town is surrounded by mangroves and shallow lagoons speckling scrub-covered plains pimpled with cactus and munched by goats. For more than a century, the lagoons have served as evaporative salt pans, which stretch for miles north of town and supply North America with much of its table salt. Where you find lagoons, you find birds. Parque Nacional Monte Cristi protects a precious habitat for manatees and more than 160 species of birds, while offshore, pristine coral reefs and the Cayos Hermanos clasp sunken galleons a few fathoms down. In fact, the park encompasses the longest barrier reef in Hispaniola, extending 25 miles (40 km) east to Punta Rucia.

Getting There and Getting Around

Monte Cristi is about 80 miles (128 km) west of both Puerto Plata and Santiago de los Caballeros. **Caribe Tours** (809-575-1946 in Santiago, 809-570-2129 in Monte Cristi; www.caribetours.com.do) has bus service from Santiago. Buses also depart Santo Domingo for Monte Cristi at 6:30, 8 and 9:30 AM and 1, 2, and 3:45 PM. Buses depart Monte Cristi at 7 and 9 AM, and 1:45, 2:45, and 4 PM from Avenida Mella, at Rodríguez Camargo.

Guaguas also depart Santiago for Monte Cristi, where *motoconchos* are pretty much your sole way of getting around. Taxis are also available for trips to Dajabón, etc.

Lodging

HOSTAL SAN FERNANDO

809-964-0250
fax: 809-724-4422

http://ecomarinamontecristi.com
Carretera al Morro km 2, Monte Cristi

The best of slim pickings, this hotel is outside town close to the entrance of Parque
Nacional Monte Cristi. The 20 lodgings in duplex bungalows are simple yet charming and
comfy (thank goodness for my firm mattress). Take a bungalow as far from the noisy gener-
ator as possible. It has a swimming pool, an airy and colorful restaurant, and a scuba diving
center, and eco-tours of the mangroves are offered. $–$$

HOTEL CAYO ARENA

809-579-3145
fax: 809-579-2096
www.cayoarena.com
Playa Juan de Bolaños, Monte Cristi

A perfectly adequate alternative to Hostal San Fernando, this condo complex is fronted by a
sliver of gray sand looking out towards the distant Cayos Hermanos floating on the horizon.
Its 7 two-bedroom apartments are pleasantly furnished and have ceiling fans and spacious
lounges. A restaurant serves seafood. $–$$

Dining

OCEAN RESTAURANT

809-579-3643
Calle Benito Monción 1, Monte Cristi
Open: Daily 9 AM–midnight

Four blocks south of Parque Duarte, this charming thatched open-air restaurant with a
raised deck and ceiling fans is the best eatery in town. Its menu ranges from seafood
(including lobster) to traditional Dominican fare, all at reasonable prices. At night the
adjoining disco packs in the locals on weekends (free). $$.

Attractions, Parks, and Recreation

Architecture

Monte Cristi is a veritable trove of fascinating historical buildings. Most are modest homes
in an eclectic amalgam of styles. Just wandering the streets is reward for visitors intrigued
by architecture. One of the most noteworthy buildings is the **Casa de Isabel Mayer** (Calle
Duarte and Calle Colón), a prefabricated two-storey home that was the residence of inde-
pendence-era Generals Desiderio Arias and Benito Monción. The house is named for a
wealthy landowner and friend of brutal Dictator Rafael Trujillo.

Parks and Plazas
PARQUE CENTRAL

Calle Duarte and Calle San Fernando

Pinned by an Eiffel Tower-style clock tower—the 19th-century **Reloj de Montecristi**—the
town's paved main square is fringed by broad-leaved shade trees and ringed by intriguing
yesteryear buildings, including a Gothic church on the southeast corner. On the northeast
corner, the most interesting structure, the **Villa Doña Emilia Jiménez** is today virtually

derelict. Prefabricated in France and erected in 1895, it features flamboyant gingerbread trim and a roof of cloverleaf shingles. On the northwest corner stands the **Museo de Montecristi** in a handsome and newly restored limestone building with antique wrought-iron lanterns and *rejas* (window grilles). It was still a work in progress at press time.

For a perspective over the square, climb the spiral staircase in the center of the clock tower.

Museums
CASA MUSEO DE MÁXIMO GÓMEZ
809-465-7003
Calle Mella 29
Open: Daily 8:30–noon and 2:30–5
Admission: Free

Dominican-born General Máximo Gómez, hero of the Cuban Wars of Independence, lived in this small, gray clapboard house during the 1890s and it was here that Gómez and José Martí (leader of the independence movement) signed the Manifesto de Monte Cristi—the Cuban declaration of independence—on March 25, 1895. A week later they sailed for Cuba to launch the War of Independence. Today, the house is a museum dedicated to the momentous effort of Gómez and Martí (who martyred himself in the first battle). It displays documents, photos, and personal memorabilia of the duo, whose busts stand beneath Cuban and Dominican flags in the garden. The enthusiastic *custodio* (caretaker), Amado Gutiérrez García, will give you a barely decipherable spiel for a tip.

Wildlife and Wilderness Parks
PARQUE NACIONAL MONTE CRISTI
No telephone
Ranger station, Playa Juan de Molaño
Open: Daily 8–6
Admission: Free

Spanning 212 square miles (549 sq km), this huge reserve protects 40 percent of the nation's mangrove forests and lagoons, as well as dry tropical forest, desert badlands, salt flats, and coral reefs and cays out to sea (in fact, two-thirds of the park is maritime).

The park spreads out to either side of **El Morro** (794 feet/242 m), a flat-topped mesa that pilgrims ascend each January 21 for the Día de la Virgen de la Altagracia. The 585-step wooden staircase to the summit is derelict and was closed at last visit, but you can follow goat trails that lead up through dry subtropical forest. It's well worth the hike for the sensational view, not least of the offshore barrier reef that stretches east as far as Punta Rucia. Start at the **ranger station**, at the end of the road from Monte Cristi. Another trail begins here and descends to **Playa Detras del Morro**, a tangerine-tinted beach where waves crash ashore beneath unstable cliffs and a huge stack (freestanding ocean-girt formation) called **Cayo Zapatillo** (Shoe Cay). Riptides make swimming unsafe.

Mangrove flats extend far inland and are edged on their eastern perimeter by miles of commercial salt pans. The flats south of town are fed by the delta of the Río Yaque del Norte and extend south for 13 miles (20.8 km) to the port town of Pepillo Salcedo. The shore is backed by a vast lacework of creeks and lagoons—home to manatees and juvenile fish such as tarpon and snook. Flamingoes parade around the two largest lagoons, **Laguna Quemado**

An Excursion into the Past

Carretera 45 runs south from Monte Cristi as straight as a slingshot into the past. After 22 miles (35 km) you arrive at **Dajabón**, a relatively prosperous border town and official entry point into Haiti, across the Río Dajabón. Try to time your visit for Monday or Friday morning, for the colorful Haitian markets.

If you have a serious bent for archaeology, 6 miles (9.6 km) south of Dajabón turn east on Carretera 18 towards Pepilo. After 3.7 miles (6 km) you arrive at the hamlet of Los Indios, where you should ask directions to **Los Indios de Chacuey**, an ancient Taíno ceremonial center on the banks of the Río Chacuey. Not much remains of this *bateye* surrounded by rocks and carved with petroglyphs. Ask a local to guide you (for a tip).

Far more interesting is to continue south on Carretera 45 to Loma de Cabrera and turn west for the mountain hamlet of Capotillo. Surrounded by pines in the middle of nowhere 1 mile (1.6 km) north of town, the **Monumento a La Restauración** commemorates the armed revolt against Spanish rule initiated here on August 16, 1863 by *independistas* Santiago Rodríguez, José Cabrera, and Benito Monción. The grandiose monument is a triptych. On one side, truncated Corinthian columns stand over a plaza. Above, a mezzanine bears two concrete monuments. The first is a massive horizontal block—Capotillo 1863—faced with a bas-relief frieze of national heroes, workers, and *independistas*. Nearby stands a spired vertical monument—Restauración 1865—engraved with the names of national heroes.

Most maps show Carretera 45 continuing south to the Valle de San Juan (see the Southwest chapter), with a portion of the road passing along the Haitian side of the border. You'll pass army checkpoints near the village of Restauración, where you must register before starting the journey (however, passage for foreigners is often denied). A 4WD is essential. Beyond Restauración it's really rugged going over the mountains! Make sure your vehicle is in good condition. And take plenty of extra water and some food.

Monumento a La Restauración, Loma de Cabrera

del Cojo (north of Monte Cristi) and **Laguna Saladilla** (the latter is on the southern edge of the park, near Pepillo Salcedo, at the mouth of the Ríos Chacuey and Dajabón). And American kestrels and wood storks nest in the scrub. They're among more than 160 bird species found here, many of them seabirds such as frigate birds and terns, boobies, and American oystercatchers, which nest on **Cayos de los Siete Hermanos** (Seven Brothers Cays). Poking up from the ocean west of Monte Cristi, these offshore cays are ringed with sands as white and as soft as snow, drawing marine turtles ashore to lay eggs. Likewise, and closer to shore, **Isla Cabrita** floats in Monte Cristi bay and has a lighthouse; boatmen will run you there from Playa Juan de Bolaños, the town's ugly beach.

Dirt roads run along the eastern perimeter of the park, granting access to hikers. And boat excursions of the mangroves are offered from **Ecoresort and Marina Montecristi** (809-964-0250; http://ecomarinamontecristi.com), and by boatmen at the funky marina next to the Politur (tourist police) station on Playa Juan de Bolaños. You can also hike a trail that begins here.

Scuba Diving

The diving hereabouts is spectacular. Not least is the barrier reef that begins immediately east of El Morro and runs for 25 miles (40 km), offering fantastic wall dives on the ocean side and calmer waters for beginners inside the reef. You can dive with sharks off Playa Buen Hombre. And many a Spanish galleon and other vessels were snared on the reefs. At least 23 shipwrecks have been identified in the crystal-clear waters, including off the Cayos Hermanos. Most famous is the **Pipe Wreck,** just east of Isla Cabrita. This 18th-century merchantman was carrying clay tobacco pipes when it sank in 15 feet (4.6 m) of water, amid fields of staghorn. Experienced divers can join archaeological excavations performed by **North Caribbean Research** (http://oldship.org/Page_1.html).

The **Centro de Buceo San Fernando** (809-224-5851; http://ecomarinamontecristi.com) dive center, at Hostal San Fernando, offers dive trips and multi-day dive packages.

Weekly and Annual Events

Every February, sleepy Monte Cristi bursts into colorful life for the annual *carnaval*. Unique in the nation, the main action is a whipping frenzy (literally) between the *civilis* (citizens) and the *toros* (bulls), dressed in bull's masks. Yes, they use bullwhips on each other

Good to Know About

Clínica Dr. Suero (809-579-2561; Calle Mella 2).
Politur (809-754-2978). Tourism police at Playa Juan de Bolaños.
Tourism Office (809-579-2254 or 579-3980; Gobernación, Calle Mella 37) In the provincial government headquarters, it has very little information.

8

El Cibao and Cordillera Central

Heartland of the Nation

The interior heartland of the country is the Valle del Cibao (colloquially called El Cibao and formerly known as Vega Real, or Royal Plain). This vast fertile flatland is framed by the ruler-straight Cordillera Septentrional to the north and, to the south, by the Cordillera Central—the Caribbean's highest mountain chain. El Cibao, which is drained eastward by the Río Camú and westward by the Río Yaque del Norte, and the mid-elevation valleys of the Cordillera Central are together the breadbasket of the nation. Rice, bananas, and tobacco are the three main products of the lowland plains. Coffee and cacao are grown on the foothills slopes. And the alpine valley around Constanza, in the Cordillera, delivers most of the fresh vegetables eaten throughout the nation.

During the 19th century, Santiago de los Caballeros (the republic's second largest city) and the neighboring agricultural centers of La Vega and Moca grew wealthy and vied with the capital for political dominance as the main centers of the independence movement. Haitian invasions and internecine warfare between ambitious *caudillos* led to most cities being repeatedly razed. Nonetheless, Santiago still retains much of its colonial architecture and, along with its world-class Centro León art gallery and museum, has enough to keep you occupied for a full day or longer. Nearby Tamboril is a center for cigar production. And the town of La Vega has a magnificent (albeit controversial) cathedral, while nearby Santa Cerro is a major pilgrimage site and also the setting for the early colonial ruins of La Vega Vieja. La Vega is also renowned for the liveliest of the nation's *carnavales*.

Meanwhile, active travelers aren't forgotten. Much of the region is protected within national parks. You can take to the Cordillera Septentrional for hiking and birding (and even spot the near-extinct solenodon) in Reserva Científica Quita Espuela. The towering Cordillera Central, which forms the island's rugged backbone, is also known as the Dominican Alps, drawing city dwellers to the cool, pine-scented mountain resort of Jarabacoa, an activity center known as the beginning point for whitewater rafting and as a gateway for challenging three-day round-trip hikes to the summit of Pico Duarte (10,164 feet/3,098 m). Pico Duarte is one of three peaks topping 10,000 feet in this remote and wild world of razorback ridges and plunging gorges sparkling with crashing cascades. And nearby Constanza, in a Shangri-La-like alpine valley, is the gateway to the equally remote and rugged Parque Nacional Valle Nuevo. Together with Parque Nacional Armando Bermúdez and Parque Nacional José del Carmen Ramírez, these parks safeguard vast tracts of virgin forest, including lush mist-shrouded rain forest on lower east-facing slopes.

Getting There and Getting Around

By Air

Cibao International Airport (809-233-8000), outside Santiago de los Caballeros, is used mostly for domestic flights. **American Airlines** (www.aa.com) connects Cibao with Miami, and **JetBlue** (800-538-2583; www.jetblueairways.com) connects with New York. Other international carriers connect the city to Haiti, Puerto Rico, and Turks and Caicos. A light metro rail system is planned to link the airport with downtown Santiago.

By Car

Autopista Duarte (officially known as DR-1) is the main highway between Santo Domingo and Santiago de los Caballeros via the towns of Bonao and La Vega. Two lanes in each direction, this *autopista* (freeway) is usually fast, although I have experienced horrendous traffic jams (including when protestors close the road for *huelgas*—political demonstrations). West of Santiago, DR-1 continues through the Valle del Río Yaque, while Carretera 132 runs east from Santiago along the foot of the Cordillera Septentrional, linking the important commercial centers of Moca, Salcedo, and San Francisco de Macorís. Once you depart these main roads, you'll quickly find yourself lost in a lacework of irrationally laid out and unfathomable country roads.

Paved highways (Carreteras 12 and 24, respectively) snake west from DR-1 into the Cordillera Central and the towns of Constanza and Jarabacoa, putting each town within a two-hour drive of Santo Domingo. Constanza is pretty much the end of the paved road. Do not believe the many maps that show a paved road connecting Constanza southward with San José de Ocoa. In reality, this is a brutally rugged Indiana Jones-style 4WD adventure. And pretty much anywhere, you'll need a sturdy 4WD to negotiate the sometimes dauntingly rugged mountain roads. There's a reason most mountain folk get around on donkeys! The good news is that in October 2008, the government announced that it would repave the Constanza-San José de Ocoa road.

By Bus

Caribe Tours (809-221-4422; www.caribetours.com.do) has 25 bus departures daily from Santo Domingo to La Vega and Santiago. Buses also depart Santo Domingo for Jarabacoa at 7 and 10 AM, and 1:30 and 4:30 PM, and 16 times daily for San Francisco de Macorís. Buses depart Santo Domingo from Avenida 27 Febrero and Leopoldo Navarro; Jarabacoa (809-574-4796) from Calle José Duran 3; San Francisco de Macorís (809-588-2221) from Calle Castillo at Gaspar Hernández; and Santiago (809-576-0790) from Avenida 27 de Febrero at Las Américas.

Metro Expreso (809-227-0101 Santo Domingo; 809-582-9111 Santiago de los Caballeros) also connects the two major cities.

Santiago and the El Cibao region do not have an efficient public transportation. However, independent bus owners operate their own routes according to demand, and there are plenty of *carros públicos* and *motoconchos* that run within and between the major cities (see the Transportation section, in the Planning Your Trip chapter).

In the mountains, *carros públicos* are often no more than open-bed pickup trucks. Uncomfortable. Unsafe. And your only option if you don't have your own wheels.

SANTIAGO DE LOS CABALLEROS

Residents of Santiago de los Caballeros (Santiago of the Noblemen) consider themselves the country's social elite. The nation's second largest city (population 750,000) was founded in 1562 by 30 Spanish noblemen *(caballeros)* in the heart of what would soon prove to be the most productive land on the island. It came into its own in the late 19th century, when Cuban émigrés settled the region, seeding a tobacco industry that boomed. The wealthy elite graced the city with fine buildings and became power brokers in national politics. Santiago remains the center of cigar production and is surrounded by bottle green tobacco fields, or *vegas*, centered on Villa González—to the west—and Tamboril—to the east. Several tobacco factories permit visits, usually by appointment, although the majority of them are in Zonas Francas, or free trade zones, that are closed to visitation.

Although ravaged by marauding Haitian and *caudillo* armies and by several earthquakes during the past two centuries, much of the historic city survived. The town straddles the Río Yaque and has a charming core—Centro Histórico—that is easily walked. Don't miss the nearby Monumento a los Héroes de la Restauración, and the Centro León (boasting a superb art gallery and museum) and adjacent Fábrica de Cigarros La Aurora tobacco factory. Santiago is also a modern city, known for its vibrant nightlife and vivacious *Carnaval*.

However, one day is sufficient for seeing the city, where the biggest downers are the sprawling, ungainly suburbs, the abysmal traffic jams, and the lack of directional signs. If you're driving yourself, arm yourself with as detailed a city map as possible.

Getting Around

Santiago is sprawling and congested. Arriving from Santo Domingo, Highway DR-1 ends at

Palacio Consitorial, Santiago de los Caballeros

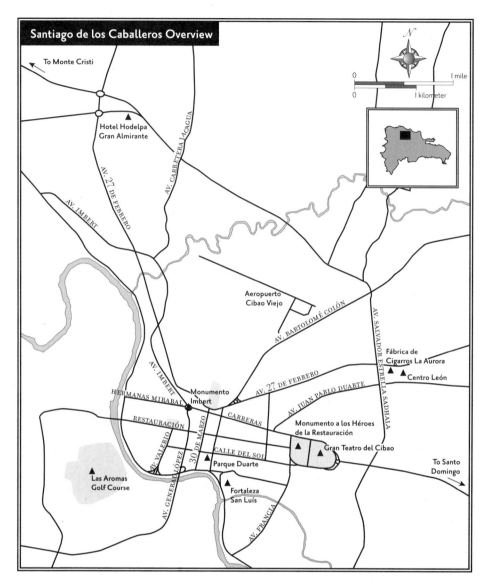

Santiago de los Caballeros Overview

To Monte Cristi

Hotel Hodelpa
Gran Almirante

AV. 27 DE FEBRERO

AV. IMBERT

AV. CARRETERA JACAGUA

Aeropuerto
Cibao Viejo

AV. BARTOLOMÉ COLÓN

AV. SALVADOR ESTRELLA SADHALÁ

Fábrica de
Cigarros La Aurora

Centro León

AV. IMBERT

AV. 27 DE FEBRERO

AV. JUAN PABLO DUARTE

Monumento
Imbert

HERMANAS MIRABAL

RESTAURACIÓN

CARRERAS

Monumento a los Héroes
de la Restauración

Gran Teatro del Cibao

AV. VALERIO

AV. GENERAL LÓPEZ

30 DE MARZO

CALLE DEL SOL

Parque Duarte

Las Aromas
Golf Course

Fortaleza
San Luís

To Santo
Domingo

AV. FRANCIA

0   1 mile
0   1 kilometer

the Monumento a los Héroes de la Restauración. In 2008, the government gave a go-head for construction of a multi-lane bypass highway to encircle the congested city, but until its completion anyone passing through the city has to deal with the aggressive and gridlocked traffic. A light metro rail system was also slated for ground breaking in 2010, with 12 stops around the city.

The **Caribe Tours** (809-576-0790) bus station is at Avenida 27 de Febrero and Avenida Las Américas (about 2 miles (3 km) northwest of the city center); the **Metro Expreso** terminal (809-582-9111) is at Calle Maimón between Avenida Juan Pablo Duarte and Avenida 27 de Febrero, about 2 miles (3 km) northeast of downtown.

Many areas are run-down and it is always best to take a taxi by night. Avoid *motoconchos*.

Lodging

There's no shortage of options in Santiago, from budget to deluxe. Hotel rooms are sold out months in advance for *Carnaval*, when you will need to book well ahead.

HODELPA CENTRO PLAZA

809-581-7000
fax: 809-582-4566
www.hodelpa.com
Calle Mella 54

My favorite steps-to-everywhere hotel in the city, in 2007 it emerged from a total refurbishing that blessed it with a hip urban vibe. Very chic. Very New York. It has 85 air-conditioned guest rooms (in five types, including junior suites and suites) done up in fashionable clinical whites, taupes, and chocolates, and you get goose down pillows and robes and slippers, plus Internet access. Suites have Jacuzzi tubs. The upper-storey Vista Restaurant offers panoramic views over the city, and there's a small casino. $$

HODELPA GRAN ALMIRANTE

809-580-1992
www.hodelpa.com
Avenida Salvador Estrella Sadhala

Busts of national heroes in Fortaleza San Luís, Santiago de los Caballeros

Considered the top hotel in the city, this 156-room facility on the northern outskirts of town is certainly stylish. I like its moderne motif, from its handsome design to its sumptuous white leather sofas and colorful contemporary art. The air-conditioned guest rooms offer eye-pleasing, predominantly white color schemes balanced by teak woods and bottle green carpets. They also come with a heap of amenities, from to-be-expected cable TVs with pay-per-view movies to WiFi access, in-room safes, and hair-dryers. It has a tapas bar and two restaurants (one chicly modern and the other antique in style), plus you can partake of a gym, spa, and swimming pool and the ever-lively casino. $$–$$$

HOTEL ALOHA SOL

809-583-0090
fax: 809-583-0950
www.alohasol.com
Calle del Sol 50

A steadfast option for value-conscious travelers, this heart-of-town hotel is fairly priced. It is comfy and slightly conservative, and makes no pretense to luxury, although my room (one of 102) was stylish and came with essential amenities. The restaurant is perfectly adequate, although not gourmet. And it has Internet service in the lobby, but not WiFi. $$

Museo Cultural Fortaleza San Luís, Santiago de los Caballeros

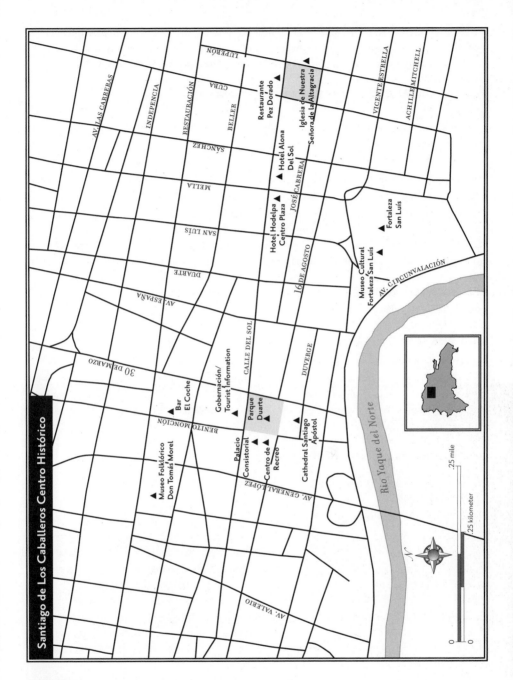

Santiago de Los Caballeros Centro Histórico

Dining

EL COCHE

809-612-4971

Calle Benito Monción 41

I like this tiny café-bar—a hangout for the local bohemian artist crowd—in a brick colonial building adorned with Lennon, Guevara, and Elvis posters. The menu is surprisingly eclectic for such a small place, ranging from soups and chicken dishes to filet mignon. It has a small roadside patio with barbecue grill. Open: Mon. through Sat. 11 AM–11 PM. $$

KOKARA MACARA COUNTRY BAR AND RESTAURANT
809-241-3143
www.kukaramacara.com
Avenida Francia 7
E-mail: www.kukaramacara.com

Go for the fascinating Western decor at this huge open-fronted restaurant built to resemble a Wild West saloon, complete with a stagecoach hanging over the entrance. The interior features cowhide chairs, John Wayne posters, and other theme regalia on the walls, plus—remarkably!—wait staff dressed as cowboys. Not surprisingly, you'll find pork ribs and sausages on the menu, but also local favorites such as *mofongo* and shrimp with rice, and even continental fare such as filet Roquefort. Open: Daily 11 AM–midnight. $$.

PEZ DORADO
809-582-4051
Calle del Sol 43
Cuisine: International

Handy for downtown hotels, this restaurant is themed as a Spanish bodega, with beamed ceiling and sturdy oak furnishings. The local business crowd gathers to enjoy well-executed continental dishes and Dominican favorites, but even Chinese dishes appear on the menu. I enjoyed a smoked salmon appetizer followed by garlic sea bass. The portions are filling, and the wait staff on the ball. Open: Daily 11:30 AM–11:55 PM. $$$.

Attractions, Parks, and Recreation

Historic Buildings, Plazas, and Religious Sites
PARQUE DUARTE
Calle del Sol and Avenida 30 de Marzo

The core of the colonial city, the tree-shaded main plaza centered on a gingerbread Victorian-era bandstand is surrounded by intriguing historical buildings. Notably, on the south side, the part neo-classical, part Gothic **Catedral Santiago Apóstol** dates from 1895, when it replaced a precursor toppled by an earthquake. After admiring the mahogany doors carved with fine Biblical-themed bas-reliefs, pop inside to view the stained-glass windows by contemporary artist José Rincón Mora (1938–); and the marble tomb of Ulises Hereaux (dictatorial president of the republic, 1845–99), who was born in Santiago in 1845. Calle Duvergé, flanking the church's south side, is one of the prettiest streets in town for its quaint and eclectic houses.

On the park's north side rises the Modernist municipal town hall, or **Gobernación**. Nip inside to marvel at the mahogany staircase and bold contemporary art.

The pedestrian-only east side—Calle Benito Monción—has two buildings of note. The pink-and-white neoclassical **Palacio Consistorial**, the former town hall (completed in 1897), is the most elegant building in town. The loggia supports bronze-painted Corinthian columns with an arched roofline topped by a weathervane. To its south, and a startling contrast, the **Centro de Recreo** has an ornate Mudéjar facade (note the crouching stucco fig-

Iglesia de Nuestra Senora de Altagracia, Santiago de los Caballeros

ures that support the metal porte-cochere atop allegorical chains); it still functions as a private social club but you can request entry to view the carved wooden ceilings and grand ballroom.

Horse-drawn carriages await custom for tours of the colonial city.

Museums and Monuments
CENTRO LEÓN

809-582-2315
www.centroleon.org.do
Avenida 27 de Febrero 146, Colonia Villa Progreso
Open: Tues. through Sun. 10 AM–7 PM
Admission: RD$70 adults, RD$30 children

Housed in a stunning postmodernist structure, this museum and cultural venue is one of the nation's premier forums for contemporary art and edification. I consider it the best all-round museum in the nation, courtesy of the Grupo León Jimenez tobacco company, whose factory adjoins.

The ground floor houses the Sala de Antropología, a superb museum with chronological exhibits dealing with Dominican society from pre-Columbian days to 21st-century living. Well-conceived dioramas include those on religious life, slave society, and Dominican

Monumento a los Héroes de la Restauración, Santiago de los Caballeros

architecture, as well as the nation's ecology and biodiversity. Upstairs is devoted to contemporary art of the past century, with many of the nation's leading exponents of Expressionism, Abstract painting, Magic Realism, etc., represented.

Ask for an English-speaking guide (RD$180).

MONUMENTO A LOS HÉROES DE LA RESTAURACIÓN
No telephone
Calle Daniel Espinal between Calle del Sol and Avenida Las Carreras
Open: Museum daily 8–5
Admission: Free

Santiago's most famous site crowns a hill to the east of the historic core. This grand phallus mounted on a monumental neo-classical marble pedestal was commissioned by self-aggrandizing Dictator Rafael Trujillo to be a colossal tribute to himself. Originally called the Monumento a la Paz Trujillo (Trujillo Peace Monument), it was rededicated following his death as the Monument to the Heroes of the Restoration. The fluted circular pillar rises 220 feet (67 m) and is twirled like a candy stick. It's topped by an allegorical bronze Victory, arms poised like Charles Atlas, with symbols of peace in its hands.

The monument and surrounding gardens were recently spruced up. The innards now include a museum with *carnaval* masks and costumes. Note the impressive social-realistic frescoes by Vela Zanetti as you ascend the caracole staircase to the top for fine views over the city. The gardens feature three plazas with statues dedicated to famous Dominican writers; Santiago's folklore; and the local baseball team, the Águilas Cibaeñas. The main entrance, on the east side, features a bronze statue of national hero Gregorio Luperón mounted on a steed.

It's at its most striking when floodlit at night.

MUSEO CULTURAL FORTALEZA SAN LUÍS
809-276-5866
www.fortalezasanluis.info
Avenida Emiliano Tardiff and Calle San Luis
Open: Daily 10 AM–5 PM
Admission: Free

The highlight of a visit to the town's crenellated colonial-era fortress, Fortaleza San Luís, this cultural museum is well worth a browse for its excellent collection of pre-Columbian artifacts; artwork ranging from Alberto Vargas's pinup females and somber portraits of national heroes to modern sculptures; and an impressive collection of weaponry spanning the colonial era to WWII. Rusted cannons, busts of national heroes, plus latter-day military hardware (including howitzers, armored personnel carriers, and yesteryear tanks) stand in Plaza Cultural, pinned by a clock tower (erected in 1895). The fortress dates from 1805 and was built atop a precursor initiated in 1674.

MUSEO FOLKLÓRICO DON TOMÁS MOREL
809-582-6787
Avenida Restauración 174
Open: Mon. through Fri. 9 AM–noon and 3–6 PM. Sat. and Sun. by appointment.
Admission: Donation

Centro Leon, Santiago de los Caballeros

For me, this homey offbeat museum is the highlight of any visit to Santiago. The venue is a simple wooden home stuffed with eclectic displays that pay homage to the Dominican passion for folk religion, including *brujería* (witchcraft). The eerie center point is a huge collection of *carnaval* masks, most of them from the collection of the museum's founder, Tomás Morel.

Miscellaneous
GRAN TEATRO DEL CIBAO
809-583-1150
Calle Daniel Espinal

Immediately east of the Monumento a los Héroes de la Restauración, this handsome post-modernist theater was built in the 1980s with a travertine facade. Note the life-size statues of important colonial-era Spanish-language literary figures that stand outside the arched entrance.

IGLESIA DE NUESTRA SEÑORA DE LA ALTAGRACIA
Calle del Sol and Calle Luperón

Completed in 1864 and looking west over Parque Altagracias, this church features twin bell towers.

FÁBRICA DE CIGARROS LA AURORA

809-755-2518
Avenida 27 de Febrero 146, Colonia Villa Progreso
Open: Mon. through Fri. 8 AM–5 PM

Beside the Centro León, of which it's a part, this small cigar factory is housed in a replica of the original, founded in 1903 by the then nascent León Jiménez company. You can view rollers at work in traditional fashion while a *lector* (reader) regales the day's news. It has a large humidor, and you can buy the company's trademark Preferidos, tapered at each end.

Culture

Casinos
Casino Gran Almirante (809-580-1992; Gran Almirante Hotel and Casino, Avenida Estrella Sadhalá and Calle Santiago de los Caballeros)

Music and Dance
Santiago has a thriving social scene with plenty of highbrow culture. The two main venues are the **Centro León** (809-582-2315; www.centroleon.org.do; Avenida 27 de Febrero), which hosts concerts, art and photography exhibitions, and lectures, and also has a Cine Club; and the **Gran Teatro del Cibao** (809-583-1150; Calle Daniel Espinal), which hosts preeminent Dominican and international artistes at two theaters for performing arts.

The **Centro de la Cultura** (809-226-5222; Calle del Sol and Benito Monción) and **Museo Cultural** (809-276-5866; www.fortalezasanluis.info; Fortaleza San Luís, Avenida Emiliano Tardiff and Calle San Luis) also host cultural events.

The **Cinema Centro Dominicano** (809-570-1358; Calle Estrella Sadhalá and Argentina) has six screens; many films are subtitled in Spanish.

Nightlife
Santiago is second only to Santo Domingo in its lively night scene. The following are the town's hotspots:

Alcázar (809-580-1992; Gran Almirante Hotel and Casino, Avenida Estrella Sadhalá and Calle Santiago de los Caballeros) Sophisticated discotheque with a dress code. The Gran Almirante hotel's Cosmopolitan Bar is a good place to warm up with cocktails before the dance crowd arrives, after midnight. And the hotel's Santiago Cigar Club is *the* place to savor a hand rolled Dominican cigar with fine cognac.

Kukaramákara Country Bar and Restaurant (809-241-3143; Avenida Francia 7) Don your Western gear for this Old West bar with live music.

Metropolis Billar Café (809-241-4727; Avenida Estrella Sadhalá 6, Santiago) Classy pool hall. Dress code.

Tribeca Lounge (809-241-2416; Avenida M. Álvarez 8, Santiago) The city's top disco. More techno than salsa.

Seasonal Events
Every last weekend in February the city bursts into riotous mayhem for the annual *Carnaval,* when scores of inhabitants dress in devil masks and costumes and most everyone else finds an excuse for sometimes salacious fun. The most colorful parades are in the rival working class neighborhoods of La Joya and Los Pepines.

Cigar roller at Fábrica de Cigarros La Aurora, Santiago

Good to Know About

There's a meagerly stocked branch of the Secretaria de Estado de Turismo, or **tourism office**, in the Gobernación, (809-582-5885; Parque Duarte at Calle del Sol; weekdays 9–5).

The **tourist police** (809-754-3102) have a branch at the airport.

BONAO AND VICINITY

This mining town, on the *autopista* 50 miles (80 km) northwest of Santo Domingo, sits at the eastern base of the Cordillera Central. Forest-clad, bottle green mountains rise sharply west of town, while to the east, rolling flatlands are farmed in tobacco and mined for precious mineral ores. The town is bypassed by most tourists yet has a few sites worth a brief visit, not least tree-shaded **Parque Duarte**, and the impressive **Monumento a los Héroes**, on Avenida Aniana Vargas.

A worthy side trip is to head west from town up the valley of the Río Yuna. The views grow ever more spectacular as you snake up through sometimes-fog-shrouded rain forest to Presa Alto Yuman, one of a series of man-made lakes.

Lodging

AQUARIUS HOTEL

809-296-2898
fax: 809-296-2360
www.aquariusbonao.com
Calle Duarte 104, Bonao

A modern and comfy state-of-the-art hotel in the heart of town. Its 29 air-conditioned standard rooms and five suites offer cozy contemporary decor and cable TV, minibars, in-room safes, and hair dryers. And the hotel boasts a swimming pool, hot whirlpool, small gym, and restaurant. $$

RANCHO WENDY

809-630-1261
www.ranchowendy.com

This is a tremendous budget option and has a fantastic riverside location at the foot of the mountains. You can choose from clean albeit simple dorm rooms, each with a basic private cold-water bath. It also has well-laid-out lawns for you to pitch your tent (US$5 per person), with shared bathrooms and hot-water showers. It specializes in guided hikes and horseback rides. $

Dining

TÍPICO BONAO

809-525-3941
E-mail: tipicobonao@codetel.net.do
Autopista Duarte Km 83, Bonao

This large, thatched-roofed restaurant (at the second Bonao exit off the *autopista*) serves *comida criolla* and is immensely popular. Open: Daily 6 AM–11 PM. $$.

Attractions, Parks, and Recreation

Golf

Non-guests can play the 9-hole, par-27 **Bella Vista Golf Club** (809-525-3565; Club Falcondo; open: 8–7).

Miscellaneous

Many of Bonao's townsfolk are employed at **Mina Falcondo**, 2 miles (3 km) east of Bonao. This opencast mine (also known as Falconbridge) extracts nickel from ferronickel ore, used almost exclusively by the stainless steel industry. Owned by the Swiss mining company, Xstrata, the mine has an annual capacity of 32,000 tons. Tours can be arranged with one week's notice through the **Fundación Falcondo** (809-686-0727 or 890-682-6041 ext 2311; www.fundacionfalconbridge.com; Avenida Máximo Gómez 30), the company's non-profit foundation designed to encourage local development and ecological preservation.

CHATEAU DE LA FUENTE
c/o 809-575-4739 in Santiago
Caribe, 3 miles (4.8 km) E of Bonao
Open: visits strictly by invitation only

Cigar aficionados may be surprised to find that none of Arturo Fuente's premium all-Dominican cigars are for sale in the Dominican Republic. They're for export only. But select visitors *can* view the *finca* where the tobacco is grown, although permission must be granted personally by Don Carlos Fuente. The immaculately maintained, 200-acre (81 ha) Chateau de la Fuente is the showcase and much-envied plantation of the world-famous father and son cigar company. Here, the Fuentes still use horse-drawn ploughs to till the rich, red soils where, uniquely in the republic, all three components of a cigar—filler, binder, and wrapper leaves—are grown for use in the exalted Fuente Fuente OpusX cigars. Father and son are usually on hand to personally escort invited guests, who get to see tobacco plants growing beneath cheesecloth *(tapados)* and thatched curing barns, and the cigar-rolling room where the silky leaves are hand-rolled into sublime smokes evoking raptures. Yes, you can even sample a divine smoke with cocktail in the gazebo and guest house on a hillock with views over the finca, studded with majestic royal palms and decorated with rows of exotic flowers.

The Fuentes closely guard their trade secrets. Don't try arriving unannounced. The well-guarded facility has a strict admittance policy. Uninvited visitors are always turned away.

Cigar Family Charitable Foundation

Poverty is so extreme in parts of the Dominican Republic that many tobacco harvesters want their children to work in the fields as young as six years of age. Lacking schools and money, many residents have little ability to improve their own lives. It's a sad scenario that prompted Carlos Fuente Jr. to act. "When we first came here, there was no electricity, there was no water. We had no idea of the problems in the surrounding villages; we were here to grow tobacco," recalls Fuente, known affectionately as Carlito by local children. "You realize you have a responsibility to help these children in some way."

Created by the J. C. Newman Cigar Co. and Tabacalera A. Fuente y Cia families three decades ago, the Cigar Family Charitable Foundation (813-248-2124 or 800-477-1884; www.cf-cf.org) is one of the foremost entities fighting poverty in the Dominican Republic through education initiatives, disease prevention, and personal empowerment. For example, the Cigar Family Complex, in Bonao, includes a Community School and Cigar Family High School providing free education and meals to more than 400 students, plus sports facilities, a theater, a health clinic, and dental services. The foundation has also provided a sanitary system and clean drinking water in the impoverished village of Caribe. The two cigar companies assume all administrative costs directly.

The Altadis cigar company, based in La Romana, is equally philanthropic. After Hurricane Georges devastated the southern republic in 1998, the company donated $1 million to relief efforts and created the nonprofit World of Montecristo Relief Organization. And Grupo León Jimenes, the biggest tobacco company in the Dominican Republic, has a similar project, Programa de Desarrollo Comunitario (Community Development Program), initiated in 1998.

Tax-deductible donations can be sent to Cigar Family Charitable Foundation, P.O. Box 2030, Tampa, FL 33601.

Tobacco leaves drying, El Cibao

Museums

The colorfully frescoed **Museo de Arte Cándido Bidó** (809-525-7707; Calle Padre Billini and Los Santos; free), on the Plaza de la Cultura, exhibits the intensely colorful works of internationally acclaimed, Bonao-born artist Cándido Bidó alongside those of lesser-known local artists. It hosts the Bienal de Bonao competition every two years. Open: Mon. through Fri. 9 AM–5 PM.

LA VEGA AND VICINITY

Today a congested and somewhat chaotic contemporary-styled city, La Vega actually has one of the island's most noteworthy pasts. The ruins of La Concepción de la Vega (founded in 1494 on Columbus's orders) bespeak the region's early import as a center for gold mining, and the first mint in the New World was founded here (as well, reputedly, as the first legal brothel). The township was leveled by an earthquake in 1562, following which a new settlement was laid out a few miles southwest on the banks of the Río Camú.

Today's La Vega is best known, however, for hosting the *Carnaval* Vegano, the largest and most flamboyant of the nation's February *carnavales*.

Carnaval Masks

Children may scream. Adults may cringe. But everyone knows that the scary and fantastical masks worn by colorfully costumed *cojuelos*—evil spirits—are what make the *carnavales* of La Vega and Santiago de los Caballeros so exciting and memorable. The fearsome papier-mâché masks typically feature sharp horns, fanged teeth, and huge bulging eyes (usually bloodshot for a more devilish effect). Many are embellished with rhinestones and/or feathers. Every town has its own style, as do separate communities within each town—a potent and easily identifiable expression of cultural identity reflecting long-standing rivalries between the neighborhoods. For example, masks from Santiago's La Joya district typically show a long pointed snout and two long horns budding with multiple smaller horns. The rival Los Pepines mask is broader, with smooth yet elongated horns, and a wide upturned snout like Daffy Duck.

Attractions, Parks, and Recreation

PARQUE DUARTE
Avenida Profesor Juan Bosch and Calle Padre Adolfo

La Vega's rather nondescript main square has none of the romantic stature of most Latin American cities, notwithstanding a sprinkling of modestly intriguing buildings to three sides: the quasi neo-classical **Palacio Municipal** (Calle Juan Bosch between Independencia and Padre Adolfo) and **Palacio de Justícia** (Calle Sánchez corner Padre Adolfo), and the Beaux Arts **Casa de la Cultura** (Calle Independencia 32 and Sánchez), built in 1925 as the Hotel Royal Palace.

Commanding the scene, however, is the jaw-dropping **Catedral de la Concepción de la Vega**, a controversial postmodernist cathedral (with Gothic and industrial elements) designed by Dominican architect Edwin Cott and inaugurated in 1992. However ungainly the exterior, the interior impresses with its stark yet striking austerity and its simple altar, featuring a wooden statue of Christ crested by a halo of lights.

PARQUE NACIONAL ARQUEOLÓGICO HISTÓRICO LA VEGA VIEJA
No telephone
Carretera Moca, 1 mile (1.6 km) NE of Santa Cerro
Mon. through Fri. 8–3; Sat. and Sun. 9–4
Admission: RD$50

This tiny national park protects the remains of the second settlement in the New World. Founded as Concepción de la Vega in 1494 at the eastern base of Santo Cerro hill, it was the setting for a small fortress and for the first Franciscan monastery in the New World, built in 1502 (Fray Bartolomé de las Casas, chronicler of the Indies, was ordained here). In 1508, large quantities of gold were discovered and the tiny settlement witnessed boom days. Alas, in 1562 a violent earthquake caused such destruction that the occupants moved away and the ruins were soon overcome by tropical vegetation.

In 1975, the government set out to protect the site, which was excavated. Today extensive remains peer out from the undergrowth. You can easily distinguish the small fortress, with circular *baluartes* (watchtowers) at each corner. The monastery ruins are some 500 yards (457 m) to the east.

SANTO CERRO

3 miles (4.8 km) N of La Vega, off Carretera Moca

You'd expect a site named Holy Hill to be one of the nation's holiest sites, and it is. This tiny hilltop village is named for an imagined miracle involving Christopher Columbus himself. Supposedly in 1494 a force led by the Great Navigator met violent resistance from local Taíno, who gained the upper hand. When Columbus planted a cross given to him by Queen Isabel, an apparition of the Virgin of de las Mercedes supposedly appeared, scaring the Taíno away.

The site is worth visiting for the Byzantine style **Iglesia Nuestra Señora de Las Mercedes** (built in 1886), a lovely church that boasts an exquisite mahogany altar and draws pilgrims en masse each September 24. A wire grille protects the supposed original site—Santo Hoyo de la Cruz (Sacred Hole of the Cross)—of the Columbus cross.

Statues of biblical scenes line the snaking road from La Vega.

Good to Know About

There's a **tourism office** (809-242-3231; Calle Mella and Calle Durangé), although it has very little literature and isn't set up to aid travelers.

LA VEGA REAL

The Royal Field refers to the vast expanse of fertile flatlands extending northeast of La Vega (and east of Santiago de los Caballeros), framed to the north by the Cordillera Septentrional, and forming the heart of El Cibao. During the colonial era, the regional towns prospered on the agricultural and tobacco trade and became the center of political power, and of the internecine warfare throughout much of 18th and 19th centuries. Ravaged and razed by marauding armies, the main urban centers (such as Moca and San Francisco de Macorís) strung out along Carretera 132 today retain relatively few buildings of historic note. The population hereabouts is distinctly more European in origin than anywhere else on the isle.

The center of cigar production is the town of **Tamboril** (8 miles—12.8km—east of Santiago de los Caballeros), with more than two dozen small-scale factories scattered along the main street. Visits can be made on weekdays by appointment to **Fábrica Anilo de Oro** (809-580-5808; Calle Real 85); **Fábrica La Caya** (809-570-9930; www.intercigar.com; Calle Real 169); and **Tabacalera Flor Dominicana** (809-580-5139; Calle Federico Velázquez 51).

Farther east, the sprawling and bustling tobacco town of **Moca**—La Villa Heroica (Town of Heroes)—is famous as the place where Dictator Ulises Hereaux was assassinated in 1899: the site, on Calle Vásquez, is marked by a monument to the hero assassins.

San Francisco de Macoris, the main and most easterly town (and birthplace of playboy race-car driver and diplomat Porfirio Rubirosa), is worth a browse of its main square, **Parque Duarte** (Avenida 27 de Febrero and Avenida Restauración), featuring a neoclassical **Ayuntamiento** (town hall); and the intriguing twin-spired **Iglesia Santa Rosa** (Calle Colón between Mella and Restauración), looking like it was made of LEGO bricks and with beautiful contemporary stained-glass windows.

The World's Finest Cigars

So you've always believed that Cuban cigars are supposedly the best in the world? Well, not so. According to expert opinion, Dominican cigars today outclass Cubans by a mile. Think of Davidoff, La Flor Dominicana, and, of course, Arturo Fuentes...the latter a very symbol of the DR. The quality of Dominican cigars has improved in leaps and bounds in recent decades, ironically much thanks to the Cuban Revolution.

Tobacco was first planted in the Dominican Republic two centuries ago, and El Cibao grew wealthy on the trade. Following Cuba's Communist revolution in 1959, that island's cigar factories were seized. Thousands of factory owners, tobacco farmers, and cigar rollers fled. Many settled in the DR where they set up production centered on Santiago, Tamboril, and Villa González. Many brought prized Cuban seeds with them. Fortunately, conditions in El Cibao proved equal to those of Cuba. Soon familiar Cuban brand names of Dominican progeny were back on the market. Today, the Dominican Republic produces more cigars than any other nation.

Of course, it takes more than good seed and soil to produce a quality hand-rolled cigar (machine-made cigars are inferior), whose individual character reflects a unique blend of leaves: filler, binder, and wrapper. The individual leaves vary markedly depending on where they are grown. And every factory has its own recipe to attain a characteristic flavor and draw to distinguish its cigars as much as possible from those of rivals.

Leaves are usually dried and fermented on the *fincas* where they are grown before being shipped to the *fábricas de tabaco*—the tobacco factories. Here they are moistened (to restore their elasticity), flattened, stripped of their hard spine, then sorted and classified by color, size, texture, and overall quality. In the *galera* (rolling room), *torcedores* (rollers, whose sole tool is a flat, guillotine-shaped knife called a *chaveta*) first select two or three *seco* leaves to provide strength to the cigar. These are rolled tightly—but not *too* tightly, or the cigar won't draw—then wrapped in *ligero* (for aroma) and *volado* (for even burning) leaves, which together form the filler. Next come *capotes*, or binder leaves, completing the bunch. The shape of the cigars can vary from the classic torpedo shape to elliptical cigars, such as Fábrica La Aurora's famous *preferidos*—pointed at each end and bulbous in the middle. The cylindrical cigars are then pressed in a tubular mold before being wrapped with a thin, elastic, and flavorful, all-important *copa* leaf. Last, a small circular piece of *copa* is wrapped and glued (with a fish-based glue) to the head to seal the cigar. The other end is then guillotined to size.

The completed cigars are sorted by color, ranging from pale brown *claro* to dark brown *oscuro*; given a paper band embossed with the brand's logo; then laid out in cedar boxes, always with the darkest cigars on the left.

Lodging

HOTEL LAS CAOBAS

809-290-5858
fax: 809-290-5859
Calle Luis Enrique Carrón, 2 miles (3 km) W of San Francisco de Macorís
Price: Moderate

The only pleasant hotel in the area, this modern motel-style property stands in expansive grounds to the northwest side of San Francisco de Macorís. Its 42 rooms are modestly furnished, but don't expect firm beds or frills. It has a pool, small casino, tennis, plus a restaurant loosely themed after Wild West movies. $–$$

Attractions, Parks, and Recreation

CASA MUSEO HERMANAS MIRABAL

809-577-2704
Conuco Salcedo, 2.5 miles (4 km) E of Salcedo
Open: Daily 9–6:30
Admission: RD$20

Justifiably a national shrine and, to my mind, a must-visit, this handsome middle-class, mid-1950s Modernist home was the birthplace of María Teresa, Minerva, and Patria Mirabal—the famous sisters (also known as Las Mariposas, or Butterflies) who led the secret anti-Trujillo resistance. In 1960, the sisters were brutally murdered, along with Minerva's husband, Manolo Tavarez. They are buried in the exquisite garden, which contains busts to the heroes. Guides lead tours of the home, furnished just as it was five decades ago.

Combine the museum with a visit to the nearby village of Ojo de Agua, where Doña Bélgica Mirabal, the sole surviving sister, still lives. Her home, **Casa Museo 'Dede' Mirabal** (809-577-4142, by appointment only), faces onto **Plazoleta Hermanas Mirabal**, with the mangled remains of the car in which the three sisters were murdered as a poignant monument to their memory.

IGLESIA SAGRADO CORAZÓN DE JESÚS

Calle Corazón de Jesús corner Morillo, Moca

Considered by many observers to be the prettiest church in the country, this confection in stone resembles a multi-tiered wedding cake. The Sacred Heart of Jesus church, belonging to the Silesian order, was inaugurated in 1956. Its lovely Italian stained-glass windows include some depicting local dignitaries. You can climb the spiral staircase behind the impressive organ to emerge atop the clock tower for a fabulous view over town.

RESERVA CIENTÍFICA LOMA QUITA ESPUELA

809-588-4156
fax: 588-6008
www.flqe.org.do
Alto La Cueva, 7 miles (11 km) NE of San Francisco de Marcorís
Open: 8–5 daily
Admission: RD$50
Guides: from RD$1050 (call ahead to reserve)

Protecting 232 acres (94 ha) of virgin montane forest on the southern slopes of the Cordillera Septentrional, this wilderness reserve lures hikers and nature lovers keen to tread trails that wend sharply through forest primeval. Birders will be enthralled, as 23 endemic bird species have been recorded, including the bay-breasted cuckoo, Greater Antillean bullfinch, and Hispaniolan parrot. With extreme fortune, you might even spot an endangered solenodon or hutia.

Three trails begin at the ranger station, 1 mile (1.6 km) above the hamlet of Alto La Cueva (it's a rugged drive; but a 4WD can make it). The Cloud Trail—**Sendero de las Nubes**—climbs 2 miles (3 km) into the mist-shrouded upper peaks; if the clouds part, you'll have sensational views from atop Loma Quita Espuela (3,091 feet/942 m). For a study of a still-thriving cacao forest (cacao is the source of chocolate), take the **Sendero del**

Iglesia Sagrado Corazón de Jesús, Moca

Faceless Dolls

Ceramic *muñecas sin rostros* (faceless dolls) are a signature product and unofficial mascot of El Cibao. These stylized dolls, in different sizes but usually no more than 10 inches (25 cm) tall, have no faces. Although no one seems exactly sure why that's so, the commonly accepted explanation is that they evolved to symbolize an inclusive society, or racial syncretism, of Taínos, Africans, and Europeans. Hence, the lack of facial features that could favor one group over any other. Most dolls depict local countrywomen—*campesinas cibaeñas*—shown carrying water vases or selling flowers and dressed in gaily colored attire plus straw hats or head-scarves. The clay dolls are still fired in traditional wood-burning ovens in family-run studios that reflect an important cottage industry dating back almost two centuries. Many are made at El Higuerito, about 5 miles (8 km) west of Moca.

Bosque del Cacao. After sweating your way through the woods, take to the **Sendero Balneario Rústico La Roca**, which leads to a natural swimming hole where you can plunge into cool waters.

Local ladies tend to the open-air kitchen at the ranger station, which has exhibits.

VALLE DE YAQUE

Hemmed to the north by the Cordillera Septentrional and to the south by the foothills of the Cordillera Central, this broad valley drained by the Río Yaque del Norte (the nation's largest river) funnels west from Santiago de los Caballeros to Monte Cristi, where the river pours into the sea. The ruler-straight Carretera Duarte highway (Ruta 1) connects Santiago to Monte Cristi. En route, you'll pass through several mostly inconsequential agricultural towns.

The easternmost part of the valley is farmed in tobacco. Many cigar factories dot the vale. Thatch-fringed tobacco-curing barns add a yesteryear note. And the **Instituto del Tabaco** (809-580-0066; www.intabaco.gov.do; Autopista Dr. Joaquín Balaguer) has its headquarters in **Villa González** (8 miles (12.8 km) west of Santiago). Most cigar factories are closed to viewing, but by prior arrangement weekday visits can sometimes be arranged to the **Tabacos Carbonell** (809-580-0228; E-mail: tabaqueriacarbonell@hotmail.com; Calle Ramón Emilio Delmonte, Zona Franca Palmarejo; free), in Villa González; and **Tabacalera Jacagua** (809-585-5702; Parque Central), in **Navarrete**, 10 miles (16 km) farther west. There are few sites of touristic interest west of Navarrete.

Badly potholed Carretera 16 runs parallel to Ruta 1 through the foothills of the Cordillera Central, linking Santiago de los Caballeros (in the east) to Sabanete (in the west), beyond which Carretera 18 connects to Dajabón, on the Haitian border.

Boasting a lovely mountain setting, **San José de la Matas**, 21 miles (33 km) west of Santiago de los Caballeros, is a center for coffee production. It's also a gateway for treks to Pico

Duarte (see the Jarabacoa and Vicinity section, below) via the mountain hamlet of **Mata Grande**, 16 miles (25 km) south of San José via a rough dirt road; the trailhead is at Antón Sape Bueno, 2 miles (3 km) beyond Mata Grande.

Carretera 16 continues west to **Moncíon**, also enjoying a lovely mountain setting beside a large fish-stocked reservoir—**La Presa de Moncíon**.

Lodging

CASA DE LAS ANAS
206-979-6016; or 809-579-9882 (Spanish only)
fax: 516-977-6016
http://sites.google.com/site/casadelasanas
28 Calle Tomas Genao, Moncíon

With only two bedrooms, this U.S.-owned bed-and-breakfast is run with loving care by a Dominican caretaker family presided over by matriarch AnaJulia and her daughter Ana-Maria. In a modest section of town, it provides a taste of real Dominican lifestyle. Hearty local fare is prepared. $–$$

JARABACOA AND VICINITY

On weekends, Santo Domingo's moneyed class head north into the Cordillera Central—a massive, dramatically rugged highland region that encompasses one of the largest untouched wilderness preserves in the Caribbean.

Remarkably, in all this vastness there are only two towns. **Jarabacoa**, the main town, nestles at a perfectly temperate 1,730 feet (528 m) elevation, where the air is scented by eucalyptus and pine. Jarabacoa is first-and-foremost an agricultural town, but tourism isn't given short shrift. In fact, it's a center for active adventures: The town is the principal gateway for climbs up Pico Duarte, as well as a base for whitewater rafting, horseback rides, and ATV tours. Easily accessed by paved road from Bonao or La Vega (via Carretera 28), its proximity to Santo Domingo (a two-hour drive) has also made it a popular year-round retreat for the nation's wealthy, many of whom have second homes in the tree-lined outskirts. An alpine retreat in the tropics? How cool! Religious orders also find inspiration in the setting: the Cistercians and Silesians have monasteries here.

There's not much to see in the town itself, which sits above the Río Yaque del Norte. Still, you can take in the airs with locals beneath a venerable mimosa tree that shades **Parque Mario Nelson Galán** (Calle Mario Nelson Galán and Colón), the central plaza. And you can take a cooling swim at **Balneario La Confluencia**, with natural pools at the juncture of the Jimenoa and Yaque del Norte rivers, at the end of Avenida La Confluence some 2 miles (3 km) north of town.

La Ciénaga de Manabao, a tiny hamlet at the end of the mountain road 13 miles (20.8 km) west of Jarabacoa, nestles at the head of the Río Yaque del Norte, at a cool 4,500 feet (1,370 m) at the foot of Pico Duarte. The trailhead for the summit hike begins here, at the ranger station for Parque Nacional José del Carmén Ramírez.

Salto de Jimenoa, Jarabacoa

Lodging

HOTEL DIANA VICTORIA
809-488-8935
Carretera La Vega, 5 miles (8 km) NE of Jarabacoa

I adore this simple country-cottage-themed bed-and-breakfast run by Victor Hugo and his charming wife, set in a quaint garden at the side of the main road into town. Its seven colorful rooms with ceiling fans are minimally furnished, but the modern bathrooms are clean, and you can recline on Adirondack chairs on your patio. The small café-style bar-restaurant serves tasty local dishes, such as grilled meats, guinea fowl in red wine, and stewed goat. $–$$

HOTEL GRAN JIMENOA
809-574-6304
www.granjimenoa.com
Avenida La Confluencia

The most impressive lodgings in town. This hotel, on the north side of town, overlooks the river and is built around a grand patriarch's summer house. Modern motel-style blocks have been added for a total of 28 large, modestly furnished rooms, all with cable TVs but uninspired bathrooms. The bar can get lively, and there's a swimming pool, a games room, and a sauna. $$–$$$

HOTEL PINAR DORADO

809-574-2820
fax: 809-574-2237
www.grupobaiguate.com/pinardorado
Calle del Carmen
Price: Moderate

I like this low-slung, two-storey hotel with interior walls of red brick. Here, the 43 spacious air-conditioned rooms offer no frills but they're comfy enough and have cable TVs, telephones, and large picture windows. The thatched restaurant (where buffets are served) and bar looks over a swimming pool. $$

RANCHO BAIGUATE

809-574-6890
fax: 809-574-4815
www.ranchobaiguate.com
Barrio La Joya, 2 miles (3 km) SE of Jarabacoa

A sibling to the Hotel Pinar Dorada, this is the main activity center in the region. Hence, the property, set amid spacious lawns with natural lagoons, draws plenty of day-trippers come to partake of the rafting, etc. It caters to all budgets. Choose from 9 meagerly furnished dorm rooms for backpackers, plus 8 standard rooms, and 10 more elegant suites. The grounds contain an Olympic pool, volleyball and basketball courts, and a thatched restaurant serving lunch and dinner buffets. $$–$$$

Dining

EL RANCHO

809-574-4557
Calle Independencia
www.ranchobaiguate.com/elrancho

Combines elegance with the rusticity of natural timbers, including rough-hewn furniture. The eclectic menu ranges from seafood to pizza, plus local favorites such as shrimp *asopao*. Has both indoor and outdoor dining. Open: Daily 9 AM–11 PM.

Attractions, Parks, and Recreation

Activity Centers

Rancho Baiguate (809-574-6890, www.ranchobaiguate.com) specializes in whitewater rafting on the Río Yaque del Norte ($50), but also has canyoning (aka waterfall rappelling, $50), mountain bike tours (from $17.50), horseback rides ($16 adults, $8 children), and a treetops challenge course ($16), as well as hikes, including to the summit of Pico Duarte.

Constanza valley

Golf

Jarabacoa Golf Club (809-574-2474 or 782-9883; Quintas de Primavera). Carved out of rugged hills, this 9-hole course—also known as Quintas de Primavera—puts up quite a challenge with its narrow pine-framed fairways and nasty bunkers. Small pro shop, plus caddies. 9 holes $10.

Miscellaneous Attractions
FINCA ALTAGRACIA
c/o in the U.S. 802-453-2776 or 802-786-2280
www.cafealtagracia.com
E-mail: info@cafealtagracia.com
Los Marranitos 7 miles (11 km) W of Jarabacoa
Occupying a ridge top with magnificent vistas,

This 260-acre (105 ha) experimental coffee and fruit farm is owned by acclaimed Dominican novelist Julia Álvarez and her American partner, Bill Eichner. A vision of sustainability and ethical farming, the project endeavors to benefit the impoverished local community (for example, by funding a local school). Tours can be arranged by advance notice, and it offers accommodations for volunteers wishing either to work on the farm or to teach with the Dominican Republic Education and Mentoring Project (809-571-0497; www.dominicandream.org).

Paragliding

Fly Vacher (809-882-1201; www.simonvacher.com) More than a decade of experience offering paragliding. Tandem flights with instructors launch from Altos de Guayabo, 2,100 feet (640 m) above Jarabacoa. $60.

Wildlife and Wilderness Parks

PARQUES NACIONALES J. ARMANDO BERMÚDEZ
AND JOSÉ DEL CARMÉN RAMÍREZ

809-472-7170 (La Ciénaga) or 557-3996 (Sabaneta)
www.medioambiente.gov.do
E-mail: ecoturismo@medioambiente.gov.do
Admission: RDS$100

The Cordillera Central—colloquially called the Dominican Alps—rise south and west of Jarabacoa. The Himalayas of the Caribbean, they form a dauntingly rugged massif rising to 10,164 feet (3,098 m) atop Pico Duarte, the region's highest peak. Three other peaks surpass 10,000 feet: Pico La Pelona (10,151 feet/3,094 m), Pico La Rucilla (10,003 feet/3,049 m), and Pico Yaque (9,055 feet/2,760 m), while the parks span an elevation range of 7,700 feet (2,347 m). Extending more than 50 miles (80 km) east-west, these mountains are the source of the island's main rivers. In 1956, the bulk of the massif was enshrined within two contiguous parks—Parque Nacional J. Armando Bermúdez and Parque Nacional José del Carmén Ramírez—encompassing 591 square miles (1,531 sq km). Together with Reserva Científico Ebano Verde and Parque Nacional Valle Nuevo, plus three smaller reserves, they comprise the Madre de los Aguas (Mother of the Waters) Conservation Area, protecting the

Pirámide Ciclópea, Parque Nacional Valle Nuevo

Whitewater Rafting

The Dominican Republic is the only Caribbean nation with whitewater rafting. The Valle del Río Yaque del Norte is tailor made for whitewater thrills (one section features a 12-foot (3.6 m) vertical drop called Mike Tyson). Prodigious rainfall feeds the Caribbean's longest river as it slaloms out of the Cordillera Central before settling into a more tranquil flow, perfect for contemplation of the valley's nature beauty.

Although trips are offered year-round, fall and winter months provide the best conditions: The river is at its peak, and the rapids at their most potent. Trips on the Río Yaque del Norte are Class II (moderately calm with minor rapids) to full-throttle Class IV (challenging rapids), depending on water levels and where you put in. Half the fun is in the teamwork of paddling your eight-person raft under instructions of an experienced guide. Typically, trips last a half day. The rafting companies provide mandatory life vests, helmets, and paddles.

Expect to get soaked (all part of the fun) as you plunge through the rapids like a log down a flume. Take a set of dry clothes and shoes to change into after the trip. Apply plenty of sun lotion: The UV factor is intense in the crisp mountain air.

forests that protect 12 major rivers and supply 80 percent of the nation's potable water.

Flora and Fauna: A pastiche of habitats, the parks are Nirvana to nature lovers. Lower elevations comprise broadleaf subtropical humid forest typified by such species as West Indian cedar and walnut, plus wild olive, and the shrubby *Palo amargo*. Above 4,000 feet (1,219 m), mists swirl amid *Palo de cruz* pines and the *Palo de cotorra* (parrot tree), forming a dense cloud forest marked by effusive epiphytes, lichens, and mosses. At higher elevations, wildflowers emblazon alpine meadows framed by Creolean pine, and ragged heather called *Palo de reina* tints marshy wind-scoured savanna.

These wilds are a last refuge for solenodon and hutia, and for wild pigs (*puercos cimarrones*), common—although rarely seen—in the dense forests of lower elevations. Vegetation thins out above the cloud forests, and wildlife is comparatively sparse. Hence, only some 50 bird species have been recorded. These include Hispaniolan parrots, the rufous-throated solitaire, and the mountain whistler.

Pico Duarte: The nation's (and the Caribbean's) highest mountain (10,128 feet/3,087 m) is topped by a cross and a bronze bust of Duarte. The first person to hike to the summit, apparently, was the British Consul Sir Robert Hermann Schomburgk (1804–65), who climbed it in 1851. Schomburgk named the mountain Monte Tina. Vainglorious President Rafael Trujillo rechristened it Pico Trujillo. Following his demise, it was renamed for Juan Pablo Duarte, the 19th-century revolutionary and father of the nation.

RESERVA CIENTÍFICO EBANO VERDE

809-565-1422 (in Santo Domingo)
Fax: 809-549-3900
www.fundacionprogressio.com
Carretera Constanza, 13 miles (20.8 km) W of Autopista Duarte

The closest mountain reserve to Santo Domingo, the 9-square-mile (23 sq km) Green Ebony Scientific Reserve is accessible to the public by prior permit application. Named for the native green ebony tree that grows here, the rain-soaked reserve was created in 1989 to

Hiking Pico Duarte

Hundreds of hikers set out monthly to attain the summit of Pico Duarte along the 14-mile (23 km) trail that begins at the park ranger station (known officially as the Centro de Visitantes del Valle de Lilís) in La Ciénaga, where you must register. It's a demanding, albeit nontechnical two-day ascent, or longer, depending on your physical fitness and the weather. The driest and best months are December through March. Last admission is 4 PM, which gives enough time to attain the first hut at Los Tablones for overnight.

Accommodations: You can bunk in a basic dorm with toilet at La Ciénaga ranger station (RD$300 for up to four people). There are seven simple cabins scattered along the trail. You can camp for free at the huts. Many hikers spend their first night at a simple hut at Las Tablones ranger station; and the second at La Compartición (7,780 feet/2,350 m), which can also easily be attained in a single day's hike from La Ciénaga. Both huts have small kitchens with wood-burning stoves, and La Compartición has solar-powered pay telephones. Note that rats forage La Compartición at night.

Guides and Equipment: A guide (*arriero*) is compulsory, even for short hikes. The community runs the **Asociación de Guías de Montaña** (809-515-7141), the Association of Mountain Guides. Guides cost RD$300 per day. You can opt to ride a mule (RD$250 per day), including to carry your equipment (RD$200 per day). Food for yourself and your guide costs RD$1,000 for three days. Your guide will cook for you. You can rent sleeping bags, tents, and ponchos in the village. Bring toilet paper and insect repellent, plus warm and waterproof clothing (it can fall below freezing at night).

THE ROUTE

Day One: The first day typically involves 6 to 12 hours of hiking. The initial going is relatively flat through the valley of the Río Los Tablones along a path used by local villagers. Broadleaf forest provides shade for much of the route, which then ascends to Los Tablones ranger station, where you can overnight at about 3,600 feet (1,200 m).

---

protect this endangered species' habitat. Despite its small size, the park is rich in endemism: a carnivorous plant (*Pinguicola casabitoana*) and two butterfly species are found nowhere else, for example. And the world's second smallest bird, the vervain hummingbird, or *zumbadorcito*, flits through the forest. Trails lead from the Estación Cazabito ranger station (1.5 miles (2.4 km) north of Carretera 12, the Banoa-Constanza highway) to the Fernando Domínguez Visitors Center, and from there through the reserve, which attains 5,135 feet (1,565 m) elevation atop Loma La Golondrina.

SALTO DE BAIGUATE

Signed off the Jarabacoa-Constanza road, 1 mile (1.6 km) N of the Shell gas station (Calle del Carmen and Calle Deligne).

Open: 24 hours (nighttime visits are unsafe).

Admission: Free.

A lovely setting awaits at the base of the staircase that leads to this spectacular waterfall 4 miles (6.4 km) from Jarabacoa. Bring your swimwear for cooling swims in the large jade-colored pool, popular with local families.

Day Two: Climbing steeply, you'll pass through forests of *Palo de cotorra* (parrot tree), West Indian laurel, and sierra palm to a rest area at La Cotorra, named for the Hispaniola parrots commonly seen here. The trail next ascends through cloud forest (of wild avocado, West Indian sumac, and effusive tree ferns) to a ridgeline and a freshwater spring (boil the water or use chlorine tablets) at the La Laguna rest area (6,900 feet/2100m). A steep 3-mile-long (5 km) climb brings you to an intersection; the Sendero Aguita Fría (Cold Stream Trail) to the right ascends to Pico Duarte, that to the left descends to the picturesque Valle Tetero, which has Taíno petroglyphs. From here, the Pico Duarte trail eases up as it follows a natural ridgeline and passes through a marshy area—Aguita Fría—that is the headwaters of the Yaque del Norte and Yaque del Sur, the nation's two longest rivers, at about 8,500 feet (2,600 m). Beyond, you'll descend along the ridgeline, arriving after another 2 miles (3 km) at La Compartición, where most hikers overnight in huts. The views down over the pine-clad mountains are superb.

Day Three: You must rise before dawn to make the summit before clouds set in. Skirting the summit of Pico La Rucilla (9,990 feet/3,045 m), the ridgeline trail switchbacks through pine forests to Vallecito de Lilis (Valley of Lilies), an open meadow named for the flowers that grow here. Beyond, the vegetation thins out as the trail climbs through bare rock terrain to the barren summit. After enjoying the stupendous view, return to La Compartición for breakfast. From here, you can descend to La Ciénaga before sunset.

Alternate Routes: You can also set out to hike Pico Duarte from Mata Grande, on the north side of the mountain (28 miles/45 km). From the south side, arduous trails begin at Arroyo Cano, north of Guanito, on Carretera 2 (8 miles/12 km); at Los Ingenitos, on the north side of Embalse de Sabaneta, north of San Juan de la Maguana (17 miles/27 km); and at Las Lagunas, northeast of Padre Las Casas (12 miles/20 km).

Organized Tours: You can book with organized group tours offered by **Iguana Mama** (809-571-0908; www.iguanamama.com), in Cabarete; and **Rancho Baiguate** (809-574-6890; www.ranchobaiguate.com), in Jarabacoa.

SALTOS DE JIMENOA
Sabanete, 3 miles (4.8 km) SE of Jarabacoa
Open: Daily 8:30 AM–7 PM
Admission: R$25

Tumbling 21 feet (14 m) into a jade-colored pool, the **Salto de Jimenoa** (sometimes called Salto de Jimenoa Uno) cascade is the closest to town of three local waterfalls. There's parking above the HEP station, where a paved track with narrow suspension bridges leads to the falls via a boulder-strewn ravine.

It's a daunting clamber over a steep and slippery and rocky trail (a guide is compulsory; you can hire one by the entrance; RD$200 for up to six people) to reach the even more sensational **Salto de Jimenoa Alto** (Salto de Jimenoa Dos), which featured as a setting in *Jurassic Park*. This cascade plunges 197 feet (60 m) from a hidden lake above the forest-shrouded rim, creating rainbows over the pool at its base. A safer route is to drive 4 miles (6.4 km) along the Constanza road to El Salto de Jimenoa, where a trail *descends* to the falls. Here, the local **Proyecto Ecoturístico Comunitario El Gran Salto** (809-541-1430; Fax: 809-683-2611) offers guided waterfall tours.

Tour operators in Jarabacoa offer trips to the falls; see Activity Centers, below.

Good to Know About

Tourism Office—Oficina de la Secretaría de Turismo (809-574-7287; Fax: 809-574-2787;
Calle Mario Galán between Duarte and Calle del Carmen). The minimally stocked
tourism office is upstairs in Plaza Ramírez, open Mon. through Fri. 8–6.

CONSTANZA AND VICINITY

Arriving in Constanza causes a double take. Squat on the floor of a broad mountain valley at
3,940 feet (1,200 m), this agricultural town enjoys a quintessential alpine setting. A kind of
tropical Shangri-La. The broad vale—supposedly caused by a meteor strike millennia ago—
is the nation's breadbasket, quilted with fields growing fresh vegetables, strawberries, garlic, and flowers. It makes a great base for hiking and horseback rides, and for 4WD
explorations of the Cordillera Central, including into the **Valle de Culata**, where you can
explore caves with Taíno pictographs.

Famously, some 900 farmers from the Japanese island of Kyushu settled outside town in
1955 as part of an effort sponsored by Rafael Trujillo to kick-start the vegetable and fruit
industry here. (Most settlers found the conditions too harsh and returned to Japan.) There
are still hints of their presence at **Colonia Japonesa**, today an impoverished settlement
about 1 mile (1.6 km) south of town. A few traditional Japanese-style homes remain,
though discreetly tucked behind walls.

Other sites in town are few. The peaceful **Parque Central** (Calle Salomé Ureña corner
Miguel Abreu) is a lovely spot to relax and watch the to-ings and fro-ings. Note the busts of
La Trinitaria— the republic's three national heroes—in triangular **Plazoleta de los Héroes,**
at the east entrance to town. And the **Fortaleza Patria** (Calle Gaston Deligne and Padre
Billini) is a vision of Beaux Arts, with its crenellated, medieval-style walls. A bronze statue
of General Luperón on horseback stands outside.

Getting There

Constanza's **14 de Junio National Airport** is served from Santo Domingo and Santiago de
los Caballeros by Air Century, which also links Constanza with Barahona and Puerto Plata.

Guaguas serve Constanza from Bonao and Jarabacoa. The road from Jarabacoa is
superbly scenic.

If driving, a sedan is sufficient for the paved (but potholed) Carretera 12 from Bonao.
However, you'll need a 4WD vehicle to tackle the rugged road from Jarabacoa; and for the
truly formidable—yet spectacularly scenic—track (Ruta 41) that connects Constanza with
San José de Ocoa via Parque Nacional Valle Nuevo. The latter is one of the most beautiful
drives in the country, peaking—literally and metaphorically—at 8,330 feet (2,525 m) just
north of the windswept potato-farming hamlet of La Nuez, the highest community in the
nation; in October 2008, the government announced that it would repair and pave the road,
but don't hold your breath.

Lodging

HOTEL ALTO CERRO

809-539-1553
Fax: 809-530-6193

www.altocerro.com
Calle Guarocuya 461

Hillside hotel with a choice of 10 modestly appointed rooms and 30 self-catering apartments, the latter with cable TV. You can pitch tent (or rent a tent) in a tree-shaded lawn. The restaurant has indoor and outdoor dining; the menu includes fowl, the hotel's specialty. It offers horseback riding. $$

HOTEL EXQUISITESES DILENIA

809-539-2213
Calle Gaston F. Feligne 7

My favorite place in Constanza, if only because of its wonderful restaurant. This small, family-run hotel in the heart of town (yet tucked up a quiet side lane) has seven simply furnished rooms, all with cable TVs and modern hot water bathrooms. $–$$

MI CABAÑA RESORT

809-539-2930
www.micabana.bizland.com
Colonia Japonesa

This modern resort has rooms, suites, and self-catering villas in two-storey units around a pool courtyard. Rooms are comfy enough, and have plenty of toiletries, and the suites are nicely furnished and have impressive modern bathrooms. All have cable TV. Swimming pool. $$

RANCHO GUARAGUAO

809-508-3333
Fax: 809-508-1212
www.ranchoguaraguao.com
Las Neblinas de Constanza, 4 miles (6.4 km) E of Constanza

A rustic yet homey hillside resort with lovely views across the valley. Popular with Dominican families, it serves as an activity center and has 30 cabins in four variations. All have cable TVs and kitchenettes or kitchens; some have fireplaces. You can camp. Facilities include a swimming pool, Jacuzzi, restaurant, and games room with pool tables and even a mechanical bull. $$–$$$

VILLA PAJON

809-412-5210
www.villapajon.com
Parque Nacional Valle Nuevo, 5 miles (8 km) W of Valle Nuevo

What a fantastic setting! This rustic alpine resort (formerly a sawmill and, later, a flower farm) in an alpine meadow thick with blackberries is surrounded by pine forest, all within the park at 7,500 feet (2,286 m) elevation. You can enjoy views of Pico Duarte from the cozy one- to three-bedroom self-catering log cabins, which have fireplaces and kitchens (bring your own food and supplies). A cook can be arranged, as can ATV tours and horseback riding. $$

Dining

EXQUISITESES DILENIA
809-539-2213
Calle Gaston F. Feligne 7

One of the republic's most endearing and rustic restaurants, the country-style restaurant of rough-hewn timbers serves genuine country fare. Here, Owner-chef Dilenia de la Rosa Durán takes pride in preparing such dishes as stewed goat in red wine, and rabbit and guinea fowl dishes. The patio is a good spot for watching hummingbirds. Open: Daily 11–11

Attractions, Parks, and Recreation

Rancho Guaraguao (809-508-3333; www.ranchoguaraguao.com; Las Neblinas de Constanza) This activity center offers ATV adventures, horseback rides, and mountain biking. It has a climbing wall.

Salto Aguas Blancas (El Convento, 8 miles (12.8 km) SE of Constanza) A mini Yosemite in the tropics, this three-stage cascade plummets 285 feet (87 m) into a jade-colored pool with frigid waters. Go ahead, take a plunge! There's a mirador and small restaurant. On my last visit, the 4WD-only track from the main road to the falls was dauntingly narrow—more like a goat track hanging on the mountainside. The alpine scenery en route makes the journey worthwhile.

PARQUE NACIONAL VALLE NUEVO
No telephone (Valle Nuevo); 809-472-4204 ext. 223 (Santo Domingo)
10 miles (16 km) S of Constanza; 36 miles (57.6 km) N of San José de la Ocoa
Admission: Free

Officially called Parque Nacional Juan B. Pérez Rancier and measuring 351 square miles (910 sq km), Valle Nuevo protects one of the most beautiful mountain zones in the republic. Anyone familiar with the Sierras of California, or even the Rockies of Colorado, will sense a certain déjà vu amid the moss-draped pine forests and alpine meadows—home to rabbits, deer, and 66 bird species, including such endemics as the Hispaniolan trogon, gray-headed quail dove, and Antillean siskin. There's even a tiny endemic freshwater crab!

Old logging trails grant birders and hikers a sublime experience. You can even follow a track to the summit of Pico Alto de la Bandera (9,379 feet/2,842 m), the fourth highest peak in the republic, pinned by 14 telecommunications towers.

Getting There: Flatbed pickup trucks serve as *guaguas* (buses) that connect the remote mountain hamlets outside the park boundaries; wear warm clothing, and be sure to have rainproof gear, and expect to share your usually overloaded ride with pigs and fowl!

A single—and *very* challenging—dirt-and-rock road traverses the park, linking Constanza with San José de Ocoa. Often you seem to be hanging on a ridge top precipice by a hair's-breadth; at other times, you cringe as you bottom out your vehicle on huge rocks and gullies. Travel with warm clothing and plenty of food and water in case you get stuck or have a breakdown.

Accommodation and Services: The ranger station is within the park at **Valle Nuevo**, 22 miles (30 km) south of Constanza and 36 miles (59 km) north of San José de Ocoa. You can camp here; most campers tend to pitch their tents in eight wooden shacks for rent. There are two outhouses, plus a makeshift *colmado* (mini-grocery). It's a lovely setting amid wildflowers and boulders at about 7,250 feet (2,200 m), on a plateau that was covered by a glacier during the Pleistocene era.

Also see Villa Pajon, in the Lodging section above.

Sites: The exact central point of Hispaniola is marked by a large pyramid—the **Pirámide Ciclópea** (colloquially called Las Pirámides), which stands in an alpine meadow in the Valle de los Frailes (Valley of Monks), 10 miles (16 km) south of Valle Nuevo. Erected in the 1950s in honor of Trujillo, who built a summer home nearby, the pyramid is named in the plural because it comprises four separate pyramidal segments that form a unified whole.

Former Dominican President Francisco Camaaño Deñó (1932–73) was executed at a spot 3 miles (4.8 km) north of Las Pirámides on February 16, 1973. Camaaño was ousted by a U.S. military invasion in 1965 that sought to end a civil war and topple Camaaño's left-leaning Constitucionalista government. He was replaced by Joaquín Balaguer Ricardo, a strongman protegé of brutal Dictator Rafael Trujillo. After secret exile in Cuba, Camaaño returned to the Dominican Republic in 1973, accompanied by guerrillas intent on inspiring a popular uprising against Balaguer. Instead, he was captured and killed in an alpine meadow, where his grave and a flagpole comprise the **Monumento a Francisco Camaaño**.

Food Purveyors

The lively **farmers' market** (Calle Enriquillo between Rufino Espino and Gratereaux) is a great place to buy fresh produce.

Good to Know About

Tourism Office—Oficina de la Secretaría de Turismo (809-539-2900; Fax: 809-539-2900; Calle Matilda Viña 18 and Calle Miguel Andrés Abreu). The minimally stocked tourism office is open Mon. through Fri. 8–6.

9

Barahona
and the Southwest

Mountain Highs, Valley Lows

The nation's southwest quarter is distinct in many regards. First, much of the zone lies in a rain-shadow, with parched dry forest and even cactus studding the landscape. The farther west you go the drier (and hotter), in general, the land becomes. In summer, the lowland vale known as Hoya de Enriquillo, at 115 feet (35 m) below sea level, can broil in temperatures well above 100 degrees F (38 degrees C). But don't think this means that the region is depauperate in flora and fauna. In fact, its main strength is its wealth of wildlife, easily seen in national parks that take up huge swaths of the region. Semi-arid dry forests lie in the lee of mist-shrouded mountains—the Sierra de Neiba and Sierra de Bahoruco (running east-west, south of and parallel to the Cordillera Central)—that are considered the prime birding spots in the country.

There's a good reason why the Dominican tourist board is promoting the region as eco-tourism central, and why much of the region—the most biologically diverse part of Hispaniola—is enshrined in national parks. More endemic bird species are found in the thickly forested mountains (with their lush epiphytes and precious orchids) of the southwest than any other part of Hispaniola. Betwixt the Sierra de Neiba and Sierra de Bahoruco, the saline waters of Lago Enriquillo teem with crocodile, and with flocks of flamingoes that feed on brine in the soupy lagoons. Iguanas are numerous, too, appearing as parched as the ground they walk on. Flamingoes are also a draw at Laguna Oviedo, a jade-colored lake that is a jewel of Parque Nacional Jaragua, known too for its sugar-white beaches where marine turtles crawl ashore to lay eggs. Together the three parks make up Jaragua-Bahoruco-Enriquillo Biosphere Reserve, covering 1,930 square miles (almost 500,000 hectares).

Although economically poor, the region is rich in Taíno rupestrine art and ceremonial sites; and with fertile soils that feed fruits such as melons and mangos in the well-watered Valle de San Juan, north of the Sierra de Neiba. Eclectic one-of-a-kind sites include Polo Magnético (a visual apparition) and the Minas de Larimar (larimar mines). Meanwhile, the coastal drive along the wave-bashed shore of the Peninsula de Bahoruco is justifiably an official Ruta Panorámica—in fact, to my mind it's the most awesome scenic drive in the country.

Getting There

You can fly into **Aeropuerto María Montéz**, Barahona (809-524-4144) with **Aero Domca** (809-826-4141; www.aerodomca.com).

Carretera 2 (Carretera Sánchez) connects Santo Domingo to the Southwest via Baní (see the South Central chapter) and the town of Azua de Compostela, gateway to the region; Azua occupies a narrow coastal corridor barely 5 miles (8 km) wide, pinched between the towering Cordillera Central and the Caribbean Sea. West of Azua the road divides. From El Cruce, where the highway splits, Carretera 2 continues northwest through the ruler-straight Valle de San Juan via the town of San Juan de la Maguana; Carretera 44 runs south through the city of Barahona and, beyond, as a Vía Panorámica to Parque Nacional Jaragua and Pedernales, a border town on the Haitian border. Just west of Barahona, a loop road (Carretera 48) leads around Lago Enriquillo.

Caribe Tours (809-221-4422; www.caribetours.com.do) operates bus service from Santo Domingo to Azua at eight times daily (6:15 AM–5:30 PM); to Barahona at 6:15 AM, 9:45 AM, 1:45 PM, and 5:15 PM; and to San Juan de la Maguana at 6:30 AM, 10:15 AM, 2 PM, and 5:30 PM.

Terra Bus (809-531-0383) connects Santo Domingo with Jimani (in the Valle de Nieba) and on to Port-au-Prince, Haiti ($40).

AZUA DE COMPOSTELA

Gateway to the southwest, this bustling town of 90,000 inhabitants, 35 miles (56 km) west of Baní, bears few reminders of its early importance. The original settlement—Puerto Viejo—was founded 11 miles (18 km) southwest of today's Azua in 1504 by conquistador Diego Velásquez de Cuellar, who arrived with Columbus's second voyage and later became governor of Cuba. Juan Ponce de León and Hernán Cortés also lived here before departing for greater glory as conquerors of Puerto Rico and the Aztecs, respectively. Puerto Viejo was an important port and rivaled Santo Domingo. Alas, the port town was destroyed by an earthquake in 1751 and abandoned in favor of a new site (today's Azua de Compostela). Foundations and other scant remains of the settlement still stand by the shore at **Puerto Viejo de Azua**, today an industrial port.

For better or worse, Azua occupied the narrowest point of the coastal plain and was a vital strategic location during the incessant 19th-century wars with Haiti. Thus, the town founded in 1752 was set ablaze by Haitian armies in 1804, 1844, and 1849. Every year, locals honor with a parade the victory here against Haitians on March 19, 1844 during the war of independence, when 2,200 Dominican troops under General Pedro Santana defeated 10,000 Haitian troops led by General Souffrand.

Attractions, Parks, and Recreation

While a few aged and quaintly colorful wooden homes remain, today's city has a modern commercial cast and Azua is mostly a place to pass through en route to other locales. In town the sole sites of fleeting interest include tree-shaded **Parque Central** (Calles Duarte and Colón), featuring a neoclassical town hall and pretty church; and, two blocks west, **Plaza 19 de Marzo** , dedicated to honoring the victory over the Haitian invasion forces in 1844 with cannon and a black marble monument.

Parque Duarte, San Juan de la Maguana

Wildlife and Wilderness Regions
PARQUE NACIONAL SIERRA MARTÍN GARCÍA

c/o 809-472-4204 ext. 223
Loma El Curro, Barahona

This rugged, mountainous 103 square-mile (268 sq km) national park, midway between Azua and Barahona, protects four distinct terrestrial ecosystems (from subtropical dry forest to low montane rain forest) plus coastal margins and waters of the Bay of Neiba. The shoreline and lagoons are fringed by four species of mangroves. Inland, endangered rhinoceros iguanas and Dominican boas—2 of 25 reptile species here—plod and slither about the dry forest at the base of a rugged limestone massif that rises sheer from the cape (Punta Martín García) and attains a cool 4,406 feet (1,343 m) atop Alto de la Bandera. Cacti stud the lowlands. Waterfowl are among the 67 bird species, which include 11 endemics, such as the Hispaniolan trogon, Hispaniolan woodpecker, and the Antillean euphonia.

The easiest access is from the impoverished hamlet of Barrera, 6 miles (9.6 km) southwest of Puerto Viejo de Azua, from where a dirt track leads to caves once used by Taíno. It is best to go with a guide, as there is no tourist infrastructure and this is tough terrain.

Catedral San Juan Bautista, San Juan de la Maguana

Weekly and Annual Events

Fiesta Patriótica de la Batalla de Azua del 19 de Marzo (March 19). A Mass followed by a military parade and public displays of patriotic fervor in celebration of the Dominican Republic's victory over Haiti at Azua in 1844.

VALLE DE SAN JUAN

The broad, flat, relatively featureless off-the-beaten-path valley of San Juan—referred to colloquially as El Valle—extends northwest from El Cruce between the Cordillera Central and the Sierra de Bahoruco. Rivers flooding down from the mountains have deposited thick soils, and the fertile vale is an important center for cultivation of rice, corn, and beans.

Carretera Sánchez (Carretera 2) runs ruler-straight through the valley via San Juan de la Maguana and Las Matas de Farfán, and extends into Haiti via the border town of Comendador and the checkpoint at Elías Piña, 90 miles (145 km) west of Azua.

The main town is **San Juan de la Maguana** (named partly for St. John the Baptist, and partly for the local pre-Columbian Taíno tribe—the Maguana), in the heart of the valley. Today a pleasant and prosperous city, it established itself as an important center of agriculture (notably sugarcane) in the three centuries following its founding by Diego Velázquez de Cuellar in 1508. Alas, the vale is the main conduit between Haiti and the Dominican Republic, and San Juan suffered mightily at the hands of invading armies during the 19th-century wars of independence. Ironically, Haitians have settled in increasing numbers in recent decades, bringing their voodoo religious beliefs with them. Hence, San Juan is colloquially called *Ciudad de las Brujas*—City of Witches.

The vale is an access point for hikes to the summit of Pico Turquino, and into Parque Nacional José del Carmen Ramírez and other remote southern sections of the Cordillera Central; and for exploring the thickly forested Sierra de Neiba—a Nirvana for birders.

Lodging and Dining

HOTEL MAGUANA
809-557-2244
Fax: 809-557-2040
Avenida Independencia 72, San Juan de la Maguana

This government-run hotel is the nicest place for miles. Formerly one of Rafael Trujillo's mansions (it was built just for his visit to San Juan), it has been restored and modestly furnished. Its 41 rather gloomy rooms enclose an atrium courtyard and have private bathrooms with hot showers; the largest and best room is the Trujillo Suite. The wood-paneled restaurant with bar features an eclectic menu, ranging from burgers to pastas and local favorites, such as guinea fowl in red wine. $$

LA GALERÍA DEL ESPÍA
809-557-5069
Calle Independencia 7, San Juan de la Maguana
Open: 11 AM–4:30 PM; 6:30 PM–midnight

Specializing in *criolla* and Mexican food, this popular café, restaurant, and karaoke bar is by far the most colorful place in town to eat. It serves filling and deliciously spicy white flour or maize flour tortillas, burritos, and tacos.

Attractions, Parks, and Recreation

Parks and Plazas

San Juan de la Maguana is one of the Dominican Republic's prettiest provincial towns at its core. An **Arco de Triunfo** (modeled on Paris's own Arc de Triomphe) stands over the eastern entrance to town. To its west, **Parque Duarte** is pinned by a statue of the national hero, who stands in front of the Modernist **Palacio de Justicia** and the neo-classical **Palacio Ayuntamiento** (town hall). **Parque Central** (Avenida Independencia and Duarte), the town's main square, is dominated by a stunning pink and green confection—**Catedral San Juan Bautista** (809-557-4823)—completed in 1958. Of eclectic design, it's topped by a fanciful wedding-cake dome.

Miscellaneous Sites

Presa de Sebana Yegua, 15 miles (25 km) east of San Juan, is a huge reservoir in the foothills of the Cordillera Central. It draws anglers who cast for tilapia and American bass. The mountain backdrop adds a note of drama. A military post guards the dam but you can request permission to enter. A trailhead to the summit of Pico Duarte begins in the hamlet of **La Loma del Yaque**, at the far north end of the lake.

Even more impressive is **Presa de Sabaneta**, another huge reservoir formed by a spectacular dam at Sabaneta, 30 miles/50 km north of San Juan de la Maguana. Another trailhead for Pico Duarte begins here (it's a challenging five-day hike to the summit). Much easier is a short hike to **Las Cuevas de Seboruco**—caves featuring pre-Taíno pictographs.

Monuments
EL CORRAL DE LOS INDIOS
Juan de Herrera, 4 miles (7 km) N of San Juan

Many of the tourists passing through San Juan do so to visit **El Corral de los Indios**, a well-preserved circular *bateye*—a ball court where the Taíno played a rough game akin to rugby—dating back more than 1,000 years. The Taíno ceremonial site is ringed by a stone pavement with a diameter of 150 yards (137 m). Goats nibble the grassy center, where a stone slab features petroglyphs of a mystical figure. Faint remains of paved road at least 0.6 mile (1 km) long reach toward the San Juan River.

This tropical Stonehenge was the site of a large Taíno settlement at the time of Columbus's arrival, when the area was ruled by Anacaona, wife of the cacique Caonabo. Anacaona attempted cordial relations with the Spanish invaders. However, the latter were not on a holy mission. In 1503, the cruel governor Nicolas de Ovando elected to rid the isle of Taíno chieftains. Arriving in Anacaona's dominion of Xaragua, Ovando invited Anacaona and fellow caciques to a feast where they were given wine until drunk, and then slaughtered. Anacaona was spared, only to be burned alive some time later.

Wildlife and Wilderness Parks
PARQUE NACIONAL SIERRA DE NEIBA
c/o 809-472-4204 ext. 223
Calle San Pedro 10, San Juan

Rising abruptly along the southern perimeter of the Valle de San Juan, the Sierra del Neiba mountain range extends west into Haiti as the Montagnes du Trou d'Eau. The entire Dominican massif is protected within the eponymous 158-square-mile (407 sq km)

El Corral de los Indios

national park, known for its varied habitats, ranging from dry forest at lower elevations to pristine cloud forests above 4,000 feet (1,219 m), and coniferous forests above 6,000 feet (1,829 m). A remarkable 25 percent of plant species on the lower slopes are endemics. The highest point is Monte Nieba (7,477 feet/2,279 m).

The park is renowned as a center for birding: 21 of the island's 22 endemics are found here, including the Hispaniolan parrot, Hispaniolan trogon, and Hispaniolan highland tanager. And the extremely fortunate hiker may spot an elusive and endangered solenodon or hutia.

Only two roads span the park: That from Hondo Valle to La Descubierta is a rugged switchback paralleling the Haitian border; another road begins at El Cercado and climbs via Derrumbadero (site of an old lumber mill) before dropping to the town of Neiba.

There are two formal hiking trails on the south side: A trail near Los Pinos leads through dry forest; and a cloud-forest trail begins near Savannah Real. Mule paths also lace the high mountains.

Ranger stations are located at El Aguacate and Savannah Real (on the south side) and at Hoyazo, on the northern slope.

Caribbean Free Flying (www.caribbeanfreeflying.com) offers paragliding in these mountains.

Liborio—the Peasant Messiah

The Valle de Río San Juan north of San Juan de la Maguana is the setting of a fascinating socio-religious movement that worships Olivorio Liborio Mateo (1876–1922), a messianic faith healer murdered by U.S. troops in 1922. Born to an impoverished family in Maguana Arriba, Olivorio was a young peasant farmer in 1908 when a hurricane swept through the southwest region. When Olivorio disappeared during the storm, his family organized a *novena* (nine days of prayer for the deceased), during which he suddenly reappeared. Olivorio claimed to have been transported to Heaven, where God supposedly entrusted him back to earth with a mission to heal the sick, and grant salvation to anyone who would believe in his mission.

He was welcomed home as an incarnation of Jesus Christ. Suddenly this short, unkempt, and illiterate middle-aged peasant had a following.

Liborismo combined aspects of Christianity (including salvation through a divine emissary) and pagan syncretism (such as quasi-magical healing rituals that make heavy use of *comarca*, Dominican religious dancing music). During the next decade, Liborio became the most important messianic leader of Dominican history. So much so, in fact, that during the U.S. military occupation of 1916–24, the authorities considered him a threat that could galvanize resistance as a guerrilla leader. Fearing for his life, he was forced into hiding. On June 27, 1922, he was ambushed and killed by U.S. Marines. His followers refused to believe he'd been killed. For decades his spirit, so to speak, lingered until eventually, four decades later, two *liborista* priests established a new commune at Palma Sola, north of Las Matas de Farfán. Following a military coup d'etat in January 1962, a right-wing military junta decided to stamp out the subversive movement: On December 28, 1962, the Dominican military used napalm bombs to destroy the commune.

The Liborista movement, however, still thrives around La Maguana (about 10 miles (16 km) north of San Juan de la Maguana). To experience it, follow the dirt road that leads east from La Maguana via Maguana Arriba to **Templo Liborio**. This sacred pilgrimage site is centered on a spring (known locally as Agüita of Liborio) considered to have healing properties. Believers come to be cured at any time, drums are often played, and a pilgrimage of *liboristas* takes place each June 27.

Weekly and Annual Events

Festival de Espíritu Santo, El Batey. This hamlet is the center of veneration of a wooden idol dressed in scarlet trimmed with gold, with two small doves embroidered on the front. Each Pentecost Sunday, Catholic faithful (many barefoot and in yellow and red costumes) make a pilgrimage from El Batey to San Juan de la Maguana. Early June.

Fiesta Patronal, Las Matas de Farfán. Religious procession plus cultural events in honor of the town's patron saint, Santa Lucía. December 13.

Fiesta Patronal, San Juan de la Maguana. A patron saint festival held over two weeks in honor of St. John the Baptist (San Juan Bautista) in June. Culminates on June 24, when locals bathe in a river to cleanse themselves of sin.

Fiesta de San Francisco, Bánica. This border town, 18 miles (28.8 km) northwest of Las Matas de Farfán, hosts a candlelit pilgrimage honoring St. Francis of Assisi, who locals believe lived in a nearby cave at Cerro San Francisco. Pilgrims wear brown (in honor of the saint) and dab their faces with water from the roof of the cave, then smear their faces with dust. September 24 through October 4.

VALLE DE NEIBA

Occupying a huge depression—the Hoyo de Neiba—between the Sierra de Neiba and Sierra de Bahoruco, the Neiba Valley stretches some 80 miles (128 km) inland from the Bahía de Neiba (Bay of Neiba) to the Haitian frontier. The valley once lay below the sea. The ocean strait formerly extended to the Bay of Port-au-Prince and divided Hispaniola into two islands. Tectonic movements about 1 million years ago sealed the channel, creating a huge landlocked saltwater lake—**Lago Enriquillo**. Evaporation has since reduced the lake, which today lies at 131 feet (40 m) below sea level—the lowest point in the Caribbean.

The lake is the rift valley's dominant feature, not least because stretching 21 miles (33.6 km) long and 12 miles (19 km) wide and measuring 100 square miles (259 sq km)—equivalent to Manhattan—it is the largest lake in the Caribbean. It also teems with crocodiles, flamingoes, and other wildlife—reason enough to visit the region.

The Río Yaque del Sur (flowing from the Cordillera Central) and the rivers that flow from the Sierra de Neiba have deposited fertile alluvial soils, and the eastern end of the valley supports a sea of banana and sugar plantations. Conditions grow more arid westward, and the southern shore of the lake is lined with salt pans and reedy marshes.

Gateway to the valley is the agricultural town of **Neiba**, on Carretera 48. The paved highway runs inland of the lake's north shore (alas, for the most part, lake views are hidden by scrub vegetation) via the town of **La Descubierta** as far as down-at-heels **Jimaní**, the principal border town with Haiti. It is worth a visit for its colorful outdoor market of Haitian vendors who arrive on *tap-taps*—brightly painted Haitian buses. Carretera 46 runs along the lake's south shore, linking Jimaní to Barahona (see the Peninsula de Barahona section, below), on the Bahía de Neiba; the desolate road passes through several middling towns beneath the magnificent backdrop of Haiti's Massif la Selle and the Sierra de Bahoruco.

Attractions, Parks, and Recreation

Miscellaneous

A statue of the Taíno cacique Guarocuya—the warrior chieftain whom the Spanish christened Enriquillo and who led resistance (1519–33) against Spanish rule in this region—stands along Carretera 46 in the hamlet of **Enriquillo**, 9 miles (14.4 km) south of Neiba.

LAS CARITAS
Postrer Río, 4 miles (6.4 km) E of La Descubierta

One of the most endearing of attractions in the country, the Little Faces are petroglyphs carved into the walls of a cave by ancient Taíno dwellers. The etchings show simple human faces smiling like the iconic Smiley Face. The cave is hollowed into former coral reefs—**Los Arrecifes de Postrer Río** (the Postrer Rio Reefs)—that contain petrified seashells and corals. Las Caritas is signed roadside about 300 yards (274 m) west of Postrer Río hamlet. The steep trail leads uphill to the cave, which offers a fabulous panorama of the lake.

Wildlife and Wilderness Parks
PARQUE NACIONAL LAGO ENRIQUILLO Y ISLA CABRITOS
c/o 809-472-4204 ext. 223
La Azufrada, 2 miles (3 km) E of La Descubierta
Open: Daily 8–5
Admission: RD$10

Wildlife viewing doesn't always come easy. But this park offers an exception. Encompassing the lake and its three islands—tiny Isla Barbarita and Islita, and the much larger Isla Cabritos—the park was created in 1974 to protect a habitat teeming with animals and birds. The super-saline lake is renowned for its vast population of American crocodiles (estimated at about 5,000 individuals). These reptiles from the antediluvian dawn can grow to 15 feet (4.6 m) long. The easiest place to see them is among the reeds and cool river-fed shoreline waters close to La Descubierta. Morning is the best time, when the crocs haul out to sun themselves (reptiles are cold-blooded and require external heat to warm up).

Migratory waterfowl flock in to join native species, totaling 62 bird species. Roseate spoonbills and greater flamingoes ladle tiny brine shrimp from the soupy waters, while sandpipers, Bahama pintails, Caspian terns, snowy plovers, and green-backed herons pick along the shoreline for tasty tidbits. Caribbean coots are often seen at the west end of the lake. And the republic's endemic and endangered rhinoceros iguanas plod about atop the dusty, sunbaked earth. They're easily seen on 5 mile-long (8 km) **Isla Cabritos** (Goat Island), which rises from the midst of the lake. The park's main **visitor center** is on Isla Cabritos; it has a small museum depicting local ecology, which includes 10 species of cactus.

You can explore the lake and island by boat with an authorized guide from the ranger station at **La Azufrada** (another good place to see iguanas). Boats operated by the **Associa-**

Locals bathing in Balneario Los Patos, Peninsula de Bahoruco

tion of Eco-Tourism Guides of Lago Enriquillo (Asociación de Guías del Lago Enriquillo; 809-816-7441; www.lagoenriquilloguides.com; La Descubierta) depart on 2.5-hour tours at around 7:30 AM and noon, or later, depending on the number of people awaiting a tour (RD$3,500/US$100 for up to 15 people). For best wildlife viewing, take the early morning departures; it's also cooler than midday, which can be broiling. Boats (which have life jackets) are uncovered: bring sunscreen, a shade hat, and plenty of water. And wear shoes that cover your feet, not sandals or flip-flops, as scorpions abound. Most guides speak only elementary English, so don't expect an in-depth David Attenborough spiel.

Back at La Azufrada, you can cool off by plunging into **Las Barias** *balneario* (natural pool), just outside La Descubierta (locals will point the way) or, on the south shore, at **La Zurza**, outside the hamlet of Vengan a Ver, just west of Duvergé, where a jade-blue pool awaits.

RESERVA CIENTÍFICA LAGUNA DE CABRAL

809-618-3045
Carretera Cabral-Peñon, 2 miles (3 km) NW of Cabral; 9 miles (14.4 km) W of Barahona
Open: Daily 8–6
Admission: free; RS$1,000 guided boat trip

This 25 square mile (65 sq km) scientific reserve protects a shallow freshwater lake (also known as Laguna Rincón) and its marshy perimeter. The Río Yaque del Sur feeds the lake, but the southern part of the lake is saline, and halophytic (salt-tolerant) mangroves grow along the edges. Together they're a vital habitat for waterfowl and for endemic and endangered slider turtles, and as a nursery for fish. Flamingoes are present in midsummer months, looking quite at odds with their green surrounds in their bright pink plumage. Ibises are also commonly seen, and northern jacanas, criollo ducks, and Louisiana herons are among the other birds to be seen. Crocodiles migrate to and from Lago Enriquillo in high-water months via the Canal Cristóbal. You can arrange boat trips at the ranger station (at the north end of Cabral), which has a few natural history exhibits plus a short interpretative trail.

Good to Know About

The Ministry of Tourism **tourist information office** (809-248-3042; fax 809-238-3183; Calle 19 de Marzo 38, Jimaní), in the town hall, has a paucity of literature . . . if you're lucky! Open Mon. through Fri. 8–5.

PENINSULA DE BAHORUCO

The shark-tooth-shaped Peninsula de Bahoruco extends south of the Hoyo de Neiba and comprises the Sierra de Bahoruco mountain range and, to its south, a rugged limestone plateau edging down to the sea. The bulk of the thickly forested mountains are protected within Parque Nacional Sierra de Bahoruco, drawing hikers, plus birders keen to spot most of the Dominican Republic's endemic bird species. And the uninhabited limestone plateau, pitted with a dog's-tooth terrain, is covered with a precious remnant of subtropical dry forest enshrined within Parque Nacional Jaragua—blessed with sensational beaches and a jade-colored lake that is the premier flamingo habitat in the nation.

Founded in 1802 by Haitian overlord Toussaint L'Ouverture, the agro-industrial town of

Barahona is the major town of the southwest. It grew to import in the Trujillo years after the dictator turned the flatlands northwest of town into a sea of sugarcane, enriching his personal coffers. Barahona became a sugar-processing town and port on the Bahía de Neiba. It still is: The *central* (sugar-processing factory) produced 60 million tons of sugar in 2008. The town, which enjoys a lovely bay setting at the base of the Sierra de Bahoruco, is famous as the birthplace of María Montez (born María África Gracia Vidal, 1912–51), the exotic beauty who in the 1940s made it big in Hollywood and became known as The Queen of Technicolor.

There are few sites in town, and the beach here is desultory, but Barahona is a good base for exploring the region.

South of Barahona—the gateway to the region—Carretera 44 (Carretera de la Costa Sur) sidles along the shore for 40 miles (64 km) or so before turning west to run along the base of the Sierra de Bahoruco, which thrust hard up against the eastern shoreline. The coast road—an official Vía Panorámica—is a spectacularly scenic roller-coaster drive, with coconut palms waving over snoozy fishing villages and shingly reef-fringed beaches washed by impossible peacock blue ocean waters. In fact, it's by far my favorite drive in the country. The road ends at **Pedernales**, on the Haitian border. The sole reason to visit this lackluster town is for the colorful Haitian market on Mondays and Fridays; or for forays into the Sierra de Bahoruco via a truly rugged dirt-and-rock road that skirts the border and clambers up over the mountain, rising to 6,000 feet (1,829 m) before snaking down to El Naranjo, in the Valle de Neiba.

Lodging

Lodgings concentrate in Barahona and the coast road south of town. Pedernales has meager options, and the few hotels here are often booked solid on weekends and holidays.

APARTOTEL PONTEVEDRA
809-341-8462
www.pontevedracaribe.com
Carretera 44 Km 16, El Arroyo, 9 miles (14.4 km) S of Barahona

This motel-style complex of bungalows slopes down to the shore. Although broad expanses of tarmac detract, palm trees add a sense of lush tropical calm. Furnishings in the 16 rooms are somewhat institutional, yet perfectly adequate for a night or two. It has an open-air restaurant and bar, plus large swimming pool. $–$$

BARAHONA CORALSOL RESORT
809-233-4882
fax: 809-524-3929
www.coralsolresort.com
Carretera 44, Km 21
Sitting on a hillside amid landscaped, albeit unkempt, grounds overlooking a pebbly beach. It has nine thatched two-bedroom cottages with tasteful but simple furnishings, plus ceiling fans and safes. They're served by twin irregular pools and a welcoming thatched restaurant. $$

CASA BONITA TROPICAL LODGE
809-476-5059

fax: 809-565-7310
www.casabonitadr.com
Carretera 44 Km 17, Barahona

One of the premier boutique hotels in the country, this one is unique for being halfway up a mountain, not at the beach. Initially a private villa retreat of politician-lawyer Polibio Díaz, it astounds for its fabulous contemporary design. Redesigned and reopened in 2006 as a luxury hotel, it exudes Caribbean comfort. The 12 guest rooms (6 with king beds) boast modern styling and state-of-the-art comforts, and each has a private deck with lounge chairs, plus gorgeous travertine-clad walk-in showers. An infinity pool seems to hang on the hillside and, together with the wooden sundeck, offers magnificent coastal vistas while all around, the bottle green forest is full of birdsong. Gourmet fare from celebrated Dominican Chef Carlos Estevez focuses on a Caribbean Fusion menu. This is one splurge you won't regret! That said, it's also a bargain. $$$

HOTEL COSTA LARIMAR

809-524-5111
fax: 809-524-7063
www.hotelcostalarimar.com
Avenida Enriquillo 6, Barahona

Barahona city's best hotel rises five storeys over a narrow palm-shaded, gray-sand beach. The somewhat jaded property, a 10-minute walk from the town center, offers older non-air-conditioned and newer air-conditioned accommodations, all with cable TVs and phones; plumbing is iffy—my bathroom delivered cold water only. Its 108 spacious rooms win no prizes but are perfectly adequate for a night or two. A modestly elegant restaurant looks over a large and angular swimming pool with swim-up bar. Kids get their own pool. $$

PLAYAZUL HOTEL-RESTAURANT

809-204-8010
Carretera 44 Km 7, Punta Prieta, 4 miles (6.4 km) S of Barahona

Run by a friendly French family, this tiny and delightful cliff top hotel offers 12 standard rooms and 6 family rooms, all with modest furniture, plus ceiling fans, cable TVs, phones, hot showers, and balconies with rockers. It sits above a cove with a pink-sand beach and the turquoise Caribbean—a lovely breeze-swept setting. There's a swimming pool, and a thatched restaurant serves Dominican and seafood dishes. No credit cards. $–$$

Dining

There are plenty of restaurants in Barahona and along the shoreline south of town, where simple barbecue joints at the many beachside *balnearios* (bathing pools) sell grilled chicken and seafoods.

BRISAS DEL CARIBE

809-524-2794
Carretera Batey Central, Barahona
Cuisine: Seafood and *criolla*

The nicest place to dine in town, this thatched open-air restaurant sits on a rise above the ocean with bay views. It also has a modern, air-conditioned section with bar. The eclectic menu ranges from creole shrimp to chicken curry and chicken cordon bleu. Open: Daily 8 AM–11 PM

RESTAURANTE LOS ROBLES
809-524-1629
Avenida Enriquillo and Avenida Nuestra Señora del Rosario, Barahona
Cuisine: *Criolla*

Where the action is at night. This rambling restaurant on a major junction by the Malecón is a great bet for bargain-priced meals, from burgers and pizza to *criolla* faves such as *mofongo*, goat dishes, and creole shrimp. The back garden has picnic tables and a take-out section. A jukebox pumps out music, and a disco kicks up out back late at night. Open: Daily 9 AM–2 AM

Attractions, Parks, and Recreation

Miscellaneous

Olivier and Marianne Messmer run **Eco-Tours Barahona** (809-243-1190; www.ecotour-repdom.com; Edificio 8 #306, Carretera Enriquillo, Paraíso de Barahona), with ecological tours and treks throughout the region.

MINAS DE LARIMAR
Las Filipinas, 9 miles (14.4 km) W of El Arroyo

Reached via a rugged dirt road requiring a 4WD, these simple pit mines are the source of larimar, the beautiful semi-precious blue stones that go into quintessential Dominican jewelry. This is the sole known source. It's sobering to see the basic and dangerous conditions in which the impoverished miners work (it's the middlemen who make the money), crawling around like ants in the scores of opencast burrows and tunnels that penetrate the mist-shrouded mountainside. Cave-ins are common and deaths are frequent, including from asphyxiation. Entering is not recommended and is at your own risk. Two cooperatives work the mines.

The turn-off from the coast highway is 100 yards (91 m) south of Apartotel Puntavedra and is signed for Las Filipinas.

Larimar
Found only in the Sierra Bahoruco, and nowhere else on earth, this lovely light blue rock is a totally unique crystalline mineral—sodium calcium silicate hydroxide—whose chemical and structural composition gives this semi-precious gemstone its translucent color, varying from whitish robin's-egg blue to deep blue, often streaked with white, gray, brown, or red. It is often mistaken for turquoise. Larimar (also known as dolphin stone) is a form of pectolite, a secondary rock of volcanic origin, formed during the Miocene era by volcanic intrusions in the limestone seabed. Vertical veins of super-hot lava absorbed calcium and other minerals before cooling and crystallizing. Dominicans attribute metaphysical properties to larimar, which is valued according to color and purity.

Wildlife and Wilderness Parks
PARQUE NACIONAL JARAGUA
809-520-5895 or 472-4204 ext. 223 (radio)
El Cajuil, 46 miles (75 km) S of Barahona
Open: 8:30 AM–4:30 PM
Admission: RD$50

A mosaic protecting 12 distinct habitats, including dry forest, wetlands, and a pristine shoreline, this 530-square-mile (1,374 sq km) park—the nation's largest—encompasses the shark's-tooth-shaped tip of the Peninsula Bahoruco and marine waters up to 15 miles (24 km) out to sea. The park is an ecotourist's dream for its magnificent flora and fauna, much of it endemic to the region or even the park itself.

The peninsula comprises a series of raised marine terraces, denuded over millennia to form knife-sharp limestone terrain called dogs' tooth, covered with thorn scrub and cactus, including many endemic plant species. Hutia and the endangered Pinocchio-nosed, long-legged solenodon survive in this inhospitable terrain, where meter-long rhinoceros iguana and the critically endangered Ricord's iguana (endemic to Jaragua) munch on prickly pear cactus. Smaller lizards abound—a veritable larder for the endemic Hispaniolan tree snake. And 11 bat species have been recorded. Offshore, vast meadows of sea grass support large populations of queen conch and spiny lobster, as well as the endangered West Indian manatee. Juvenile green turtles and hawksbills also abound in the sea grass meadows and around Jaragua's pristine coral reefs.

Most of the park is inaccessible except for Laguna de Oviedo, in the northeast; Bahía de las Aguilas, at the extreme west; and **Fondo Paradí**, a designated bird-watching site (good for such endemic species as the Hispaniolan parakeet, Hispaniolan woodpecker, and Greater Antillean bullfinch) amid dry deciduous forest festooned with epiphytes, accessed by trail 2.5 miles (4 km) from the roadside community of Los Tres Charcos.

Laguna Oviedo: The park, which is named after a Taíno cacique, Xaraguá, was initially created in 1983 to protect the seasonal flamingo population (the republic's largest) of Laguna Oviedo, which is separated from the sea by a sandy spit. Main entry point to the park, this 6-mile-long (9.6 km) saltwater lake is just off Carretera 44, at El Cajuil, which has a **visitors center** and *mirador* (lookout tower). The jade green lake is one of the prime birding spots in the country. Roseate spoonbills, ibises, terns, and various species of heron are among the more than 130 other bird species (76 are residents, 47 are migratory, and 10 are endemics) that frequent the lake and mangroves. The huge breeding colony of white-crowned pigeon is the largest in the Caribbean. And some 20,000 waterfowl flock annually, including the West Indian whistling duck.

You can hike the lake perimeter with a compulsory guide (RD$500); or take a two-hour boat tour (RD$2,000 with gasoline, up to five people) that typically includes a visit to Cueva Mongó, containing pre-Columbian pictographs.

The Oviedo visitor center has four rustic cabins.

Bahía de las Aguilas: The remote and serene Bay of Eagles lines the western edge of the peninsula and is renowned for its 5-mile-long (8 km) sliver of sugar white sand dissolving into larimar blue ocean waters. The beach is a prime nesting spot for hawksbill and leatherback turtles. Supposedly the offshore waters of Jaragua support the greatest density of hawksbill turtles in the world; fortunately, the other nesting beaches in the park are off-limits to humans. Inland of the beach is semi-arid terrain that attracts thousands of migratory birds. In February 2006, a presidential decree freed Bahía de las Aguilas for tourist development, bowing to pressure from hotel groups; development here has been a hot potato issue and previous efforts to permit hotel construction have been scrapped following public outcry.

Getting There: Bahía de las Aguilas is reached off Carretera 44; the turn-off is 7 miles (11 km) east of Pedernales. It's a flat, dusty drive past the Cabo Rojo bauxite mine and processing plant to the park entrance (RD$50) at the impoverished fishing community of **Las Cuevas**. Beyond the entrance station 1 mile (1.6 km), you'll arrive at a cliff top cactus garden with trails and a *mirador* offering fabulous views over the bay. From here, you'll need a sturdy 4WD vehicle to tackle the dauntingly rugged track that descends sharply to the beach through a rocky canyon. Note that it's easy for your vehicle to get bogged down in the sandy track that parallels the beach.

Alternately, you can hire a boat and skipper at Las Cuevas (RD$1,500 round-trip for up to five people); it's a 15-minute ride in each direction.

Lodging and Dining: You can camp (free) at Bahía de las Aguilas, which has no services. Bring all food, water, and camping gear. The residents of Las Cuevas have turned several cliff-face caves into *parrilladas* (grills) serving fresh-grilled fish and lobster; typically for about RD$80–100; and the humble Ranchito Las Cuevas restaurant also has more varied fare, such seafood *criolla* (in tomato sauce), and *ajillo* (in garlic sauce).

Jeep at Bahia de la Aguilas, Parque Nacional Jaragua

Isla Beata and Alto Viejo: Seeming to float on the horizon south of the mainland, these two scrub-covered islands—3 miles (4.8 km) and 13 miles (20.8 km) offshore, respectively—and their satellite coral cays—**Los Frailes** and **Piedra Negra**—are important nesting sites for seabirds, including brown pelicans, frigate birds, and brown and red-footed boobies. Alto Viejo is also the Caribbean's premier nesting site for sooty terns (80,000 pairs). And in 1998, the world's smallest lizard was discovered on Isla Beata; the endemic gecko is just 2/3 of an inch long (small enough to curl up on a dime) and is also the world's smallest terrestrial vertebrate.

These islands require a permit to visit: You can request one from the Jaragua ranger stations, or from the **Dirección Nacional de Parques** (809-472-4204; www.medioambiente.gov.do; Avenida Reyes Católicos and Avenida Máximo Gómez, Santo Domingo). You can then hire a skipper in Las Cuevas or Oviedo for the bumpy hour-long ride, accompanied perhaps by bottlenose dolphins, which are frequently sighted around Alto Velo.

Guides and Guided Tours: You can hire guides through the local **Asociación de Guías de Naturaleza de Pedernales** (Pedernales Nature Guides Association; 809-771-9120; Calle Segunda, Barrio Alcoa, Pedernales); and through **Grupo Jaragua** (809-472-1036; www.grupojaragua.org.do; Calle Paseo Mondesí 4, Oviedo).

Tody Tours (809-686-0882; www.todytours.com; Calle José Gabriel García 105, Zona Colonial, Santo Domingo) offers guided birding tours led by company owner and expert ornithologist Kate Wallace, a former U.S. Peace Corps volunteer.

PARQUE NACIONAL SIERRA DE BAHORUCO
809-515-0484
Calle 141, Puerto Escondido
Open: Tues. through Sun. 9–4:30
Admission: RD$50

Rising south of the Valle de Neiba, at the extreme southwest of the country, the heavily forested Bahoruco mountains extend west into Haiti as the Massif de Selle. On the Dominican side the mountains rise westward to 7,811 feet (2,367 m) atop Lomo del Toro. This wild and rugged terrain harbored Taíno leader Enriquillo's rebel forces during their guerrilla war (1519–33) against the Spanish. Little has changed in the interim.

The park, created in 1983, protects 310 square miles (800 sq km) of virtually undisturbed forests. Below, cactus stud lowland dry forests. Higher up the habitats meld into broad-leafed subtropical montane forest; above that into pine forest. The north-facing slopes differ markedly from the drier south-facing slopes. Regardless of aspect, the sierras are particularly rich in orchids: The 166 identified species (20 percent of these endemic to these mountains) represent 52 percent of the orchid species in the republic.

Access: The easiest access is from the south side, via Carretera 44; a turnoff (opposite the turnoff south to Bahía de las Aguilas) 7 miles (11 km) east of Pedernales leads uphill via the superbly scenic and paved **Vía Panorámica El Aceitillar** to a *centro de control* entrance gate (pay your RD$50 here) and, beyond, the ranger station at El Aceitillar. From here, a dirt road leads 4.5 miles (7 km) to **Hoyo de Pelempito** (6,335 feet/1,931 m), with a visitor center and 360-degree lookout.

Access from the north is via the town of Duvergé (pronounced doo-ver-HEY in Spanish) on Carretera 46, where a yellow and green Parques Nacionales sign points the way to the park via a dirt road to the foothills hamlet of Puerto Escondido; pay your RD$50 entrance fee at the ranger station here. Trails begin here, including the **Sendero Sierra Bahoruco** trail, which connects to El Aceitillar and can be driven by 4WD vehicle by advance permit from the Secretario de Estado de Medio Ambiente, in Santo Domingo.

From Puerto Escondido, you can also drive via El Naranjo and turn south for the remote border post of **El Aguacate** and the isolated **Loma del Toro** ranger station, from where you can continue south for Pedernales. This rocky and badly eroded mountain track paralleling the Haitian border is more fitting for mules than vehicles, and I barely managed it (scraping bottom now and again) in a 4WD in 2007.

Sendero Quisqueya, a ridge top trail, runs the length of the park, connecting Hoyo de Pelempito to El Aguacate and Haiti.

Birding: Notwithstanding limited amenities for tourists, the park is extremely popular with birders (but is otherwise one of the least-visited parks in the country). The park boasts more than 150 species including, uniquely, all but one (the Ridgeway hawk) of the Dominican Republic's 22 endemic species. The diverse habitats draw more than one hundred other resident and migratory species.

What can you hope to see? Well, the dry forests are a great place to spy the endemic bay-breasted cuckoo, Antillean piculet, and flat-billed vireo. Higher up, the cloud forests are a rare habitat of the even rarer La Selle thrush. Look, too, for the endemic Hispaniolan crossbill and Antillean siskin in the pine forests festooned with Spanish moss. One of the best birding sites is **La Charca**, a lagoon 3 miles (4.8 km) south of El Aceitillar; it's a short hike from the road.

Seeing these birds takes a keen eye and a sound understanding of the very limited locations in which many of these endemics can be spotted. Go with a guide or guided tour.

Recommended birding guides include Steve Brauning (stevebrauning@yahoo.com) and Miguel A. Landestoy (mango_land@yahoo.com); and Kate Wallace, a former U.S. Peace Corps volunteer who now operates **Tody Tours** (809-686-0882; www.todytours.com), specializing in individualized birding tours in the Dominican Republic.

Accommodations and Services: You can camp at El Aceitillar, which has camping toilets, showers, and picnic benches and barbecues (you'll need to be self-sufficient).

Villa Barrancoli (http://puertoescondido.tourism.googlepages.com), at Puerto Escondido, is a safari-style camping lodge with sheltered tents on decks (RD$300 single, RD$500 double). Right on the edge of the park, this small eco-tourism project (a joint venture of Tody Tours and the Duvergé-based Committee of Local Ecotourism Initiatives) is the perfect spot for early morning birding. The tents come with mattress and sleeping bag, plus there's a bathhouse with shared showers and toilets, plus a kitchen attended by women of the community. Meals, services of a cook, plus campground caretaker all cost extra. Make reservations through Tody Tours or c/o CIELO, E-mail: puertoescondido.turismo@gmail .com.

There are also a few rustic dorm cabins and a site for camping at **El Cachote**, a remote mountain hamlet at about 3,000 feet (914 m) elevation in the eastern sierras; access is via La Ciénaga, on the coast road south of Barahona. Part of a community ecotourism initiative, this facility has a rudimentary visitors center, kitchen, and dining area, plus basic cold-water showers and latrines. Trails lead into the nearby cloud palm forest, with many endemic palm and fern species and a habitat for the endemic Eastern chat tanager.

POLO MAGNÉTICO

La Cueva, 12 miles (19 km) S of Cabral (Carretera 46, 9 miles (14.4 km) W of Barahona)
You can be forgiven for doing a double take when you arrive at this apparent dip in the road in the foothills of the Sierra Bahoruco. You'll absolutely swear that the road ahead runs downhill, southward. However, if you stop your car and put it in neutral, instead of rolling forward, you'll be amazed to find yourself rolling backwards, uphill. Locals are convinced that this is a result of a subterranean magnetic charge—hence the name for this spot: Magnetic Pole. Others accredit the occurrence to spiritual matters. In fact, it's a simple optical illusion caused by the particular topography. It's about 500 yards (457 m) south of the village of La Cueva.

Good to Know About

Freelance guide Julio Féliz (809-524-6570 or 809-429-9671) is recommended for local ecotours; he operates out of the Hotel Costa Larimar, in Barahona.

Grupo Jaragua (809-472-1036; www.grupojaragua.org.do; Calle Paseo Mondesí 4, Oviedo) is the best resource for information on tourism. This environmentally focused community group can arrange naturalist guides and tours.

There's a minimally stocked local **tourism office** (809-524-3650; Avenida Enriquillo and Carretera Batey Central) next to Restaurant Brisas del Caribe, in Barahona. The **Tourist Police** (809-754-3035 or 524-3573) is in the same building.

Optical illusion at Polo Magnetico

The Republic's Most Spectacular Scenic Drive

Load up on the film or break out the digital camera for the Vía Panorámica—the coast highway between Barahona and Pedernales. Unspooling along the Caribbean shore for some 45 miles (72 km) before cutting west, inland of Parque Nacional Jaragua, for another 35 miles (56 km) to Pedernales, this is a scenic drive par excellence. Throw in some fun twisty bits and coiling climbs over headlands and Carretera 44 has the hallmarks of one of the world's great drives.

The scenery builds quickly out of Barahona. First stop should be the rose petal pink, pocket-size beach tucked below **Punta Prieto** (see Playazul Hotel-Restaurant, in the Lodging section). Next up, **Playa Quemaito**: The shingly beach is no great shakes, but the traditional fishing boats here are photogenic.

At the hamlet of **El Arroyo**, and with a 4WD vehicle, you might turn inland for the 9 miles (14.4 km) via rugged dirt road to see the larimar mines at Las Filipinas (see Minas de Larimar, above). Continuing south and passing through the fishing village of Bahoruco, you'll be amazed at the brilliance of the waters. Suddenly you round a bend and a staggering vista over **Playa Bahoruco** unfolds ahead, with waves breaking over a reef protecting an ocean of impossible Maxfield Parrish blues and greens.

Grilled fish at Balneario Playa San Rafael

Playa San Rafael, Peninsula de Bahoruco

Be sure to stop at **Playa San Rafael**, where a river that pours onto the pebbly beach has been chan-neled into several pools, popular with Dominican families on weekends. San Rafael is a fabulous experi-ence—a must visit—enhanced by lunch at one of the shady *balneario* barbecues selling fresh-grilled fish.

Just when you think coastal vistas can't get any better, 2 miles (3 km) farther south you ascend to a *mirador* (lookout) with views that simply astound. The next 20 miles (32 km) is an unending parade of beaches, *balnearios*, and fishing hamlets squeezed between the Sierra de Bahoruco and the sea. The loveli-est of settlements is **Enriquillo**, 34 miles (54.4 km) south of Barahona. Poised atop a limestone terrace, this lovely little town is graced by charming clapboard houses painted in tropical ice cream colors.

Beyond Enriquillo, the road moves inland from the shore. The mountains recede. The landscape turns arid. The bottle green forest fades into tawny and thorny acacia scrub. Farther south 10 miles (16 km) you arrive at El Cajuil and **Laguna Oviedo**, beyond which Carretera 44 turns west. The serpentine road is a wonderfully winding roller coaster, like something Disneyland might have dreamed up, and with fabulous vistas to boot: On your left, the vast expanse of Parque Nacional Jaragua, while raised marine platforms that form the Sierra de Bahoruco foothills rise in dramatic tiers on your right. Gorgeous!

10

IF TIME IS SHORT

Hopefully your visit to the Dominican Republic will be long enough to make the most of many of the attractions listed in the Culture and Recreation chapters, plus a healthy sampling of restaurants. But if your time is limited and you're scratching your head over so many options, then why not follow an itinerary that samples my personal favorites? Not everyone might pick these particular spots, but I feel confident that you won't go home disappointed.

PLACES TO STAY

Casa Colonial (809-320-3232; www.casacolonialhotel.com; Playa Dorada) Perhaps the finest boutique hotel in the country, this Italianate beachfront villa has sumptuous accommodations, fabulous dining, a world-class spa, and an oh-so-chic rooftop pool and Jacuzzis.

Hotel Atarazana (809-688-3693; www.hotel-atarazana.com; Calle Vicente Celestino Duarte 19, Santo Domingo) This tiny, lovingly restored gem offers plenty of colonial-meets-contemporary charm; the location is just steps from the main sights and nightlife; and the budget pricing seals the deal.

Contemporary art in lobby at Casa Colonial, Playa Dorada

Altos de Chavón and Chavon gorge

PuntaCana Hotel (888-442-2262; http://puntacana.com; Puntacana Resort and Club, Punta Cana) The original hotel that initiated the tourism boom hereabouts has been remade and is one of my favorite hotels in a region replete with fabulous options. Major pluses are the choice of superb restaurants, and furnishings by courtier and local stake-holder Oscar de la Renta.

CULTURAL ATTRACTIONS: DAY

Altos de Chavón (809-523-8011; www.altosdechavon.com; Casa de Campo, La Romana) It's slightly surreal to find a faux Tuscan village in the hills atop the gorge of the Río Chavón, but this irresistibly charming place is full of art galleries, boutiques, and fine restaurants.

Catedral Primada de las Américas (809-541-5652; Parque Colón, Calle Arzobispo Nouel and Arzobispo Meriño, Zona Colonial, Santo Domingo) In a historic district that justifiably deserves the moniker U.N. World Heritage Site, this cathedral stands out as *the* site to see. Completed in 1546, it is the New World's oldest church. The western Plateresque facade astounds.

Cueva de las Maravillas (809-951-9009; Carretera 3, Ramón Santana, 10 miles (16 km) east of San Pedro de Macorís) Of the many caverns in the republic, this is the shining star. Well laid out trails lead you into a jaw-dropping environment, featuring stupendous dripstone formations and Taíno pictographs, enhanced by voice-activated state-of-the-art lighting.

Catedral Primada de América, Santo Domingo

CULTURAL ATTRACTIONS: NIGHT

Kandelá: The Show (809-523-2424; www.kandela.com.do; Altos de Chavón Amphitheater, Casa de Campo, La Romana) The setting—an open-air neoclassical amphitheater—is almost as thrilling as this sexy Caribbean-themed cabaret. Beyond the gratuitous skin, solo singers perform everything from *boleros* to romantic opera.

La Guácara Taína (809-533-1051; Avenida Mirador del Sur, Parque Mirador del Sur, Santo Domingo) The venue for this sizzling nightspot is an underground cavern. No air-conditioning is required to keep things cool as well-heeled and young-at-heart locals perform sizzling salsa just a little closer than cheek-to-cheek.

Lax (809-571-00421; www.lax-cabarete.com; Cabarete) Cabarete's legendary beachfront night scene centers on this no-frills but guaranteed fun lounge serving up cool sounds and killer cocktails that can be enjoyed with sand between your toes.

RESTAURANTS

CaféCito Caribbean Bar and American Grill (809-586-7923; www.popreport.com/CC2; Plaza Isabela, Carretera 5, 2 miles (3 km) east of Puerto Plata) Tim Hall's laid-back, bohemian café-restaurant makes a fine break from the all-inclusive routine. Here you can enjoy eclectic fare such as sea bass in sherry. The music is soulful. And free Wifi is a bonus.

Mesón de Barí (809-687-4091; Calle Hostos 302, Santo Domingo) This colorful bohemian haunt in the heart of the capital city's Zona Colonial delivers satisfying Dominican fare, plus a tremendous yet unpretentious ambience that draws society figures. For something fancier and more romantic, dine upstairs.

Opio (809-552-6371; www.grupoanthuriun.com/opio/web.php; Cocotal Golf and Country Club, Avenida Real, Bávaro) Recreating the mood of Morocco or Rajasthan, this fusion restaurant delivers sensational dishes. It's away from the beach, requiring a taxi for most hotel guests, but the drive is worthwhile.

RECREATION

Dolphin Dive Center (809-571-3589; www.dolphindivecenter.com; Sosuá beach) Sosuá has top-notch diving and this outfitter will take you on scuba trips to the *Zingara* wreck and Airport Wall.

Laurel Eastman Kiteboarding (809-571-0564; www.laureleastman.com; Cabarete) Among the best of half a dozen kiteboarding outfitters at Cabarete, this one is run by a literal champion. A great way to learn this thrilling sport.

Ocean World Adventure Park (809-291-1000; www.oceanworldadventurepark.com; Cofresí, 3 miles (4.8 km) west of Puerto Plata) Acrobatic dolphin and sea lion shows; Bengal tigers; and a chance to snorkel with harmless rays and nurse sharks are all draws to this marine-based theme park. Swimming with dolphins is a joyful kick you won't soon forget.

Teeth of the Dog (fax (809-523-8800; E-mail t.times@ccampo.com.do; www.casade campo.com; Casa de Campo, La Romana) Ranked as one of the world's premier golf courses, this challenging Pete Dye-designed course launched the republic to fame as the Caribbean's top golf destination when it opened three decades ago.

Tody Tours (809-686-0882; www.todytours.com) Birders need look no further than this company, run by ex-U.S. Peace Corps volunteer Kate Wallace. She'll take you into the Sierra de Bahoruco and other prime spots where you're guaranteed to see many of the island's endemics.

Swimming with dolphins, Ocean World Adventure Park, Puerto Plata

About the Author

Born and raised in Yorkshire, England, Christopher P. Baker—the Lowell Thomas Award 2008 Travel Journalist of the Year—earned a Bachelor's degree in Geography, plus Master's degree in Latin American Studies and Education. He settled in California in 1980. Since 1983, he has made his living as a professional travel writer, photographer, and lecturer, and has established a reputation as the world's leading guidebook author specializing in Central America and the Caribbean. He has also authored Countryman *Palm Springs and Desert Resorts,* plus guidebooks on The Bahamas, Cuba, Jamaica, Panama, Puerto Rico, and Turks and Caicos, and California and Nevada for Frommer's, Prentice Hall, Lonely Planet, and the National Geographic Society, among others.

Baker is acknowledged as the world's foremost authority on travel to Cuba, about which he has written six books, including *Mi Moto Fidel: Motorcycling Through Castro's Cuba,* a two-time national book award winner.

His feature articles have appeared in most major U.S. daily newspapers as well as in publications as diverse as *Caribbean Travel + Life, Elle, Maxim, National Geographic Traveler,* and *The Robb Report.* A nine-time Lowell Thomas Award winner, Baker is also an accomplished photographer with many front-cover credits to his name.

A gifted public speaker, he has lectured aboard various cruise ships (including currently for National Geographic Expeditions) and has been privileged to address such entities as the National Press Club, the National Geographic Society (*Live...from National Geographic* series), and the World Affairs Council. He currently escorts cruise-tours as an expert for National Geographic Expeditions.

In addition, he has been profiled in *USA Today* and has appeared on dozens of syndicated national radio and TV shows, including CNN, Fox TV, ABC, NBC, and NPR, and Canada's Shaw TV and CBC.

In 2005, the Caribbean Tourism Organization named him Travel Writer of the Year.

He promotes himself through his websites: www.christopherbaker.com and www.cubatravelexpert.com.

General Index

history, 14–47; books, 81–82; natural, 14–31; social, 32–47
Hodelpa Caribe Colonial, 92
Hodelpa Centro Plaza, 303
Hodelpa Gran Almirante, 303–4
Holiday Spanish School, 132
holidays, 76
Hollywood Café (Santo Domingo), 127
Hollywood Plaza (La Romana), 172
horseback riding, 66; Cabarete, 280; Constanza, 332; Hato Mayor, 223; Juan Dolio, 146; La Romana, 170–71; Las Terrenas, 244; Playa Lavacama, 219–20; Santo Domingo, 131
horse-drawn carriages, in Santo Domingo, 90–91
Hospital Pablo A. Paulino, 246
Hospital Padre Bellini, 78
hospitals, 49, 78
Hospiten Bavaro, 215
Hostal Nicolás Nader, 92–93
Hostal San Fernando, 292–93, 296
hotels. See lodging; and specific hotels
Hotel Aloha Sol, 304
Hotel Alto Cerro, 330–31
Hotel Atarazana, 93, 356
Hotel Bahía Blanca, 283
Hotel Bahía Las Ballenas, 240
Hotel Bahía View, 229
Hotel Bayahibe, 178
Hotel Caribani, 156
Hotel Castilla, 254
Hotel Cayo Arena, 293
Hotel Conde de Peñalba, 96
Hotel Costa Larimar, 347
Hotel de Caobas, 318
Hotel de Salinas, 157
Hotel Delta, 96
Hotel Diana Victoria, 323
Hotel Discovery, 96
Hotel Don Carlos, 186
Hotel Doña Elvira, 93
Hotel Duque de Wellington, 96
Hotel Europa, 97
Hotel Exquisiteses Dilenia, 331
Hotel Fior di Loto, 144
Hotel Frano, 165–66
Hotel Garant International, 136
Hotel Gran Jimenoa, 323–24
Hotel La Catalina, 283
Hotel La Loma, 222
Hotel Magnifico Condominiums, 275
Hotel Maguana, 339
Hotel Montesilva, 254
Hotel Monumental, 97
Hotel Najayo Beach, 149
Hotel Pinar Dorado, 324
Hotel Playa Palenque, 149, 151

Hotel Rancho La Cueva, 217, 218
Hotel Residence Playa Colibri, 240
Hotel Residence Santo Domingo, 95
Hotel Restaurant Casa Club, 186
Hotel Restaurant La Casona Dorada, 97
Hotel Restaurant Mira Cielo, 187
Hotel Restaurant Sinai, 283–84
Hotel Restaurante El Viejo Pirata, 187
Hotel Riu Naiboa: nightclub, 213
Hotel Santo Domingo, 97
Hotel Tortuga, 287
Hotel Villa Colonial, 97–98
Hotel Villa Taina, 275, 278
Hotel Zapata, 137
Howard Johnson San Pedro de Macorís, 144
humpback whales. See whale watching; whales
Huracan Café Bar, 212

I

Iberostar Bávaro, 197
Iberostar Costa Dorada, 255
Iberostar Hacienda Dominicus, 178
Iberostar Punta Cana Casino, 214
Iglesia Cristiana El Buen Samaritano, 263
Iglesia de la Regina Angelorum, 113
Iglesia de Santa Bárbara, 113
Iglesia del Convento de Santa Clara, 110
Iglesia Nuestra Señora de la Altagracia (Santiago), 310
Iglesia Nuestra Señora de la Altagracia (Santo Domingo), 112
Iglesia Nuestra Señora de la Consolación, 151
Iglesia Nuestra Señora de las Mercedes, 113, 317
Iglesia Nuestra Señora del Carmen, 112–13
Iglesia Sagrado Corazón de Jesús, 319
Iglesia San Dionisio, 189
Iglesia San Pedro Apóstol, 147
Iglesia Santa Rosa (San Francisco), 317
Iglesia Santa Rosa de Lima (La Romana), 171
Iglesia y Convento de los Padres Dominicos, 114
Iguana Mama, 59, 63, 260–61, 280, 329
Ilsa Internet Cafe Bar, 149
Ingenio Porvenir, 147
insects, 30–31, 78–80
Institute of Languages, 132
Instituto del Tabaco, 321
Instituto Intercultural del Caribe, 132
Instituto Postal Dominicano, 76
International Film Festival, 75, 265
International Sand Castle Competition, 74
Internet service, 77
Isabel Villas Country Club, 64
Isla Beata, 351
Isla Cabrita, 296
Isla Cabritos, 344
Isla Catalina, 61, 170, 180
Isla Catalinita, 184

Lodging by Price

Inexpensive($)   Up to $100
Moderate ($$) $100–150
Expensive ($$$) $150–250
Very Expensive ($$$$) Over $250

Santo Domingo

Inexpensive
El Beatrio Guest House, 91
El Refugio del Pirata Guest House, 94–95
Foreigners Club Hotel, 92
Hotel Residence, 95
Plaza Toledo Bettyes Guest House, 95

Inexpensive to Moderate
Hotel Atarazana, 93
Hotel Delta, 96
Hotel Discovery, 96
Hotel Restaurant La Casona Dorada, 97
La Hacienda, 95

Moderate
Boutique Hotel Palacio, 95
Coco Boutique Hotel, 91–92
Hodelpa Caribe Colonial, 92
Hostal Nicolás Nader, 92–93
Hotel Conde de Peñalba, 96
Hotel Doña Elvira, 93
Hotel Duque de Wellington, 96
Hotel Europa, 97
Hotel Monumental, 97
Mercure Comercial, 98

Moderate to Expensive
Hilton Santo Domingo, 98
Hotel Santo Domingo, 97

Expensive
Courtyard Marriott, 95–96
Hotel Villa Colonial, 97–98
Sofitel Frances, 94

Expensive to Very Expensive
Meliá Santo Domingo, 98–99

Very Expensive
Renaissance Jaragua Hotel and Casino, 99
Sofitel Nicolás de Ovando, 94

South Central

Inexpensive
Hotel Caribani, 156
Hotel Fior di Loto, 144
Hotel Garant International, 136
Hotel Playa Palenque, 149, 151
Hotel Zapata, 137

Inexpensive to Moderate
Hotel Las Salinas, 157
Hotel Najayo Beach, 149
Howard Johnson San Pedro de Macorís, 144
Neptuno's Refugio, 137

Moderate to Expensive
Barceló Capella Beach Resort, 142
Barceló Talanquera Beach Resort, 142–43
Costa Caribe Coral, 143–44
Don Juan Beach Resort, 135–36
Embassy Suites Los Marlins, 144
Oasis Hamaca Beach Resort, Spa, and Casino, 137

Punta Cana and the Southeast

Inexpensive
Coco Loco, 222
Hotel Bayahibe, 178
Hotel Don Carlos, 186
Hotel La Loma, 222
Hotel Rancho La Cueva, 217
Hotel Restaurante El Viejo Pirata, 187

Inexpensive to Moderate
Hotel Frano, 165–66
Hotel Restaurant Casa Club, 186
La Posada de Piedra, 197–98
Paraíso Caño Hondo, 222

Moderate
Cortecito Inn, 195–96
Hotel Restaurant Mira Cielo, 187

Moderate to Expensive
Barceló Bávaro Resort, 194
Dreams La Romana, 177–78
Meliá Caribe Tropical, 198
Oasis Canoa La Romana, 178–79
VIK Hotel Arena Blanca, 200–201
Viva Wyndham Dominicus Palace, 179

Moderate to Very Expensive
Barceló Premium Punta Cana Resort, 194

El Cibao and Cordillera Central

Inexpensive

Inexpensive to Moderate

Moderate

Moderate to Expensive

Barahona and the Southwest

Inexpensive to Moderate

Moderate

Expensive

Dining by Price

Inexpensive ($)   Up to $10
Moderate ($$) $10–20
Expensive ($$$) $20–35
Very Expensive ($$$$) $35 or more

Santo Domingo

Inexpensive
Andrea Panaderia, Cafeteria and Heladeria, 106
Auto Sandwich Payano's, 106
La Cafetería, 105
Segafredo Café Boutique and Lounge Bar, 106

Inexpensive to Moderate
El Conuco, 99–100
Restaurante Boga Boga, 104

Inexpensive to Expensive
Restaurante del Lago, 104

Moderate to Expensive
Aka Sushi en Rojo, 99
El Mesón de la Cava, 100
Hard Rock Café, 100–101
Pepperoni Café, 103

Moderate to Very Expensive
Lina Restaurant, 101–2
Pat'é Palo, 103
Red Grill, 103–4

Expensive
El Catador, 99
Mesón de Barí, 102

Expensive to Very Expensive
Fogaraté, 100
La Briciola, 101
La Résidence, 101
Mitre Restaurant and Wine Bar, 102
Mix, 102–3
Samurai, 104
Scherezade, 104–5
Vesuvio del Malecón, 105
Yatoba, 105

South Central

Inexpensive
Fela's Place, 151
Punto Gourmet Italia, 141

Inexpensive to Moderate
Deli Swiss, 145
Di Lucien, 138
Restaurante El Concón, 145
Robby Mar, 145

Moderate to Very Expensive
Italy and Italy, 138
Neptuno's Club, 138
Pequeña Suiza, 138–39
Restaurante Boca Marina, 139

Punta Cana and the Southeast

Inexpensive
Bamboo Beach, 179
El Navegante, 218
Le Boulanger, 166
Mesón de Cervantes, 187

Inexpensive to Moderate
Caribbean Coffee and Tea, 166
Don Quijote Restaurante, 167
El Pulpo Cojo, 202
Ristorante Barco Bar, 180
Shish Kebab, 168
Trigo de Oro, 168

Inexpensive to Expensive
Capitán Cook, 202

Moderate
Tau Restaurant, 218

Moderate to Very Expensive
Chinois, 166–67
Jellyfish, 202

Expensive
Blu II, 201
Gourmond Restaurant, 218
La Palapa, 203
Mare Nostrum, 179–80
Onnos Tapas Bar, 167

Dining by Cuisine

Santo Domingo

American
Hard Rock Café, 100–101

Bakeries/Coffee Shops
La Cafetería, 105
Segafredo Café Boutique and Lounge Bar, 106

Dominican/Criolla
El Conuco, 99–100
Mesón de Barí, 102
Restaurante del Lago, 104

Fast Food
Andrea Panaderia, Cafeteria and Heladeria, 106
Auto Sandwich Payano's, 106

Fusion
Mitre Restaurant and Wine Bar, 102

International
El Mesón de la Cava, 100
Fogaraté, 100
La Résidence, 101
Lina Restaurant, 101–2
Mix, 102–3
Pat'é Palo, 103
Red Grill, 103–4
Yatoba, 105

Italian
La Briciola, 101
Pepperoni Café, 103
Vesuvio del Malecón, 105

Japanese
Aka Sushi en Rojo, 99
Samurai, 104

Spanish
Restaurante Boga Boga, 104

Steaks
Scherezade, 104–5

Sweets and Treats
Helados Bon, 106
Helados Nevada, 106
La Casa de los Dulces, 106
Surtidora Pura, 107

Tapas
El Catador, 99

South Central

Dominican
Fela's Place, 151
Restaurante El Concón, 145

Fondues
Pequeña Suiza, 138–39

International
Restaurante Boca Marina, 139

Italian
Di Lucien, 138
Italy and Italy, 138

Seafood
Deli Swiss, 145
Neptuno's Club, 138
Robby Mar, 145

Punta Cana and the Southeast

Bakeries
Le Boulanger, 166
Trigo de Oro, 168

Continental
Caribbean Coffee and Tea, 166
Don Quijote Restaurante, 167

Dominican
Cocoloba, 202
Mesón de Cervantes, 187
Paraíso Caño Hondo, 222

French
Bamboo Beach, 179
Gourmond Restaurant, 218

Fusion
Beach Club by Le Cirque, 166
Blu II, 201
Jellyfish, 202
Mitre Bar and Restaurant, 204
Opio, 204
Ristorante Barco Bar, 180
Vesuvio, 180

Italian
La Piazzetta, 167
Mare Nostrum, 179–80
Vesuvio, 180

Mediterranean
La Yola, 204
Laveranda Restaurant, 218

Middle Eastern
Shish Kebab, 168

Pan-Asian
Chinois, 166–67
Tau Restaurant, 218

Seafood
Capitán Cook, 202
El Navegante, 218
El Pulpo Cojo, 202
La Palapa, 203
Mare Nostrum, 179–80

Tapas
La Tasca, 203
Onnos Tapas Bar, 167

Samaná

Bakeries
El Pan de Antes Boulangerie, 246

Dominican
Santi Rancho, 243

French
La Mata Rosada, 229

International
Chez Denise, 235
Mi Restaurante Terraza Bar, 229

Italian
Restaurante Xamana, 229–30
Ristorante Pizzería, 236
Ristorante Pizzería La Capannina, 243

Mediterranean
Club de Playa Cayenas del Mar, 229

Seafood
Baraonda, 242
Paco Cabana Bar Restaurant Beach Club, 242–43

Snacks
Tiki Snack, 243

Tapas
La Yuca Caliente, 236

North Coast

American
Hemingway Bar and Grill, 257
Sam's Bar and Grill, 257

Breakfast
Eze Bar and Restaurant, 281
Panadería Repositera Dick, 281
Rocky's, 269–70

Dominican
El Buzo, 288
Ocean Restaurant, 293

Fusion
Casita de Don Alfredo, 276–77
Castle Club, 277
Joseph's Grill and Grape, 268
La Roca, 268
Veranda Restaurant, 257
Wabi Sabi/Miró on the Beach, 278

International
Cafécito Caribbean Bar and American Grill, 256
Casanova, 276
El Paraíso, 288
Hotel Restaurant Sinai, 283–84
Lax, 277
Morua Mai, 269
The Upper Deck, 288

Italian
Marabú Restaurant and Club, 277
Ristorante Stefy and Natale, 257

Seafood
El Buzo, 288
Escape Al Mar, 256–57
Los Gringos Beach Bar, Grill, and Cabañas, 285
Ocean Restaurant, 293
Restaurant Luperón Lobster House, 288
The Upper Deck, 288

El Cibao and Cordillera Central

Chinese
Pez Dorado, 306

Continental
Kokara Macara Country Bar and Restaurant, 306

Dominican
Pez Dorado, 306
Típico Bonao, 313

Eclectic
El Rancho Dominican, 324

El Rancho
Dominican
Exquisiteses Dilenia, 332

International
El Coche, 305–6

Barahona and the Southwest

Dominican/Criolla

Eclectic

Seafood